To/

Mum

Merry Christmas 2008

CLIFF RICHARD
The Biography

Lots of Love

Susie + Bryce

xxx

To my Dad and Mum,
Gordon and Ivy Turner,
with thanks for all their
love and encouragement,
and to the memory of
George Hoffman

CLIFF
RICHARD

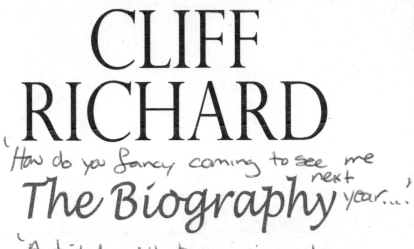

The Biography

'How do you fancy coming to see me
next year...'

'A ticket will be winging its
way to you shortly!'

STEVE TURNER

LION

A Lion Book
an imprint of
Lion Hudson plc
Mayfield House, 256 Banbury Road,
Oxford OX2 7DH, England
www.lionhudson.com
ISBN-13: 978-0-7459-5175-1
ISBN-10: 0-7459-5175-9

First edition 1993
Second edition 1994
Third edition 1998
This updated edition 2005
10 9 8 7 6 5 4 3 2

The text paper used in this book has been made from wood
independently certified as having come from sustainable forests

A catalogue record for this book is available
from the British Library

Typeset in 10/12pt Baskerville BT
Printed and bound in Great Britain
by Cox & Wyman Ltd

Steve Turner is a journalist, author and poet. He has written for many top music papers and journals, including *Rolling Stone*, *New Musical Express*, *Mojo* and *Q* magazine. He has also contributed music and travel articles to *The Times*, *The Independent* and *The Mail on Sunday*.

His books include *A Hard Day's Write*, *Amazing Grace*, *The Man Called Cash* and *Trouble Man*.

Steve Turner's four collections of poetry, *The Day I Fell Down the Toilet*, *The Moon Has Got His Pants On*, *Dad You're Not Funny* and *I Was Only Asking*, have established him as a best-selling writer for children. He lives in London.

CONTENTS

PREFACE TO NEW EDITION

This is a revised and updated version of the book that was first published as a hardback in 1993. It was an important book for me because it was my first opportunity to write a full-length biography and it became a best-seller in Britain within weeks of its release. I had been fortunate in my debut as a biographer to pick on someone whose life hadn't been seriously scrutinized and yet who was of great interest to millions of people.

The changes I've made in this edition appear in four main areas. First, I rewrote Chapter 1. In the original book, this was titled 'Only a boy from Cheshunt' and focused on the then fairly recent concert at Wembley Stadium called 'The Event'. That concert is now sixteen years in the past so, to bring the account up to date, I took a similar approach to a 2004 concert at Leeds Castle.

In common with 'The Event', this concert happened to be filmed although I didn't know this when I arrived on site. Also in common with 'The Event', it was a show that accurately took the temperature of Cliff's career at a particular moment in time. In the late 1980s, the emphasis had been on huge audiences and extravagant staging. Post millennium, the emphasis was on intimacy and durability.

Secondly, I went through the entire text to improve it where I could. I didn't need to add anything other than to note the passing of a few key characters because no significant facts had come to light that would alter the overall story and no new witnesses had emerged. The main need was to edit the language because a decade of writing biographies has led me to be much more precise in my use of words.

Thirdly, there was new material to be added. In 1998, I had added a chapter on *Heathcliff* for the first mass-market paperback edition but it now needed two more chapters to take the book through to the present day. I devoted one of these chapters to events leading up to and including the millennium and the other to his career since taking his well-publicized year away from show business.

Fourthly, I needed to overhaul savagely the book's last two

chapters. These had summarized his lifestyle and then put his career into historical perspective. I had thought that my conclusions in 1993 could have been set in stone but since the turn of the millennium there have been so many changes that virtually nothing I had said back then remained true.

In the past five years, there have been significant modifications to Cliff's lifestyle, career, circle of friends, management team, recording contract, income and general outlook. After being a very settled character for around 35 years, he appears to have become much less predictable than many had assumed him to be.

There would be no benefit in updating such a biography if there was not a continuing interest in its subject. Paradoxically, Cliff is one of the most popular and famous British pop stars and yet one of the least known. He always seems to be there, being interviewed or singing us his songs, and yet he remains a mystery. Of all the people I have written about, he's the one of whom people always ask 'But what's he really like?'

It would be presumptuous to claim that this book solves the mystery once and for all but at least I hope that it asks the right questions and shines a light in the right corners.

Steve Turner, January 2005

INTRODUCTION

I was nine years old when I first became aware of Cliff Richard. I can remember hearing 'Living Doll' on the radio – the 'wireless' as we then called it – and have a clear memory of children singing 'Travellin' Light' on the way back home from junior school.

At that age I didn't know anything about Cliff having 'softened up' his sound. I had no knowledge of Little Richard, Jerry Lee Lewis, Chuck Berry and Gene Vincent because Uncle Mac didn't play their kind of music on 'Children's Favourites', one of the few BBC wireless shows in those days to play pop records. All I knew was that Cliff wasn't like the Perry Como and Alma Cogan sound that seemed to dominate pop through my childhood, and I liked what I heard.

I also liked what I saw. I wanted a striped shirt like Cliff's ('too jazzy,' said Mum). I wanted pink socks ('girls' clothes,' said Mum). Most of all I wanted a hairstyle which swept back at the sides and tumbled forward at the front ('you're having a short back and sides and that's it,' said Mum).

I'd like to say that I have all Cliff's early singles in mint condition, but the fact is that in those days my parents had a gramophone that only played 78 rpm records. My first Cliff purchase (other than a comb in a grey plastic case bearing his image and signature) was the sheet music to 'Please Don't Tease'. It cost two shillings and I only bought it for the photograph on the cover.

It's easy to look back and see what a 'nice' boy Cliff really was, but at the time, to someone not yet in his teens, he seemed like forbidden fruit. The only people I knew who dressed in such outrageous colours and wore their hair without a clean parting were Teddy boys, Rockers and the boys who operated the bumper cars at fairgrounds.

Those were the days, it has to be remembered, when a solid-body electric guitar was regarded as a symbol of teenage discontent. Rock 'n' roll, whether original and from Memphis or derivative and from London, was nothing more than a 'noise' which the older generation associated with juvenile delinquency.

My parents certainly didn't see Cliff as a good thing. I'm sure they had never checked out his worthy opinions but he just looked like a rock 'n' roll person. I can remember wanting to buy a book about him (it must have been a paperback version of *It's Great To Be Young*, his 1960 autobiography) and my dad said, 'You don't want that. It'll be full of sex.' If only he had known.

I didn't meet Cliff until 1970, at a party in London. By this time I had started to write about rock music. We passed on the stairs and I stuck my hand out and said, 'Hi, I'm Steve Turner,' and Cliff stuck his hand out and just said, 'Hi'. It was then I realized that when you're as famous as Cliff you no longer have to bother giving your name. I saw him at various times after that during the early seventies, but didn't interview him until 1977 while he was recording his album *Small Corners*.

The genesis of this book, though, lies in a four-part documentary series for BBC TV called 'Cliff!' (1981) for which I was researcher and interviewer. I interviewed many of his friends and colleagues for these films, travelled with Cliff on the road, visited him at home and joined him on a tour of America.

At the end of it all I realized I would be well-positioned to write a much more comprehensive book about Cliff than had ever been written before. I had the access, the contacts and a pile of research material.

That Christmas I was given a copy of Albert Goldman's *Elvis*, a book which set new rigorous standards for rock biography. The previous 'definitive' biography of Elvis, written by Jerry Hopkins, had listed 112 interview sources and began the story at Elvis' birth.

Goldman listed 160 interviews and started the story with David Pressley (the original spelling of the family name) who had come to America some time during the 1740s.

Early in 1982 I made my first approach to Cliff's office suggesting there was room for a more expansive biography of Cliff. They eventually agreed but there were long delays because they felt the market was saturated with Cliff products, and they didn't want fans to be overwhelmed.

Final approval wasn't given until March 1991. By this time I had amassed even more material, and had the additional perspective of having co-written a song for Cliff which became the title track of his album *Now You See Me... Now You Don't*.

I didn't come to the project with a theory to prove. I wanted simply to provide as full a portrait of the man as I could, because I considered that anyone who had been that successful for that long was deserving of detailed investigation.

There were areas I was particularly interested in though, because I thought they offered clues both to his success and to his character.

There was the question of his enigmatic sexuality. If he were a bank manager or a captain of industry I wouldn't consider this relevant, but it is when you are dealing with a man who trades in romantic fantasy. Understandably people want to know why he has never married, or whether he's interested in women at all.

The fact that Cliff has survived so many changes in musical fashion is remarkable. He has been at the top of the music business for over thirty years, and yet his success in Europe and Australasia has not been repeated in America. I wanted to find out why.

Then there is Cliff's Christian faith – not very fashionable for a popular entertainer – and his image of being a 'nice guy'. Just how much of that is due to his upbringing, and how much is a result of his conversion to Christianity? I was intrigued to know if his faith had changed or matured over the years. And whether he's a nice guy when he's not on show.

Finally there is his youthfulness. His apparent failure to grow old has become an important part of his image. I wanted to discover how much his youthful looks have to be worked on now, and how bothered he is by changes in his appearance.

Since starting work on the book the two questions I've been asked most often are, 'Hasn't there already been a book about Cliff?' and 'Is it an authorized biography?' The answer in both cases is, … er, well, sort of.

There have been at least thirty books about Cliff published in Britain. But surprisingly enough, only three of these are adult biographies, and none have been in-depth studies. In addition Cliff has written two autobiographies: *It's Great To Be Young* (1960) and *Which One's Cliff* (1977). Both attempted a very different job from the book you now hold in your hand.

I felt that there was room for a more detailed account of Cliff's life because the expectations of a rock biography have been significantly raised by books such as Goldman's *Elvis* and *The Lives of John Lennon*, Philip Norman's *Shout* (the Beatles) and David Ritz's *Divided Soul* (Marvin Gaye). No longer is it sufficient to speak to half a dozen colleagues and stitch their comments together with material from newspaper cuttings.

For this book I carried out over two hundred interviews and discovered, very early on, that despite the volume of words written about Cliff over the years, I was not tramping a well-worn path. Almost all my interviewees had never been questioned about Cliff before. No one had spoken to his aunts, uncles, schoolfriends, childhood neighbours, former girlfriends and early business associates. No one had ever bothered tracing his family tree or tracking down the members of his early groups.

The book is authorized in as much I have had the full support and cooperation of Cliff and his management team during the writing, but they have not had authorial control and have no financial stake in the project.

I consider this to be the perfect arrangement. Without Cliff's blessing I would have had limited access to his friends, colleagues and office diaries. People are very suspicious about cooperating with unapproved biographers.

Yet if my involvement with Cliff had extended to include editorial approval the book would have lost any hope of objectivity. It's impossible to write an honest biography with the subject looking over your shoulder.

As it was, Cliff has given me as much of his time as I asked for. I was given an introductory letter to smooth the way in setting up interviews, and there has been no evidence of anyone having been warned against talking to me. In fact some interviews, like the one with Cliff's mother, Mrs Dorothy Bodkin, were organized on my behalf by the office.

It was very brave of Cliff to allow me to nose around in his past, digging up long-forgotten associations and asking impertinent questions. I hope that he discovers his trust has been rewarded with a book which accurately and fairly sums up his life so far.

ACKNOWLEDGMENTS

This book couldn't have been written without the support of Bill Latham who, in giving me the green light to go ahead with it, had to give the red light to a number of other well-qualified potential biographers.

It was Bill who ultimately had to reassure worried interviewees that I was alright when they called up to check with the office. Throughout the project he encouraged me to fight for objectivity knowing that this would be a difficult task in view of the closeness I had enjoyed with Cliff in the past.

Another vital support has been Gill Snow, secretary (and much, much more) to Cliff Richard. She has supplied me with phone numbers, answered all my little queries and opened the office diaries.

At Lion I'm grateful to Becky Winter not only for seeing the potential of a full-length biography of this kind but also for helping me focus my vision. Melanie Watson has overhauled the book for errors both historical and grammatical, and collected many of the photos.

All my interviewees deserve thanks for giving up time and information, but I must mention some who have given special help.

Cliff's mother, Mrs Dorothy Bodkin, had not been interviewed for 25 years but graciously consented to speak to me for this book.

Peter Gormley, famed for his reticence, not only gave me an interview but was ready at the end of a phone any time I had a query.

From Cliff's family I must thank Vincent Bridgwater for his time and the use of his photographs. Joyce Dobra not only lent me photographs from the Webb side of the family but gave me access to some documents and copies of birth certificates which greatly speeded up my completion of the family tree. Olive Dazely spent long hours on the phone telling me about life in India.

Delia Wicks, Janice Berry and Betty Clarke had never spoken of their romances with Cliff to anyone in the media before and I am grateful to them for their time and openness.

Ian 'Sammy' Samwell not only spoke to me frequently on the phone but met up with me in London and gave me a small suitcase full of photographs, cuttings, sheet music, and scrapbooks. A real gold mine!

Dick Teague, who thought I was a practical joker when I first called him to ask about the days when Cliff sang in his group, sent me invaluable information about the brief career of the Dick Teague Skiffle Group. This included pages from a diary kept by his father who managed their affairs, engagement sheets, letters and cuttings.

Royston Ellis was another great discovery. Back in Britain for a short break, he went through his cupboards and discovered all sorts of helpful photographs and cuttings. He lent me copies of his books *The Shadows By Themselves* and *The Big Beat Scene*, as well as an autographed proof copy of Cliff's *It's Great To Be Young*.

Ray Mackender, who has a great memory for the 'Oh Boy!' days, sent me lots of details about incidents he remembered and was always readily available to check facts.

There were some deleted albums and videos which I needed and Christine Whitehead, coordinator of Britain's Cliff Richard Fan Club, tracked them down and sent them to me.

Rachel Melville-Thomas cast a psychologist's eye over some of my research and Mick Brown, Richard Branson's biographer, was one of the first to encourage me to take on this book.

Of Cliff's current circle of close friends, Graham Disbrey was very generous with his time and Peter Graves was a reliable source of information when it came to dates of holidays and meetings. John Davey very kindly photocopied material which helped me with the chronology of events around Cliff's Christian conversion.

Finally, much of the burden of this book has fallen on my family – daughter Lianne, son Nathan and wife Mo – and I thank them for their love and patience.

CASTLES IN
THE AIR

Cliff Richard wakes up in the Turret Room of Leeds Castle, Kent. Last night he played to 12,000 fans on the Cedar Lawn just over the moat. Tonight he will repeat the performance, this time with a camera crew tracking his every move. The plan is to produce a DVD of the concert that will be released at the same time as his next album.

The Turret Room, furnished and decorated by the celebrated French interior designer Stephane Boudin, has all the grandeur and elegance that you'd expect of a luxury bedroom in a castle once lived in by kings and queens and now regularly visited by celebrities, leaders of industry and heads of state. Eighteenth-century oil paintings hang on the walls, the bed is a four-poster and the couches are upholstered in velvet.

After 46 years in show business, most of them spent at the top, Cliff is no stranger to luxury. He lives on an exclusive private estate at St George's Hill, Weybridge, drives a Mercedes convertible and owns multimillion pound holiday homes in Portugal and Barbados. Wherever he goes, he is fêted. It is customary for him to be given the best table in the restaurant, the best box in the theatre, the best seat on the plane.

Not that he takes it for granted. He's permanently conscious that at the time of his first hit single, he and his family were living in a small council house in Cheshunt, Hertfordshire. He remembers the struggles his parents went through to find work and to fill their home with even the most basic furniture. The image of the packing

16

cases that served for chairs and tables has in many ways been his spur to fame.

After showering, shaving and dressing in a dark patterned shirt over a T-shirt, he leaves the Turret Room and descends the stone staircase to the oak-panelled dining room where he's met by his personal assistant, Roger Bruce. For breakfast he has two slices of toast and a cup of coffee. He will only have one more meal during the day. It's a diet that has held his weight at 11 stone for over 40 years.

Although fast approaching his 64th birthday, there is still something undeniably boyish about him. It's not just the lithe frame, the spring in his step and the lack of unsightly folds in his skin. It's his unflagging enthusiasm. After almost half a century of singing 'Move It', he could be forgiven for dropping it from his set or at least singing it through gritted teeth. But he still attacks it with gusto.

He's excited about the day ahead and by 11 a.m. is embarking on a filmed tour of some of the castle's attractions with Cilla Black, his surprise guest of the night. Cilla has been a fan of Cliff's since she was a Liverpool teenager and saw him on the 'Oh Boy!' TV show. Now she's a near neighbour of his in Barbados and in recent years they've become close friends.

They visit the vineyard where they taste some wine, he plants a Cliff Richard rose in the garden and then they both get lost in the maze. As Cliff feeds a falcon in the falconry, crowds gather to catch a glimpse. The castle is open to the public until early evening.

In the middle of the afternoon there is a session with photographer, Andy Earl. Dressed in a white suit and with the castle prominently in the background, Cliff moves around and adopts a range of familiar poses. The photos may be used on the cover of the DVD or just as a promotional handout.

At 5.30 p.m., Cliff retires to a fenced off 'village' area behind the stage to get himself ready for the concert. There are caravans for himself, the backing vocalists, the band and the opera group, Amici Forever, who are supporting him on this show. In his caravan there are the fruit juices and herbal teas that he drinks to loosen his throat up. After a period of relaxation, he spends twenty minutes alone going through a routine of vocal exercises set for him by a voice coach.

Roger Bruce has laid out his clothes for the concert. A make-up girl comes in and applies powder to his face and forehead to prevent any unnecessary glare when he's being filmed under the stage lights. His hair, that has started to thin on top, is combed forward to disguise the loss.

The stage backs on to the moat and is flanked on either side by huge screens. The audience is spread out over a huge field, seated in rows of collapsible chairs. Behind the stage, on the other side of the moat, is the stirring sight of one of the most beautiful and well-preserved castles in Britain.

When Cliff makes his entrance on the stage at 8 p.m., he is partly hidden by six dancers until he steps out from among their writhing figures to sing 'Heartbreak Hotel', the song that converted him to rock 'n' roll in 1956. He's wearing a dark jacket, faded blue jeans and a white shirt with a pleated front. He moves slowly and jerkily in a routine that alludes to Elvis's choreography in the movie, *Jailhouse Rock*.

This is followed by 'Move It', his first single and first hit, a song that many still regard as one of the best British rock 'n' roll records. In the past he has said that he doesn't like to give what he calls 'history lessons' in concert but this is exactly what the first half of this concert is designed to be. It is taking his audience from his first major musical inspirations and through his early hits up to the point where the Beatles became his main challengers.

He calls it a 'potted view of pop-rock'. Although he includes some versions of other artists' songs – Chuck Berry's 'No Particular Place To Go', Little Richard's 'Good Golly Miss Molly' and a doo-wop medley – it's really a potted view of his own early career. He sings the theme songs from his two big movies, *The Young Ones* and *Summer Holiday*, obscure album tracks such as 'Baby It's You', 'Without You' and 'Baby I Could Be So Good At Loving You' and top ten hits like 'Please Don't Tease', 'Bachelor Boy' and 'On the Beach'.

Most of the audience don't need the lesson. They were buying singles when these hits came out. The front few rows in particular are made up of hard-core Cliff fans who faithfully attend every concert they can. They already know what songs are in the set so when Cliff performs 'No Particular Place To Go', a small crowd of them stands up with a large banner that reads 'Essex: A Particular

Place To Go'. Two women at the back of the front section are wearing T-shirts that say 'Once a Knight Is Great' on the front and 'But Twice a Knight Is Better' on the back.

Cliff's relationship with his fans, in concert at least, is one still based on the myth of his availability and their desire to have him, although this has now become ironic because he hasn't had a girlfriend in almost 20 years and most of his fans are long-since married. So when he rubs his thighs or shakes his rump and all the ladies shriek, it's a form of pantomime. Cilla Black plays up to this when she later joins him on stage to sing 'It Takes Two'. 'Cliff! I want you!', she says as she walks on. 'I need you. I love you. Take me. I'm yours.'

This is the final concert in a series of nine held at six stately homes and castles. Two nights ago, he was at Blickling Hall in Norfolk. Five nights before that he was at Edinburgh Castle in Scotland. It seems appropriate that the country's senior practitioner of rock and pop, a man who started out playing for teenagers in a Soho basement, should now be playing against a backdrop of ramparts, towers and turrets on a summer evening in the Kentish countryside.

Some have brought thermos flasks and sandwich boxes. Threatening black clouds have been gathering in the distance since the late afternoon and the long-range forecast isn't good. The better prepared are equipped with plastic macs and umbrellas. By the time the intermission is over, the daylight has gone and there's a warm orange glow in the windows of the castle across the moat. The inside of the stage set is pinpricked with small lights designed to look like the night sky.

For the second half of his show, Cliff skips forward from the mid sixties to his revival of fortune in the mid seventies and early eighties with songs like 'We Don't Talk Any More', 'Miss You Nights' and 'Dreamin'. His voice has lost none of its power and range and he wheels around the stage with the energy of a 30-year-old.

Although he retains his enthusiasm for his back catalogue and never performs it in a desultory or slapdash way, his excitement is always reserved for his latest project. Tonight this is his album, *Somethin' Is Goin' On*, that he recently finished recording in Nashville. He explains that he used over twenty songwriters, all but one of whom were American. The exception is Chris Eaton, whose previous hits for Cliff include 'Saviour's Day'. He sings two of Eaton's songs that will be on the album, the gospel flavoured 'Faithful One' and 'I Don't Want To Lose You'.

As he carries on with songs from the album, the heavens open and the plastic macs come out. It's the first bad weather of the tour but very few people leave their seats as the rain drives down. He finishes the set with 'Willie and the Hand Jive', a hit for him in 1960, and then returns to do an encore of 'Thousand Miles To Go', the opening track from the new album, and his eighties hit 'Wired For Sound'.

He leaves the stage with an umbrella held over his head by Roger Bruce and is led back to his caravan where he relaxes with his favourite post-concert tipple of champagne and pineapple juice. It's not just the end of a show but the end of a tour.

After mingling at a small reception in the hospitality tent and greeting old friends like Helen Hobson (Cathy in *Heathcliff*) and theatre producer Ray Cooney, he is driven back to Weybridge by Roger Bruce. Although it's after midnight by the time he gets home, there's time for a light supper with friends and family before going to bed.

ROOTS IN *two* THE RAJ

The fact that the boy who became Cliff Richard was born in India and baptized Harry Rodger Webb has been presented a million times. But nothing has ever been said about how his parents, Rodger and Dorothy Marie, came to be on the subcontinent and there have been only the sketchiest descriptions of his grandparents.

Perhaps because of this it has often been rumoured that Cliff's dark good looks are due to mixed race. When he was a teenager in Cheshunt the question for his friends was not whether he had Indian blood, but from which parent it came. Most of them plumped for Mrs Webb because she was most like Cliff in appearance and had the same darker skin tone.

Cliff has never been a good source of information on family history because he has never been interested. The most he has ever said is that his grandparents were 'as English as roast beef,' and that it had been they who had made the move to India. He once told a journalist that he thought one of his grandfathers was born in Threadneedle Street, in the City of London, but that 'every time I pass through there all I can see are banks and insurance offices'.

The truth is that only one of his grandparents was born in England, but not in Threadneedle Street, and it's possible that some of his great-great-grandparents never knew any country other than India. The mystery of the skin pigmentation is partly solved by the records of baptism, marriage and burial held by the India Office Library in London. They show that a great-grandmother on his mother's side was half Welsh and half Spanish, born to George David Smith and Emiline Josephine Rebeiro who had married in Calcutta in 1869. Photographs of her in middle age show that she had distinctively Mediterranean looks which passed to her children.

The Portuguese had planted themselves in India in 1510 when they captured Goa on the west coast and turned it into a colony. A steady flow of Portuguese and Spanish workers came to that first settlement and soon moved northwards to Bombay.

The British didn't come into India for another hundred years, when the East India Company began building trading posts and forts. Although the company hadn't intended to govern, merely to make money out of such commodities as spices, cotton, sugar, jute and silk, effectively it became an imperial power dividing the country into the presidencies of Bombay, Bengal and Madras and organizing its own massive private army.

By the time Victoria came to the throne in 1837, Westminster was firmly in control of India and the Crown had appointed a governor general. Whereas the original merchants of the East India Company had set up in the ports and worked alongside the indigenous population, the Victorian imperialists had no such respect for the natives and their ways. They saw the Indians as people to be tamed.

Cliff's ancestors came to India as part of this exercise. His father's family came to join the task force needed to build the railway system that would transform India from a collection of outposts to a modern nation. On his mother's side they came as soldiers, equipped to defend the British Empire against restless natives.

The earliest ancestor on record is Thomas Webb, Cliff's great-great-grandfather, who was born in London's East End in 1805. He became a book-keeper, married a woman called Mary Taynton, who was two years his junior, and lived at 2 Wilson's Place, a small cul-de-sac near Commercial Road in Limehouse. Here, in 1841, Mary gave birth to Cliff's great-grandfather, Thomas Benjamin Webb, the man who was to lead the Webb family to India.

Wilson's Place today is an area of lock-up garages with the outline of Canary Wharf visible in the distance. The houses that Thomas Benjamin Webb would have known were torn down long ago.

Nothing is recorded of his life until 1865 when he married Amelia Sophia Smart, a West Ham girl, and moved over the river to Woolwich where they settled at 135 Plumstead Road.

The 1871 census shows that Amelia was then a dressmaker and Thomas Benjamin was working as an engineer at the Woolwich

Arsenal. This meant that they were affluent enough to employ a live-in nursemaid, Jane Brown, to look after their first child, probably their eldest son Thomas.

It was in this house in 1872 that Cliff's grandfather, Frederick William Webb, was born. Again we don't know much about his early life, but the stark facts show that he was frequently hit by tragedy. Two more children were born to his mother in quick succession. Then shortly after his second birthday she died, age 33, of typhoid fever, leaving her husband with four children to care for.

In view of this new responsibility it's hard to account for what happened next. In 1877, the year Queen Victoria became empress of India, Thomas Benjamin packed his bags, left his children and went to work as a mechanical engineer on the South India Railway.

There may have been sound economic reasons for the move. The railway system in India was in its infancy and British labourers were being recruited to lay new track. Maybe the wages of an engineer at the Woolwich Arsenal weren't sufficient to cover the care and education of his children, whereas those of a covenanted engineer in India were. No one knows who looked after his children or whether he ever intended to return.

All that is known is that the young Frederick William received a grammar school education in Holborn and then, at the age of twelve, left England to join his father. On 10 April 1885 we find him in Perambur in South India where, according to the ecclesiastical returns, he was baptized by a chaplain of the Madras Railway. His brother later joined him, but the fate of his two siblings remains a mystery. Neither of them went to India or saw their father again.

Two years after Frederick William arrived in Perambur, further tragedy struck. On 27 August 1887 Thomas Benjamin was tending a damaged valve on an engine when it burst open. The escaping steam could have caused an explosion so he laid himself across it to prevent a disaster, and died of terrible injuries.

Thomas was buried the same day, which happened to be Frederick William's birthday. Conducting the funeral service was the same railway chaplain who had baptized the boy two years before. At fifteen Frederick was an orphan, alone in a still strange land, and with no means of returning to the familiar streets of South London.

No one alive today can remember him mentioning this calamitous time. 'We didn't ask our parents about their backgrounds in those days,' says his daughter Joyce Clarkson. 'It just wasn't done.'

The next entry in the ecclesiastical returns is Frederick's marriage in 1896 to Donella Eugenie Woodfall, Cliff's paternal grandmother. Donella Eugenie, known because of her initials as Dewy (a nickname that passed briefly to Cliff's oldest sister who was baptized Donella Eugenie Webb), had slightly oriental looks. Rumour had it they were due to a Burmese princess who had married into Donella Woodfall's mother's family. Her direct ancestry was Dutch and English but, if the Burmese connection is true, it would further explain Cliff's dark colouring.

Donella and Frederick started their married life in Negapatam but by 1899, when their first daughter Dorothy May was born, they had moved to Burma where Frederick William was involved in bridge construction in the capital city of Rangoon.

He was a handsome man with a commanding manner, but had a foul temper which sometimes lost him work. 'But there was another side to his character,' his granddaughter Joyce Dobra points out. 'He would spend a lot of time in the juvenile courts where he would bail out young men, take them home, get them good apprenticeships and see them on the right path.'

Donella Eugenie gave birth to a total of eleven children. Rodger Oscar Webb, Cliff's father, was born on 23 December 1904 at Tramway Quarters, Rangoon. Although it was company accommodation, the Webbs were well-off by the standards of their contemporaries back in England. They enjoyed the services of a cook, a bearer, a sweeper, a washer, and an *ayah*, the servant who looked after the small children.

They stayed in Burma until 1914 when the family began to move around Indian railway towns such as Howrah, Allahabad and Lucknow. By the time Rodger started at Allahabad High School his oldest brother, Harry, was seventeen and his youngest sister, Joyce, was a baby.

Frederick William was a tough disciplinarian who caned the boys and took the attitude that if girls misbehaved while boys were present it was the boys' fault for letting it happen. He kept his servants in order and told them that a spare glass eye which he kept in a drawer was able to see everything that they did in the house. (He had lost his left eye in an accident.)

He was also deeply religious, reading the Bible regularly and making notes of his studies in the margins. 'We were always taught from the Bible,' says his youngest daughter Joyce Clarkson. 'I remember having to go to Sunday school when I was young. The local priest, Reverend Vetichan, was a wonderful man and it was through him that we became regular churchgoers.'

The Webbs were a happy family and the children enjoyed the sheer fun of being let loose in a country of exotic smells, wild animals and brilliant sunshine. Rodger was often dragged around with his older brothers and sisters and unwittingly got involved in their mischief.

'Once they went to a Hindu cremation,' Joyce Dobra remembers being told. 'They hid in the bushes to watch and as the heat affected the muscles of the body being burned it began to sit up and the children fled in terror. Rodger was only a toddler and he had terrible nightmares for a long time afterwards.'

During the First World War life changed dramatically for the Webbs. Harry was sent to fight in Tanganyika, German East Africa. He was killed there in Dar es Salaam at the age of twenty. Around the same time Rodger's older brother Frederick died of typhoid at fifteen. The one bit of bright news was that Doncella Eugenie was expecting yet another child, but even this turned into tragedy. She died of 'malarial cachexia and childbirth' in Lucknow. Eight months later the child, a little boy baptized Valentine, died of a heart defect.

Frederick William was badly affected by these tragedies. He locked himself away in a room alone for several weeks and drank heavily to numb the pain. 'When he finally came out his hair was absolutely white,' says Joyce Dobra.

Rodger must have left school around this time. No one is sure what he did immediately afterwards. His sister, Joyce Clarkson, thinks that he returned to Burma to work in a factory that made chocolate. What is certain is that he eventually took an office job with G.F. Kellner and Co., a Calcutta-based company described at the time as being 'wines, spirits and provision importers, wholesale and retail distributors'.

Established in India during the middle of the nineteenth

century, Kellner's was well known to the European community for its railway catering. Rodger became a steward on trains travelling between Calcutta and Dehra Dun and then a regional manager, which is what he was doing when he met his future wife.

Cliff's maternal lineage is a military one. His grandmother, Dorothy Edith, was the daughter of William Brock Bridgwater and his wife Marie Beatrice. William Brock had been born in the Vale of Health, a beautiful hamlet tucked into a fold of Hampstead Heath.

He joined the army as a boy, trained in Ireland and went to India with the Essex Regiment. It was here he met Marie Beatrice Smith, a dark-eyed half-Spanish beauty who was living in the hill station of Naini Tal looking after the children of a high-ranking military officer. They fell in love and married in 1898 in Allahabad.

Their daughter, Dorothy Edith, was born with a club foot and grew up to be a short, plump girl. The children at school made fun of her and called her *'lungi'* ('lame one'). She visited England for operations to correct the foot but it only made matters worse. William Brock instead taught her to defend herself by giving her boxing lessons.

When the First World War broke out William was far too old to serve and had already done seven years' service in the army but he insisted on re-enlisting.

'They were taking people up to the age of forty,' remembers his son Vincent Bridgwater. 'He was 45 and put his age down as 40 and five months, and he was accepted.

'He returned to England where he was reunited with his family and then he was sent to France. He fought in the second battle of Ypres in April 1915 where the Germans used poison gas for the first time. He was gassed and the trench he was in was blown up. Fortunately he was discovered. They took him to hospital and found that he had broken his spinal cord. He came back to us in India in 1916 as a cripple.'

He spent the rest of his life in a wheelchair and Dorothy Edith had to look after him. Perhaps to escape the pressures of home life, at sixteen she married William Edward Dazely, a young soldier stationed in Bangalore with the Supply and Transport Corps. Nine months and three days later, in Lahore, she gave birth to a baby she had baptized Dorothy Marie.

Although she never discussed the marriage with her children, it can't have been happy. Two years after Dorothy Marie's birth there was a second daughter, Olive Queenie, born in Jubbulpore. Then in the spring of 1924 William Edward 'disappeared'.

Vincent Bridgwater, who was ten years old at the time, remembers being told that his brother-in-law had been sent up to the north-west frontier where British troops were defending themselves against Afghan tribesmen, and had never returned. There was no death certificate, he was told, because the body had never been found, but that in itself was not unusual in a conflict where soldiers were often captured and slashed to pieces with swords.

'He was attached to the army in some respect and he vanished,' he says. 'We never heard from him again. My sister and mother tried to find out where he was but they couldn't come up with anything. The army gave no details at all.'

Dorothy Marie and Olive Queenie grew up believing that their father was dead. They knew nothing about him because everything connected with him, including photographs, had been destroyed after he failed to return.

'She seemed to blame him for dying,' says Olive Queenie. 'She wouldn't talk about him and yet sometimes, when I had done something wrong, she would say, "You're just like your father". But how I was like my father I didn't know because I didn't know anything about him. I didn't even know what he looked like.'

It was only during research for this book that, after seventy years, the true story finally emerged. There are no records of a William Edward Dazely having died in India between 1924 and 1948 but there is a record of a William Edward Dazely arriving in Karachi in 1929 and marrying a 23-year-old woman named Maizie Sherard. Thirteen weeks later Maizie gave birth to a child. Mr Dazely's given age, 33, was exactly that of Dorothy Edith's husband who had been born in Kirkee in February 1896. Significantly he described himself in the church register as a 'widower'.

Clearly he wasn't telling the truth, but whether he abandoned Dorothy Edith and his daughters or whether there had been an agreement to split up and start their lives anew will never be known. The fact that she harboured such long-lasting resentment towards him suggests that his disappearance was half expected.

Olive Queenie remembers overhearing her mother discussing the matter with an aunt. 'They were saying that he couldn't be dead and that he had only been reported missing,' she says. 'They were suggesting that he might still be alive and other bits of gossip.

'I used to ignore it and then one day a friend of the family showed my sister a photograph of him and she was more or less saying the same thing. I never believed it though. As far as I was concerned no one in the British Army could possibly get away from his family and live because he couldn't get out of the country.'

Yet he did manage to get away from his family. In Karachi he worked first as a policeman and later as a motor mechanic. He fathered five sons in fourteen years, though he was known always to have wanted a daughter.

In 1944 he moved his family to Poona and then four years later left for England where he settled in Balsall Heath, Birmingham, and worked as a storekeeper at the Rover factory in Solihull.

William Edward Dazely died of coronary thrombosis in 1969 never knowing that Cliff Richard was his grandson, and never having told his family about the wife and two daughters that he had left behind in Ambala in 1924. When, during the writing of this book his family found out, the news was a great shock to them.

Within two years of William Edward's 'disappearance', Dorothy Edith had found a new love in Richard Dickson, an Anglo-Indian who claimed Indian royal blood. In 1927 their first daughter, Edna, was born.

As a chief inspector on the railway, Richard commanded respect, perks and a good salary. When the family travelled by rail they had their own special carriage and at home there were up to fifteen servants doing everything from cooking and washing to nursing the children and gardening. Dorothy Marie and Olive Queenie loved him as if they had never had any other father.

'I had no feelings for my real father,' says Olive Queenie. 'The only father I knew was my step-father and I thought the world of him because he was a very clever person and he was very good to me.'

Dorothy Edith ruled her family with a rod of iron and had a fierce temper. 'When she went wild she would nearly kill you,' says Olive Queenie. 'People would have to grab hold of her to stop her. I remember once we were at a Railway Institute dance and a soldier turned and said something to my sister which involved referring to her as a "fair wench".

'My mother came up to this fellow and caught him right across his head with her hand. It sent him flying. He was enormous, she was only five-foot tall, but it sent him reeling backwards.

'She became known as "the battle-axe" but everyone respected her. She was good and kind but you couldn't act the fool and you couldn't use bad language when she was around. If she heard soldiers using bad language she would order them out of the room. She wasn't afraid of anyone.

'There was nothing religious about her morals though. She was just plain Victorian. My grandmother, on the other hand, was slightly of the religious kind. Behind her way of talking and teaching was always the Bible. Her point of view was that God wouldn't like that.

'She wasn't a Bible thumper but a lot of her goodness came from the fact that she always read the Bible and we all had to say our prayers at night before we went to sleep. If she wanted something done her way she would bring the Bible out to prove it.'

Dorothy Marie and Olive Queenie had spent most of their early life as boarders at the Lawrence Royal Military School in Sanawar, which offered a limited number of free places each year to children who had lost fathers in military service.

When William Edward Dazely went missing in 1924, Dorothy Edith was living in an army cantonment in Ambala, close to Simla, and of the five Lawrence schools in India the one at Sanawar was the closest. Shortly after the two little girls entered the kindergarten their mother moved down to Asansol to be with Richard Dickson and so the girls spent their early years hardly ever seeing her.

'For the first few years we never went home at all,' remembers Olive Queenie. 'We were just kept at school because it was a good ten-day train journey to Asansol. We used to go for treks into Simla and further on up into the Himalayas. Then we went home when it was Christmas time but not for the summer holidays.'

Sanawar was a beautiful location high in the foothills of the Himalayas, close to the glamorous hill station of Simla where the Viceroy and his government spent their summers. The Lawrence school was mixed, and designed to produce soldiers, nurses and the wives of soldiers.

The two girls were very different. Dorothy Marie was outgoing, sporty and good at knitting and sewing; Olive Queenie was desperately shy and bookish. Dorothy Marie shone at tennis, badminton and hockey and was renowned as an aggressive team player, a quality that her son was to inherit along with her love of sport.

It was while at Sanawar that she started wearing glasses. 'Some children started calling her "four eyes" and "goggle eyes" but she was such a good fighter that very few of them would call her names except behind her back,' says Olive Queenie. 'She would fight anybody tooth and nail. I wouldn't fight anybody and I used to rely on her to defend me.'

Her second family now well established, Dorothy Edith decided in 1934 that it was time that the girls came to live at home, and they were enrolled in a local Roman Catholic school in Asansol, the Loretta Convent. It was at Asansol that Dorothy Marie was to meet her future husband.

'HE WAS A *three* TERROR FOR MUSIC'

Although she was an attractive girl with many admirers, especially from the nearby Catholic boys' school, Dorothy Marie had never loved a man before Rodger Webb. Up until then there had only been coy looks and flirtatious chatter. Actions more serious couldn't be contemplated in the climate of the times, especially with Dorothy Edith keeping a keen eye open for anything that might suggest misbehaviour.

It often fell to Vincent Bridgwater, her mother's younger brother, to discourage potential suitors. 'I had to warn some of them off because they weren't the type that I thought should be mixing with my niece,' he says.

Olive Queenie remembers the time: 'You could say she had boyfriends before Rodger but they were kept secret and they weren't boyfriends like young girls have nowadays. You didn't go out with them. You met them after school and cycled home with them or you'd go into the park and chat to them. To our way of thinking at the time they were boyfriends though.'

The British India of the nineteen-thirties was still in a Victorian time warp. Children whose parents had grown up in Britain were considered terribly modern, and slightly dangerous. A girl was treated as a child until she was at least sixteen and then, on leaving school, she would be expected to clean, wash and darn at her parents' home until a man with an appropriate income came to ask for her hand in marriage. Except for those bold few who learned to type and thought in terms of a career, the late teens were spent learning how to be a housewife.

'We were terribly old-fashioned,' says Olive Queenie, looking back. 'The atmosphere we were raised in was the same one I was reading about in books written in nineteenth-century England.

'You weren't supposed to speak to a boy unless you were actually introduced to him and you certainly wouldn't be able to go out with a boy unless a *duenna* [governess and chaperone for young women] or your parents were with you. You weren't allowed to go out alone with a boy not even when you were engaged. I used to smile when Dorothy was engaged. She used to have to kiss Rodger in the sitting room. She couldn't go outside and kiss him.'

Dorothy met Rodger Webb in Asansol in 1936 when he came to visit his sister, Dorothy Cooke, who lived in the apartment above. The Cookes and the Dicksons had become close friends and were always in each other's homes. Now sixteen years old with dark bobbed hair and large flashing eyes, Dorothy Marie fell for this smartly-dressed man with his impeccable manners. She thought he looked like a matinée idol. 'He was a thorough gentleman,' she says. 'And handsome too.'

Remembers Olive Queenie, 'In those days he had smoothed-down hair and he was very good looking. He used to remind me of the actor Leslie Howard. He had the same bone structure.'

There were drawbacks though, the biggest being the difference in their ages. Rodger was 31, almost twice Dorothy Marie's age and only two years younger than her mother. Then there was the question of distance. Rodger was based in Howrah, a district of Calcutta, and wouldn't be visiting Asansol more than twice a year. Dorothy Edith made it clear that much as she admired Rodger, she didn't think him a suitable boyfriend for her daughter.

Nevertheless Rodger and Dorothy Marie courted for three years, mostly by letter. When they were able to see each other in Asansol there wasn't much opportunity for intimacy because the visits were turned into huge family affairs with the Cookes, the Dicksons and the Webbs gathering to eat, sing and play parlour games. Rodger had a sister, Marjorie, and a brother Tom, who also lived in Howrah and they would travel up for these parties. They were quite unlike the debonair Rodger and were both, in their own way, eccentrics.

Tom appears to have been the black sheep of the family whose life consisted of a cycle of making money and giving up his job for a life of pleasure, before he eventually returned home broke. Marjorie, who worked as a ticket collector on Howrah station, frightened the younger children with her loud voice and her strong language. She dressed in men's clothes and smoked a cigar. 'You didn't think a woman could be like me, did you?' she once asked a rather timid Olive Queenie. Neither Tom nor Marjorie ever married.

The two brothers were very close and teamed up to make music, Rodger with his guitar and mandolin, Tom singing while playing ukulele or banjo. Later, Tom would provide Cliff with one of his earliest musical memories by sitting at the foot of his bed and singing him to sleep.

To the impressionable Dorothy Marie, Tom was as smooth and accomplished as Bing Crosby and she would sit out on the steps of the quarters as he sang songs like 'Ramona', 'The Bells Of Sorrento' and 'Red Sails In The Sunset', while Rodger accompanied him and Marjorie puffed away on tissue paper and comb.

On 26 April 1939 Rodger and Dorothy Marie were married at St Paul's Church, Asansol, and moved north west to a large company bungalow in Dehra Dun. Life was wonderful for Dorothy Marie. Rodger was doing well in his job, managing the local Kellner's restaurant, and she was happy in her home where most of the housework was carried out by servants.

Although she had lived in India all her life she would never have known a native Indian as a close friend. The Indians had their homes on the outskirts of the big towns and lived entirely separate lives. Although she would have respected them there was no question of them being regarded as equals.

'The Indians didn't like the idea of a mixture of races,' says Olive Queenie. 'They thought that any white person who mixed with an Indian was trash, any white girl who went with an Indian man was trash to them. They wouldn't respect her. Similarly any of their girls who went with a white man was automatically considered trash.'

The largest employers in British India were the post and telegraph, the railways, the civil service and the army, and each occupation bred its own community.

'There was a very great class distinction,' Joyce Dobra remembers. 'I had the education of a civil servant and could get into almost any club. But because my father had been born in India he was looked down on by those who had been born in Europe. We in turn looked down on the railway people who, like the post and telegraph, lived in rented accommodation.

'There were very strict social codes laid down by the wives of army officers and diplomats. The rich Indians were allowed to socialize with the whites but even they weren't admitted to any of the clubs.'

Rodger and Dorothy Marie's club was the local Railway Institute where they regularly went to play cards or tennis and badminton. 'There were dances almost every day,' remembers Dorothy Marie. 'It was a lovely life.'

In 1940 she discovered she was pregnant. There were no large British hospitals in Dehra Dun, which then had a population of fewer than 250,000, so she planned to travel three hundred miles south east to Lucknow where Rodger's father was now living in retirement, to have the baby at the King's English Hospital in Victoria Street.

Britain was by now feeling the effects of the war with Germany. There had been skirmishes with fighter planes over South-East England and bombs had been dropped on London. There was little danger of India being attacked but there was a feeling that the days of the British Empire might now be numbered.

When Dorothy arrived in Lucknow the local papers were running stories on the ambitions of the Axis (the alliance of Germany, Italy and Japan) to capture the oil fields of Iraq, and Mahatma Gandhi's plan to fast for the cause of Indian independence. The big films in town were Laurel and Hardy's *Saps At Sea* and *Broadway Melody Of 1940*, starring Fred Astaire.

On Monday 14 October 1940 Dorothy gave birth to the dark-haired boy who would one day be known as Cliff Richard. He weighed nine pounds. That day the *Lucknow Pioneer* printed the text of the first BBC Radio broadcast by Britain's Princess Elizabeth which read, in part: 'When peace comes remember it will be for us, the children of today, to make the world a better and happier place.'

Rodger didn't see the new baby until his wife returned to Dehra

Dun, where they agreed to name him Rodger Harry Webb – 'Harry' in memory of Rodger's eldest brother. This was the name they had prepared as they set off on Saturday 2 November to take the child to his baptism at St Thomas' Church.

'When I got to the church I saw his godmother and mentioned that I was naming him Rodger Harry,' remembers Dorothy Marie. 'She immediately said, "Oh no. I think it should be Harry Rodger." I just stood there unable to do anything and of course the vicar was holding the baby at the font as they do and I heard him saying, "I baptize thee Harry Rodger Webb." '

Harry was placid but tough. Many white children were susceptible to tropical disease but he remained strong and healthy, playing around the house under the eye of his *ayah* while his mother embroidered, sewed and knitted. She made all his clothes until he was six years old.

A year after Harry's birth she became pregnant again, this time returning to her mother in Asansol where, on 10 June 1942, she gave birth to a boy whom they named Frederick William, after Rodger's father.

The baby Frederick William hardly features in Cliff's biographies and autobiographies, the only mention coming in *It's Great to Be Young* where he says, 'Back in India Mum's second child had been a boy but the poor chap died very shortly after birth. Things like that don't mean much to children, and much as I wanted a brother then, I can't think what life would be like without my perky younger sister, Joan.'

There's disagreement over how long the child lived. Olive Queenie thinks he was over twelve months old. Dorothy Marie thinks it was less than three weeks. The ecclesiastical returns don't record his burial. He must have been alive at the age of eighteen days because that was when he was baptized at St Paul's Church in Asansol.

He was born a 'blue baby' and never enjoyed full health. Often he cried all day. Dorothy Marie and Rodger went out dancing one night and returned to find him so ill that a doctor had to be called. The next morning young Frederick William was dead.

'Dorothy always felt she was to blame,' says Olive Queenie. 'But it would have made no difference if they had stayed at home that night. He would have died anyway.'

Dorothy Marie now thinks the death had a far deeper effect on Harry than she had at first thought.

'He was too young to explain what he was feeling but Rodger and I felt that he had lost something in that moment,' she remembers. 'I think he is always conscious that the brother he had was lost. When he was young he didn't show anything but when he grew older he would sometimes say, "I had a brother." Funnily enough when I was in Bermuda once I heard him say, "If my brother had lived he would now be forty." It's obviously never left him.'

After three years living in Dehra Dun Rodger was promoted, and the family moved to Calcutta where Kellner's had its headquarters in the prominent thoroughfare of Chowringhee Road. They were given a small first-floor apartment over a chocolate factory close by Howrah Station, Calcutta's teeming gateway to the rest of India, where a rickety wooden staircase on the outside of the building took them to their front door. Soon after moving in their first daughter, Donella Eugenie, was born.

Harry was remarkably even-tempered as a child. Interviewed in 1964 by Bob Ferrier for his book *The Wonderful World of Cliff Richard* his mother said, 'I never found any fault in that child. He never lied to us, he never hurt anybody, he still doesn't.' Today her opinion is much the same. 'He was very good,' she says. 'He has all his life been that way. He has always been very kind and I can honestly say that he has never driven me to despair like some children can.'

Yet he wasn't spineless. 'Cliff was undoubtedly a toughie,' says Olive Queenie. 'He was always very fit and was able to weather all the sicknesses. His sister Donna had a habit of deliberately getting him into trouble with his mother and he would get soundly walloped but because he was such a tough little guy he never used to let on that he was innocent.'

In the summer months they would leave Calcutta and holiday in Lucknow with grandfather Webb and then go on to Buxar where grandmother Dickson was now living. These times away from home provided Harry with some of his few lingering memories of India – chasing bees, watching monkeys jumping in the branches of trees, fishing, flying kites; and hearing tales of his father's exploits as a tiger hunter.

Rodger was a typical chauvinist of the period who expected everything to be done his way. He would come home from work and sit in his favourite chair while Dorothy Marie and the servants arranged things according to his wishes.

'If things weren't going exactly the way he wanted them to go he would become very Puritanical,' Olive Queenie recalls. 'He could be very strict with Dorothy. She would be quite tired by the time he came back home from work and yet he would want to go out to one of the company dances.'

It was in Howrah that Harry discovered that he could operate the family gramophone and sing along to records.

'He was pretty smart with that machine and would always choose the exact records that he wanted to hear,' says Dorothy Marie. 'He would wind it up himself. We asked him how he knew which records he liked and it was because he recognized different marks on the labels. After discovering the gramophone, music was his number one thing.'

His three favourite records were 'Ragtime Cowboy Joe' by Geraldo and his Orchestra featuring Dorothy Carless, 'Chewing A Piece Of Straw' by Jack Payne and his Orchestra and 'Jersey Bounce' by the Glenn Miller Orchestra.

'He was a terror for music,' remembers Olive Queenie. She was in the army, and used to take the children out for walks in Calcutta's Botanical Gardens when home on leave. 'He used to stand by the gramophone with his finger in the air beating time to the music as if he was a great conductor.'

In September 1945 Harry started at St Thomas' Church School in Church Road, Howrah, a building set among banana trees. He remembers one of the family servants, Habib, bringing his lunch up to him each day wrapped in a napkin.

He was already learning to speak Hindi, which his father spoke fluently, and at school he learned Bengali. His best friend Lal spoke no English and so all their conversations were in Hindi.

The war had only just ended, Japan had been crushed by two atomic bombs and the British, who had promised Home Rule to the Indians in return for their wartime cooperation, were now nervously working out the details of a transference of power.

For those like Rodger and Dorothy Marie who, although British by family origin had never known any other home but India, it was a worrying time. Their days living in the sun with servants at their beck and call were numbered because there would be no place for the old ruling class in an India run by Indians.

Harry began to notice that gradually schoolfriends were leaving, saying that they were going to a place called 'home' which was small, cold and thousands of miles away and which most of them had only read about in books.

The prospect of independence reawakened old religious feuds. Under British rule the Moslem and Hindu factions had no political power and so they set aside their differences. Now the Moslems were wanting to ensure that they would get their own state within the boundaries of the old British India.

In June 1946 the Moslem League voted to accept a British plan that granted them the territory of Pakistan but within seven weeks they withdrew their acceptance and accused Britain and the Congress Party of going back on their pledges. The All-India Moslem League in Bombay called for 'direct action' and set up a committee to launch a struggle 'as and when necessary'.

At this point violence spilled into the streets. Dorothy Marie was jostled while out shopping and Indians shouted at her, 'Go back to your own country white woman.' The young Harry was frightened. 'Leave her alone,' he screamed. 'She's my mummy.' The old India his parents knew, where the natives 'knew their place', was fast vanishing.

On 16 August 1946 riots came to the streets of Calcutta. The Moslem League mounted a Direct Action Day as a protest against the British independence plan, and were attacked by Hindus. British troops and police had to fire on crowds as shops were burned and looted. In three days there was damage estimated at one million pounds, a death toll of 3,000 and 10,000 casualties. The Calcutta Fire Brigade dealt with 900 fires and the streets were littered with bodies.

The Webbs, who lived in a predominantly Sikh area, were terrified. A family of Moslems nearby had been attacked and killed by Hindus leaving only one boy who they could see was hiding in his garden. They kept him alive by dropping food parcels on a rope from their window at night and eventually got in touch with Dorothy Marie's uncle who was serving in the Calcutta Police and he came over in an armoured car to take the boy to safety.

'When he drove up we looked out of the window and we could see that there was human flesh hanging off the tracks of his vehicle,' remembers Dorothy Marie. 'It was a terrible sight. We could see a bit of the Hooglie River from our apartment but that day you couldn't see the water for dead bodies. It was dreadful.

'That was when we knew we had to leave eventually. We knew that if this was what it was going to be like then it wasn't going to be worth living in India.

'My uncle Harry made sure that we got safely out of our apartment and we went and stayed with Rodger's sister, Marjorie. But we hadn't been there for two days when threats were made to burn the place down. Some Moslems guided us out and they didn't hurt us but the whole street was strewn with dead bodies and glass and bricks. They took us to a cinema for safety.'

Thus began the speedy wind-down of British rule. In February 1947 Lord Louis Mountbatten was despatched from London to replace Field Marshal Lord Wavell as viceroy of India and to begin negotiations with Hindu and Moslem leaders over the future of their land.

Although the Hindus were fiercely resistant to the idea of partition it was obvious, with such hatred abroad, that this was the only workable solution. By June both the Congress Party, led by Pandit Nehru, and the Moslem League accepted a plan which would set up a state of West Pakistan in the north west and the much smaller state of East Pakistan in the north east.

On the stroke of midnight, on 14 August 1947, 163 years of British rule in India ended and the transference of power was complete.

But freedom for India didn't bring immediate peace. Months of turmoil followed as millions of refugees fled over the Indo-Pakistan borders in both directions and an estimated 400,000 Moslems and Hindus were slaughtered.

Into this India, on 21 November 1947, came Jacqueline Ann, the Webbs' second daughter. Two months later, in New Delhi, a Hindu fanatic assassinated Mahatma Gandhi, one of the inspirational figures behind the independence movement, as he made his way to a prayer meeting, thus precipitating a further series of riots. By now the British were streaming out of India towards destinations that they hoped would provide them with as good a life as they had left behind.

It was Rodger's inclination to go to Australia where Charlie Holder, one of the men who worked for him, had emigrated, but Dorothy Marie wanted to follow her mother to England where she had gone with her new family of seven, the youngest of whom was the same age as Harry.

A scheme had been set up where those who could prove British ancestry had half of their fare paid by the British government and so the Webbs put all their savings towards getting Bombay to London tickets and packed their few belongings into suitcases. They had always lived in company accommodation so there was no house to sell, no furniture to put into storage and most of the clothes they owned they knew would be hopelessly impractical in the English climate. Their pet dog was left with Dorothy Marie's uncle Vincent, who was staying on in India along with Tom and Marjorie Webb and Frederick William.

They left their home in Howrah for the last time on Saturday 21 August 1948 and took a train from Calcutta to Bombay where, three days later, they boarded their boat for England.

The *Ranchi* was a 23-year-old P&O passenger liner which had spent the war as an armed merchant cruiser and then as a troopship in the Middle East. This was its first round trip since being refitted as a passenger ship. (All other books have mistakenly identified this as the *Ranghi*.)

Built as a liner for 587 passengers, including a first-class section, it had been redesigned for 950 'tourist class' passengers, which meant that it was functional rather than luxurious. Rodger was told that this was to be the ship's last voyage before being scrapped – which wasn't true – and so they were pleasantly surprised to have a comfortable cabin to themselves. (The *Ranchi* stayed in service until the end of 1952 and was then sold to the British Iron and Steel Corporation.)

'The dining rooms were alright,' remembers Dorothy Marie. 'They had a cinema on board and I remember Cliff crawling under the tent without paying to see the films.

'He and I were quite ill when we started on the journey and couldn't even leave the cabin. We felt a little better during the middle of the journey and then when we reached the Bay of Biscay we both fell ill again.'

Having left Bombay on the evening of 24 August the *Ranchi* sailed through the Arabian Sea, arriving in Aden on the morning of the 29th where it docked for four hours, before setting off through the Red Sea towards the Suez Canal.

While sailing up the canal Harry learned how to whistle by imitating other passengers who cat-called the Egyptians watching from the banks. His father's response was to give him a memorable belt around the head. After a six-hour stop-over in Port Said on 2 September the liner made its way across the Mediterranean, arriving at Tilbury Docks at 6 a.m. on Monday 13 September.

The story that Cliff has always told is that after disembarking, his father hired a taxi to Carshalton with his last five pounds (or seven pounds as it was being reported in 1960) but Dorothy Marie remembers it differently.

She believes they were picked up by a private car from Tilbury and that their first few days in England were spent with an aunt of her mother's who lived somewhere in South-East London. It was only then that they made it down to Carshalton where the Dicksons, Dorothy Marie's mother and her family, had set up home.

Harry's first impression of his new country was the typical one of those who had never seen the motherland – the appearance of well-watered vegetation after a lifetime surrounded by brown dust.

'I can remember nothing of the white cliffs of Dover or even of Tilbury,' he once said, 'but I shall never forget the green fields, the trees and the flowers; particularly the flowers on Carshalton station.'

More striking to Rodger and Dorothy Marie must have been the effects of the wartime rationing of clothes, food, petrol and confectionery, which was still in force, and the bomb sites which blighted London. This was not the colourful, confident Britain of the picture books but a nation suffering austerity.

The latest news in the *Wallington and Carshalton Times* was of a serious bread shortage and a worrying lack of telephones.

Apparently there were only 8,000 phones in the whole area and even the chief engineer at the local exchange could not get one installed.

For Rodger, whose whole life had been spent promoting fine wines and good food, the prospects of work in the home country didn't look at all promising.

'LIKE *four* A DREAM COME TRUE'

Richard and Dorothy Dickson had bought their three-bedroomed house at 47 Windborough Road, Carshalton, for £2,500 but it was barely big enough for them and their children – Edna, Jean, Nora, Vincent, Peggy, Geraldine and Christopher.

Then had come the news that Rodger and Dorothy Marie – their daughter and her family – were on their way with Harry, Donella and Jacqueline. It didn't seem possible that they could all fit into a suburban semi-detached so the neighbours at number 45, Norman and Elizabeth Luscombe, agreed to let the Webb family sleep in their small front bedroom until they found a home.

'The room was the size of a box,' remembers Dorothy Marie, 'and everything had to be done in that small space. Because the children were young I had to have a little cooker there to boil their milk and make them porridge.'

The arrangement didn't last long and the Webbs soon returned to number 47, where they were put in an equally small room. This meant that the Dicksons' house now had fourteen people sleeping in it, including two married couples and two children who were over twenty.

'We were sleeping all over the place,' remembers Vincent Dickson, the eldest son. 'We hadn't been in the house very long ourselves so it was a big upheaval.'

Soon after their arrival Harry started at Stanley Park Road Junior School which was only a five-minute walk away. Here he learned for the first time that he didn't have the milky-white skin that most English-born children had during the winter.

His deep tan hadn't stood out in India. In fact, there he had been the 'white boy'. But here in South-West London, where very few children had ever seen a person who wasn't white, he was thought exotic. The difference was accentuated by his Anglo-Indian accent.

Discovering that he was newly arrived from India his classmates concluded that he must be an Indian and, in 1948, the only Indians that British school children knew much about were the ones who threw tomahawks and attacked cowboys in Hollywood films.

Harry was teased and asked where his headdress was. It didn't make it any easier that most of his relatives were part-Indian and stood out in the street with their dark hair and brown skin.

To this day there are those in Carshalton who are convinced that Cliff is part Indian. 'I think there was Indian blood in him because the Dicksons were Indian weren't they?' says Dorothy Willis, who as Miss Olstead taught him in Sunday school.

The most effective way of gaining respect, Harry soon learned, was to hit back rather than to trade insults. Rodger wanted to lodge a formal complaint, especially after a teacher had said to his son, 'Come on Webb, you can't run off to your wigwam any more.' But Harry wanted to stand up for himself.

It was while in Carshalton that he had his first experience of evangelical Christianity. He had sung in the choir of St Thomas' in Howrah, a traditional Anglican church, but at Stanley Park Evangelical Mission, a crude corrugated hut in Stanley Road where he started to go to Sunday school, they talked about 'asking Jesus into your heart' and sang lively choruses.

'His interest in religion in those days was no more than any of the other kids in the class,' remembers Dorothy Willis, who taught him for half an hour each week. 'And he certainly had no thoughts of singing.'

In photographs taken at the time his Sunday school friends beam cheekily and confidently at the camera where he appears subdued and worried. His front teeth were beginning to protrude and he had a noticeably fang-like upper left tooth. His father had told him to straighten his teeth by sucking them in.

His insecurity was a natural part of finding a new place in the world. Back in India he had been treated like a prince by adult servants. Here he was being made to feel racially inferior by white children. Also his father was penniless and out of work and they had no home to call their own.

'The British in India were top dogs,' says his cousin Joyce Dobra. 'We were white and were always brought up with the idea that one day we would be going "back home to England". We were used to telling other people what to do. Our servants were all adults and yet we treated them as if they were children.'

Rodger finally found work as a wage clerk in a local hospital. It gave him money but it was a blow to the pride of a man who had been used to running the show. Dorothy Marie was so unhappy that she wondered whether it might not be best to find another country to live in.

'I was making all sorts of plans to leave England,' she admits. 'I had a brother-in-law who had gone somewhere in the East and he had written and said he could get Rodger a job. I wanted him to go.

'I told him that he could have a job and we'd have free accommodation but he felt that Britain was losing colony after colony and that soon that place would go. And it did.

'A year later my brother-in-law was in England himself and living not far from us but I still hated it here. Rodger hadn't wanted to come in the first place but he never once reproached me.'

Rodger's sister Dorothy Cooke and her husband had by now left Asansol and were living at the opposite end of London in Waltham Cross, Hertfordshire, in a semi-detached house. They suggested easing the situation in Carshalton by having the Webbs stay with them.

Their local council was building a lot of rented accommodation as part of the post-war resettlement and they believed the Webbs could then be put on the waiting list. So, on Harry's ninth birthday, after one year and a month in Carshalton, they went to live with Dorothy and Ernest Cooke and their two boys, Rodger and Ernie.

It may have been slightly less cramped than the Dicksons' house but the Webbs still found themselves squatting in a small room with mattresses on the floor. The only difference was the glimmer of hope that within months they might get their own council house.

Harry was taken to the nearby King's Road school where his teacher was the second-year junior mistress Mrs Tonks.

'I'll always remember the day he came into my class,' she says. 'The headmaster, Harold Cooper, brought in this lad who was very dark with big brown eyes. He was holding his hand because he was quite young and he said to me, "Well, there you are Mrs Tonks. Here's another one for you," because the term had already started and I already had between thirty and forty children in the class. Harry stood there and he bowed. I'll never forget that. He bowed!'

One of Harry's new classmates was a tall blond-haired boy named Norman Mitham whose family lived near the Cookes. The two boys took to each other straight away. They shared a love of football and other sports and would stay close friends right through school, then becoming musical partners in Harry's first major venture.

Mitham remembers the racial taunting starting up again at Waltham Cross, this time with Harry being nicknamed 'Sabu' after the subject of Alexander Korda's 1937 documentary film *The Elephant Boy*.

'In those days anyone who didn't come from Waltham Cross was an alien,' he says. 'He was very unafraid of it all though. He didn't try to hide from the fact or kowtow to them. He stood up for himself. He could certainly lose his temper and he knew how to handle himself.'

On 6 January 1950, Rodger, who was now working as a clerk in the City for Eastwood's Ltd. at 158–160 City Road, filled out his first application form for a council house. He explained to Broxbourne Borough Council that his family of five had lived for a year with nine other people in a three-bedroomed house and now, with his wife expecting a fourth child, they were still having to live and sleep in one small bedroom.

They were added to the waiting list but by the summer he still hadn't heard anything so on 7 August he filed a second application. Christmas 1950 came and went without any news.

After fourteen months with the Cookes, tensions were rising, especially between the two women who found themselves trapped together in the house for long hours each day.

'We had to sleep on two mattresses which just fitted into the room and we had to stand on them when we got dressed,' says Dorothy Marie. 'She wouldn't let us use any other part of the house except to eat.'

Dorothy Marie began to get friendly with the woman next door, Marcelle Henrit, who was outraged that a young family was expected to live in such appalling conditions. Her son Bob Henrit (later to drum for the Roulettes, Argent and the Kinks) remembers the time well.

'We had a family friend who was on the Waltham Abbey Council,' he says, 'and she started to pull some strings. She wasn't able to get anything going in Waltham Abbey itself but she had a friend in Cheshunt who she got in touch with and asked for things to be speeded up.'

In March 1951 things finally started to move. 'It all happened so quickly,' says Dorothy Marie. 'Within a week this fellow came and I told him that I couldn't take him over the house because that was out of bounds but he could come to the room where we all lived, slept, ate and drank.

'He got such a shock when he saw it. By that time Joan had been born and there was a line running across the room with nappies hanging out to dry, a burner to boil her milk and absolutely no room to move about.

'In two weeks' time we had the key to a brand-new council house. We went there to three bedrooms, a kitchen, bathroom and a huge living room downstairs. It was like a dream come true!'

Cheshunt, at that time a small town, is in the Lea Valley just north of London. It is only five miles from Enfield and a short train journey from Liverpool Street Station. After the war it had attracted some industry from the city and was a centre for garden nurseries.

The Bury Green Estate, where the Webbs had been housed, represented the post-war ideal of reasonable rented accommodation surrounded by wide streets and playing areas for children. Hargreaves Close had eighteen houses, with number 12 part of a terrace at the far end looking down the close. The Webbs moved there on 11 April 1951 – two years after arriving in England.

Rodger and Dorothy Marie soon found work at Thorn Electrical Industries on the Great Cambridge Road in Enfield which incorporated the Ferguson Radio Corporation and Atlas lighting. Rodger became a blue-collar worker in the credit control office while Dorothy Marie sorted components on the assembly line.

Their total wages barely added up to twenty pounds a week and it became a struggle to feed and clothe four children while furnishing a new home. Shoes had to be shared around, a lot of rice was eaten and Rodger improvised by making dining-room chairs and tables out of old packing cases he picked up at work for a pound. There was no television set, telephone or gramophone.

'There was no furniture as such,' remembers Norman Mitham. 'When they first moved in you'd have to sit on boxes and quite often on the floor. None of us was rich but they probably had less than any of us.'

The values that the Webbs brought with them from India seemed strangely out of place in a world that was frantically trying to rid itself of Victorianism. Rodger didn't like the new air of informality. He was determined that in his family, at least, the old values of honesty, courtesy and diligence would be upheld.

Although not a church member, Rodger Webb had a firm belief, possibly inherited from his father, that the Bible was the supreme guide for living, and he would regularly read chapters of it to the children by the fireside in the evenings. When he admonished them it was always with an appeal to what the Bible said.

'He would always tell us that this was what God said,' recalls his daughter Jacqui. 'I remember him saying that we shouldn't do this or that because God wouldn't approve of it.

'I think he felt there was a lot wrong with the church system and that you didn't need to go to church in order to be a Christian. I suppose he sent us all to Sunday school because he felt that at least it was better for us to be doing something.'

This moral code was rigid and enforced quite severely at times. He demanded unquestioning obedience and was a stickler for the letter of the law. The children would be punished for being five minutes late. Harry would get a slap.

To his daughters, whom he never hit, he was a warm and friendly figure. 'I saw my dad as the most wonderful person in the world,' says Jacqui. 'What I most remember is sitting on his lap. He would always sit on the armchair and leave a little corner for me to sit on.'

But to Harry he was a prickly character who never openly displayed affection and in whose presence he was very wary. In some children this would have created wilful disobedience but in Harry it created respectful conformism. 'I knew I couldn't get away with anything,' he explains, 'and I never tried.'

He went to his mother for consolation. Whereas his father seemed old and crusty she was young, vivacious and attractive, and a big hit with the schoolfriends he would bring home for tea.

'She became a great guiding light for Cliff,' says Olive Queenie. 'In all the old-style families the father was respected. He was the master. He dished out the punishment. There wasn't the same close-knit attachment that there was with the mother.

'After coming to England things did drift between Cliff and his father because he saw a lot less of him than when he was in India. Rodger didn't have the time to take him out anywhere because he was either working or too tired.

'She adored Cliff and a bit of spoiling would go on. Sometimes Rodger would arrive home and find that Dorothy had allowed her son to do something which he had said he couldn't do.

'Cliff never argued back though. He would get chastised but wouldn't then turn round and say that his mother said he could do it. He knew that would have got her into trouble and Rodger could be very strict with her too.'

'His father could be unyielding,' remembers Mitham. 'If he wanted Cliff in by 9.30 and yet the film we wanted to see didn't end until 9.45 he'd say, "I don't care. It's 9.30 and that's that." Cliff would never argue with him. He set the law and that was it.'

'His family wasn't as flexible as most of ours were,' says Pete Bush, one of Harry's closest schoolfriends. 'We were the first generation to be a lot more free and easy with our parents but it didn't seem to apply to him. He respected his father but I think that it was respect out of fear rather than respect out of love.'

The Webbs stood out among their neighbours for their strictness. Harry didn't seem to enjoy the rough and tumble of life out on the streets and was only allowed out of the house at certain times to play. 'He was a mummy's boy,' says Ivy Clare, the Webbs' next-door neighbour. 'Mrs Webb had a real hold over him. I never saw him out at all.'

Another neighbour, Richard Holmes, had twin daughters who sometimes played with Joan and Jacqui.

'He may have had his own friends at school but I didn't see much of him playing outside,' he says. 'The only time I can remember seeing him is when he was flying his kite out in the close with his dad.' His daughter Linda confirms this. 'He just didn't mix with the other boys,' she says. 'He didn't play with other people outside.'

The only person who saw another side of Harry and his father was Norman Mitham. He remembers Rodger hiding coins around the house and getting the boys to find them. He also remembers being entranced by Rodger's stories of hunting tigers in India. 'To a boy in Cheshunt, hearing someone describe life in the jungle was quite amazing,' he says.

Norman and Harry would sometimes go 'scrumping' – stealing apples – or knocking on doors and running away. 'During the conker season we would fill our pockets with conkers and we would run down the road throwing conkers at people's front doors,' says Norman. 'I can remember he was absolutely over the moon one night because he had thrown a conker and it had hit a doorbell and made it ring.'

The biggest blow of Harry's early life came in the summer of 1952 when he failed the eleven-plus. The blow was all that much harder to take because it had been assumed that he would pass without any problem.

'I was top boy at my junior school,' he says. 'I have a book somewhere which I was given as a prize and then, within weeks, I had failed the eleven-plus and people below me had passed. I was shattered.'

In September 1952 he went to the newly-built Cheshunt County Secondary School which was taking in 800 pupils, and he soon fell in with a crowd of high achievers.

It was for his accomplishments on the sports field rather than in the classroom that Harry would be remembered. He played soccer for Hertfordshire, rugby football for the school, broke the over-13's javelin record with a throw of 106 feet 3 inches, was a top sprinter and had a reputation for fierce tackling that equalled his mother's tough tactics on the hockey pitches of Sanawar.

'He was good at football and played rugby like a lunatic,' says Brian Cooke. 'Also he was undoubtedly the best scrapper in the school. You didn't play around with Harry Webb. I think he had to look after himself when he arrived in this country and that toughened him up.'

By the time he arrived in the second year, in September 1953, he was well established and popular. 'He was different from the other boys,' says his classmate Frances Slade. 'He seemed quieter and more gentle. He wasn't sloppy. I think a lot of it was due to his background in India. He was definitely the most polite and charming boy I knew.'

One woman Harry was able to charm was Jay Norris, a young English and drama teacher who, like Harry, had come to the Cheshunt school when it opened in 1952. They established a relationship which still continues and she was to become the first person to persuade him to get up on a stage and sing.

'I remember him coming to me one day because he hadn't done his homework' she remembers. 'He had this really charming smile and he said something about having had to go out the night before and I said, "I'll tell you something, Webb. When you leave school you'll go into a job where the measure of success is smiling at women because you do it very well."'

Jay Norris had a unique ability in getting teenagers excited about poetry and drama. She read them Shakespeare and brought in a reel-to-reel tape recorder so that they could hear themselves recite. After school she ran a drama society which entered productions into local competitions.

'We were just an ordinary bunch of secondary modern kids,' says his schoolfriend John Vince, 'and she had us acting and singing and recording. We got to learn what a stage was and how to put theatrical make-up on. I'm sure a lot of kids today from backgrounds like ours wouldn't even know who Shakespeare was.'

Harry was only average at his schoolwork but he responded to Jay Norris. He joined the drama society and discovered that despite his shyness he had a real feel for acting.

His acting debut was in *The Price of Perfection* by Sheila Buckley in February 1954. This was followed up in October by A.A. Milne's *The Ugly Duckling* in which he played the chancellor and then, in February 1955, he had a part in *Willow Pattern* which won first prize in the Youth Drama Festival.

'He had the right kind of voice,' says Jay. 'He had a feeling for words and a feeling for putting something over. It's very rare to find a boy with a really good, interesting voice.'

'I think Jay was very instrumental in getting him motivated,' says Frances Slade. 'He was very shy when he first came to the school but she spotted something in him. He could read aloud so well.

'To get a class of idiots like us to sit down and listen to someone reading was quite something and she managed to get us all doing it with Shakespeare and the sorts of things you normally have to bludgeon kids with.'

Life at 12 Hargreaves Close had been complicated by the arrival of Harry's grandfather, Frederick William Webb, who was now in declining health. 'When everyone else left India in 1948 he didn't want to come to "Freezeland", as he called it. It was too cold,' says granddaughter Joyce Dobra. 'Then suddenly when he was about eighty he decided he wanted to come.'

He looked out of place in England. He insisted on wearing the lightweight linen suits he had always worn in India and with his long white beard and walking stick the local children believed he was Father Christmas. The fact that he frequently handed out sweets and apples to them reinforced the suspicion.

He took over the small front bedroom and Harry had to move in with his three sisters. It wasn't to be for long though. In 1954 Frederick went to stay with the Cookes where he died one morning of a sudden heart attack.

Dorothy Marie was now cycling every day to a wiring factory in Broxbourne where she would work until five o'clock. This meant that Harry had to look after Donna, Jacqui and Joan from the time they left school until she arrived home.

In September 1955 Jay Norris became Harry's form teacher and the school's Christmas production was to be A.A. Milne's *Toad of Toad Hall* based on Kenneth Grahame's *The Wind In The Willows*. Harry was her choice to play Ratty. 'That should tell you what sort of boy he was,' she says. 'Ratty was the sympathetic one, the nice one, the sensible one.'

The only problem was that if he took the part he would have to sing and although he had enjoyed singing since childhood he was not a confident performer. 'As far back as I can remember he had enjoyed music and he was always singing,' says Jacqui. 'But if anyone was around he would hide behind the settee. He wouldn't stand up and sing in front of our aunts and uncles if they could see his face.'

He told Jay that he wanted the part of Ratty but, unfortunately, he couldn't sing. 'I told him that was rubbish,' says Jay. 'I said, "It's actually quite simple. If you can't sing you can't play Ratty." Of course he did sing it and he sang it beautifully. I can see him now in his Ratty suit, twirling his tail.'

At the same time that Harry was fronting his first audience as a singer, a new form of American music had come over to Britain. It was called rock 'n' roll and 'Rock Around The Clock', a record by Bill Haley and the Comets, had come into the *Record Mirror* charts at number twelve on 15 October 1955 and had risen to the number one spot on 12 November, staying there through to the second week of January 1956.

Haley was a most unlikely looking hero for teenagers. Thirty years old, with an egg-shaped face, he appeared on stage in a tartan dinner jacket with a silk collar and had a precious kiss curl sprung on his forehead. With their receding hairlines, moustaches and spectacles, the Comets didn't look any more youthful.

Born in Michigan in 1925, Haley's musical background was in country and western but in 1951 he became the first white singer to cover a rhythm and blues song when he recorded Jackie Brenston's up-tempo song 'Rocket 88' with his group the Saddlemen.

At the time music like this made by blacks was categorized as 'race' music. It was produced mainly for what was then termed the 'negro' market, which didn't have the purchasing power to make an impact on the national charts.

'Rock Around The Clock' was recorded in New York on 12 April 1954, produced by Milt Gabler of Decca Records, and was an immediate hit in America. Its international success though happened only when the producers of *The Blackboard Jungle*, a film about rebellious New York schoolchildren, seized the opportunity to use what was then considered a novelty song over the credits.

The effect of Haley's record on British teenagers was profound. The pop music of the day was dominated by Rosemary Clooney, Dickie Valentine, Alma Cogan, Ruby Murray, Teresa Brewer and

Frankie Laine, singers who soothed rather than excited. It was music that appealed to those who had come through the war and were now looking forward to a future of peace, prosperity and family life.

But their children wanted something more vigorous and stirring. Rock 'n' roll, with its brash American vocabulary and pulsing beat, pointed to the sort of future they wanted.

'I think we were all desperate for something new,' says Frances Slade. 'We all had been born either just before or during the war, many of us had experienced separation from our fathers, we had gone through rationing and everywhere looked grey. There was no colour anywhere. It was just dull, grey and boring.

'The word "teenager" had hardly been conceived. Entertainment for people in this age group was non-existent. We couldn't buy the clothes we wanted. The thing is, we didn't really know what we wanted. All we knew was that we wanted something different.

'Then along came Bill Haley and rock 'n' roll and suddenly there was something we could relate to and, what's more, it was something we could do.

'I think we were all being cloned into becoming very good safe little factory workers and office girls or, if possible, into doing some further education in order to become a teacher. But we weren't supposed to rock the boat because we were putting the country back together again. I think we just thought that there was more to it than that.'

Bill Haley inspired Harry. He never wanted to look like him or to emulate his stage act but at least he knew there was more to pop music than Jimmy Young singing 'The Man From Laramie'. For the real epiphany, the one that was to change his life, he had to wait. But only for another five months.

'I HEARD *five* ELVIS AND THE NEXT STEP WAS TO DO IT'

One Saturday in May 1956, Harry was walking with friends in the Four Swannes area of Waltham Cross when he passed a Citroën parked outside Asplan's the newsagents, with its engine ticking over and its radio playing. What he heard from that car radio transfixed him.

It was a pop song but it was unlike anything he had ever heard. It seemed like a surge of energy, an attitude transformed into noise. He had no idea what it was and had to tune in regularly to AFN (American Forces Network) to find out that it was 'Heartbreak Hotel', by an American singer named Elvis Presley. There were no BBC radio or television programmes at the time which were likely to play such music.

The effect of that moment has never left him. It marked a change in his aspirations. 'The day I first heard Elvis' voice I thought of it as a sound or an instrument,' he says. 'I had never heard anyone sing like that before. I had liked songs by Perry Como and Frank Sinatra but I had never wanted to be like them. When I heard Elvis the next step for me was to try to do it.'

Bill Haley had introduced the rhythm to the young white

audience but Elvis brought the style. He was 21 when he cut 'Heartbreak Hotel' and had been recording for only eighteen months after having been discovered by Sam Philips whose Sun Records label in Memphis had released Jackie Brenston's 'Rocket 88' in 1951.

Philips' great idea – which must have been encouraged by Bill Haley's cover version of 'Rocket 88' – was to find a white boy with a black-sounding voice who could make rhythm and blues widely acceptable to the racially-prejudiced white community.

Hip white American teenagers were already tuning into black radio stations but as yet there were no artists they could identify with. There were no James Deans or Marlon Brandos singing rock 'n' roll.

Elvis was white with a voice that sounded black, and he looked great. He had the lips and nose of a young Greek god, held his long dark hair back with grease and wore flash pimp's jackets that would have branded a white man a homosexual in many parts of America.

'He had a strange kind of appeal to both sexes,' commented Jerry Leiber, who co-wrote many of his hits. 'He didn't intimidate or look too much like a grown man. He was innocent but still provocative. There was a feminine undertone to his features. He wasn't handsome, he was beautiful.'

Not that fifteen-year-old Harry even knew what Elvis Presley looked like in May 1956. All he knew was that he needed to buy a copy of 'Heartbreak Hotel' and he needed to try to sing like Elvis. The first that his friends knew about his Four Swannes experience was when he arrived at school one morning with the record begging them to listen to it.

'We had managed to commandeer the school record player,' says Frances Slade. 'We had it hidden in our stock room for months and we were allowed in school before everyone else because we were prefects. In Room 9 we used to have our own private club.'

Harry put 'Heartbreak Hotel' on the turntable and raved about his discovery. 'He came in at around half past eight and he played this record over and over again,' remembers Pete Bush. 'He then tried to mime to it. That to me was the first sign of his fascination for Elvis. He used to take the microphone from the tape recorder and sing through it as the record was playing.'

He soon saw photographs of Elvis in weekly magazines and developed a passion for wanting to look like him. He pushed Brylcreem through his dark hair, combed it back into a huge wave and then practised curling his upper lip and staring moodily beneath lowered eyelids in the mirror over the fireplace.

'He used to keep asking us if he looked like Elvis,' remembers Jacqui. 'He used to do his little movements and then he'd say, "Do I look like Elvis? Do I look like Elvis?"'

There was a weekly dance on Saturday nights at Holy Trinity Youth Club in Waltham Cross. Harry would go with a group of friends and dance to chart records played on a small Dansette gramophone. Two of the girls, Betty Clarke and Freda Johnson, liked singing to the records and when Harry, John Vince and a girl called Beryl Molineux began to join in it took on the shape of an informal group.

They harmonized on songs like 'Water' by Frankie Laine and 'Only You' by the Hilltoppers but had a special affection for the doo-wop sounds of the Crew Cuts ('Sh-Boom') and the Teen Queens ('Eddie My Love').

Doo-wop was a convenient label to describe the new vocal harmony music coming out of New York from groups like the Clovers, the Moonglows, Frankie Lymon and the Teenagers and the Cleftones. It wasn't strictly rock 'n' roll but it was inspired by rhythm and blues and a lot of the groups were black.

There had been no serious intentions behind the sessions around the record player but when, in July 1956, Trinity Youth Club put on an Anglo-French dance as a fundraiser for Holy Trinity School the five were asked to perform a cabaret spot. They called themselves the Quintones, a suitably doo-wopish name, and began rehearsing in a friend's house.

'Harry would sing the song,' remembers John Vince, 'the girls would harmonize and I would do the boom-de-boom bass line.' One song, however, wouldn't require any help from the others. Harry was going to do 'Heartbreak Hotel' on his own.

When it came to the event on Bastille Day, 14 July 1956, at the Holy Trinity School in Waltham Cross, Betty Clarke suffered stage fright at the sight of an audience of 250 people and was substituted at the last minute by her friend Irene Fowler.

The brief performance, which included Harry's 'Heartbreak Hotel' solo spot, has gone down in history as his first concert. It also earned him his first publicity. *The Cheshunt Weekly Telegraph* carried a large photo of the Quintones with Harry clearly distinguishable in his light jacket and greased-back hair.

'The dance, which was in connection with the school's birthday and fête, also Bastille Day, raised £20 for the school funds,' ran the report above the picture.

'Posters, supplied by the French Embassy, advertising the day and the beautiful French countryside, decorated the hall, and the stage accommodating Jack de Benham and his band, represented a French cafe. Appropriate lighting completed a most effective scene.

'Cabaret turns were provided by members of the club; Mr Eric Frith, the leader, impersonated Liberace.

'Proceeds from the competition were given to the Duke of Edinburgh's playing fields fund.

'Refreshments were provided under the direction of Mrs Rix and Mrs Mathews.'

The Quintones rehearsed more than they played. The only other event that anyone is certain they performed at was the 21st birthday party of John Vince's sister Pamela, in September of that year. A photograph taken of the cake-cutting shows Harry still looking shy and out of place. While John Vince and his brothers are sniggering and wearing casual white shirts Harry is standing behind them in a dark jacket and tie with his lips gripped together.

Besides giving him his first performing experience the Quintones brought Harry closer to Betty Clarke, a petite girl with dark hair who he'd known since junior school in Waltham Cross. They had always liked each other but now they were both fifteen things became more serious.

'I think Betty Clarke was my first girlfriend,' he says. 'In those days you took bets on who you could catch and kiss. We used to say, "Well, if you're so crazy about her then grab her in the corridor during the break and kiss her."

'So from chasing girls, catching them and kissing them suddenly you found that you were with someone and you were seen as a couple. Betty and I were boyfriend and girlfriend and went to the pictures and to parties together.'

One of their first times together had been at the 1955 school lunch. 'It was usual that a boy and a girl would choose a member of staff to take to the lunch,' remembers Betty. 'This year both Harry and I had chosen to take Jay Norris and she said, "I think really it's Harry taking Betty!" At school we were just friends but then, at the youth club, we walked out together for a little while.

'He didn't send me flowers because none of us had that sort of money in those days, but he would send me cards and once he put a box of chocolates inside my desk at Christmas. It was just those little things that meant you were a closer friend than just an ordinary schoolfriend and other people regarded you as boyfriend and girlfriend.'

Teenage relationships in the fifties were still very innocent, unaffected by commercial pressure to pair off and become 'sexually active'. Over 80 per cent of English children still went to Sunday school, so in many cases there was a moral foundation for chastity, but the biggest fear was putting a girl 'in the family way', which inevitably meant an early marriage. Teenagers who went 'all the way' were generally considered a bit fast and not 'nice'.

Harry and his friends were definitely a 'nice' bunch who believed in socializing as a group rather than pairing off for intimate moments. With little money and no commercial teenage culture they spent their time swimming, walking, bike riding and going for picnics. They spent more time in one another's homes than they did in cafes or cinemas.

'We didn't have the opportunity to go to many different places so we used to take our bikes and go to Epping Forest,' says Betty. 'Sometimes we went out as a group. There weren't discos in those days, only the record player down at the youth club.'

What struck Betty about Harry was his respect towards girls. He never used his good looks to flirt outrageously.

'He never pushed himself around,' she says. 'I think it was to do with the way he was brought up. He was taught that it wasn't nice to go out with one girl after another and that you should never take advantage of anyone.

'I'll always remember someone asking him whether he had a girlfriend and he said, "Yes. I've got her picture in my pocket," and he dived into his pocket and brought out a photograph of his mother.'

Most of the children in Harry's year, including Betty Clarke, left school that summer but he was included as part of an experimental group of fifteen pupils who stayed on to sit O level GCE examinations. Their relationship didn't survive the summer holidays as Betty started courting another boy from the youth club.

'We parted good friends,' she says. 'We just went our separate ways. When I saw him on TV just a few years later I couldn't believe that I'd actually been out with him and he'd been in my home.

'I'd always remember him whether or not he had become famous. Harry Webb was an important part of my schooldays.'

There were two other girlfriends from those days that he can still remember – Sheila Bevan and Heather Harman. 'Sheila was the girl that all the guys wanted to go out with,' he says. 'I also remember being besotted with Heather when we were doing *HMS Pinafore*. I went out with her for a short period.'

In the group that had stayed on in Jay Norris' fifth form there were thirteen boys – including John Vince, Pete Bush and Brian Cooke – and two girls – Janice Berry and Frances Slade.

They were an unusually close-knit form. Brian Cooke can remember the time when Pete Bush received a cuff around the head from a member of staff and the whole class walked out and protested to the headmaster. Groups of them would often go for tea at Jay's home.

'They were the first class that I knew I'd miss because they were so nice,' says Jay. 'We had been together such a long time and had developed a mutual trust and goodwill.'

Harry studied for O levels in Religious Education, English Language, English Literature and Maths, but he was never a star student. No one would have picked him out as a boy who was going to do great things.

'His problem wasn't in being lazy but in wanting to do too many other things so that he didn't want to sit down and do essays,' says Jay Norris. 'He was also extremely interested in rock 'n' roll. That didn't leave an awful lot of time for school work.'

At the age of sixteen Harry was a mixture of respectful conformism and determined individualism. In his reluctance to blaspheme, smoke, drink or argue back with his parents he seemed, even to his contemporaries, to be a little old-fashioned.

But no one mistook his politeness for compliancy, because beneath the well-mannered surface was grit. He showed this in his competitive nature on the sports field and in his reputation as a fighter.

'He was not a guy that you would upset,' says Cooke. 'He'd knock your block off. There was a really big lad in our class, and I remember that one day he said something Cliff didn't like, and Cliff punched him in the mouth.'

For his final Christmas play at Cheshunt School Harry took the part of Bob Cratchit in *A Christmas Carol*. It was then, according to Cooke, that the future rock 'n' roll star began to emerge.

'For his part in *A Christmas Carol* he had to dress up in tight black trousers and you suddenly noticed that the girls were looking at him as a bit of all right. Up until that time there had been nothing. During rehearsals he used to sing "Heartbreak Hotel" and "Hound Dog" just as a joke.'

A Christmas Carol earned him his first review. 'Harry Webb acted well as Bob Cratchit,' said the *Cheshunt Weekly Telegraph*, 'but he was rather let down by the make-up team and, hard as he worked, he could not dispel the impression that he was a teenager and not a harassed father.'

That Christmas he visited his grandmother in Carshalton and his aunt Ruth (married to Vincent Dickson) can remember him singing Tommy Steele's two hits 'Rock With The Caveman' and 'Singing The Blues', which were the first attempts at British rock 'n' roll, and telling her, 'I'm going to be famous one day.'

Although rock 'n' roll, was being heard more frequently it was still considered a passing phase and wasn't receiving any specialized television coverage until '6.5 Special' started in February 1957 on BBC TV, the same month that Bill Haley arrived in Britain for his first tour.

Pete Bush remembers that by this time Harry was becoming increasingly conscious of his looks. 'In our last year at school he became very meticulous about his appearance. He was always combing his hair. It wasn't a fashion show because none of us had a lot of money. It was just that he liked to keep looking good.'

There was enormous anticipation for Haley's concerts. *The Daily Mirror* had been orchestrating a publicity campaign which would culminate in the organization of a four-hundred-seater Rock 'n' Roll Special train. It was to travel from Waterloo Station in London to Southampton to greet Haley and the Comets when they docked on 6 February.

The film *Rock Around The Clock*, which starred Bill Haley, had gained notoriety because Teddy boys had decided that they shared an affinity with rock 'n' roll and were turning up at the cinemas to jive in the aisles and slash seats. The film was banned in some cities and Bill Haley was given space in the *Daily Mirror* to declare how sorry he was that his music had got people overexcited and to explain how virtuous it really all was.

In hyping Haley to such an extent the *Mirror* was walking a fine line between promoting a series of events and inciting teenage frenzy. When Haley finally arrived he was faced with a crowd of 5,000 at the dockside and more at Southampton station. The fans were so out of control at Southampton that he was virtually carried by the force of the bodies towards his train. All along the route to London those who'd read the *Mirror*'s timetable for the progress of the Rock 'n' Roll Special stood beside the tracks and waved.

The behaviour so alarmed Haley that he threatened to cancel the concerts if any rioting occurred. Strict security was enforced, dancing in the aisles was banned and the *Mirror* soberly advised its teenager readers to 'take it easy'. The warnings proved worthwhile. When he took to the stage at London's Dominion Theatre, Tottenham Court Road, there was a full house of 3,000 but no riots.

On 23 February Haley was able to write in *Melody Maker*: 'There haven't been any disturbances at the concerts. The boys and girls clap and they sing with us. That is the general pattern that we follow in our presentation. If we entertain the crowd, then the crowd will watch and listen quietly.'

The tour, as originally planned, was to be no more than a brief incursion but shortly before Haley arrived in Britain a further twelve dates were added, one of them at the Regal in Edmonton, just a few miles down the road from Cheshunt. Harry and his friends were in line for tickets the morning they went on sale, which was a school day.

The plan had been to go on to school but by the time they were served it was after midday so they killed the afternoon at Terry Smart's house. What they didn't know was that a member of staff had seen them in Edmonton and so the next day they received a dressing down from the headmaster, with the prefects among them temporarily losing their badges.

The concert was on Sunday 3 March 1957, and was an eye-opener for these sixteen-year-olds from Hertfordshire who had never been able to see a live rock 'n' roll performance.

'We were absolutely bowled over by the whole thing,' remembers Frances Slade. 'It was so exciting. At last there was something we could relate to instead of all this Guy Mitchell and Perry Como stuff that was being churned out at us.'

Haley was preceded by a 50 minute set from the Vic Lewis Orchestra and then came on playing 'Razzle-dazzle' dressed in his tartan jacket. The volume, although low by today's standards, took the audience by surprise. *Melody Maker*'s Laurie Henshaw had described it as 'hitting the crowd like a battering ram' even though it only came through three small speakers.

Bass player Al Rex threw his stand-up bass around, eventually straddling it like a horse, while tenor sax player Rudy Pompilli climbed on his back in what appeared to be wild abandon to youngsters more accustomed to a band seated behind its music stands.

'What struck me was that everyone was standing up,' remembers Norman Mitham. 'It was electrifying. We'd never seen anything like it before. The sound seemed so full. We came home afterwards on the bus and talked about the concert for days.'

Says Cliff: 'I can still feel the excitement I felt that night. We were in the circle and we had to stand up to see and you could feel the balcony shake when he came out singing, "On your marks, get set, now ready, ready everybody, Razzle-dazzle..."

'It's hard for me now to think of anything that has been as good as that. There must have been, but that was my first encounter. I had never been to a concert before and suddenly everything we had heard on the radio was happening right before our eyes!'

In 1960 he wrote: 'This, I think, was the moment when I knew what I wanted to do above everything else in the world.'

The month of the Haley concert saw another musical phenomenon, skiffle, gripping Britain. Like rock 'n' roll it was an American music but its origins were further back in negro spirituals, folk songs, jug band music and acoustic blues rather than the electrified Chicago blues.

Unamplified and largely unrecorded, skiffle tended to appeal to the better-educated and more middle-class teenagers who wore thick pullovers and corduroys rather than coloured shirts and drainpipes. They admired the music for its 'authenticity' and 'purity' and rather scorned rock 'n' roll because of its deliberate commercial appeal and its associations with Teddy boy hooliganism.

Nevertheless, that didn't stop the music papers from gleefully declaring the death of rock 'n' roll and predicting that skiffle would be the next big thing. The point was considered proven when the Vipers scored a hit with 'Cumberland Gap', Chas McDevitt with 'Freight Train' and Lonnie Donegan with 'Don't You Rock Me Daddy-O'.

Harry never really liked it. To him it was as far removed from rock 'n' roll as was opera. He bought Donegan's records but the releases that he really loved were those by Elvis, the Everly Brothers and the Platters. He could never have imagined himself singing skiffle.

'I UNASHAMEDLY USED SKIFFLE'

During July and August 1957 Harry took a summer job picking tomatoes in a local garden nursery while waiting to hear how he had fared in his GCE O level exams. He had a horrible feeling as he trudged home each night with his hands stained dark green that he could be doing a job like this for the rest of his life.

When the results came through they were a severe disappointment. His father opened the letter and broke the news that he had passed only in English Language. In real terms this left him no more qualified than his classmates who had gone out into the world after the fourth year. Career opportunities for people with one O level were limited. If he didn't take up an apprenticeship he was left with the options of being a manual labourer or an office junior.

Fearing the worst, his father had already been making enquiries at Thorn Electric and knew of a vacancy in the credit control department at Atlas Lighting. It was an unskilled position checking orders against the different trade discounts and passing the information on to regional despatch centres. It wasn't a demanding job but there were 'prospects' for the right hard-working lad and it brought in extra money for the still-struggling family. Most of his four pounds a week wage packet would be handed straight over to his mother.

Thorn Electric was a major employer in the area but didn't offer the ideal work environment for a sixteen-year-old boy. The average age of its workers at that time was forty and many of these were housewives working on the assembly lines. June Pearce, who, as June

Turner, was a personnel officer when Harry joined the company, remembers him mainly because he was one of the few young people on the payroll.

'He just seemed like most other young people of the day,' she says. 'He was very quiet, very polite and sort of orderly. He wasn't a tearaway by any means. He belonged to the Sports and Social Club and used to play a lot of badminton with his father.'

While sorting out the orders and looking up maps to find out where the closest despatch centre to Macclesfield was, he secretly dreamed of being Elvis. He had been doing his best to look like his idol, studying the photos that Donna was collecting and pinning up in the girls' bedroom, but he now wanted to be able to do what Elvis did – to sing, make records and appear in films.

He had been encouraged by singing with the Quintones but since then he had entered some local competitions as a solo act. In one talent show, held at the Capitol Theatre in Winchmore Hill, he had sung a version of Frankie Laine's 'A Woman In Love' and taken second place.

'I wasn't frustrated at the office,' he says, 'because I never thought about it that much. I was only thinking about becoming a singer. I was convinced I could do it but I was frustrated that I didn't know how to start. If only there had been a door marked "Show Business" with a list of vacancies posted outside. I had no way of knowing where to go. If there is such a thing as luck, that's where luck came in.'

Luck in his case, came when his bicycle broke and he had to take the bus into work. On the top deck he met his schoolfriend, Frances Slade, who was now a student commuting daily to Hornsey College of Art. Somewhere between Cheshunt and Enfield, where Harry had to get off, Frances mentioned that the singer in the skiffle group her boyfriend Terry Smart was drumming for had just been called up to do his National Service and they were looking for a replacement. Harry's name had been brought up, apparently because Smart remembered from the school plays that he could sing. Harry indicated his interest and, the next evening, Smart came knocking at the front door of 12 Hargreaves Close.

Harry was a year older than Terry Smart who had left school at fifteen to become a butcher's mate but he knew him from playing in the school's rugby football team and from playing the role of The Ghost Of Christmas Yet To Come in *A Christmas Carol*.

He had started drumming after seeing a trio playing at a wedding reception in the Flamstead End Community Hall. 'I sat watching the drummer and I thought, "That's what I want to do," ' he says. 'I used to have a paper round and I bought myself a bass drum, snare drum and high hat with my earnings. Later I bought a twenty-inch crash cymbal. A friend of my dad's had played drums in an army band and he used to come round and give me lessons.'

News that there was a drummer living on the estate came to the attention of Dick Teague, a fairly serious-minded accounts clerk whose big musical love was traditional jazz. When his younger brother Mick left the navy and bought a guitar he was inspired to start playing skiffle in the front room of his family's home at 19 Kingsley Avenue, with their mother Kathleen joining in on a washboard.

It wasn't long before the windows and doors were thrown open and friends would sit on the garden wall clapping along to these informal concerts. Eventually a neighbour complained to Broxbourne Borough Council who threatened the Teagues with eviction unless the music was halted at 10 p.m. each night.

By the time Smart was recruited in June 1957 it had become a fully fledged skiffle group with the Teague brothers playing guitars, Terry Harness singing and playing guitar, Allan Crouch on washboard and Ken Simmons on tea-chest bass. An insurance salesman who was a friend of the Teague family heard the boys rehearsing and booked their first public appearance at a pub in Stoke Newington, North London, after which Dick's father, Walter Teague, began to manage the group, getting them regular work at local youth clubs, fêtes, pubs, jazz clubs and carnivals.

Terry Smart took Harry to meet the rest of the group at Frances Slade's home in Churchgate. 'It was an audition in a very loose sense of the word,' remembers Dick, who never had a high opinion of his group's musicianship.

'It would have been very presumptuous of us to consider we were auditioning someone. Basically it was a question of finding someone who could sing better than we could and none of us could sing a bloody note. Everybody was doing skiffle in those days. You didn't even have to be good at it.'

Harry turned up wearing a brown duffle coat and seemed shy and lacking in confidence as he ran through a couple of numbers in the front room of the bungalow, but his singing was distinct and impressive.

'There was a very musical, pleasant quality to his voice even then,' says Dick. 'As a matter of fact it wasn't the best sort of voice for the material we were doing, which often sounded better with a jazz voice that was slightly raspy and unpleasant. But Harry made everything he sang sound good.'

On 19 September 1957 Walter Teague wrote in the group's engagement diary: 'Harry introduced to group and enlisted right away. Good luck to the group's additional member.'

The next day Harry signed his first contract, a handwritten note made out on a sheet of paper torn from an exercise book. It read: 'We, the undersigned (members of Dick Teague's Skiffle group) hereby agree not to leave the group to take an individual engagement with any other musical concern without previously discussing the matter with the full group and its controlling manager.' It was signed by Harry Webb, Dick Teague, Mick Teague, Terry Harness, Allan Crouch, Terry Smart and Ken Simmons

British skiffle, which reached its commercial peak in 1957, had developed from a fascination with American folk blues and was pioneered by traditional jazz musicians like Ken Colyer (trumpet), who had spent time in New Orleans in 1952, Chris Barber (trombone) and Lonnie Donegan (banjo), which is why a jazzer like Dick Teague found himself getting involved. It was Donegan's 1955 recording of 'Rock Island Line' which triggered off the national craze when it became a hit.

'Rock Island Line' was the perfect skiffle number. It was frantic, it was easy to play and it was splattered with Americanisms. The story of how it was discovered by the American folklorist Alan Lomax, who picked it up from a convicted murderer called Huddie 'Leadbelly' Ledbetter in 1934, gave it absolute credibility in the eyes of the purists who liked to think that the best songs were written from the soul without any thought of posterity or financial reward.

Donegan, who played in Chris Barber's band, had initially been given a spot to play 'Rock Island Line' as a novelty interlude in Barber's programme of New Orleans jazz but by 1957 he was a major star in his own right with a string of top twenty hits including 'Lost John', 'Cumberland Gap' and 'Putting On The Style'.

Although the songs were inevitably American and skiffle was supposed to have started at rent parties (parties put on by impoverished musicians to raise money for their rent) in Chicago during the twenties, skiffle in the hands of Lonnie Donegan and his friends was a peculiarly British phenomenon which appealed not only because it was vibrant and unstuffy at a time when young people were looking for an excitement that would lift them out of the sea of post-war blandness, but because you didn't need to be an accomplished musician to play it and the equipment was inexpensive and largely improvised.

You could get by with three chords, a song book and a lot of enthusiasm. An upright bass could be made out of an empty tea chest, a broom handle and a length of string, while percussion was produced by dragging a thimble across the ribbed metal of a domestic washboard.

It wasn't rock 'n' roll but it drew from the same well of black American culture and appealed to young people. It created a ready-made audience for blues singers like Big Bill Broonzy, Sonny Terry, Brownie McGhee and Lonnie Johnson when they later came to England and at the same time led to the folk music revival of the early sixties.

'It was also an ideal place for potential rock 'n' roll musicians to get started in Britain. Trade embargos introduced after the war meant that electric guitars made in America weren't available in British music stores and few teenagers in this country had enjoyed the long exposure to black gospel music, country and western and blues that people like Elvis Presley and Chuck Berry had. Six months before Harry Webb joined Dick Teague, John Lennon had started singing skiffle with the Quarry Men, and was later joined by Paul McCartney.

Alan Lomax himself saw the movement in glowingly positive terms. In August 1957 he commented: 'Before skiffle, even three or four years ago, relatively few people in London made their own music. Singing and playing was for show-offs or professionals. Pub singers mulled over the dry bones of the Cockney music hall songs which had little meaning for the younger generation. Nowadays the young people of this country have songs they like to sing.'

Harry hated skiffle. It was too worthy and folkish for him and lacked the raw energy of Memphis rock 'n' roll. But he saw the sense in keeping his mouth shut about his personal musical preferences and regarded the job in Teague's group as his first step into show business. He even dared to think that maybe he could introduce a little rock 'n' roll into the act.

'For me it offered a way of singing,' he admits. 'Skiffle was just a vehicle to take me where I wanted to go. I couldn't have possibly sung like a skiffle singer. I didn't find it very exciting but I liked being able to sing in front of an audience. There wasn't another skiffle singer who looked like Elvis. I unashamedly used it to further my own ends.'

Once he had signed the contract he rehearsed every night, learning the words to such songs as Woody Guthrie's 'Bring A Little Water Sylvie' and the Donegan hits 'Rock Island Line' and 'Don't You Rock Me Daddy-O'. The group's sources were mainly the singles by Donegan and Ken Colyer's song book, *Skiffle Album*, which had the words and chords to such skiffle favourites as 'This Train', 'John Henry', 'Down By The Riverside' and 'The Grey Goose'.

Before Harry joined the group Dick Teague's opinion was that they were 'basically rubbish'. His revised opinion was that they were 'basically rubbish', but with an added 'bit of quality'. The speed at which the new singer could pick up songs amazed them all. 'We would pick a record we liked and work out the chords in rehearsal,' says Dick. 'Harry could come back the next day and he would know the piece inside out.'

One of the group's regular gigs over the coming months would be an 8.30 spot at the Flamstead End Youth Club during a Friday night jazz evening known as the Saints' Rhythm Club.

'What used to happen was that while the jazz bands were on, the kids flopped round the hall looking bored,' says Dick. 'Then when the skiffle came on they would go mad dancing.' It was here, on 4 October, that Harry made his debut as the lead singer of a group.

With the departure of Terry Harness – after a couple of performances sharing the stage with Harry – the group had lost a guitarist. Harry couldn't yet play guitar but he did like to strap one over his shoulder and have it hanging behind him as he sang, Elvis Presley style.

'He used to embarrass me with it,' Dick admits.

Two weeks later Harry roped in Brian Parker, a friend from Cheshunt Secondary School who had played violin in the National Youth Orchestra, to play guitar. Parker was to go on to become an important figure in the rock 'n' roll scene around Cheshunt and Waltham Cross, playing with Dave Sampson and the Hunters and the Parker Royal Five before forming Unit Four Plus Two with an old school friend and scoring a number one hit in 1965 with 'Concrete and Clay'.

'I knew him mostly through sport at school,' says Parker. 'Then because I had owned a guitar for a couple of weeks he thought I must be very proficient and so he asked me to join.'

Over the next three months the Dick Teague Group played an average of twice a week and rehearsed furiously in between. A look at the date sheet meticulously kept by Walter Teague shows that they played Flamstead End Youth Club once a week and then usually played another local event such as a Boy Scouts' party, a dance at Goff's Oak or a function at Waltham Town Hall. The group's fee was one pound, raised to three pounds and five shillings for bigger events such as the one at the town hall.

At the same time they were entering local talent contests but finding themselves unplaced. On 22 October Walter Teague wrote rather proudly in his diary, 'Received confirmation of group's entry in Haileybury Boys' Club competition in Hoddesdon, which was a skiffle group contest with a first prize of a silver challenge cup autographed by Tommy Steele.'

On 2 November there was the forlorn addition 'Played in competition at Haileybury Club. Not in first 4 out of 12. Alleykats 3rd.' The Alleykats were their main local rivals.

Skiffle inspired dancing and quiet appreciation rather than screaming, but Harry was consciously introducing a rock 'n' roll element to his act by dressing sharp in patterned pullovers and emulating Elvis's pelvic thrusts. Sometimes, after his set, he would go out on the floor and dance with the girls but the partner most of the group remember him dancing with was his pretty fourteen-year-old sister Donella, who now called herself Donna and was catching the eye of all the local boys.

Surprisingly, in view of his Victorian contempt for the modern world, Rodger Webb supported Harry's skiffling, perhaps seeing in it some of the same unsophisticated fun that he had enjoyed in India with his brother Tom when they had played old Irish and Scottish folk tunes.

June Pearce remembers that he would regularly stop her at work to tell her how well his son was doing with his music.

'We used to have mid-morning breaks in the canteen and Mr Webb would come over and say that Harry was playing at such-and-such a place last night and they got on very well. He was obviously very proud of him.'

Yet, at the same time, he seemed surprised to find that Harry could succeed at something. Maybe his expectations had been lowered after his son's examination failures or maybe, with his own status in the world diminished, it was important for him to see Harry as a dependent child.

Walter Teague was taken aback when Rodger told his wife Kathleen that he was worried that Harry would hold the group back.

'He came along to one of the boys' local appearances,' remembers Walter, 'and he started talking to my wife. He said, "If only my son had the confidence that the rest of the group had, they would go far. But I'm afraid Harry will never do any good because he is so nervous."'

He was indeed nervous. In his early shows he found it hard to look directly at the audience and preferred to slink away afterwards. Although he was friends with Terry Smart and Brian Parker, whom he'd known from school, he never got close to anyone else in the group and didn't socialize with them.

Kathleen Teague remembers him as 'reserved and shy. He wouldn't push himself forward at all.' Her daughter Sheila picked up the same impression from seeing him rehearse at their home. 'I remember him with dark hair, jeans and a leather jacket, just standing there looking very edgy. He used to have a nervous cough. They would hang a microphone from the light fixture in the middle of the room and start playing. I was extremely impressed with this boy's voice though. It seemed to boom out and fill the room.'

At twenty-two, Dick Teague was five years older than Harry. Whereas Harry couldn't wait to leave his office job and saw music as the key to his escape, Dick was rather happy in the accounts office of a local chemical company and didn't want anyone to take the group too seriously. It had started out as fun, he thought, and when it stopped being fun the group should end.

Yet although he wasn't serious about a musical career he was serious about the type of music he thought they should play. He insisted that they be a purist group not swayed by pop or gimmick songs. Dick Teague was a man for whom even Lonnie Donegan was suspect. He had about as much interest in rock 'n' roll as Harry had in skiffle and thought that Elvis Presley was 'a great greasy wop'.

By December 1957 Harry was pushing Dick to let him sing 'Heartbreak Hotel' and 'All Shook Up' in a special spot. The suggestion appalled Dick, who saw it as a compromise with commercial pop. He wouldn't allow it. Already he was worried about Harry's swivelling hips and vocal 'uh-huh's which he found totally inappropriate for songs expressing the anxieties of rural blacks and dustbowl migrants.

'He had slightly long sideboards and he used to do himself up as a dead ringer for Elvis,' Dick remembers. 'When Harry started shaking himself about I got uptight about it because we were supposed to be a traditional jazz outfit. I was very old-fashioned for a young guy.'

In October, unknown to his sons, Walter Teague had written to the BBC requesting an audition for the *Saturday Skiffle Club*, an experimental half-hour show on *The Light Programme*, which was produced by Jimmy Grant and later turned into the highly influential pop and jazz show *Saturday Club*. To Walter's surprise, a letter came back offering an audition at BBC's Studio 4, Maida Vale, on 13 January 1958.

The first that Dick knew of the audition was when he arrived home from work and his father told him not to bother changing out of his office clothes as they were going straight out.

'All the others knew about it, but they knew I was a perfectionist. I thought the group was rubbish and that they were rushing to places I didn't want to go yet,' he says.

The group went to Maida Vale that evening and played 'Stackerlee Blues', 'Sporting Life', 'This Train' and 'This Little Light Of Mine' in front of a clerk from the variety booking section.

'It was ridiculous really. They asked us who the lead guitarist was but we didn't really have one,' says Dick. 'We were just a bunch of guys thrashing away on guitars. They asked who the lead singer was and so we stuck the mike on Harry and he took the lead while the rest of us stayed in the background churning out our rubbish. The woman who had auditioned us came down from her cubicle after we had finished and said to Harry, "You've got a very good voice. You ought to have it trained." That was the only comment she made.'

What no one else knew at the time was that Harry was already planning to leave. He hated the songs he was having to sing and could see that there was no scope for his plans to emulate Elvis with Dick Teague policing his movements. The only person he grumbled to though was Terry Smart who he found shared his grievances.

'We both found rock 'n' roll far more exciting than skiffle,' says Smart. 'A few times during rehearsals we had asked to try some of these new numbers but Dick didn't want to. He didn't like the sound.'

So they planned to form their own rock 'n' roll group which would rehearse on the evenings that they weren't needed to play skiffle, only breaking the news to Dick when they felt confident enough to get their own engagements. The most immediate problem though was that they were only a duo and neither of them could play guitar, even though Harry had recently bought one from a mail order firm and had been shown the rudiments by his father.

They tried to coax Brian Parker away from Dick because Parker was becoming recognized as one of the brightest guitar talents in the area. 'I can remember actually getting on a bus to go down to Hargreaves Close saying to myself, "Yeh, I'm definitely going to join this rock 'n' roll group,"' Parker remembers. 'But by the time I arrived I'd changed my mind. I told him that I was going to stick with the skiffle group.'

Eventually they decided they'd recruit Norman Mitham, Harry's old friend.

'He came to me and said that if I could learn to play guitar I could be in his band,' says Mitham. 'Up until that point I'd never had a music lesson and really knew nothing about music at all.'

What he did have though was an uncle, Philip Spur, who had played professionally in dance bands and who was willing to give Norman and Harry lessons on his Gibson guitar.

'First of all uncle Philip told us what key Harry sang in and then we'd play the record we wanted to cover and he would work out the chords,' says Mitham. 'He'd teach us the chords, show us where the chord changes came and we built up a repertoire like that.

'We didn't have the musical ability to play instrumental breaks so we improvised with a sequence of chords. It was similar to what the skiffle boys did but Terry made it more rock 'n' roll by playing a definite beat. In the skiffle group he tended to play with brushes but now he was using sticks to play a more prominent beat.'

Dick Teague sensed that something was happening behind his back when Harry's legendary talent for picking songs up overnight seemed to disappear. He also noticed that Harry's friend Norman was now coming along to the group's gigs and studying his guitar chords.

Then one evening, while returning young Joan from a play session with his daughter Sheila, Walter Teague heard the sounds of a rock 'n' roll group rehearsal coming from the open windows of 12 Hargreaves Close.

'After telling Dick not to teach him how to play guitar,' says Walter, 'there he was playing as lively as you like.' A crisis meeting of the group was called for 17 January at which Harry argued that the skiffle group should include rock 'n' roll.

The other guys said that they liked what we were playing,' remembers Dick. 'They thought that the type of material we were playing was most suited to the instruments we had. Rock 'n' roll required more competence.

'Then Terry Smart piped up that he also wanted to play rock 'n' roll. I said that there was no question about it. Either they played our sort of music or we had a split. Harry said he'd rather play rock 'n' roll but he'd prefer to do it with me because we had a good thing going. I said it wouldn't be with me.

'It wasn't unpleasant but it was a sort of agreement that the music we wanted to do was different and we just packed up that night. I just said to Terry, "Well, off you go," and I lost contact with both of them after that.'

Walter Teague solemnly recorded it in his diary: 'Harry and Terry left group after full discussion of all matters relating to future policy.' Coincidentally, the local paper ran its first feature on the group that evening beneath a photo of Harry singing at the Saints' Rhythm Club. The headline was, 'Local Skiffle Group Get BBC Audition'.

'Many people are saying that skiffle music is on the way out, but for a local group, Dick Teague and his Skiffle Group, it may well be just on its way in,' read the report.

'This local skiffle group had an audition with the BBC on Monday evening for the "Saturday Skiffle Club," which is heard every Saturday morning at 10 a.m. The result of the audition will not be known for some time.

'Dick Teague commented afterwards: "The audition went very well, and I hope that we have passed it..."

'The group was formed just over six months ago, and its motto is "The surest way not to fail is to determine to succeed." Since its formation, the group has been rehearsing at every opportunity.

'For the first four months the group were in existence the instrumentalists sang the songs, but in September Harry Webb joined the group as their singer.

'In its early days the group entered for many skiffle competitions but was never placed. Now they have ceased to enter for them. Dick Teague explained: "At these competitions a group is generally expected to sing Lonnie Donegan style numbers, and we don't like them. We specialise in true traditional skiffle."'

A week later Walter Teague received a letter from the BBC letting him know that the Group had not passed the audition for 'Skiffle Club'. 'Heard from BBC re. audition,' he noted in his diary. '(No go). If at first you don't succeed etc. Something attempted is something done.'

Harry's only response, when he saw the newspaper report, was to think how much he looked like Elvis. His mind was already made up to leave skiffle behind and concentrate on rock 'n' roll.

Left Cliff's maternal great-great grandparents, William and Martha Bridgwater

Below India, c.1924: Cliff's mother as a young girl (front, left) with her sister Olive Queenie (front, right), her uncle Vincent Bridgwater (standing, centre), her mother Dorothy Edith (standing, right), her aunt Beatrice Bridgwater (standing, left) and her grandparents, William Brock Bridgwater and Marie Beatrice Bridgwater (seated)

Above Burma, India, c.1905: Cliff's paternal grandparents – Frederick William Webb (front, right), and Donna Eugenie Webb (back, right) – with Frederick's brother Thomas Webb (front left), Harry Webb (front, centre) – who Cliff was named after – Dorothy Webb (standing, left), Beryl Webb (on lap, centre), Marjorie Webb (on lap, right), Frederick Webb (standing, right), wife of Thomas Webb (back, left), Gertrude Woodfall (back, centre)

Left India, 1920s: Cliff's father, Rodger Webb, with two of his sisters, Joyce and Donella

Above Anasol, India, 1935: Cliff's mother (seated, right) with Olive Queenie (seated, left) and their step brothers and sisters

Above Dehra Dun, India, 1941;
Cliff learning to crawl at home

Above India, 1943: Cliff as a toddler

Above India, 1946: Cliff (front, right) with
his aunt Edna Dickson (back, left), his
mother (back, right), and Donna (on lap)

Left Cliff with his sister, Donna

Above: Carshalton, 1949: Cliff (right) with Sunday School friend Peter Maynard

Right: England, 1954: Cliff's cousin Joyce Dobra (holding her son Stephen) with grandfather Frederick William Webb

Right: July 1956: The Quintones – (from left to right) Cliff, Freda Johnson, John Vince, Irene Fowler, Beryl Molineux – Cliff's first gig as featured in the *Waltham and Cheshunt Weekly Telegraph*

Left September 1956: Cliff and his fellow Quintones at a party at John Vince's home. Cliff can be seen third in from the left. His childhood girlfriend Betty Clarke is third from the left in the back row

Right 1957: (clockwise from bottom) John Vince, Norman Lockwood, Doug Lee, Jay Norris, Cliff, Pete Bush, Chris Green, unidentified, at Jay Norris' home

Left The same occasion at Jay Norris' home: (left to right) Cliff, unidentified, Chris Green, John Vince, Irene Fowler

Right Cliff's first serious
girlfriend, Janice Berry
(picture taken some years
after their romance)

Below December 1957:
Dick Teague's Skiffle
Group – (left to right)
Mick Teague, Brian
Parker, Terry Smart, Cliff
and Dick Teague

Above February 1958: Cliff in the kitchen of his parents' home in Cheshunt

Above February 1958: The Drifters in its original line-up – (left to right) Cliff, Terry Smart, Norman Mitham. Taken on Bury Green Estate, Cheshunt

Above July 1958: (left to right) Terry Smart, Cliff and Ian Samwell in the front room of 12 Hargreaves Close, Cheshunt

Right April 1958: The Drifters with new member Ian 'Sammy' Samwell (seated with guitar) at the 2 I's coffee bar, Soho

Left 25 May 1958: (left to right) John Foster, Cliff, Jerry Lee Lewis, Terry Smart and Ian Samwell backstage at the Kilburn State Theatre

'SOMETHING TOLD ME HE WAS GOING TO BE REALLY BIG'

seven

For Harry Webb, 1958 was to be the last year of normal life; the last year he could walk along a British street without being recognized, go out on a date with the assurance that he wasn't being used for his social position, or have what most people refer to as a private life. It was also the last year he would have to worry about money.

He began it as a shy young office clerk playing skiffle in Hertfordshire village halls, and ended it under another name as a national celebrity who girls wanted to paw and their boyfriends wanted to punch.

The speed of the transition was mind-blowing. Twelve months after his first appearance with Dick Teague he was closing the show on a major tour. Elvis Presley had to wait a year and a half after cutting his first single before he was on national television, and John Lennon, who started playing skiffle in 1957, didn't become a celebrity until 1963.

The opening months of the year were charged with excitement. Not only had his picture appeared in the paper but he was rehearsing every night at home with his own rock 'n' roll trio.

Between them Harry, Terry Smart and Norman Mitham would buy the latest American rock 'n' roll singles on a Friday night and then Donna would painstakingly transcribe the lyrics while they worked out the chord changes. In this way they quickly learned to play 'Blue Suede Shoes', 'Heartbreak Hotel', 'Rock Around The Clock' and 'Blueberry Hill'.

Cliff's musical preferences were for the sweeter style of singers like Ricky Nelson and the Everly Brothers rather than the vaguely threatening screams and wails of Little Richard and Gene Vincent. He even admired Pat Boone, a white boy from Tennessee who made his name by recording cover versions of black rock 'n' roll hits in the knowledge that in a society still racially divided he could sell them to the conservative white audience.

Smart suggested calling the trio the Planets. It was a topical enough name – the space race had just been inaugurated with the launch of Russia's Sputnik-1 satellite – but Harry and Norman Mitham didn't think it was quite right.

'It sounds crazy now,' says Mitham, 'but almost as soon as we started playing we decided on the cover of our first album. We hadn't recorded a single song but we said that if we ever made an LP we could have a picture of us sitting on a toboggan driving into a snow drift.'

The Drifters made their debut in March 1958 at the Forty Hill Badminton Club, between Cheshunt and Enfield, where Harry and his parents were members. It was the annual dinner and dance and they played the cabaret spot, getting the then enormous fee of five pounds.

'I was elated that all these people were applauding me,' says Cliff, 'but it probably gave a false impression because these were people who knew me and who I played badminton with every week.'

Harry's life was incredibly full and even though he was donning a suit and tie each day to go to work, the fact that he was singing in a group reassured him that he was somehow different from all the other people there. At least he had the hope of one day breaking out. He knew that British teenagers were starved of live rock 'n' roll. There had been Tommy Steele and Terry Dene but neither of them had successfully captured the American sound.

In his already busy schedule he now found time for romance. During his last year at school he was attracted to his classmate Janice Berry who, unfortunately for him, was wrapped up in a serious relationship with Brian Cooke. A bright pupil, Janice had become head girl and passed six GCE O levels. She was working in a two-year secretarial job with ICI in Welwyn Garden City with plans to train as a teacher when she was eighteen.

'All the time I was going out with Janice I knew that Harry wanted to go out with her,' says Cooke. 'Then one day she told me that she wasn't going out with me any more and the next thing I knew she was going out with Harry. I think she must have had him in mind when she got rid of me.'

Janice admits as much. 'It was the day I finished with Brian that he [Harry] knocked on my door and that evening we went to the cinema in Waltham Cross,' she says. 'I have to be honest and say that it wasn't entirely a coincidence. He had heard about the break-up.'

When in later years Cliff was to talk about the 'couple of times' he really believed he had fallen in love, Janice was certainly included although he has never before mentioned her by name and Janice has never told her story.

In a fan booklet published in 1959 she was referred to as 'June', a 'sixteen-year-old brunette' whom he dated for five months. 'They quietly held hands at the local cinema,' it read. 'They went to teenage parties together (spending most of the time in a corner alone), and took long country walks.'

Four years later in an interview he spoke of 'Janet', the girl he had been 'courting steadily' before he broke into show business. 'I guess she was the most serious girl I ever had,' he said.

Today he says, 'If love came into it at all, that was the first time.'

She was a dark-haired girl who lived with her mother at 242 Turner's Hill, a fifteen-minute walk from the Webbs' home. She was an only child, and her father had died suddenly while she was still at school.

She had always been part of the close-knit gang that centred on the school drama group and had often been to Hargreaves Close for tea. 'She was a lovely girl,' says Cliff's mother. 'We were very fond of Janice.'

Their brief relationship in 1958 typified the teenage innocence of the time. They would talk over coffees at the Blue Bird Café, go off on country rambles, visit the cinema or just see each other at home.

When she came along to group rehearsals she would sit in a corner quietly listening and supplying them with cups of tea. They even used her front room to practise in, setting up in the bay of the front window and leaving a threadbare patch of carpet behind as a memory.

Once, while on an evening walk, Harry surprised Janice by vaulting over the wall of a garden and picking her a flower.

'There was a beautiful magnolia bush,' she remembers. 'It was at its peak and I just happened to say something about how beautiful it looked in the evening light and he leapt over the wall, picked this flower from the tree, leapt back and gave it to me. It was a terribly romantic thing to do but it wasn't typical. That's why I remember it!

'A lot of what we did together was built around the Drifters' rehearsals. We were the same as any other boyfriend and girlfriend really. It was a loving relationship. People in those days didn't leap into bed together as they do now. Maybe some people did, but we didn't and it wasn't something that the crowd of people I was with did.

'I was certainly in love with him and, I don't know... I can't answer for him. Maybe it was one-sided but we both seemed to be in love.'

Dates with Janice had to be fitted in between dates with the group. They had been offered a spot at the Five Horseshoes, a pub up the road in Burford Street, Hoddesdon, where the publican was experimenting with live music during the week.

The stage was a small raised platform next to the door to the gents' toilet. There was no amplification and anyone who played had to compete with customers' chatter and the sound of darts thudding into cork boards.

When the Drifters took on the challenge one mid-week evening in March, a well-built local lad with a Tony Curtis haircut and a black leather jacket was standing at the bar. John Foster was, in his own words, a 'bit of a Ted' but he considered himself wise in the ways of rock 'n' roll because, unlike most young people in the area, he had visited the legendary 2 I's coffee bar in London's Soho. Once when he was there he found himself standing next to Terry Dene, who in 1957 had been touted as 'Britain's answer to Elvis Presley'.

What John Foster saw at the Five Horseshoes that evening impressed him deeply. It wasn't the musicianship – the group was barely mastering the most basic chords – but there was something about the singer that transcended all the failures of the act.

'I didn't look at Terry and I didn't look at Norman,' he admits. 'I looked at the singer in his white shirt and black trousers and I saw Elvis. Something told me, yes, he's going to be big. He's going to be really big. I don't know what made me do it because I was drinking with my mates at the bar, but I just walked up to the group and asked them if they wanted a manager.'

It was pure bluff. He had no experience of show business management and had never booked an act into the 2 I's. He was a driver employed on the local sewage farm. But he was on speaking terms with the manager Tom Littlewood, a former film stunt man who had the unusual business practice of paying groups to play in the cellar and then charging them a 10 per cent commission for the privilege.

Being asked if you wanted to play at the 2 I's was like being asked if you would like your latest film to be shown at Cannes. For aspiring British rock 'n' rollers it was *the* place to play. It was where Tommy Steele and Terry Dene had been 'discovered' by their future managers and it had become the best-known coffee bar in Britain.

They did need a manager, especially one with such apparently good contacts. Foster even had a telephone in his home, something that neither Terry, Norman or Harry had.

'I knew I was being rather flash when I gave them my phone number,' he says. 'It was a rather impressive thing to do in those days.'

He promised them that if they met him that weekend he would arrange a spot for them at the 2 I's. No trouble.

'Foster told us to be prepared to go up to London on the 715 Green Line bus that Saturday,' remembers Mitham. 'He said it would be coming through at two o'clock and that he would be sitting on the nearside. We were to wait at the Old Pond bus stop in Cheshunt and get on when we saw him.

'We talked about it all week among ourselves. We didn't know if we were being taken for a ride. However, we turned up and waited and John was on the second bus that came, sitting up against the window. I think Harry had a lot more faith in him than I did. I didn't think he would be there.'

The 2 I's was at 59 Old Compton Street, not far from Shaftesbury Avenue. It was a small street-level coffee bar with live music in the cellar. It had been taken over in 1956 by two Australian wrestlers, Paul Lincoln and Ray Hunter, who bought it from the Irani brothers (hence the 'I' of the 2 I's).

It was at a time when coffee bars were the latest teen sensation, providing a meeting space that was neither church youth club (where adults were concerned about your moral welfare) nor public house (which required that you be eighteen). The Gaggia machines which gushed and gurgled on the counters provided an exotic new beverage from the Continent known as 'espresso' coffee.

At first the 2 I's had been a financial disaster. Then, on 14 July 1956, a young commercial artist called Wally Whyton dropped by and asked whether he and his skiffle group the Vipers could busk there.

'Paul Lincoln said it was OK, and within about three weeks the place was literally packed to the doors. Instead of letting us busk he charged a shilling admission and paid us two pounds a night each,' remembers Whyton. 'The basement had been a store room and when we became the resident group down there I went with Lionel Bart and a couple of others and painted designs on the walls.'

Even though they lived on the fringes of London none of the Drifters had ever ventured into Soho before. As they walked through its narrow streets they felt a frisson of excitement at the sight of the jazz clubs, foreign food stores and striptease clubs. Soho had not yet become the sleaze pit of the sixties but there was enough of an air of strangeness and naughtiness to cause a provincial lad's eyes to widen.

'I can remember someone pointing to some girls and mentioning that they were prostitutes,' remembers Mitham. 'We had never had anything to do with prostitutes and we couldn't believe that we were right in the middle of it all.'

They were met at the 2 I's by Tom Littlewood who listened to them perform two songs before telling them that they had passed the audition and could play their first show that night.

We weren't the star attraction but at least we were on and got invited back the next day and then the day after that,' says Mitham. 'There was no screaming. The kids just listened.

'What we talked about afterwards was the fact that people had paid and they had stood there and listened. We weren't there as incidental entertainment like at the Five Horseshoes or the Badminton Club. People had paid to watch us and they seemed to like us.

'By the time I got home that night my parents were asleep but I actually woke them up to tell them that I had played at the 2 I's.'

John Foster's bluffing had paid off. The audition had led to what was in effect a two-week residency during April 1958.

'It was all very exciting for him,' says Janice, who was by this time seeing even less of her boyfriend than before. 'He obviously wanted to succeed and the fact that everybody applauded at the 2 I's reinforced the idea that he was going to.'

During the first week a sandy-haired young man on leave from the RAF, where he was just finishing his National Service, came up to them and asked if they needed a lead guitarist to boost their sound.

He was Ian Ralph 'Sammy' Samwell and like Harry had been playing in a group – the Ash Valley Skiffle Group – while really wanting to play rock 'n' roll. What the Drifters were doing encapsulated everything he hoped to do.

'They asked me to audition for them on the Saturday afternoon,' says Samwell. 'That became my first group rehearsal and that night I played with them and effectively joined the Drifters.'

The same night Jan Vane, a teenager from Rainham in Essex, was visiting the 2 I's as part of a treat for her sixteenth birthday from her boyfriend Eddie. The cellar was so packed that they sat on a Coca-Cola fridge and craned their necks to see.

'I can't remember what he sang that night but I just thought that he was so unusual,' she remembers. 'He was so handsome and so different.

'He was young and exciting and I had never been anywhere like that before. I was caught up in the whole atmosphere of the evening; of seeing someone live and of thinking that if he was playing at the 2 I's he must be extremely famous.'

A chatty, confident girl, she stayed behind to get Harry's autograph. After asking the usual questions about how long he had been playing and where he usually performed she asked him whether he had a fan club. Harry laughed at the question. He explained that he had only been playing rock 'n' roll for just over four weeks and apologized for having to leave so soon to get the last bus home.

'I told him not to worry because we would run him home,' says Jan. 'Eddie had a car, which was quite impressive in those days.

'So that night, we all squeezed into a small green Morris Minor and drove back to Cheshunt. The group all lived in different places too so we spent half the night finding their houses.

'The main point was that we exchanged addresses. I told him I would keep in touch to see what he was doing and I started writing. Sometimes he would write back to me and sometimes his mum would write back and eventually I got invited back home.'

This was to be the beginning of the official Cliff Richard Fan Club. It started with half a dozen members who Jan would personally write to with the latest information, and rose to a 42,000-strong membership which required a full-time staff of four.

Harry Greatorex was the closest thing to an agent to spot Harry Webb at the 2 I's. He was a 35-year-old dance hall manager from Derbyshire who scoured London to find talent worth promoting in the north of England.

He heard the Drifters during their second week and told John Foster that he could give them work at the Regal Ballroom in Ripley. He offered a fee of five pounds with an additional ten pounds for expenses.

There was just one thing that Harry Greatorex wasn't happy with. He didn't want to bill them as a group act, but as a singer with a backing group. He didn't think Harry Webb and the Drifters sounded convincingly rock 'n' roll enough. Foster assured him that the problem could be solved within minutes and he called the boys to The Swiss, a pub in Old Compton Street, to dream up a new name for Harry Webb.

It wasn't unusual for English rock 'n' roll singers to ditch their given names for something more evocative. Manager Larry Parnes had made an art of it – contrasting warm and friendly first names with tough and aggressive surnames: Tommy Steele for Thomas Hicks, Marty Wilde for Reginald Smith, Billy Fury for Ronald Wycherley.

'All the American people had cool names anyway,' says Samwell. 'They were Chuck, Rick, Carl, Gene and things like that. None of them were called Ian or Norman.'

They started by playing on variations of Russ Hamilton, a British singer who'd had a couple of hits the year before, and came up with Russ Clifford and Cliff Russard before hitting on Cliff Richards. Samwell then suggested dropping the 's' as a tribute to Little Richard. John Foster then returned to Harry Greatorex and told him that it would be Cliff Richard and the Drifters who would be appearing in Ripley.

'I can remember him coming back home and saying that from now on he would like to be called Cliff and not Harry,' says his sister Jacqui. 'I don't think Dad ever called him Cliff but Joan, Donna and I started calling him it fairly quickly. Mum took a bit longer just because she kept slipping up. I mean, after calling your son Harry for seventeen years it is a bit difficult to call him something else overnight.'

The Ripley show, booked for Saturday 3 May, was their biggest engagement so far and their first outside London and Hertfordshire. They took a train to Derby and, on arriving, they were impressed to see posters announcing, 'Direct from the famous Soho 2 I's Coffee Bar – Cliff Richard and the Drifters'.

The Regal Ballroom was a converted snooker hall with a mock Tudor frontage which Greatorex had taken over two years before and turned into a dance hall with events ranging from old-time dancing to skiffle. On the night Cliff and the Drifters played there was a 'top twenty record session' and support from Keith Freer and his Dixielanders.

'They had a stage with curtains which was quite something to us after the 2 I's,' says Samwell. 'The curtains parted, we were standing there and that night we really rocked. The place was absolutely jam-packed and the response was fantastic.'

After the show they had to bed down on hard benches in the venue because they were too late to get a train back home. 'It was a very exciting gig because it felt much more like the big time,' says Cliff. 'Suddenly I was fronting the band.'

Three weeks later Jerry Lee Lewis, one of the group's favourite American artists, played his first British concert. The tour was surrounded in controversy because news had leaked out that the new bride accompanying him was actually his fourteen-year-old cousin and he hadn't divorced his previous wife before the wedding.

Exposing the moral corruptness of a rock 'n' roll star was a job that the British press took to with great relish. They hounded Lewis during his stay in London and wrote editorials suggesting that the Home Secretary should deport him and teenagers should boycott his concerts.

Jerry Lee Lewis wasn't an avuncular figure like Bill Haley or a Southern gentleman like Elvis. With his narrow eyes and tight mouth he looked to be in a permanent state of insubordination. His music was the look perfectly portrayed in sound – wild, sleazy, lustful, dangerous.

Cliff and the Drifters played 'Great Balls Of Fire' and 'Breathless' in their set and when they found that he was playing at the Kilburn State Theatre on Sunday 25 May they bought tickets as soon as they went on sale. The anti-Lewis publicity put out by *The People* and the *Daily Sketch* had an effect because on the night only a quarter of the seats had been sold.

'Jerry did a heck of a show that night to a poor audience,' remembers Samwell. 'There were one or two cat-calls and the people in front of us made rude noises when he stopped to comb his hair. John Foster, who was wearing his leather jacket, leant over and said, "One more peep out of you and that's your lot." They didn't make another noise.'

After the show John Foster thought of his greatest wheeze yet. He would take Terry Smart, Sammy Samwell and Cliff backstage so that he could brag about his future star. They found Lewis in his dressing room, wearing a ribbon tie and black gambler's jacket with leopardskin lapels, being photographed by a man from the *Daily Mirror*.

'I basically conned my way into the room by saying that Cliff was the latest British rock 'n' roll sensation,' says Foster. 'Of course, at that time he was nowhere near it. He'd hardly got used to the name Cliff Richard and had never been near a recording studio. Anyway, I asked if we could have our picture taken and we did, with Cliff standing right next to Jerry Lee.'

It was the closest any of them had come to a rock 'n' roll legend. Within a week Cliff was to have his own first taste of the fury and excitement that could attend rock 'n' roll.

Foster had booked the group into the Gaumont Teenage Show, a Saturday morning show at the Gaumont Theatre in Shepherd's Bush which mixed films, music, variety acts and celebrity appearances.

It was here that Cliff-mania began in a wave of frenzied screaming.

'We just weren't used to that sort of reaction from people,' says Mitham. 'It was the first reaction we had ever had to Cliff as a sex symbol. In Soho and Ripley you thought they were getting excited at the music but in Shepherd's Bush the audience was seated and they were screaming at Cliff.'

He had been playing rock 'n' roll for less than four months and had already stumbled on his natural audience. 'It didn't make sense and it felt unreal but I loved it,' he says. 'In those days the sound of girls screaming was the gauge of success.'

'I WANTED A CAREER SO I GOT RID OF THE GIRLFRIEND'

On Saturday 14 June 1958 Cliff Richard and the Drifters returned to the Gaumont, this time as 'special guests' on a talent show.

Knowing that it was almost guaranteed to be another storming success, Sammy Samwell had been scanning entertainment newspapers to find an agent he could invite along. The names he saw meant nothing to him and so, at random, he picked on George Ganjou of George Ganjou Ltd. Entertainments, who regularly advertised on the back page of *The Stage*, and called him.

What Samwell didn't know was that Ganjou was the least likely agent to launch the career of a teenage rock 'n' roll group. Already in his late fifties, he had spent most of his life in Poland before coming to England as part of an adagio act, the Ganjou Brothers and Juanita, and after retiring as a performer he had become an agent for several variety acts. He knew nothing about rock 'n' roll beyond the fact that he didn't like it, and he proudly referred to himself as a 'square'.

Yet, to his credit, when John Foster and Sammy Samwell visited him at his Albemarle Street office on 6 June he agreed to come to the show despite the fact that it meant cancelling a weekend game of golf. He thought they were 'nice boys' and liked the looks of the singer whose photograph they showed him.

Ganjou suggested that Cliff and the Drifters should cut a demonstration record which he could play to his friends in the record industry. Early the next week they recorded two songs at a small studio above the HMV record shop in Oxford Street. They chose Elvis Presley's 'Lawdy Miss Clawdy', written by Lloyd Price, and Jerry Lee Lewis' 'Breathless', written by Otis Blackwell.

When they returned to the Gaumont that Saturday it caused an even greater sensation than the debut. The audience was now primed and when Cliff hit the stage it was as if a dam had burst. His voice was barely audible above the screams and wails.

'As soon as Cliff started to sing, they all, especially the girls, went mad,' Ganjou remembered. 'They started to shout and rush towards him, and after seeing this I decided I'd better go backstage and have a talk to him.'

Ganjou's interest was aroused by show business common sense. Cliff looked good, seemed to have a pleasant personality and there was a demand for what he was doing. You didn't have to like rock 'n' roll to know you were on to a good thing here, and he had excellent connections with record companies through former dance band musicians who had gone on to become musical directors.

Samwell remembers being staggered when Ganjou came into the dressing room after the show and asked, 'Would you like to be on Decca or Columbia?' Samwell faked nonchalance and said his preference would be Columbia and so Ganjou said he would pass the demo disc to Norrie Paramor, a friend of his who was head of artists and repertoire for the EMI-owned Columbia label.

The scene in the dressing room that morning was a mixture of excitement and tension. There was a palpable sense that something very big was going to happen for them but also a slight fear of the teenage power that was being unleashed.

John Brunel, a reporter on the *Shepherd's Bush Gazette & Post* had been a judge on the morning talent show (won by a local skiffle group called the Avro Boys) and described what he saw in his weekly column.

'Black-haired Cliff Richard had just been "sending" the fans and I found myself in a top floor room with the orders "Don't leave the building".

'No, I wasn't a political prisoner of the Rank Organization, but there were three hundred screaming fans down in the road below, the exit doors were being rattled and if we went out there it would have been like being thrown to the lions. So we stayed put, Cliff got out some buns (he had not had any breakfast) and we started the long wait.

'I asked a girl who introduced herself as the leader of Cliff's fan club how old he was. She did not know. Cliff ate another bun. The girls outside screamed more and we had to pretend we had left the building to kid them into leaving too.

'Who'd be a rock star? Not me.'

These experiences at the Gaumont convinced Cliff that something important was about to happen for him and because of this he thought it was time to cool his relationship with Janice.

'I enjoyed being with her,' he says, 'but I can remember at that time feeling that I had to make a choice. I thought even then that if I was going to be a pop star my fans wouldn't want me to be married or to have a girlfriend. I could see how my sister Donna would quickly go off a pop star that she'd liked if she found out that they were engaged or married. The rock 'n' roll singer became a sex symbol and belonged to the fans.

'With Janice I had to make the decision that if I was going to go all out to be a pop star I didn't want any attachments. I didn't want anything to get in the way of me being famous and having loads and loads of girls chasing me all over the place.'

Janice had separately come to the same conclusion. She had too much self-respect to imagine herself as a bit-part player in a drama of rock 'n' roll and screaming girls.

'I can remember seeing mounted police outside the theatre and I had to stay inside while they got him out and it all worried me slightly,' she says. 'I remember thinking, Well, this isn't me. I don't like this. I don't really like coming to these concerts.

'Cliff knew that if he was known to have a girlfriend it wouldn't be good from the point of view of his girl fans. It obviously looked better if he was a single fellow and available.

'So all these things meant that it was his and my decision that it was better if we separated.

'I remember the evening that it happened. He brought me home and we knew we were going to part anyway because we had been talking about it. We were standing in the porch of my house and he gave me the words of a song he had written for me. It said:

> *When teenagers love*
> *They love for ever*
> *When teenagers love*
> *It's bound to be true*
> *I'm a teenager in love*
> *A teenager in love*
> *I'm a teenager in love with you.*

'I was literally crying on his shoulder after he handed me the piece of paper. It wasn't me saying that I'd had enough of him, it was a joint decision that this was the only thing we could do.

'I wanted Cliff to be successful. I wanted him to do well because he wanted to and I could actually see that I was in the way. I could see that he was better without a girlfriend. I don't mean without me in particular but that he was better off being single.'

It was the first of many times that Cliff would consider the options and always he has made the same choice with the same measure of apparently dispassionate calculation.

'It was far easier than it might appear looking back,' he says of the end of his romance with Janice. 'I wanted a career, I didn't want a girlfriend. So I got rid of the girlfriend. That's as brutal as I can put it. It didn't mean I liked her any less but I just made the cold-blooded choice to go for that. That's what I wanted.'

Within days of ending the relationship he was sitting in Norrie Paramor's office in Great Castle Street under consideration for the Columbia record label.

Norman William Paramor, known to everyone as 'Norrie', was 44 years old and had been in the music business since leaving school at fifteen. He'd been a pianist, a band leader and, since 1949, a record company music director.

In common with George Ganjou he had no real experience of rock 'n' roll because he'd grown up in the big band era and, as a producer, was best known for working with old-style singers like Michael Holliday and Ruby Murray. His most recent hit was 'Lollipops' by a group called the Mudlarks.

Rock 'n' roll was still dubious music to these men who couldn't believe that the big band era was really over. They thought it was an American craze that would soon die out. Paramor had had a stab at producing the sound with jazz drummer Tony Crombie and his Rockets, Britain's first rock 'n' roll combo, back in 1956.

Older musicians who'd sweated through apprenticeships in dance bands and orchestras were angry at the new wave of guitar strummers and tea-chest bassists who were able to earn twice as much money with an eighth of the skill. The musical style that was liberating for a generation of teenagers was putting an older generation of professional musicians out of work.

Paramor was open-minded. He was a warm and gentle man with young daughters who were already dancing to the new music and he knew that in his position personal taste had to give way to market trends.

Although the acetate by Cliff Richard and the Drifters was crude and amateurish by record company standards, there was something about it which convinced him that they should be given an opportunity. He took it home and played it to his teenage daughter Caroline.

'She flipped when she heard it,' Paramor wrote a year later, 'and she double-flipped when I showed her Cliff's photo. This photo was not of Cliff alone but included the Drifters and American star Jerry Lee Lewis.' He arranged a meeting with Cliff. 'When he eventually turned up he brought his whole group along with him, complete with instruments. My immediate reaction was that if this youngster could go to the trouble of bringing his group along, the least I could do was to listen to what they had to offer.'

The boys plugged in their guitars and played to Paramor in his office. He later claimed that he was 'instantly filled with excitement by this thrilling sound,' but if he was, he managed to contain it for the moment and told the boys that he would make a decision over the next two weeks while he went on holiday to Tangier with his family. Cliff has since described this period as the longest fortnight of his life.

It wasn't wasted time. John Foster made up reel-to-reel tapes of a Drifters' performance and hawked them around to anyone who cared to listen. He mostly faced indifference, sometimes hostility.

One record company told him that Cliff would never be a singer in a thousand years. Tommy Steele's agent told him to advise Cliff not to give up his day job.

The group carried on playing and rehearsing. On 15 June they played at the Freight Train, a coffee bar at 44 Berwick Street owned by skiffle star Chas McDevitt and named after his 1957 hit with Nancy Whiskey. Sammy Samwell wrote a letter of thanks to the coffee bar's manager who was obviously absent for the show.

'Despite the late arrival of your staff they [the Drifters] thoroughly enjoyed the evening and were pleased by the most appreciative audience. Unfortunately playing for almost three hours proved rather too strenuous. This was, however, compensated by the addition of eight new members to our "Fan" club.'

A week later they were at the Tudor Hall, Hoddesdon, supported by the Missin' Links, their main local rivals, and on 6 July they played the Astoria in Ware, sharing a double bill with a Kim Novak film. On the nights they weren't playing they would meet at Cliff's home and run through new songs.

An amusing note in the Broxbourne Borough Council files from 1958 records that on 5 July the occupant of 11 Hargreaves Close complained to them that a 'skiffle group' was playing every night at number 12 until eleven o'clock and that they should 'ask them to stop these long noisy evenings'.

The council officer obviously relayed the message to the Webb family for beneath the entry of the complaint was added the handwritten comment, 'Son not willing to cooperate.'

When Paramor returned from Tangier in mid-July, the news was good. Franklyn Boyd of the music publishers Aberbach Music had sent him a song called 'Schoolboy Crush' which had been a hit in America for Bobby Helms and Norrie thought it was a good number for Cliff to cover.

In those pre-Beatle days most artists neither wrote nor chose their own material. The power resided with the publishers and record companies. In Britain during the late fifties there was a tendency to depend on cover versions of American hits. Terry Dene had made it with Marty Robbins' 'A White Sports Coat' and Mary Wilde, Britain's latest new Elvis, had just scored with 'Endless Sleep', originally recorded by Jody Reynolds.

'Schoolboy Crush' was not a great song. It was a formulaic number of teenage angst in which a young student tells his 'baby doll' that even when they graduate she will be his 'steady date' because she's more than a 'schoolboy crush'.

Cliff was sent an acetate and learned the song in a day. 'Then he phoned me and told me that he'd like to come in and sing it to me,' said Paramor. 'He came up the same day with the Drifters and gave a faultless performance of the song. It impressed me enough to offer him a contract with Columbia.'

Even though it was Cliff Richard and the Drifters who had passed the audition, it was Cliff who was awarded the contract. This meant that although the group's name would appear on the record label, they would not be getting a percentage of the royalties. They would only be paid a fee for taking part in the recording session.

The most immediate problem was to find something to put on the B-side, the side of the record which wouldn't be getting radio play. The normal practice was to add a 'filler', a song with no real commercial potential. Because the 'mechanical' royalties (based on record sales rather than stage performances or radio plays) were the same as the A-side, producers often made themselves extra money by composing throwaway songs for flip sides and publishing them under assumed names.

Fortunately Samwell had just written his first song, called 'Move It', and they played it to Paramor. 'The arrangement was pretty rough,' said Paramor, 'and Cliff was not sure of the melody, but they gave such a spirited performance that I wasted no time in fixing up a session which would include Samwell's "Move It", which was to be the backing of "Schoolboy Crush".'

At the time it was virtually unheard of for a British rock 'n' roll group to record a song written by one of its members. The closest was perhaps Tony Crombie's co-writer credit on 'Rock 'n' Roller Coaster' (1957) or the writing of 'Rock With The Caveman' (1956) by Tommy Steele's friend Lionel Bart. That the song should become an A-side and then a national hit was unprecedented.

A rockabilly song with lots of American slang ('babe', 'honey', 'groove'), Samwell had written 'Move It' in June while travelling from his mother's home in London Colney to Cliff's house in Cheshunt on a Green Line double-decker bus. He had wanted to create an authentic sounding rock 'n' roll song that would expose the pale British imitations. He sat upstairs in the back seat with his guitar on his knee and hit on the tune while deconstructing Chuck Berry licks to discover their secret.

The lyric was partly his response to a recent *Melody Maker* article by broadcaster and music writer Steve Race bemoaning the effect of rock 'n' roll on popular music. 'So rock 'n' roll is dead, is it?' 37-year-old Race, a graduate of the Royal Academy of Music, had challenged. 'All right then. My funeral oration consists of just two words: good riddance.'

He went on to wonder whether ballads might be coming back into fashion and concluded, 'As of early June, 1958, there is no clear sign about what the next craze will be. Indeed, there may not be another craze at all. The record-buying public has not shifted its allegiance to some other kind of music: it has merely stopped buying so many records. That, too, is all to the good. Perhaps now we shall see some sense of proportion returning to the pop music business.'

It wasn't an unusual rant for the time. There were many of his generation who were only too glad to leap in and write the obituary of rock 'n' roll. Samwell's response was:

> They say, it's gonna die: Oh! Honey please, let's face it;
> They just don't know what's a-goin' to replace it.
> Ballads and Calypsos, have got nothing on
> Real Country music that just drives along.
> Oh! Honey move it.

'By the time I got to Cliff's house the song was complete,' he remembers. 'I just played it to the rest of them, including my introduction. I had to rewrite the lyric out because it was full of bits and pieces and Cliff needed to be able to read it. I used to put the "ah"s and the "uh-huh"s in because you need to have every nuance there.'

Mitham became the first casualty of the new-found success. Samwell felt that his guitar added nothing to the overall sound and that it was a waste of money having three guitars when two would be adequate.

'Sammy was older than us and having served in the RAF seemed much more a man of the world, and he said that I was only duplicating Cliff's guitar work,' says Mitham. 'What you have to remember is that Cliff and I had been friends since we were nine or ten and we had gone through a lot together. Now it had got to the stage where an outsider had turned round and said, "I think you ought to get rid of Norman." I'm sure Cliff gave it a lot of thought but he told me that was what had been suggested and I said I agreed but it's not going to stop a friendship. Then that was it. I was out of the story.'

For the recording at EMI Studios in Abbey Road on 24 July Paramor hired two seasoned session men. His original plan had been to use the Ken Jones Orchestra, whom he had used to back Michael Holliday, but Cliff was insistent on a group sound. In 1958 there could be re-takes of a song but no overdubbing or mixing because it was all recorded onto a single-track tape, and for 'Schoolboy Crush' and 'Move It' there was only three hours of studio time booked.

Paramor brought in Frank Clarke on double bass and Ernie Shear on electric guitar. Both men were in their early thirties and had a wealth of experience playing in orchestras. To them it was just another session, Cliff was a fresh-faced young kid, and rock 'n' roll was a new musical craze they knew they'd have to get used to if they wanted to keep working.

'Schoolboy Crush', the first track of the evening, didn't really showcase their talents. It had no fire in its belly and was covered in a soufflé of background vocals from the Michael Sammes Singers. But on 'Move It' their talents combined to produce a sound that could have come straight out of Memphis, Tennessee.

The guitar introduction has become such a classic of early British rock 'n' roll that there have been arguments ever since about who invented it and how much they got paid for it. The truth is that the idea was Samwell's, and the execution was Shear's. Samwell was smart enough to know he didn't have the competence to play lead guitar on the single so he showed Shear the riff he'd come up with, and Shear then translated the sketch into a full-colour masterpiece. Samwell, meanwhile, played rhythm guitar.

'I think we just talked about it in the studio and it developed,' says Shear. 'It was really a busking session for us even though we read music. I didn't even have a solid-body electric guitar then so I used to use a Hoffner acoustic with a D'Armond pick-up which I bought in America. To get the top sound I used to push it near the bridge. I wanted to get the toppiest sound I could get.'

When the session started, Peter Bown had been engineering but he had to leave for an appointment at the opera and so he handed over to his assistant Malcolm Addey, a junior engineer who had only been with the studio four months. There were rule books at EMI Studios in those days which stipulated the volume at which music should be recorded. Addey allowed 'Move It' to go over the limit, and this added to its authentic sound.

It was a great performance. British rock 'n' roll records up until this date had been insipid affairs that had none of the clarity and attack of the Americans. With 'Move It' there was, at last, a single that offered a challenge to the originators.

Hearing it for the first time some twenty years later Carl Perkins, author of 'Blue Suede Shoes' and a former Sun Records artist, commented:

'That sound could have been made in Sun Studios in 1954. It's basic rockabilly music. That guitar is doing what we did. He's got some echo and he's working on more than one string. He's getting three of the bass strings and he's doubling up on the bottom. That's very good.'

Paramor quickly had test pressings made up and circulated them to his contacts, and seven days after the recording Cliff was featured in a prominent *Daily Mirror* article written by record columnist Patrick Doncaster under the headline 'New Recruit For The Disc War'.

Although Doncaster committed himself to no more than the claim that Cliff had 'a personality that shines through the grooves,' and that 'he could succeed in Discland,' the article took up an impressive amount of editorial space for an office lad who had yet to release his first record.

Publisher Franklyn Boyd was also doing the rounds with test pressings because of his stake in 'Schoolboy Crush' and he wanted TV and radio exposure. His first contact was Dennis Main Wilson who was producing '6.5 Special'. Wilson liked the record but couldn't use Cliff for six weeks so Boyd contacted his counterpart on independent television, Jack Good, who earlier in the year had done two pilot shows of 'Oh Boy!' and was planning an autumn series.

Good was one of the geniuses of British rock 'n' roll, whose understanding of the medium was at least a decade ahead of its time. He cut an odd figure in the world of greasy-haired teenage school-leavers with tight jeans and James Dean scowls. He was a 27-year-old Oxford graduate with thick glasses and a booming voice, whose eyes would pop out with excitement when he heard something he liked. But his taste was impeccable and his faith in pure rock 'n' roll remained, and remains, unshakable.

Boyd made an appointment to see him and played a white label of 'Schoolboy Crush' on Good's office record player. Good listened politely but was non-committal. He recounted what happened next in his 'Sidetracks' column in *Disc* on 9 August, when he told the story of how he had just heard 'the most amazing first recording made by any teenage artiste in Britain'.

In a full-page article under the headline 'Just another beginner? No – this boy is really terrific!' Good wrote, 'Then he [Boyd] spins what he laughingly refers to as the "flip-side". Wham! This disc could sell 50,000 on its first eight bars alone.

'It kicks off with a forceful, dramatic guitar phrase that runs an electric shock down the spine. In comes the drum, driving a vicious beat right through the heart of the number. Then the voice rides confidently over this glorious backing – a voice with an amazingly 'non-imitative' style, considering that this kind of music ought by rights to be foreign to anyone who is not a native of the southern States.

'The diction is clear; the phrasing authentic, professional – there is a real feeling for this country-and-western style. If this disc had been a product of Sun Records of Memphis, Tennessee – the original recording company of Elvis Presley and Jerry Lee Lewis – I should not have been surprised, but would still have rated it as important and good enough to be compared, though not, of course, on equal terms, with those two giants of the beat.

'But when one considers that this is the product of a seventeen-year-old boy from Cheshunt, Hertfordshire, the mind just boggles.'

Good was eager to see the artist in the flesh. He couldn't believe that he would look as good as he sounded. He was sure that there would be some physical drawback and that 'Move It' was just a fluke of the recording studio. An audition was arranged for the following evening at Max Rivers Rehearsal Rooms at 10–11 Great Newport Street, just around the corner from Leicester Square underground station.

In a room on the third floor Cliff and the Drifters played while agent George Ganjou lurked hopefully in the corridor outside.

'I thought it was wonderful,' says Good. 'I thought he was a good singer but there was nothing special about his physical performance. He just bounced up and down adequately and I thought he looked a bit trashy with his sideburns.'

Good's recollection is that he agreed to book him there and then and walked Cliff down to the underground while explaining to him that the guitar and the sideburns would have to go before he made an appearance on 'Oh Boy!' Boyd doesn't think he decided that quickly.

'Jack loved him but Jack's wife, Margit, didn't like him at all. So when we came away Jack said, "Look, I like him." So I said, "Are you going to use him?" He said he didn't know and that he would try to sort it out. But his wife was quite adamant that she didn't like Cliff. He then rang me a couple of days later and said, "OK, I'm going to use him but he's not going to be singing 'Schoolboy Crush'. He's going to be doing the B-side."'

Margit Good can't remember the audition but says that it's quite likely that she was apprehensive. 'I tended to be the more pessimistic one,' she admits. 'Jack was always totally enthusiastic about everything. I would imagine that the fact that Cliff looked like a shy little boy, definitely non-show-business, would have made me wonder – what on earth are you going to do with him?'

Coincidentally, the day that Good's article hit the news stands, and alerted the music industry to the 'exciting newcomer', was Cliff's last day working at Atlas Lamps. Ganjou, who was the sole entertainments booker for Billy Butlin's holiday camps, had offered him a two-week contract singing at their 2,000-capacity Clacton camp and the only way to fulfil the engagement was for Cliff to leave his job and turn professional.

Cliff had only ever spent one night away from his mother and father. Most young people in the fifties were naïve compared to later generations but Cliff struck those he met as having been particularly protected. Tulah Tuke was a young actress employed by Radio Butlin and recalls that her chalet mate, who was known as 'Randy Rene', made a play for him one night.

'He was very young and very unsophisticated and didn't know what on earth was happening. She managed to get Cliff back to the chalet but I think he brought John Foster with him as protection. I remember thinking that he was very young even for his age. He was seventeen but I thought of him as sixteen.'

Foster remembers it as a time of good clean fun. Only he and Samwell smoked (which is why they shared a chalet), none of the boys were big drinkers and no one had time for girlfriends.

'In those days it was big news to sleep with a girl,' says Foster. 'You didn't want to set up a lasting relationship with someone who slept around. We were still all innocent boys and women were up on a pedestal somewhere.'

During the first week the camp's entertainment manager moved them around because he couldn't find the right venue for a rock 'n' roll trio. Drinkers in the camp pub, The Jolly Roger, weren't of the right generation to appreciate Cliff Richard and the Drifters and the ambience of the Hawaiian-style cocktail bar wasn't enhanced by their presence, so they were finally assigned to the Rock 'n' Roll Ballroom.

A poor-quality tape recording of one of their sets survives. It was made by Stan Edwards, a fellow Red-Coat entertainer, who set a reel-to-reel tape recorder on a chair in the middle of the ballroom. The guitar sound is unsurprisingly thin and limited but Cliff's vocals are already well developed although hampered by an obvious affection for Elvis. He puts a little too many 'uh-huh's into every song and doesn't yet have the confidence to match the looseness he's striving for.

The set list is dominated by songs made popular by Elvis and Jerry Lee Lewis. He starts with Eddie Cochran's 'Twenty Flight Rock', then sings 'Move It' and 'Breathless'. This is followed by five Elvis songs – 'Money Honey', 'Heartbreak Hotel', 'Hound Dog', 'I Got A Woman' and 'Milkcow Blues Boogie' – before closing with 'Move It' and 'Whole Lotta Shakin' Goin' On'.

On 'Milkcow Blues Boogie' he even follows the pattern of Elvis' Sun Records recording where the song is started as a lazy blues before Elvis stops the musicians and says, 'Hold it fellows. That don't move me. Let's get real real gone for a change' before launching into a rocked-up version. In a jive American accent Cliff can be heard saying, 'Wait a minute fellows. That don't move none. Let's get real real gone for a change, huh?'

Pre-release copies of 'Move It' had been sent by EMI to Radio Butlin which broadcast throughout the camp.

'When Cliff's acetate came in I was just grateful to have something that I could chat about,' remembers Tulah Tuke. 'I could say that he was playing on site and announce the venue. I gave the record a great plug and the next thing I knew was that Cliff and John Foster were standing at the door saying "That's the first time we've heard it. It's great. Thanks a lot. Can we hear it again?" So they came in to my studio and I played it to them. That must make me the first person ever to play a Cliff Richard record to the public. I was certainly the first person to play a Cliff Richard record to Cliff.'

It was also while at Clacton that the group first heard the record on Radio Luxembourg. 'It was unbelievable,' says Foster. 'They may have played both sides of the single but I definitely remember "Move It" and after that they started to play it quite regularly.'

When they returned home from Butlin's there was more good news waiting for them. Mark Forster, who worked for top promoter Arthur Howes, was offering them a spot on an October tour of Britain headlined by the Kalin Twins. Their fee would be two hundred pounds a week, the most money they had ever earned.

Then there was a letter from Jack Good, who had auditioned Cliff and the Drifters for 'Oh Boy!'. They would be needed the next day, Sunday 7 September, for the first rehearsals of 'Oh Boy!'

'I DIDN'T *nine* WANT
THE REAL
CLIFF RICHARD.
REAL PEOPLE ON
TELEVISION ARE
BORING'

Jack Good invented rock 'n' roll television. He was working as an actor understudying Wilfred Lawson on a 1956 television drama when he went to see the film *Rock Around The Clock* one afternoon when he wasn't needed at the rehearsal room in Islington. The experience was to change his life.

Whereas the film *The Blackboard Jungle* had simply used Haley's song in the soundtrack, *Rock Around The Clock*, directed by Sam Katzman, was chock full of rock 'n' roll. There was not only Bill Haley but Little Richard, the Platters, and Freddie Bell and the Bellboys. For Good it was an experience of pure primitive theatrical excitement.

'I had always hated pop music,' he says, 'and therefore this rock 'n' roll appealed to me in a perverse way because I immediately realized that Frank Sinatra would hate it, and I loathed Frank Sinatra. Rock 'n' roll had a raw excitement and that was what I liked about theatre.

'To me, Laurence Olivier was an exciting actor, and Shakespeare done right was exciting. There was nothing like it. It seems ridiculous to say it, but there was something electrifying in good rock 'n' roll, and that's what I liked.'

Shortly afterwards he abandoned his short-lived career as an actor to work for the BBC where he thought there might be opportunities to translate the excitement of rock 'n' roll into television.

His chance came when he was paired with Josephine Douglas and asked to come up with a winning formula for a teenage programme that would fit the space immediately after six o'clock in the evening. Up until then it had been left 'dark' so that parents could use the time to put children to bed. What they came up with was the '6.5 Special'.

The first show was broadcast in February 1957 but there were too many compromises for Good's liking. There was a bit of rock 'n' roll – a duo he had discovered on a United States Air Force base, called Bobby and Rudy, singing 'I'm Gonna Teach You To Rock', and a clip of Little Richard from the film *The Girl Can't Help It* – but there were a lot of features that certainly weren't rock 'n' roll: a boys' choir, a team of Hungarian acrobats, trumpeter Kenny Baker and Pouishnoff playing Mozart.

There was a conflict of ideas between Josephine Douglas, who wanted healthy Boy Scout-type features on such hobbies as stamp collecting and mountaineering, and Good who wanted to terrorize adults and excite teenagers with his vision of wild abandon.

Realizing that he was never going to have his way with the BBC, who were warning that rock 'n' roll was on its way out, Good left and joined the independent television company ABC. They allowed him to trial two live rock 'n' roll programmes at the Wood Green Empire in June 1958. Good called the shows 'Oh Boy!' after Buddy Holly's song.

These two half-hour shows were topped by Marty Wilde, a lanky South Londoner who had shot to prominence after an appearance on '6.5 Special', and they moved faster than anything seen before on British television.

'I wanted pace, attack and no chat,' says Good. 'I hated light entertainment. I wanted next number, next number. I'm bored with that, next number... so by the time you were sick of somebody they were off and the next act was on flash, flash, flash! I wanted it to jump. I wanted action. I wanted the lights to go on cue, the music to go on cue and the audience to go up in the air and everything to be like a Cadillac zooming down a freeway.

'The lighting was very important. I had seen a photo of Ricky Nelson standing in a strong spotlight which was circled on the floor, and that shot was seminal to the look I wanted. Also there was a company called Theatro Nationale Populaire who put on Shakespeare but they did it all with black and white lighting and very little in the way of sets.

'At the time I was into the psychological effect of rhythm and lights. I was into all sorts of strange books about brainwashing and the effects of voodoo. I thought I was doing the public a favour by introducing these things to television. William Sargent's book *Battle For The Mind* (subtitled 'A Physiology of Conversion and Brain Washing' and first published in 1957) was very influential.

'I wanted to create tremendous tension and excitement which I justified in my mind as being a form of catharsis as described by the Greeks. I thought that the kids would let off steam in the theatre and would then be peaceful and passive when they went back on the streets. Absolute rubbish! It worked quite the other way. I should never have been let loose.'

It was a powerful concoction and knocked spots off '6.5 Special', which was cosy and amateurish in comparison. ABC knew they were on to a winner and gave Good a spot between 6.00 and 6.30 p.m. each Saturday evening beginning on 13 September 1958 and lasting for as long as they could see.

Good began pulling together a show that would be transmitted live from the Empire Theatre in Hackney. He planned to keep the line-up that he'd had at Wood Green – instrumentals from the John Barry Seven, vocal harmonies from the Dallas Boys and the Vernons Girls, a Fats Domino style rhythm blast from Lord Rockingham's XI led by Harry Robinson, Hammond organ music from South African Cherry Wainer and solo spots from Marty Wilde, Bernice Reading and Ronnie Carroll. The last-minute addition, made after hearing 'Move It', was Cliff Richard and the Drifters.

Rehearsals for 'Oh Boy!' were intensive. Cliff was needed for a full week to go through 'Move It' and 'Don't Bug Me Baby' because Good wanted to plan every move and build a persona for Cliff that would make him instantly recognizable in a crowded marketplace.

His plan had swung into action the first evening they met when he told Cliff that the obvious similarities with Elvis would have to go. 'Although we were keen to have someone on "Oh Boy!" who would have the impact that Elvis did, we didn't want an Elvis impersonator. Also, Cliff clearly couldn't play the guitar very well and this would prove very limiting for the shots.'

Having eradicated the most obvious of the Elvis traits, Good set about building Cliff Richard. He was to be a young naïve teenager surging with sexual energy, but apparently unaware of it.

'He was very slim and innocent looking,' says Good. 'We presented him as if it was beyond him not to smoulder and yet he didn't mean to. That was the excitement. Elvis looked as though he'd knocked around a bit and he would bump and grind and sneer. Cliff didn't do any of that. He would be withdrawn, and the audience would come to him.'

Every day for the week before the first show Cliff would go to the 'Oh Boy!' rehearsal room at the Four Provinces of Ireland club in Canonbury Lane, Islington. Vernons Girl Maggie Streader remembers him coming in looking like a little boy lost, obviously overawed at being surrounded by hardened professionals, television executives and music business hangers-on.

'He was so sweet,' she remembers. 'He was around the same age as us but when you saw him you just wanted to look after him. There was no brashness. He wasn't "of the business" as it were. I think we girls were a bit overpowering for him.'

Good would work through the songs with Cliff line by line. Cliff was so self-conscious that he had to be tutored in a room away from the rest of the cast. Good taught him to hide the pointed tooth that still bothered him, to tilt his head at the camera and raise his eyes up and, most effectively, to suddenly grab at his arm 'as if stuck with a hypodermic syringe' at key emotional points in the songs. The word 'sex' was never mentioned.

In February 1959 Good wrote about these rehearsals in his *Disc* column.

'"Move It" was probably the most difficult number I have had to produce so far,' he said. 'Cliff and I spent some hours getting the thing absolutely right for his first TV appearance... Every blink, every change in the pose of the head, every gesture, had to be worked out and made meaningful.

'The whole song was broken down into fragments. At last, each fragment was right. Then came the very difficult job of putting all the component parts together and creating not a mass of details, but a complete and meaningful whole. Above all, the finished product must not seem to have been worked over to the nth degree. It has to seem quite fresh and unconsidered.'

For stage wear Cliff had a pink jacket and black tapered trousers (which he had made to measure by a tailor in Dean Street, Soho), pink tie, black shirt and pink socks. It was his decision to develop this image although the idea wasn't original. Elvis had been buying pink and lime-green jackets from Lanksy Brothers clothing store on Beale Street in Memphis and wearing them with black peg-legged trousers. But, in those grim post-war days when most fathers were still wearing the black or grey suits they had been issued with on leaving the armed forces, it was a fashion statement which excited the young and worried the old.

'If a woman wore shocking pink in those days it was considered quite brave,' says *Observer* journalist Janet Watts, who saw Cliff in concert in 1958 when she was a teenager. 'For a man to wear pink was alarming! For us it was liberation. It was a splash of fun and colour into what had become a very grey world.'

On the day of the broadcast there were two further rehearsals: one in the morning for vision only, one in the afternoon for sound and vision. The director was Rita Gillespie, a woman in her mid-twenties who had little experience of rock 'n' roll but saw it as an opportunity to experiment with television. It was from her carefully-prepared camera scripts, based on listening to the songs, that Good developed his stage directions.

'Cliff was very inexperienced and he wanted to be told what to do,' says Rita. 'I loved shooting him. He had the perfect face for television. I never tired of close-ups and profiles of him.

'Once, by sheer accident, I caught him singing something with a "t" or an "s" in it, and his spit was highlighted by the arc lights as a glittering tiny speck. After that I kept waiting for the same thing to happen again.'

It would complete the fairytale to say that Cliff tore the house down on his TV debut, but the response was muted. The screams were reserved for Marty Wilde, already a TV star, who was at four in the charts with 'Endless Sleep'. But the effect of the national exposure was undeniable. The following week he returned to sing 'Schoolboy Crush' and by the week ending 27 September 'Move It' had entered Melody Maker's top twenty chart at number twelve.

Good's coaching had paid off. The reserved boy from Cheshunt was now regarded as both 'moody' and 'sexy'. Before the year ended, he would be accused of 'crude exhibitionism' and 'short-sighted vulgarity' by *New Musical Express* (in an unsigned attack by its publisher Maurice Kinn), and the *Daily Sketch* would ask, 'Is this boy TV star too sexy?'

Good just used to laugh at these stories. Cliff took up Elvis' argument that he meant no harm – it was the beat that made him do it.

'I can't help it if people say I'm too sexy in my singing,' he said. 'I can't help it. I don't push it, believe me. I just get carried away. It's just that I do exactly what the songs tell me inside I gotta do.'

For the Kalin Twins' tour new musicians needed to be drafted in to work with Cliff. They had met a guitarist called Ken Pavey at Butlin's who had filled in for them but he'd been offered a residency in a pub in Wood Green and didn't want to pass on what looked like a secure job for the sake of a rock 'n' roll tour. This left Cliff with Samwell now playing bass, Smart playing drums and a tour due to start on 5 October. Foster went down the 2 I's to find a replacement.

'I went to meet Tony Sheridan, a very good guitarist. While waiting for him I met Hank Marvin who got his guitar out and played a few Buddy Holly riffs and something by Ricky Nelson's guitarist James Burton. It turned out that he was already on the tour playing for the Most Brothers so I asked him to double up by playing for us as well. Hank agreed to it but he wanted to bring his mate Bruce Welch who played rhythm guitar.

'The next I heard of Tony Sheridan was when he cut his first single in Germany with the Beatles as his backing group.'

Hank Marvin and Bruce Welch were two sixteen year olds who had come to London from Newcastle to play in the finals of a talent contest with their skiffle group the Railroaders, and had never returned.

Their recent past was remarkably similar to Cliff's. They had both started playing skiffle in 1957, flunked out of school with no qualifications, changed their names to sound more American (Hank's real name was Brian Rankin, and Bruce's Bruce Cripps). Both had played rock 'n' roll and headed for the 2 I's because they had heard that this was the place where things happened.

When they arrived in London in April 1958, Cliff was already playing at the 2 I's but they didn't catch sight of him until July when Welch, who took a job in the coffee bar working the orange juice machine, went back and told Hank about the most exciting British rock 'n' roll singer he had ever seen.

Hank was by then in the Vipers, the one-time skiffle group which Wally Whyton was updating to meet the challenge of rock 'n' roll by adding drums and electric guitars. What Whyton didn't know was that he was creating the Shadows in embryo. Besides Hank on guitar he had Tony Meehan on drums and Terence 'Jet' Harris on bass.

'We went out and had a bit of a disastrous tour,' remembers Whyton. 'We had new amplifiers which blew up and at that point I decided I didn't want to be involved with electric music. So I went off busking in the South of France and the lads asked me if it was alright if they went out with Cliff who was touring for three weeks. I said, "Do exactly as you want."'

The first rehearsal of the new Drifters was at 12 Hargreaves Close. Cliff, Hank Marvin, Bruce Welch, Terry Smart and Sammy Samwell worked through a set of 'Baby I Don't Care', 'Don't Bug Me Baby', 'Blueberry Hill', 'Move It', 'Whole Lotta Shakin' Goin' On' and 'King Creole'.

'The drum kit was set up in the living room,' remembers Hank. 'The rest of us played electric guitars through amplifiers that were the size of cornflake packets which meant that it wasn't particularly noisy. But we could see straight away that Cliff really had something going for him.'

116

Two days before the tour Cliff recorded another Samwell song at Abbey Road, 'High Class Baby'. Again Paramor hired Frank Clarke and Ernie Shear to beef up the sound, but this time it didn't work. It wasn't their fault. 'High Class Baby' was a colourless song.

When Cliff got home that evening he broke down and cried. He thought his career was over, that everything he had attained had been through a recording fluke. 'I thought that was it,' says Cliff. 'It just didn't compare in any way to "Move It".'

The Kalin Twins' tour began on 5 October at the Victoria Hall. Hanley and Cliff Richard and the Drifters were booked to open up the second half of a show that started with sets from the Most Brothers, the Londonaires and Eddie Calvert.

Calvert was a veteran trumpeter, produced by Norrie Paramor for Columbia, who'd had several hits (including two number ones) since his chart debut in 1953 with 'Oh Mein Papa'. The Londonaires were a jazz-based trio and the Most Brothers were, according to Mickie Most, 'an Everly Brothers with bad harmonies'.

At the time the Grade Agency booked the tour, the Kalin Twins had a number one single with 'When' but it had since fallen while 'Move It' was still climbing. This put the Kalins in the unenviable position of closing the show after a set by one of the hottest acts in the country.

Hal and Herbie Kalin were not a rock 'n' roll act. They were 24 years old at a time when pop stars were expected to be teenagers, and had started out singing Frankie Laine and Johnnie Ray songs. What made them acceptable to a rock 'n' roll audience was the fact that they looked younger than they were, they had a hit record and they were American.

The Kalins had come to Britain expecting to discover that Cliff Richard was a nice-looking boy who couldn't sing. They had worked in America with Fabian, a handsome Italian who had trouble holding a tune in his head or keeping to the beat. But what they saw on stage in Hanley on that opening night made them realize that Cliff not only had a hit but had a voice to carry it off on stage.

'He tore the house down,' says Hal Kalin. 'Then the audience would have to go from that to, "And now ladies and gentlemen the Kalin Twins" and you'd hear a five-piece jazz band trying to outdo what the Drifters had just played. Our volume alone was half theirs! It was a constant battle.

'Then there was a shift during the last four or five dates when they arranged to put Cliff on last because it was obviously not working out with us. There was no way we could compete with an up-and-coming seventeen-year-old. It had become a nightmare for us.'

The second night of the tour, at the Odeon, Blackpool, was reviewed in the *West Lancashire Evening Gazette* by someone who, in common with a lot of show business correspondents of the day, persisted in evaluating a rock 'n' roll performance as if it was a new music hall turn.

'The package, tied up by wisecracking, crew-cut compère Tony Marsh, contained a collection of 'pop' musicians to the exclusion of comics, jugglers and tumblers who used to be measured amongst the choice of the music hall,' wrote the anonymous critic.

'The show pleased teenagers, but there were not enough there to fill more than a third of the house.

'The American Kalin Twins, whose disc "When" has only just slipped from the top rung of the hit parade, made the boys and girls yell for more. And Cliff Richards [sic], a new British recording star, generated almost as much excitement as he rocked and roared in a "shocking pink" jacket, surrounded by four bandsmen, dressed in sinister style in black shirts and wearing sunglasses, and the jumble of wiring and amplifiers which transmit the latest sound.'

Standing in the wings as Cliff and the Drifters played those opening nights was Jet Harris, Wally Whyton's nineteen-year-old bass guitarist who had been picked up for the tour by Mickie Most.

'I still maintain that "Move It" was the turning point for British rock 'n' roll,' he says. 'It certainly shook me because I was a staunch jazz man. Then, part way through the tour, Cliff asked me if I'd like to beef up the sound by playing bass with the Drifters. I said "yes" straight away.'

Jet was not only older than the rest of the group but he was more worldly-wise and more experienced as a musician. Whereas Cliff and Hank looked like home-loving lads, Jet with his bleached blond hair kept in place by Vitapointe and his permanently dangling cigarette could have been the member of a street gang.

He had started playing clarinet in jazz clubs at the age of fifteen and had then switched to double bass and worked with Terry Dene, Larry Page, Tubby Hayes, Ronnie Scott, Don Lang, Wee Willie Harris and Tony Crombie. It was the jazz drummer Crombie who suggested that he switched to a bass guitar.

'Jet played a Framus with a thin semi-acoustic body which sounded great at a time when everyone else was playing stand-up bass,' says Hank. 'He was also a very driving player who liked to turn up the volume and give it a lot of bottom end.

'He'd been around a lot longer than we had and had a concept of advanced chord sequences and how to play against them. To us he was like the old man of music.'

His image of brooding bohemianism added a rebellious hint to the Drifters. Where Cliff abstained from alcohol, Jet would drink it until he fell down. Where Cliff seemed unfazed by female attention, Jet was never without a woman. Where Cliff went home to life with mum and dad in Cheshunt, Jet returned to a basement flat in Eccleston Square, behind Victoria Station, which he shared with a collection of musicians, a fox, two monkeys, a dog, a cat and a skunk called Sam. His bedroom was carpeted with newspapers, had a broom handle fixed in the doorway as a wardrobe and was lit with a single bare light bulb.

'He looked incredible,' remembers Cliff. 'He had a quiff, he was gaunt... he was everything I wasn't. Jack Good once described him as "the moody, magnificent Jet Harris" and said that only Cliff Richard could ever stand in front of him.'

Even at the age of nineteen Jet had a reputation for being edgy and unreliable. Wee Willie Harris, an eccentric piano player who was dyeing his hair pink in 1957, employed Jet and found him difficult to be around.

'He was always a bag of nerves,' he says. 'He used to drive me mental. Whenever we shared a dressing room he would be up and down like a yo-yo pacing backwards and forwards. Just watching him would get me going.'

In 1958 touring conditions were primitive. All the artists on the tour travelled in an unheated Bedford coach driven by Ron King of Timpson's Coaches, and everyone but the headlining act had to find their own accommodation on arrival.

'They all had to pay for their own digs out of their wages,' remembers King, 'They would take the cheapest digs they could find even if it meant sleeping on the bus, which they nicknamed the "Hotel Bedford".'

The sound for performances was normally fed through two house speakers which would be positioned high up at either side of the stage. The drums wouldn't be miked and so the only sound worth checking was the sound made on the stage.

'There were no PA systems as such,' says Bruce Welch, 'and as for lights, it was just a matter of whether you wanted them on or off.'

Performances were brisk – the closing act was only on stage for eighteen minutes – and backing musicians were shared around to cut costs. Eddie Calvert's band supported the Kalin Twins and Hank was putting in performances for all the acts except the Londonaires. Jet was now playing for the Most Brothers and Cliff.

After playing Manchester on 10 October Cliff returned to London to appear on 'Oh Boy!'. He was in Liverpool on the 12th, where in the audience was a sixteen-year-old local boy called Paul McCartney. 'My dad had a mate who used to work on the stage door,' says McCartney. 'And I can remember he got me Eddie Calvert's autograph.'

Two days later, at the De Montfort Hall in Leicester, it was Cliff's eighteenth birthday. The fans threw birthday presents on the stage and the whole audience of 2,500 sang 'Happy Birthday' to him. On 19 October, at the Colston Hall, Bristol, the tour came to an end. 'Move It' was now at number four in the charts.

'THE KIDS LIKED HIM, BUT HE DIDN'T HAVE AN ACT'

ten

George Ganjou, who had been used to booking variety acts, was already out of his depth as an agent. John Foster, not as good at business as he was at bluffing, stood no chance at negotiating with the power brokers of British show business.

Norrie Paramor spoke to Cliff and his father about the situation and recommended Franklyn Boyd, the publisher of 'Schoolboy Crush', as the man to manage Cliff's career as he was older and well-connected in the music industry.

Franklyn Boyd had the advantage of having been a singer himself. He had left the RAF in 1946 and worked with Teddy Foster's Orchestra for three years, later singing with Oscar Rabin and Eric Winstone. He agreed to handle Cliff's affairs as long as he didn't have to leave his job with Aberbach Music. John Foster was retained as road manager and put on an uncontracted salary of twelve pounds a week.

Then there was the question of the Drifters. Cliff was well satisfied with the addition of Hank Marvin and Bruce Welch but he was aware that their proficiency now exposed the weaknesses of Samwell and Smart. He knew that eventually they would have to go, and first of all he decided to get rid of Sammy.

He wasn't told right away. After the Kalin tour there were no immediate dates to play and Samwell took a break What he didn't know was that although the Drifters weren't playing, they were hard at work practising and that his replacement on bass guitar was Jet Harris.

It was only when he turned up with a new song that he realized he had been ousted. Still he wasn't told by Cliff. 'I think it might well have been John Foster who had to break me the bad news,' he remembers.

'Even though I didn't have to do the telling, it was a hard decision because Sammy was a friend,' says Cliff. 'This sort of thing never becomes easier but I have to be single-minded when I want something new. In 1958 the decision was based on the fact that Hank was the best guitarist, Jet was the best on bass, and that meant there was no room for Sammy.'

Cliff was now becoming the star of 'Oh Boy!', much to the chagrin of Marty Wilde's manager Larry Parnes who had seen the show as the perfect showcase for his boy and others, like Vince Eager, who he was currently grooming. While Cliff and Marty remained friends, sang together on the shows and admired each other's work, Larry Parnes tussled with Jack Good over the lack of attention he felt his protégé was getting.

Parnes was the most important rock 'n' roll manager in Britain and was determined to control as much of the scene as he could. He was born in north-west London to a Jewish family in the clothing trade. After school he managed women's clothing stores before being attracted to the theatre, where he invested a small amount of money in a touring play.

His big break came in September 1956 when John Kennedy, a publicity agent, told him about rock 'n' roll and introduced him to Tommy Hicks, a merchant seaman he'd seen playing at the 2 I's. The two men took over his career, and as Tommy Steele he became Britain's first rock 'n' roll star. Marty Wilde was their second discovery.

The battle that Parnes was creating between Marty and Cliff was partly built out of resentment that Cliff didn't belong to him. A major league rock 'n' roll star had developed in Britain in London and he didn't have a share.

On 18 October this resentment spilled over into a full-blooded row. Both Cliff and Wilde were scheduled to appear on the show and Marty turned up in a steel-grey mohair suit which Good said he couldn't wear because it wouldn't work with the lights.

'When I told him that, Parnes flew into a rage and threatened to pull him out of the show if he couldn't wear the suit,' says Good. 'In the end I had to call a security guard to usher Parnes out of the theatre.'

Wilde did the show but Parnes pulled him out of the series and didn't allow him to come back until 7 February 1959. By this time he had been eclipsed by Cliff who was now in such demand that he didn't have the time to appear regularly on 'Oh Boy!'.

Wilde then lost out on the role of Bongo Herbert in *Expresso Bongo* which Cliff was eventually offered. The reason was mainly because producer Val Guest thought that Wilde, who stood six feet three inches tall, was 'too big to feel sorry for'. Parnes put an amusing spin on the rejection when he told the press that he thought it was 'a suitable part for a smaller talent than Marty'.

The Cliff versus Marty feud made great newspaper copy and kept both their names alive.

'The "Oh Boy!" row was the best thing that ever happened to Cliff Richard and the biggest boost to his career,' says Franklyn Boyd. 'It made the front page of the *Daily Mirror*. It was unbelievable. Cliff was immediately a big star because he made the front page of a national newspaper. Having a number one record doesn't make headline news but this hullabaloo did.'

What concerned Boyd was Cliff's inexperience as a performer. Television and radio commitments were keeping him in London during the week and he was only playing out of town on Sunday nights.

'Cliff was terrible in those Sunday night concerts,' he admits. 'You had people like Rory Blackwell who had come out of the jazz clubs and they were killing him. Cliff was top of the bill but all these other stars knew what to do on stage and it killed him. I mean, the kids liked him but he didn't have an act. He didn't know how to come on and off stage. He didn't know how to take a bow.'

So Boyd booked him into three weeks of variety shows during November and December – a week at the Metropolitan, Edgware

Road, a week at the Chiswick Empire and a week at the Finsbury Park Empire. Cliff was to stay with Boyd and his wife Daphne at their apartment in Barons Court. He would rehearse his 'Oh Boy!' shows during the day and then give two performances a night with the Drifters at 6.15 and 8.15, the aim being to give him an intense forty-two-show crash course in stagecraft.

The variety bills make strange reading today. At the Metropolitan, for example, Cliff shared the stage with Little Beaver and Maree, a roller-skating tap dancer called Checker Wheel, someone called Bernard Landy who mimed to records, comedian Michael Roxy, multi-instrumentalist Michael Hill, puppeteer Janet Fox and comic double act Roy Hudd and Eddy Kay.

It wasn't a happy mix. The rock 'n' roll fans weren't interested in tap-dancing roller skaters and didn't take up their seats until Cliff appeared, and the admirers of old-time variety hall acts found rock 'n' roll too loud and brash.

'If there is one thing that the appearance of Cliff Richards [sic] demonstrates at the Met this week it is the deep gulf that exists between teenage taste and the conventional variety act,' reported *The Stage*.

'It is not unbridgeable, for the youngsters often appreciate the novelty of variety, but if the bridging is to be done I do not think this bill is going to do it. It provides, in fact, a strong argument against mixing the old and the new. Young Cliff Richards [sic] is an advanced example of his kind, an acquired taste that is quite as likely to antagonize as it is to please.

'I found his almost savage approach, backed by an overloud battery of guitars and drums, most impressive and without, so far as I know, being "sent" anywhere in particular, I quite enjoyed the demonstration. But one needs to be teenage, I think, really to know what it is all about.'

Tulah Tuke, back from her stint at Butlin's, saw one of the Metropolitan shows and remembers how unpolished it seemed.

'The Drifters went on stage with their chords written out and sellotaped to their guitars. Cliff seemed very inexperienced. He was only eighteen and here he was topping the bill on a variety circuit.

'Kids weren't as streetwise as they are today anyway and Cliff's background was even more protected than most. When he became a star he hadn't had the experience of knocking around Liverpool and Hamburg that the Beatles had had by the time they started having hits.' (By the end of the Kalin Twins' tour, Cliff had been on stage fewer than a hundred times in his whole career. The Beatles, by contrast, played the Cavern Club alone 292 times before recording their first single.)

The reviewer who caught him at the Chiswick Empire was even more disdainful. After chiding a duo called Reggie Redcliffe and Desmond Lane, who had apparently moved around a bit too much on stage, he went on to deal with 'young Cliff Richard' who he said, disapprovingly, was 'another young artist in the long line of those who find it necessary, in order to express themselves, to jerk a leg or wave an arm as they string together a succession of extraordinary words and phrases, often repetitive, each jerk or wave producing more or less non-stop screams from youthful fans who hang on to his every word and gesture. Master Richard is backed by his Drifters – drums and electric guitars which, to the uninitiated, appear to be grossly over-amplified.

'How pleasurable, therefore, to sit back and watch someone who restricts movement to a minimum – Vendryes, who silently produces a succession of doves seemingly from thin air...'

Because he was so obviously popular with the girls, the boys were becoming jealous. They didn't like this pretty, smooth-skinned boy who was becoming an icon to their girlfriends. He particularly wasn't liked by Teds and Rockers who fancied themselves as hard men.

At the Finsbury Park Empire a group of Rockers turned up threatening to cause trouble.

'They were the yobs of the time,' remembers Stan Edwards, who hadn't seen Cliff since they worked together at Butlin's. 'Cliff invited them to come and meet him. We were in the dressing room and these guys arrived in heavy leather gear and they turned out to be really great blokes. So they said, "We like you and we'll make sure no one gets on stage." They had come as the aggressors and became the defenders!'

By this final week of concerts Cliff was flagging. He was now not only rehearsing 'Oh Boy!' and doing two concerts a day but was playing a small role in *Serious Charge*, a film being shot in

Borehamwood. He wasn't used to working under such pressure and was clearly suffering from exhaustion.

'When it came to the last night Cliff just couldn't go on stage,' remembers John Foster. 'He came off after the first show and he just couldn't talk. So I threw everyone out of the dressing room, made him sleep and gave him honey and melted butter.

'While I was doing this Franklyn Boyd knocked on the door and when I opened it he asked, "How's my boy?" I said, "Look, get in your car, drive to Piccadilly Circus, go to the all-night chemist and get 'your boy' something for his throat because you're murdering him." I threw him out.'

He stayed in bed at home for a few days and his father began consulting a man called Ray Mackender, at the time a fringe character in the music business, whom Cliff had met at a party thrown by Cherry Wainer, one of the cast of 'Oh Boy!'.

Mackender was a handsome 26-year-old homosexual with thick wavy hair and a public school accent. By day he worked as a non-marine broker at Lloyds of London and by night donned a pair of jeans and headed down to Battersea Town Hall where he organized a rock 'n' roll dance night. He desperately wanted to be part of the scene but hadn't yet found a role. He wrote some features for *New Musical Express*, became a disc jockey at the Poplar Theatre, and befriended many of the 'Oh Boy!' stars.

On Sunday mornings he organized coffee parties at his flat in Danvers Street, Chelsea, where the cream of Britain's young talent would gather for chat and drinks. In his visitors' book from that period are the names of Vince Eager, Jess Conrad, Sammy Samwell, Cliff Richard, Jimmy Page (later to form Led Zeppelin) and Gerry Dorsey (later to be renamed Engelbert Humperdinck).

'It was the fact of getting together in those days that was so exciting for us,' says Jess Conrad. 'We weren't drinkers. We just liked meeting and playing records and back then you really had to go somewhere else to play your records because your parents complained too much about the noise if you played them at home.'

Cliff's parents warmed to Mackender. Rodger, who was forever believing that his son was being exploited, was impressed with Mackender's position in the City and started calling him up for business advice.

'Rodger saw me as a complete Godsend at that time,' Mackender admits. 'He confided that he was thinking of getting rid of Franklyn Boyd and he thought he could become Cliff's manager if I was willing to help him out.

'Initially I thought I could but, after a few meetings with the accountants, I realized it was a much bigger job than anyone could manage part-time. I was also reluctant to give up the security of my job with Lloyds.'

Rodger Webb went ahead anyway and sent a letter of dismissal to Franklyn Boyd, who had never signed a contract. The next day the story was splashed over the newspapers: 'Cliff Richard In Rumpus. Father Gives Manager The Sack.'

'I never had any quarrel with Cliff or his mother,' says Boyd. 'It was his father who was a pain in the neck. I think Cliff should have been strong enough to say, "Look Dad, I know you're my father but this is business." But he never said it.

'I knew he was struggling a bit rehearsing and doing the variety shows but I also knew he had to learn show business very quickly. If he had stuck doing Sunday concerts it would have taken him a year to get the same experience. I knew he would have a hard time but everyone goes through that.

'His father was working in a rather dull office, cycling eight miles to work each day, and now show business managers had started to wine and dine him. He was becoming quite impressed with it all. Tito Burns, Cherry Wainer's manager, had been sending limousines up to Cheshunt to bring his mother to shows. In other words, everyone was winning the parents over because they could see the pound signs in Cliff Richard.'

Boyd left at around the same time that it was decided that Terry Smart, Cliff's last link with the original Drifters, was going to have to go. It wasn't a difficult decision to make because Smart knew that he couldn't keep pace with the professionals and he was keen to join the Merchant Navy when he was eighteen anyway.

The obvious first choice as his replacement was Tony Meehan, the drummer who had worked with Hank and Jet in the Vipers.

Although only fifteen, Meehan had been drumming since he was thirteen, playing in small dance bands in the Irish belt of

North London and then graduating to Soho where he played in backing groups for Adam Faith, Vince Eager and Vince Taylor.

'I went because they were complaining about how lousy their drummer was and they felt they just couldn't handle it any more,' he says. 'They were putting out feelers to see if I would be interested. So I saw him and I was impressed with what I saw. I thought he was terrific. He really was hot at that time and I was stimulated.

'Terry Smart was a real sweetheart but not a great player by any stretch of the imagination. It was a big wrench for Cliff when he left but he was quite ruthless about getting on. He was very determined. He knew that he couldn't put friendship before business.'

It was a hard time for Cliff because he was having to learn his stagecraft in the full glare of the national media and thousands of adoring fans. He was being projected as a star, yet he still found it hard to look directly at an audience. It took Cherry Wainer to coach him in the art of holding a microphone, and Franklyn Boyd to tell him how to take a bow.

By the end of 1958 he was starting to put it all together. With the addition of Tony Meehan, he had an experienced group behind him who could help paper over some of the remaining cracks.

eleven

'I WORRIED FOR HIS LIFE. I DIDN'T WANT ANYTHING TO HAPPEN TO HIM'

As his life expanded because of his stardom, so he became less and less the ordinary boy from Cheshunt. He could no longer travel on the bus or walk out alone without being surrounded by fans. Girls turned up and sat outside his home in Hargreaves Close and he often had to spend hours waiting inside the Hackney Empire until crowds dispersed. Then there was the additional threat from the Teddy boys and the slighted boyfriends.

'He didn't seem to know what had hit him,' remembers Tulah Tuke. 'When I saw him at the Metropolitan he seemed amazed and somewhat horrified that there were these little girls screaming outside. I think he was knocked back by it. He was as excited as any teenager would be but there was also that frightening dimension of not knowing exactly what might erupt.'

One night in Romford, while the girls stood outside the dressing room windows yelling for Cliff, a mob of boys started throwing bricks through the windows of the tour bus. Cliff had to be smuggled out of the building though a toilet window and driven to a rendezvous point on the road back to London.

At the Chiswick Empire some lads threw a fire hydrant from the balcony and two girls in the stalls were injured. At the Lyceum, off the Strand, he was forced to abandon a concert after being pelted with vegetables and coins with sharpened edges.

'If one of those things hit you it would take your eye out or give you a nasty cut,' says Tony Meehan. 'We tried to play on and then one of these things came right across my cymbal and I said, "Right, that's it." So, after three numbers, we pulled the plugs. I think that was the only time we ever stopped a show. There was absolute uproar. There were hundreds of people squashed against the stage and there didn't seem to be any control. Then these people at the back started breaking up chairs and hurling them through the air. It was a horrible, horrible atmosphere.'

Events like this began to trouble Cliff's mother.

'I never worried about him being a rock 'n' roll singer but I did worry about what could happen to him. I used to try and go everywhere with him. Rodger wouldn't come. He said I was daft. But I told him that these people were doing rotten things to him and I could save him.

'There used to be rows of policemen linking arms trying to protect him from the crowds. These boys would be shouting, "Kill him! Kill him!" It was dreadful. I used to go to all these shows because I didn't want anything to happen to him and me not to be there. I used to go everywhere.'

Within months of his first hit single being released he was adapting to the abnormal lifestyle of the rich and famous. His earnings were phenomenal by the standards of his contemporaries – £15,000 for a 30-week contract with the Grade Agency in March 1959 – but there was no time to spend it and few places to go. At the age of eighteen he was hermetically sealed into a way of life that he has never been able to escape.

His old friendships gradually fell away, partly through his friends' inability to deal with his fame, partly through Cliff's unavailability. His new friends and acquaintances were from the world of show business: people who lived the same hours and experienced the same problems. From the cast of 'Oh Boy!' he became particularly close to Cherry Wainer, who responded to this 'little boy lost' by taking him under her wing.

Cherry was something of an oddity on 'Oh Boy!'. She was neither from the same musical background nor the same generation as the regular stars of the show. She had come to Britain from South Africa late in 1957 with her drummer Don Storer and Jack Good had spotted her playing at a US Air Force base.

'Cherry always seemed so worldly wise,' remembers Maggie Streader from the Vernons Girls. 'She was older than all of us. She was a star! She knew everybody, knew everything and called everyone "darling".'

She met Cliff at his first rehearsal and began gently to coach him and advise him on how to handle himself in the business. She saw him as vulnerable and easily exploited.

He began to share his hopes and fears with her and together with John Foster and other performers from the show he would spend evenings with her at the Lotus House, a Chinese restaurant in the Edgware Road which was a late-night hang-out for the 'Oh Boy!' crowd. Because Cliff had no means of transport and no telephone at home she also began to chauffeur him around and take messages.

Through Cherry Wainer's influence Cliff was brought together with her manager Tito Burns, who was then introduced to his parents over a meal at the Lotus House.

'His mum and dad knew nothing about show business,' says Cherry. 'Cliff became so big so fast and everywhere he went people were trying to get at him. I think he was thankful and grateful that it was happening, but it bothered him.'

Tito Burns was everything that the Webbs could have imagined a show business manager to be. He had slicked-back hair and a Groucho Marx moustache, smoked cigars and liked talking about 'wheeling and dealing'.

He was born Nathan Burns in the East End of London and had joined a dance band on leaving school. *Melody Maker*'s annual polls voted him Britain's top accordion player, and he was also a good enough comedian to play support to Alma Cogan.

Unlike Cliff's previous managers, he already controlled several acts he could use as bargaining tools. George Ganjou had now been shunted on to the sidelines. He was still paid his 10 per cent in line with the contract signed when Cliff was seventeen, but he no longer played any active part in Cliff's career.

Burns made no secret of the fact that he had no love for rock 'n' roll. He saw it as a short-term phenomenon and thought that the best insurance policy Cliff could take out would be to distance himself from the Drifters and introduce more classic cover songs into his act. Whereas Cliff had always seen himself as Elvis, Burns saw him as Frank Sinatra.

The move away from rock 'n' roll though was eventually to come through Lionel Bart, Tommy Steele's songwriter. He had been approached by film producer Mickey Delamar to write songs for a film version of *Serious Charge*, a British play about a vicar who helps a juvenile delinquent who then tries to frame him on a charge of indecent assault.

At the time homosexuality was a risqué subject for cinema, and Delamar wanted a rock 'n' roll soundtrack to broaden its appeal. 'He asked me if I knew of an English kid who was an Elvis clone,' says Bart. 'I put Cliff's name forward.'

The director was 43-year-old Terence Young, later to make his name with the early James Bond films. 'I think we thought that if we put a few kids in it would draw a younger audience,' he admits. 'Otherwise it would have been strictly a television sort of audience. So the part of Curly was added for the film version.

'There were two or three singers that I went to see. I saw Cliff at the Chiswick Empire and I was sold on him right away. He seemed terribly self-assured and had a very good stage act. I thought if he could do that, then he could act.'

The film had a strong cast with former child star Andrew Ray playing the teenage delinquent, Anthony Quayle the vicar and Sarah Churchill, daughter of Sir Winston, a middle-aged parishioner with marriage on her mind. Cliff took the part of Curly, the delinquent's younger brother.

Filming took place at MGM's studios in Borehamwood and in the new town at Stevenage. Andrew Ray calls the film 'a poor man's *The Wild Ones* set in Stevenage'.

Cliff didn't have many lines and the ones he had he spat out of the corner of his mouth in a pseudo-hip accent that was out of keeping with his innocent face.

'I remember Cliff was a lovely fellow,' says Ray, 'but he was very nervous about acting. He really wanted to get on with the songs in the film.'

While filming was going on, Tommy Steele, still the reigning king of British rock 'n' roll with eleven top thirty hits, paid an unexpected visit to the set. He asked to see Cliff in his dressing room. Jess Conrad, who was playing the leader of a local gang which disrupts the vicar's youth club, remembers the tense scene as the king met the pretender to the crown.

'There wasn't friction, but Tommy was the established star and now this new boy was coming up and he asked Cliff if he had ever played "knuckles", where you had to touch knuckles and if you couldn't move away fast enough you got hit.

'Tommy was very good at it and very fast. He cut Cliff's hands to ribbons. I'll never ever forget it. It was the most devious thing I had ever seen because Tommy had decided that he wanted to draw blood from the new idol. It was really awful. Cliff could never get out of the way quick enough and it went on and on. Cliff kept saying he'd play on, and yet his knuckles were red raw where Tommy had been whacking and whacking him.'

Steele had learned the game as a merchant seaman on board the liner *Mauretania*.

'To lose at "knuckles" on that ship was as bad as walking the plank,' remembers Steele. 'A young man intent on entering the arena needed to be strong, sly and very quick. Cliff was not very good at it.'

One of the songs from Lionel Bart's soundtrack was 'Living Doll'. He had written it one Sunday morning in October 1958 while reading the *Sunday Pictorial*.

'I was looking at the back pages and there was a small advert for a doll which could apparently do everything,' Bart remembers. 'I wrote the song in ten minutes.'

The advert that caught his eye was for a 99/6d 'Darling Doll' which was said to 'kneel, walk, sit and sing'. He linked this idea with the Mills Brothers' wartime hit 'Paper Doll', in which the singer asks for a cut-out paper girl because others wouldn't steal her, and she would be easier to be with than a 'fickle-minded real live girl'. Bart added his own twist to the tale.

As performed for the soundtrack, 'Living Doll' was a fast song in four-four time which Cliff hated singing. Paramor tried to thwart its release as a single by writing a song with a similar title, 'Livin' Lovin' Doll', which Cliff released in January 1959. So that no one would know who was behind it he used the pseudonym Johnny May and his friend Bunny Lewis was credited as Jim Gustard. (Paramor and Lewis went on to write Cliff's 1960 hit 'A Voice In The Wilderness', this time not hiding their identities.)

But the public was not satisfied with 'Livin' Lovin' Doll', and it only reached number twenty in the charts. There was demand for a soundtrack EP from the film and so, at the end of April 1959, Cliff re-recorded the songs.

'We told Norrie that we didn't like "Living Doll" the way it was,' says Cliff. 'We were at Sheffield City Hall doing a sound check one afternoon [14 February 1959], sitting around thinking what we could do with the song, when Bruce started strumming his guitar and he said, "What about having it as a country song?"'

Since 'Move It' had reached number two in the charts and stayed around for over four months, Cliff had been struggling to maintain momentum as a singles' artist.

He tried to achieve this initially by recording more rock 'n' roll numbers, but after 'High Class Baby' reached number seven his chart positions became less impressive. 'Livin' Lovin' Doll' only just made the top twenty and 'Mean Streak', because it was competing in the charts with its own flip side 'Never Mind', stalled at ten. The number of records sold had slumped to below 200,000 from a high of well over half a million.

His first LP, recorded days before the concert at Sheffield City Hall, was to be the last all-out burst of rock 'n' roll. Paramor wanted to capture the feel of those early live performances, but to do it in the controlled environment of Abbey Road's studio two. Cliff and the Drifters played to an invited audience on a make-shift stage beneath the control room.

Over two nights, Cliff belted out his favourite hits, including 'Whole Lotta Shakin' Goin' On', 'Be Bop A Lula', 'Donna' and 'That'll Be The Day'. The result was *Cliff*, which went on to reach number four in the LP charts.

The slowed-down version of 'Living Doll' became his most

important recording since 'Move It'. It redefined him as a singer, was his first number one and sold almost two million copies.

'It wasn't an out-and-out rocker. But by then I was coming to see that rock wasn't a tempo but a musical culture, and that a song like "Living Doll" fitted into it,' Cliff says.

'What we were discovering was that rock 'n' roll seemed to be fairly limited as a beaty form of music because the public weren't buying it in hundreds of thousands. We were the first rock teenagers and ten year olds had no money to spend so in the end records like "Living Doll' sold because they appealed to parents who had money.

'We helped the audience to grow. By the time the Beatles came along those ten year olds were fifteen and had money. They could make a stand for rock 'n' roll. The Beatles had the benefit of all the groundwork that we had put in.'

At around the time that Cliff hooked up with Tito Burns, he moved away from home for the first time, and rented a three-bedroomed flat at 100 Marylebone High Street. At first he just shared with John Foster, but it soon became a crash pad – not only for the Drifters – but also for such singers as Billy Fury, Dickie Pride and Vince Eager. Comedian Jimmy Tarbuck often used the small spare bedroom.

'I didn't have a thing to my name back then,' says Tarbuck. 'Cliff used to let me stay at his flat when I was in London.' Cliff's mother and sister Donna would come up regularly to keep it clean and Donna would often stay for extended periods.

'We were on our own a lot of the time,' says Foster. 'We weren't really meeting new people. There weren't the clubs like you can go into today in London, and he had become so big so fast that he couldn't go anywhere. He couldn't even walk out on the street.'

The move had to be made because in 1959 Cliff started what was to become a familiar pattern of one-nighter shows which would almost always start with everyone being collected from a pick-up point in Marylebone – either Great Cumberland Place or Allsop Place – and it was too much to travel in from Cheshunt continually, especially as he didn't yet drive.

In February and March he toured the Granada circuit as part of a package which included Wee Willie Harris, Tony Crombie and Johnny Duncan with Jimmy Tarbuck as compère.

'Cliff was top of the bill,' remembers Tarbuck. 'They were fun days but the tour was so disorganized. You might be in Hull one day, Bournemouth the next and then Glasgow after that, and all of it done by coach.'

During one show, when Cliff lost his voice, Wee Willie Harris was positioned at the back of the stage to sing while Cliff mimed.

'It just shows you what it was all about in the fifties,' says Harris. 'I don't think the girls were bothered who was singing. Every time he made a sexy movement with his legs they screamed even though I was singing in full view of the audience.'

In April Cliff played for a week each at the Birmingham Hippodrome and the Chiswick Empire. It was while in Birmingham that he sent away for Hank's Fender Stratocaster, the first solid-body electric guitar to be sold to anyone in Britain.

Hank had been playing an Antoria, but the neck was bent and the tuning suspect. Like Cliff he admired the playing of James Burton, whose guitar breaks on Ricky Nelson's records epitomized American rock 'n' roll. Hank knew that Burton's instrument was made by Fender Instruments of Fullerton, California.

Hank and Cliff acquired a catalogue, pored over it and decided that Burton must have been playing a Stratocaster. The most expensive of Fender's guitars, it had revolutionized the guitar industry when it was introduced in 1954. Cliff offered to buy it for Hank (the cost was about five weeks of Hank's salary in 1959), and wrote to Dave Lilley, Ray Mackender's flatmate, to ask if he would order it:

'Dear Dave,
    We've decided to have the "Red" Fender Guitar. With A. Three pickups. B. With tremolo lever. C. Gold platted [sic] Hardware
    The guitar is a "Stratocaster". Have marked in catalogue. When you send for it please order spare set balanced strings and also a 'Fender Case'.
    Well Dave thanks a million. All the Best, Cliff.'

Hank remembers it arriving.

'A magnificent flat case with plush red lining came, and inside it was this magnificent guitar – flamingo pink with a maple finger board. You didn't have to play it. You just had to hang it around your neck and the audience would be totally impressed.'

The guitar, which at the time was considered to be very strange-looking, changed the image and sound of the group. It was much easier to play, there was greater tonal versatility and with the tremolo arm Hank was able to 'bend' notes. Within a few years solid-body guitars would be standard equipment for all rock groups.

At the Chiswick Empire Jet met a sixteen-year-old girl in the bar. Her name was Carol Costa, and she came from Hounslow.

'She was with a chap but he wasn't her boyfriend,' remembers Jet, 'and I thought she looked terribly Brigitte Bardot-ish.' A relationship was started and the two of them moved into the spare bedroom at Cliff's flat.

Although Cliff was charming towards all the girls in his social sphere, it became obvious quite early on that he and Jet's new girl were developing a crush on each other.

They started eyeing each other at the flat. They would even hold hands discreetly at the cinema, even though Jet was sitting on Carol's other side. Then there would be parties at Carol's home in Cedar Road, Hounslow, after which everyone would crash out overnight on the floor and again there would be looks and touches between her and Cliff.

'I had always fancied Brigitte Bardot,' Cliff says. 'When I was a teenager I had a poster of her on my bedroom wall which was made up of three parts given away in *Reveille* magazine. Bardot wore eyeliner and I remember Carol being like that.

'I fell for her. It was a strange time. It was the period I refer back to when I say that all my friends got married really young. All the Drifters were going steady with girls they would marry, and there was great pressure on me to get married. That must have played a great part in our relationship, brief though it was.

'I think Jet must have been aware that she fancied me. I don't think we were as discreet as we could have been really but at that stage it was only looks and glances.'

Cliff's mother began to suspect something was going on when she visited the flat one day to clean. She discovered that Carol had slipped a letter beneath Cliff's pillow before going out. Cliff told his mother that he was frightened of her and that he didn't like what was happening, but that was only part of the truth. The other part was that he was developing feelings for her. The fear came from the fact that she was the girlfriend of one of his closest friends.

What he didn't tell his mother he poured out to Cherry Wainer in long emotional conversations. He told her that he was very fond of Carol but that he didn't want to do anything that would hurt Jet or hurt his career.

'I think Carol was prepared to break off with Jet if she knew that she could have gone with Cliff,' she says, 'but at that time Cliff's mother didn't want anything to happen to him that would affect his career. I think although he felt very deeply for her, he didn't want to argue with his parents – to say, "Yes, I'm going to do this." So that's why he stayed put.'

Matters came to a head one night at a party where Jet was sitting on a sofa with Carol perched on his knee. Without explanation, Cliff suddenly rushed out of the room and didn't return. Carol assumed he'd been taken ill.

'I asked the road manager what was wrong with him, and he said, "You know what's wrong with him," ' she says. 'I went out and found him in one of the bedrooms. He was crying. He told me that he loved me and asked me what we were going to do about it. He wanted me to tell Jet that it was over. But when I did break from Jet and move back to my parents' home he dropped me. It was just like that.

'I think someone had been talking to him. I suppose he was worried about about breaking the group up. Maybe he was worried about the effect it would have on the fans.'

At that time it was important for a young male singer to preserve his single image. His fans, who were mostly female, needed to be able to nurse the fantasy that they could be his dream girl. Terry Dene married in July 1958 and never had another hit. Marty Wilde put an end to his career as a teenage idol when he married one of the Vernons Girls in 1959.

'Without a shadow of doubt my marriage affected my record sales and my popularity,' says Wilde. 'Directly after that I really struggled. You had to change your career to survive. But we knew that would happen. I had a long meeting with my manager and he said, "I'll leave the decision to you, but you must know what you're up against." '

Cliff had thought right from the start that marriage would limit his career but an incident in 1959 confirmed it for him. He was dating a dark-haired girl called Jean who worked in a bowling alley in Wembley and had got on well enough with her to be taken back to meet her parents. Jet Harris remembers her as 'the most gorgeous girl'.

She came along to several concerts with Cliff and after one show, at the Finsbury Park Empire, she left the theatre with him and sat on his lap in the waiting car. Cliff looked out of the car window long enough to see that his fans were in tears and some of them had thrown their concert programmes into the gutter and were grinding them in with their heels.

He was shocked at the intensity of their feelings. 'When I started seeing Jean I thought, well, perhaps I could have a girlfriend but this experience underlined the fact that I couldn't,' he says. 'The fans wanted to own me, and I was happy with that.'

Franklyn Boyd reckons that early in his career Cliff's mother was also influential in keeping him single.

'She always told him not to get romantically involved with girls because it would be the end of his career.'

There can be no doubt that his image as a lonely boy just waiting for Miss Right to come along helped his career. One of the most popular magazine story ideas of the time was 'Cliff's Ideal Girl'. Cliff would always say that he liked plain-looking girls who wore no make-up and weren't too forward. In this way even the most ordinary-looking fan could think that she fitted the bill.

A typical story (featured in a romantic comic for girls) was headlined 'Cliff Richard Reveals – If Only I Could Find The Right Girl' and began, 'Although I meet pretty girls wherever I go – I haven't got a girlfriend.' What sort of girl would he like? Of course she must like rock 'n' roll, cowboy films and Chinese food but 'I like a natural looking girl... a girl who can let herself go without worrying if her hair is going to lose its curl in the rain, or her nose get shiny.'

Later the same year he told a fan magazine that the girl he would marry (at 27), 'needn't be too good-looking, as long as she's got a personality of her own'.

His ideal, he told *Boyfriend* in May 1959, was Hollywood actress

Carol Lynley, who had been in two teen films, *Blue Jeans* and *Hound Dog Man*, because 'she seems so wholesome... so quiet. She's not specially good-looking. But in her very plainness there's a special kind of beauty.'

He couldn't have put it better if he'd been handed a script by a marketing executive. He was the boy with everything, surrounded by beautiful women, and yet all he wanted was a good old-fashioned plain girl who could cook him a meal and listen to records. Everyone was in with a chance. The challenge had been laid down. Even the prettiest of girls could leave off her make-up, tousle up her hair and affect just the right degree of plainness.

Jack Good was right. Cliff was too innocent to suggest the pleasures of forbidden fruit in the way that Elvis did. He was more suited to offering the promise of a romantic meal, a night at the cinema and a kiss on the doorstep that was guaranteed not to go too far. Whereas a lot of parents might have had a hard time adjusting to having Elvis around the house, Cliff was the ideal boy to invite back home: traditional but not fogeyish, proper but not prim.

Interviewed in 1964, Sammy Samwell suggested that Cliff's broad appeal was because he was a rock 'n' roll star whom parents were comfortable with and that this was more important in Britain at the time than it was in America for very practical reasons.

'In England not every home has a record player,' Samwell said. 'In many of the homes that have one, it is still something of a prized possession and if the youngsters want to play a record on it which annoys the parents, then there is trouble.

'Cliff broke this down by having the clean-cut "wouldn't mind having him for my son" type of thing. His records in this way became acceptable, so the kids were free to buy his records and play them, and still retain their own private inner image of Cliff, different from that of their parents.'

When Cliff went away in the summer of 1959 it was his first holiday since the days when he visited his grandfather in Lucknow and his first time out of England since arriving in 1948. In *It's Great To Be Young* he wrote, 'Ronnie, a chum of mine from the old days, was going out [to Italy] in his car and wondered if I'd like to join him. Would I? I jumped at it.'

'Ronnie' was Ronnie Ernstone, a 21-year-old car mechanic from Notting Hill Gate who had met Cliff at an EMI Studio party. They probably wouldn't have got so close if Ronnie hadn't had a car and promised to run him back to Cheshunt.

He was soon giving Cliff driving lessons. When, in April 1959, he wanted a Lambretta motor scooter Ernstone ordered one from friends in the motorcycle business and had it sprayed nasturtium, which was the colour of the moment. Much later, in August 1959, he organized the purchase of Cliff's first car – a grey Sunbeam Alpine with red leather seats.

Ernstone's other useful connection was clothes. His father was a textile importer and it occurred to Ernstone that if there could be Fred Perry shirts there could also be Cliff Richard shirts.

'In those days people were wearing striped cotton shirts in bright colours,' he says. 'As it happened my father had just bought in some material like this. I showed it to Cliff and asked him what he thought about having some shirts made.'

'He thought it was a good idea so I had some samples made up. I got Cliff wearing them, had him photographed, and did a deal with Tito Burns whereby Cliff got a royalty. I interested some teenage magazines in what we called the "Cliff Richard Shirt Offer", which was a shirt in either small, medium or large, presented in a box which had a picture on the lid of Cliff wearing one of the shirts.'

The holiday in Italy came about spontaneously. Cliff had a break in his work schedule and Ernstone suggested driving on the Continent, something he had been doing with his parents since he was a child. Both Cliff and Tony Meehan agreed to go and Ernstone brought along a platonic friend called Pam who looked like Audrey Hepburn.

They drove down through Belgium, Germany and Switzerland in Ernstone's red and grey Morris Oxford Estate. Ernstone drove, Meehan map-read and Cliff sat in the back with Pam, who attempted to snuggle up to him but was apparently kept at arm's length. They made it to Viareggio on the coast of Italy in 36 hours.

They checked into the Hotel Regina, an old seafront hotel with creaky wooden floorboards and a grand marble staircase. After crashing out for a few hours they went out for a meal of Steak Bismarck (steak with eggs) in a local restaurant, washing it down with a large bottle of Chianti. 'We were all eighteen then and felt we were really great,' says Ernstone (actually Meehan was still only sixteen). 'We were really putting the steak and wine away, and the truth is that we all got absolutely paralytic. We staggered back down the main street swaying all over the show and feeling as sick as dogs.'

'It was the first time for all of us,' says Meehan. 'Cliff threw up. I sat outside the hotel with my head in my hands feeling absolutely smashed. It was a beautiful evening and somehow I didn't get sick.

'But when I got back to our suite Ronnie and Cliff were just vomiting into the sink. They were very badly sick. Then they had to keep going into the shower. I cleared off out again because I couldn't stand the smell. The next day we all felt pretty fragile.'

For the next twelve days they sunbathed and swam, and listened to music from the Italian pop charts. One night they went to a cabaret club where Cliff was pulled out of the audience and asked to sing a song. The owner, a friend of Ernstone's parents who knew who Cliff was, handed him a guitar and said, 'Now, ladies and gentlemen. From London, England – Richard Cliff!'

Cliff remembers it as a wonderful experience. In one way it was the last time he could be a lad among lads and spontaneously elect to drive off. In another way it was the start of his globetrotting.

'It was the beginning of it all,' he says. 'It was the first holiday I had ever afforded. I can remember we stopped to clean our teeth in a Swiss mountain stream on the way down. It was my first feeling of real freedom. I was not only able to leave my family and go off on holiday but I could afford to go to another country.'

Ever since his first press interviews Cliff had said the same thing when asked what his personal ambition was. It was 'to meet Elvis Presley', and it was on his way back from Viareggio that he made the first of several attempts.

Inducted into the US Army in December 1957, Elvis had left America in September 1958 to join the Third Armored Division in West Germany and was eventually posted to the small town of Bad Nauheim, north east of Frankfurt, where he rented a three-storey white stucco house, Goethestrasse 14.

It was well known that Elvis lived in Bad Nauheim but Cliff and his friends knew no more than that. They decided to give it a try, to drive into the town and ask around to see if they could track down the king of rock 'n' roll.

'We got to the army camp and told one of the guards that we had come to see Elvis Presley and they told us where we could find him,' says Ernstone. 'I seem to remember that his house was the third one on the left and we pulled up outside and then we just sat there in the car for about ten minutes deciding who should be the one to go and knock on the door. Tony wanted me to go and I wanted Tony to go and then I said I thought it should be Cliff who went first because he was the rock 'n' roll star.

'In the end we voted and it was decided that Cliff was going to be the one to do it. I said, "I'll tell you what. If you go and knock on the door I'll film you with my ciné camera and then when he comes out and shakes your hand, we'll have a record of it."'

The footage, exhumed after 34 years in Ernstone's mother's attic, shows Cliff, dressed in a striped shirt and jeans, walking slowly to the white wooden gate. He goes up a short flight of steps on the left side of the house where he drags his fingers through his hair and presses a door bell.

The door is answered by a friend of Elvis' who tells him that unfortunately Elvis is on leave in Paris but that he'll pass on Cliff's good wishes. A dejected Cliff comes back down the steps and then the camera pans along the wall in front of the house where girls have scribbled their messages of love. The picture ends up on Elvis' parked car.

'It was very disappointing for all of us,' admits Meehan. 'We were very keyed-up and thought it had been quite a feat for us to find his house. The guy who answered the door said that if Elvis had been around he would have loved to have met Cliff. It felt like a big let-down.'

'It would have been a great time to have met him because that's the Elvis I remember,' says Cliff. 'The second Elvis, the big fat Elvis, was not the one I wanted to meet.'

What Cliff didn't know was that Elvis was away meeting Cliff's old manager Franklyn Boyd in Paris at the time. 'I spent ten days with him there with his Memphis friends Charlie Hodge and Lamont Fike,' says Boyd. 'I'd had a call from my boss in the States, Jean Aberbach, who told me to meet Elvis at the Gare de Lyon in

Paris. I talked Elvis out of coming to England. He wanted to come and I told him that he'd never get out of his hotel.'

On the same day, nineteen-year-old Terence 'Jet' Harris married seventeen-year-old Carol Ann Costa at St Paul's Church, Hounslow Heath, in London. Even though Cliff must have realized that nothing was going to develop from his flirtation with Carol, he still wasn't ready for it to end.

'I knew it was going to happen,' says Cliff. 'I must have been disappointed but I don't think I'm cut out to be married. I think I wanted the trimmings but I didn't want marriage. So, in point of fact, it was probably a good "out" for me.'

Left July 1958: first publicity portrait taken at EMI studios, Abbey Road

Below August 1958: (left to right) Terry Smart, Cliff and Ian Samwell playing at Butlins as the Drifters

Right 1958: Cliff with 'Oh Boy!' producer Jack Good

Left Cliff puts Good's 'hypodermic syringe' move into action

Right 13 September, 1958: Cliff's debut on 'Oh Boy!'

Left February 1959: Cliff and Donna at the first 'Oh Boy!' party at Ray Mackender's Chelsea flat

Below February 1959: (clockwise from left to right) Cliff, Donna Webb, Tito Burns, Joe Lee (chauffeur), Hank Marvin, Tony Meehan, Bruce Welch, Jet Harris, Len Saxon (road manager), George Ganjou and Dorothy Webb

Above On the road, 1959: Royston Ellis (second right) with Cliff, band members and friends

Right May 1959: Cliff modelling Ronnie Ernstone's sample 'Cliff Richard Shirt'

Below May 1959: The 'Oh Boy!' line-up. Among the group, Cherry Wainer (front, standing), Dallas Boys (left), Billy Fury (back, third from right), Cliff (back, fifth from right)

Left and above June 1959: Cliff enters the gate of Elvis Presley's home in Bad Nauheim, Germany (top left), knocks on the door (top right) and returns disappointed (bottom left)

Below July 1959: filming *Expresso Bongo*

Left 1960: Cliff with David Kossof in 'Stars in Your Eyes'

Left August 1959: (from left to right) Rodger Webb, Dorothy Webb, Cliff and Ray Mackender

Right 1960: Cliff and Carol Costa (left) at a party during the time of their affair

Above February 1960: Cliff with fans in America

Above right On tour in the US: (from left to right) Freddy Cannon, Jet Harris, Hank Marvin and Johnny Paris (of Johnny and the Hurricanes)

Below The Shadows – Britain's first instantly recognizable rock group

Above Cliff with friend and confidante, Cherry Wainer, at the Lotus House restaurant, Edgware Road

Above Summer 1961: Cliff with girlfriend Delia Wicks in the garden of 2 Colne Road, Winchmore Hill

Above June 1961: Filming *The Young Ones* – (from left to right) Cliff, Carole Gray, Melvyn Hayes, Annette Robertson, Richard O'Sullivan and Teddy Green

'AMERICA WAS A REAL EYE-OPENER FOR US'

twelve

Within a day of returning from Italy, Cliff plunged into a string of concerts around Britain. Travelling on the tour was Royston Ellis, an author who had been commissioned to ghost-write a book for Jet Harris called *Driftin' With Cliff*.

Ellis was Britain's first teenage pundit. He'd started by writing poetry about coffee bars, motorcycles and rock 'n' roll and the newspapers seized on him as an erudite beatnik, an Allen Ginsberg of suburban London. The fact that he wore a beard and had worked as an office boy, duster salesman, gardener, milk-bottle washer, building labourer and farm hand by the age of eighteen helped confirm the image.

'I guess you'd call the boy in the picture a weirdie,' said the *Daily Mirror* in 1959 below a photograph of him dressed in a fur-collared jacket. 'And you'd be right. He's strictly, as they say in beatnik language, from Weirdsville.'

His first volume of poems, *Jiving To Gyp*, was dedicated to Cliff and he was soon asked by television programmes to explain what teenagers were all about. He ended up with his own series, 'Living For Kicks', in which he explored the controversial issues of the day such as pep pills, and sex before marriage.

A cogent musical commentator – his 1961 paperback *The Big Beat Scene* still stands up as an appraisal of early British rock 'n' roll

– he was soon to meet the fledgling Beatles (in May 1960) and show John Lennon and Paul McCartney how to break down a Benzedrine inhaler and sniff the strips inside to produce a mild high. This was, Lennon later recounted, their first experience with drugs.

'I wrote to Cliff saying I wanted to meet him and write about him,' says Ellis. 'I got a letter back from Ray Mackender, who was by now helping Cliff's mother deal with all the fan mail, inviting me to a broadcast that Cliff was doing with the Drifters at Radio Luxembourg.

'Cliff didn't really take me on at all because he didn't really relate to anyone in those days but Jet Harris did immediately and so my first friendship was with Jet. It was only after quite a while that Cliff decided I was harmless.'

Ellis and the Drifters worked together on some poetry and music projects, a Soho version of what America's beat poets had been doing for some years in the North Beach area of San Francisco. Ellis called it 'rocketry'.

'We did a television show and some gigs with him,' remembers Meehan. 'We didn't play our normal style of music though. It was more jazz-orientated as far as I can remember. It was different, it was interesting, and it was a bit of extra money.'

Driftin' With Cliff wasn't an in-depth account of life on the road but it did supply interesting snapshots: the communal singing of American rock 'n' roll songs on the coach, the cushion fights, the pit stops at transport cafes where they'd all have greasy fry-ups and Cliff would have his favourite drink of Tizer with a scoop of icecream.

Off stage Cliff was wearing 'a blue continental-style jacket, fawn tapered trousers and white calf-skin shoes which he had brought back from Italy'. At night he wore pink pyjamas. His favourite reading matter was science fiction and his favourite singers Connie Francis, Ricky Nelson and Elvis Presley.

Before the show the musicians would often go out to see a film. After the show, they would play cards until the early hours of the next morning. Cliff stayed in a separate hotel to the Drifters.

'Cliff was always a mystery to me,' admits Ellis. 'He kept himself to himself. He wasn't a part of the gang. Often, when all the others were on the coach, Cliff would be in a car with his manager Tito Burns. It was very difficult to get close to him.'

One of the most noticeable differences between Cliff and the rest of the musicians was in his attitude to girls. Whereas he obviously enjoyed the mass hysteria his performance could provoke he never attempted to capitalise on it when he came off stage. As Bruce Welch puts it, 'If there were women available we in the Drifters would be having them but Cliff wasn't interested.'

It wasn't just that he appeared to believe that sex was for marriage – there were many other boys of his age at that time who felt the same way – but that he didn't seem moved by sex at all. This was an observation made by almost all who knew him.

'From the moment I met him women were of no interest to Cliff,' says Tito Burns. 'I'm not by any means saying he's gay. Not at all. I just don't think sex meant anything to him. People find it hard to understand that there is such a thing as being completely sexless, totally unaffected by sex.'

Ronnie Ernstone thought he was 'undersexed – it just wasn't important to him,' and Maggie Streader says, 'I think there was so much going on in his life that sex played the smallest part. I think he had a very low sex drive.'

His friends didn't know what to make of this behaviour. Some thought he was simply naïve. Some thought he'd grown up with an overly protective attitude to women as a result of having to look after his younger sisters. Others believed that he was constrained by his relationship with his mother.

When he moved back to Cheshunt from his London flat one national newspaper took the opportunity to say that Cliff was 'running back to mummy'. The accusation stung him badly and it is one of the reasons why his mother became so wary of the press. Alluding to this incident, Royston Ellis (writing as Jet) defended Cliff against the charge of being a 'mummy's boy' by arguing that this couldn't be so because he spent so much time away from home.

'True, he is attached to his family, but then most normal sons are,' he said. 'Then there is the question most girls are wondering – why hasn't Cliff Richard got a girlfriend? The answer is simple. Cliff hasn't found the right girl, and he has no time.'

For *Expresso Bongo*, which he started filming at Shepperton Studios almost as soon as he came off the road, his role as a virginal young pop singer discovered in a Soho jazz cellar was remarkably close to the truth although it had not been written with him in mind.

Created by writer Wolf Mankowitz as a satire on the Tommy Steele phenomenon, it had originally been a West End play starring Paul Scofield as the manager and James Kenny as the manipulated boy star.

Bongo Herbert is supposed to be an eighteen year old so madly devoted to his music that he has no time for anything else. 'For me, it's more like a drug,' he confesses. 'Takes my mind off a few things.'

His sharp-talking manager Johnny Jackson (Laurence Harvey) introduces him to the glamorous but fading American star Dixie Collins (Yolande Donlan) who agrees to have him as a guest on her London show and is eventually eclipsed by him.

Dixie clearly wants to seduce Bongo but he is more interested in talking to her about his love for Lambrettas. She asks him what he'd like to have behind him on the pillion seat if he was to get his motor scooter and he tells her that he was thinking of having a box fitted for his sandwiches.

In one scene, set in her luxury apartment late at night, Dixie purringly asks him whether he has a steady girlfriend.

'Why's everyone always on with this girlfriend routine?' responds a defensive Bongo. 'It's not unnatural or illegal, you know,' says Dixie.

'Girlfriends just pin you down,' says Bongo. 'They're always wanting things.' Dixie slowly sinks into a sofa and looks up at Bongo. 'Sometimes,' she says, 'the feeling is mutual, you know.'

In another prescient scene Johnny Jackson (whose character was modelled on that of Larry Parnes) tries to add a fresh dimension to Bongo's image. He suggests a song about mother love but the songwriter hired to supply the material can't come up with anything that gels.

'So far, what have we got?' asks Johnny. 'Sex. Beat. Violence... we've got it all. We've got it all except for one thing – religion! We've got to get religion!'

'I put that in because religion is always exploited in the common music hall reference out of which this type of music came,' says Mankowitz. 'Mothers and religion have always gone very well together. This suited Cliff too, I think.

'Cliff wasn't our ideal choice for the part because he didn't have the acting experience but he had the right sort of androgynous look. You could start him off quasi-innocent and have his lack of innocence as a singer come through.'

Although he had a clean-living image at the time (noted newspaper journalist Maureen Cleave had called him 'an abstemious paragon'), Cliff was not religious. He had abandoned confirmation classes because, he says, 'I couldn't understand what it was all about.' He didn't doubt the existence of a God and he would pray in times of difficulty but that was the extent of his belief. The crucifix he wore, which fans thought must have religious significance, had belonged to John Foster, who had promised to give it to him at the first sign of success.

His first public connection with a religious organization came when he opened the 59 Club in Hackney Wick and became the club President.

The 59 Club was a new kind of church youth club set up by John Oates, a 27-year-old motorcycling curate, who wanted to create a club which felt more like an espresso bar so that local teenagers could wander in and out without feeling conspicuous.

'I chose Cliff to open the club because I knew he was someone who would attract the young people,' says Oates. 'On the opening night we had 450 people turn up. The following week they all came back and brought their friends. It was chaotic!'

By the autumn of 1959 the effects of stardom were starting to tell on Cliff. The persistent clamour of fans and the lack of privacy brought him a sense of isolation.

'I honestly can't say I enjoy it much,' he grumbled when asked by *Melody Maker* to comment on his status as a 'teenage idol'. He said he worried about the 'innocent faithfulness' of the girls who screamed at him night by night and he couldn't understand why he'd lost all his friends from Cheshunt.

'When I was at school I had lots of pals. Now I've only got one real one from those days,' he said. 'Look, I'm no different. My house is still there and any of my old mates are welcome to come any time and my mother takes care of us all. But it isn't like that any more.

'Suddenly these old friends, my one-time gang, are all peculiar and stiff and strange. And they take the mickey too and try to impersonate me. Mickey-taking in any shape I can't stand – not by anybody or about anybody – but why should they? What bites them?'

The interview displayed what the fan magazines chose to ignore: his tetchiness about being criticized, his doubts about the rewards of stardom and his sense of having lost out on a normal experience of teenage life. It also revealed his competitive attitude towards the charts.

'I've just slipped from top spot in the Hit Parade,' he told the interviewer. 'Craig Douglas has taken over... However I think I've got something in store for Craig to worry about. It's a new song called "Travellin' Light" that I've just recorded... Simplicity is everything on this one and it's got a real smooth easy tempo. I think it's an even better song than "Living Doll" and I'm banking heavily on it.'

All Cliff's singles so far had been British-written but 'Travellin' Light', a lazy country-flavoured number, was the work of Sid Tepper and Roy Bennett, two veteran New York songwriters who had been writing together for over twenty years. By 1959 they had contributed songs to two of Elvis' films, *Loving You* and *King Creole*, writing them to order from early drafts of the scripts handed out to a pool of songwriters.

'Travellin' Light' had been written in this way for a scene which was subsequently cut from *King Creole*. It was then offered to others and picked up by Cliff who, until the writing of this book, hadn't realized that it had been written for Elvis.

The sparse, almost acoustic arrangement, with Jet's stalking bass line accentuated with Meehan's tambourine and Hank's whining guitar, acknowledged the country mood of 'Living Doll'. Like 'Living Doll' it reached number one.

To rock 'n' roll die-hards, such as Jack Good, this change of pace was the beginning of the end. 'Living Doll', he claimed, was his least favourite song ever. Its lyrics were twee and its tune trite. Cliff had backslidden from the true faith of rock 'n' roll.

'There was a period of cooling off between me and Cliff,' admits Good. 'I was moaning about these songs and Cliff abandoning rock 'n' roll. I think I moaned a bit in my *Disc* column. I got no direct feedback but I think he got a bit fed up with me.'

Speculation about rock 'n' roll's death had been rife since the first records were released but 1959 marked the start of a hiatus which would last until the coming of the Beatles. Elvis was in the army, Jerry Lee Lewis had been disgraced over his teenage bride, Little Richard had given up rock 'n' roll to study the Bible, Chuck Berry had been arrested on a sex charge and Buddy Holly was dead.

When Royston Ellis asked Cliff whether rock 'n' roll was dying out he had answered, 'No. It's not dying out at all. Just cleaning up.'

Asked what he thought would take its place he had said, 'I don't know, but rock is leading to a strong beat ballad style of singing,' a plug perhaps for his second album, *Cliff Sings*, where Norrie Paramor split the repertoire between rock 'n' roll and such orchestrated standards as 'The Touch Of Your Lips' and 'As Time Goes By'. No one expected to be singing rock 'n' roll into adulthood. In *Expresso Bongo*, Bongo is asked by Dixie Collins whether his manager has made plans for his career when he's no longer a teenager. Bongo slowly shakes his head. He can't imagine what it must be like to be twenty.

Recording standard songs with an orchestra was considered to be the natural way of extending stardom beyond the initial hysteria; of proving that you were a mature entertainer.

'He wants to cover everything in show business,' wrote Ellis. 'He would like to tackle every medium there is and make a success of it. This way, and this way only, will he be able to prove that he is a more talented youngster than people care to credit.'

The implication was that talent in rock 'n' roll alone was not real talent. The goal was to become an 'all-round entertainer', and Cliff was well on his way. Ballads suited his voice and, unlike a lot of rock 'n' roll singers, he had never abhorred the older songs.

'Although I was in at the beginning of rock 'n' roll I was also in at the end of the era that preceded it,' Cliff says. 'I knew all the songs of Bing Crosby, Frank Sinatra, Teresa Brewer and Rosemary Clooney. When Norrie suggested recording with an orchestra I thought it was a wonderful idea.'

In November he made his debut on 'Sunday Night at the London Palladium', the biggest entertainment show on British television at the time, and Sir Winston Churchill appeared at the première of *Expresso Bongo* (which had been rated X certificate because of its strip club scenes. Today it is rated PG.)

Cliff started to dress more conservatively. In October 1959 he was wearing a black leather jacket and white buckskins but by 1960 they were hung up in favour of smart jackets, neckties and suede shoes.

'We used to talk about the teenagers and the mums and dads,' Cliff admits. 'We were very conscious that our careers depended on the mums and dads and that we needed to appeal to them to get going.'

His accent, which in *Serious Charge* sounded like a mid-Atlantic teenage drawl, was becoming more well-rounded. He was losing the Anglo-Indian lilt that he had brought to Britain and, remarkably, he hadn't inherited the North London tones of his schoolfriends.

'His most lasting influence... [has been] his speaking voice,' wrote rock critic Nick Cohn at the end of the sixties. 'Before him, all pop singers sounded what they were, solidly working class. Cliff introduced something new, a bland ramble, completely classless.

'It caught on. David Frost uses it. So do [disc jockey] Simon Dee, Sandie Shaw and Cathy McGowan... it has become the dominant success voice. I'm not suggesting anyone deliberately copied it from Cliff, but he was where it first broke through.'

That Christmas he and the group appeared in their first pantomime – *Babes in the Wood* – at the Globe in Stockton. Here Cliff made another tentative approach towards starting a relationship with a girl.

Diana Ward was a nineteen-year-old member of the chorus who came from nearby Derby. Cliff appeared to be attracted to her but was obviously too shy to do anything about it. In the meantime Hank asked her out.

'Cliff didn't pair off with anyone, and yet every single girl was out to get him,' says Diana. 'When I went to a party with Hank, Cliff just followed us everywhere we went, and then the next night he asked me out.'

They saw each other throughout the season, which went on into January, but almost always with other people in tow. Their first date – a run along the beach at Redcar – included Jet and Carol and subsequent dates had a friend as chaperone.

It was in Stockton that Jet drove into an oncoming car while returning from a late night party with Hank, a road manager and a heavily-pregnant Carol. The boys were only slightly injured but

Carol, who was thrown out of the car door, suffered broken ribs and a fractured skull. She was hospitalized and it was feared that she would lose the baby.

Jet was subsequently fined for 'dangerous driving, failing to display L-plates and driving unaccompanied by a qualified driver'.

The Drifters were by now known as the Shadows. They had recorded an instrumental, 'Jet Black', and it was when they tried for a release in America that they discovered the existence of the original Drifters, who threatened them with an injunction over the name. To avoid further problems they called themselves the Four Jets for this release.

It was Jet who came up with the name the Shadows one day while they were drinking at the Six Bells in Ruislip after a ride out on their Lambrettas. He'd thought of the idea because when the spotlight shone on Cliff, as it invariably did, they were performing in the shadows. Also that year a film was released, directed by Jon Cassavettes, called *Shadows*.

On 17 January 1960 Cliff and the Shadows topped 'Sunday Night at the London Palladium' and drew a television audience of 19 million, the most that had ever watched a light entertainment show in Britain. Eddie Cochran, on tour in England at the time, saw the broadcast and thought Cliff was 'quite a good performer but I have seen a lot better in Britain'.

'Living Doll' was Cliff's third American single and had by now become a minor hit, reaching a high point of number thirty in the *Billboard* charts. This was a considerable breakthrough at a time when British artists rarely had transatlantic success. His first two American singles, 'Move It' and 'Livin' Lovin' Doll' had flopped dismally.

Sensing an opportunity of reversing the fortunes of British pop in America, Tito Burns planned to tour Cliff and the Shadows. He eventually signed a deal with Irving Feld of the General Artists Corporation, one of America's biggest booking agencies, who specialized in putting together top-rate rock 'n' roll package tours.

His 'Biggest Show of Stars 1957' had featured Fats Domino, Chuck Berry, Frankie Lymon and the Teenagers, the Everly Brothers, Paul Anka, Clyde McPhatter, the Drifters (the American

161

group) and Buddy Holly. It was on his 1959 tour, 'The Winter Dance Party', that Buddy Holly had been killed.

For the 'Biggest Show of Stars 1960', Irving Feld planned to feature ten acts on 33 dates that would stretch from Montreal to Dallas and across to New Jersey and Philadelphia. His bill reflected the change that was happening to rock 'n' roll with good looks now taking precedence over great talent.

Before Elvis Presley, American pop had been dominated by Italian Americans – such men as Frank Sinatra, Perry Como, Tony Bennett, Al Martino and Dean Martin. Now that rock 'n' roll was apparently on the ropes the Italians had returned.

Feld's bill-topper was Frankie Avalon (age twenty, real name Francis Avallone), who sang anaemic high school rock and had become a star on 'Dick Clark's American Bandstand'. Symbolically, it had been Avalon who replaced Buddy Holly on tour the night after he died.

Supporting Avalon on the 1960 bill were Bobby Rydell (age seventeen, real name Robert Ridarelli) and Freddy Cannon (age nineteen, real name Frederick Picariello), both of whom sang the same bowdlerized rock 'n' roll.

Then there was Johnny and the Hurricanes who'd met at high school in Toledo, Ohio, and had had hits with instrumentals 'Reveille Rock' and 'Crossfire', Clyde McPhatter (who'd led the original Drifters), the Isley Brothers, Sammy Turner, the rhythm and blues group the Clovers, the Crests ('16 Candles') and Linda Laurie.

Cliff's name was added at the foot of the poster (misspelled Cliff Richards) as an 'Extra Added Attraction: England's No. 1 Singing Sensation'. No mention was made of the Shadows. Cliff had insisted they should back him despite pressure from the promoter to use the resident tour band.

America was a thrilling place for a group of teenagers to be going to in 1960 when few of their contemporaries in Britain had ever travelled abroad. It was the land where the future had already arrived; where there were highways instead of main roads, Cadillacs instead of Morris Minors and Hollywood instead of Borehamwood.

'It was a real eye-opener for us,' says Bruce Welch. 'It seemed so far away from home at the time and it was where rock 'n' roll had come from. Just to be flying on a plane was mind-boggling enough but we were going to be meeting all these American acts and playing in front of crowds of 10,000.'

Sammy Samwell, who had become the Shadows' unofficial manager, remembers the anticipation.

'I was already steeped in American culture because I had two uncles who worked on American air bases,' he says. 'They brought back magazines which had adverts for wonderful wide cars which did about six miles to the gallon and had four happy people driving in them. I had all these wonderful images in my mind as I set off!'

The tour was booked to start in Montreal, Canada, on 22 January and so Cliff and his father, the Shadows, Samwell and Burns flew from London to New York on 18 January and were met at Idlewild Airport (later renamed JFK) by two limousines, one black and one white.

Once in New York the Shadows bought themselves trendy 'pork pie' trilby hats and checked out such legendary jazz clubs as Birdland and the Metropole. Cliff appeared on 'The Pat Boone Show', where he sang 'Living Doll' and 'Pretty Blue Eyes' and engaged in some tame scripted banter.

All the musicians on the tour met up on 21 January and left New York for Montreal on two Greyhound buses which, with their reclining seats and air conditioning, seemed luxurious to Cliff and the Shadows who'd spent the last year toiling around the B roads of Britain on a Bedford coach.

For the first show Cliff had worked out a set of five songs: '40 Days', 'My Babe', 'A Voice in The Wilderness' (from *Expresso Bongo*), 'Living Doll' and 'Whole Lotta Shakin' Goin' On'. The only change made before the end of the tour was that 'My Babe' was replaced by 'Dynamite'.

The reaction to Cliff's set was beyond all expectations. Every night the show-stopping acts were Cliff and the Shadows, Bobby Rydell and Clyde McPhatter.

'No one could follow after we had finished,' Cliff remembers. 'The crowd were still screaming for more. It was very difficult for the next act to go on. That happened right from the first show.

'I remember there was a big black tour manager and he would get on the coach and say, "Well, I think we should all give a big hand to our friends from England," and they would all applaud us. It was fantastic and I thought we were really going to make it.

'The trouble was that I never saw anyone from my record company [ABC/Paramount] in the whole six weeks. They should have been there. My career in America is littered with lost opportunities.'

From Montreal they drove down to shows in Rochester, New York, and then to Philadelphia before returning to Toronto and Kitchener. Most of the travelling was done at night to avoid traffic and as the winter weather set in and the air conditioning failed everyone would be forced to sleep in their overcoats.

After Canada they wound down through the Midwest to Kentucky, home of the Everly Brothers, and then on to the East Coast. After five dates in North and South Carolina they flew the longest leg of the tour on to Fort Worth, Texas.

'We ran into an electrical storm and everyone was terrified,' remembers Tony Meehan. 'The plane was an old Dakota and the fact that Buddy Holly had died in an air crash on the last tour was still pretty fresh in our minds. I went to sleep though. I was that young and that optimistic.'

In Texas they played Fort Worth, Houston, San Antonio and Dallas before coming to Buddy Holly's home town of Lubbock where they played the Coliseum. Holly's family came to the show and they were moved to tears by the sight of Hank Marvin on stage with his Fender Stratocaster and horn-rimmed spectacles. From the back of the auditorium he looked to them like a visitor from beyond the grave.

The segregation in the southern states bemused them. They could visit clubs and see black performers such as James Brown and Bo Diddley but they couldn't eat out with black musicians like Clyde McPhatter and Sammy Turner who were on the same tour. They even had to travel on separate buses for a while.

It was after the 19 February show in Wichita, Kansas, that Cliff flew back to London via New York to appear at the *NME* Poll Winners concert at Wembley Pool and then, later the same day, on 'Saturday Night at the London Palladium'.

It had been too expensive to bring the Shadows back as well so Tito Burns advised Cliff to surround himself with the best session musicians available. Cliff ignored this advice and instead hired his old Cheshunt friend Brian Parker's new group, the Parker Royal Five.

It was a mistake. Jet-lagged on arrival, he had to rehearse that night until half past four in the morning and didn't sleep until after the Wembley show that afternoon. When they tried to wake him in time for the Palladium he was in such a deep sleep that they had to throw cold water in his face to bring him to.

He sleepwalked his way through the performance and was roundly criticized for being lacklustre. He later apologized to his fans, admitting that 'I was just too tired to give you my best,' and then flew back to Milwaukee with his mother for the last night of the tour.

'I honestly was homesick by then,' he explained later that year, 'and I know it isn't just a place you get homesick for, it's the people. And of all the people in the world I miss most, Mum tops the list.'

With the tour finally over he headed to New York with his parents for a series of press interviews to promote *Expresso Bongo*, which was opening at the Sutton Theatre in a fortnight. They even managed a meeting with Colonel Tom Parker, Elvis' illustrious manager, at the Warwick Hotel where he was staying as he awaited Elvis' arrival from Germany. There was talk in the air of Colonel Parker being able to do something for Cliff in Hollywood.

The Colonel made an immediate impression on Cliff and his parents by asking them if they would like to join him for lunch. After they eagerly accepted the great man's offer he reached into an office drawer and pulled out three packets of sandwiches which he then handed around.

On 2 March Cliff flew back to London and was met at the airport by Ray Mackender. The next day, in Frankfurt, Elvis Presley boarded a plane for Fort Dix, New Jersey, where he was demobbed after two years as an army private.

Before he left Germany he had given an interview in which he said that he knew Cliff Richard's work and owned some of his records.

'Sure I'd love to have met him,' said Cliff later that year. 'But I wanted to get home even more. Some day we'll meet and I can think of nothing I'd like more than sharing a bill with him. That would really be something, wouldn't it?'

'WITH *thirteen* CAROL IT WAS THE FIRST FULL-BLOODED ROMANCE'

Despite the thousands of miles travelled and the great success of his act, Cliff hadn't made the slightest impression on the American market.

'I'm afraid they had about 4,000 Cliff Richards over there already,' says Tito Burns. 'They just didn't have the appetite for yet another one.'

Sammy Samwell says more or less the same thing. 'The timing was all wrong. He was a little too late and a little too generic. He was somewhere between Elvis Presley and Ricky Nelson and they already had both.'

In Britain he was rapidly becoming the country's highest-paid entertainer, commanding upwards of £1,000 a week for variety shows and £4,000 for a single television appearance. This was in addition to income from record sales, films and the granting of merchandising licenses to companies who were making everything from 2/6d photo books to 5/11d Cliff Richard pillowcases. ('You can soon misplace lockets or bracelets, but you will never lose your own pillowcase. Will last for years, and will not fade in the wash.')

All of this meant that at nineteen years of age Cliff Richard was rich. His contemporaries would have been lucky to have been going home on a Friday night with ten pounds. One newspaper calculated that he was earning more than the entire government cabinet put together. True he was paying Burns 10 per cent of his income, George Ganjou a further 10 per cent and had four musicians each on 25 pounds a week, but it still left a sizeable income.

Yet Cliff was not a conspicuous spender. He was happy to have been able to allow both his parents to relinquish their jobs and regain their dignity after years of hardship, but he was never tempted to live particularly ostentatiously.

His pocket money was rationed to ten pounds a week until September 1960 when it was raised to fifteen pounds. His one luxury was cars. Having had the Sunbeam Alpine for almost twelve months, he traded it in at Lex Garage in Brewer Street, Soho, and bought a red American Thunderbird with a white roof for £4,000.

His parents still didn't own their own home and so in May 1960 he bought them a corner house at 2 Colne Road in Winchmore Hill, North London, for £7,000. It was unexceptional by show business standards – a neat suburban semi with a front gate and slatted garden fence – but it was equipped with what were called 'luxuries' at the time: a telephone, a stereo record player, a 21-inch television set, a radiogram, a leather-topped bar and wall-to-wall carpeting.

For a family that hadn't so long ago been sitting on chairs made out of deal packing cases and squashing four children in one bedroom it was paradise. 'This house and everything in it is all paid for,' he proudly announced to visiting members of the press. 'It will last us a lifetime.'

He tried to live as normal a life as was possible, the only difference being that 2 Colne Road was often besieged by fans and so the front gate had to be padlocked and the garden fence had to be raised two feet to prevent intruders.

Dick Teague's sister Sheila was still close to Cliff's youngest sister Joan, and would spend weekends at Winchmore Hill. She remembers that Cliff's room was in the roof and was reached through a door on the landing which looked as if it was the airing cupboard.

'When you opened the door you went up this beautiful deep blue velvet carpet to Cliff's room,' she says. 'It was like a concealed room and I remember it being all green and yellow with sheepskin rugs.'

To a ten-year-old like Sheila, who was still living on a council estate in Cheshunt, the house at Winchmore Hill seemed like another world.

'We were all very poor and so seeing a taxi arrive for Cliff's mum to take her to the hairdresser was like watching royalty,' she says. 'Cliff wasn't big-headed though. He was very calm, very relaxed and casual.

'He showed a lot of love to his sisters and he'd often spend time in the garden with his dog getting it to bite on the end of a rag and then swinging it around. He took us all out in his car sometimes but when he tried to park he would get recognized and he found he just couldn't go shopping.'

From the outset Tito Burns' plan had been to loosen the bond between Cliff and the Shadows. He wanted to establish the idea of Cliff Richard – solo artist, so that when the beat boom was over Cliff would survive.

'The way I saw his career advancing was to turn him into Cliff Richard rather than "Cliff Richard and the...". The "and the" was alright, providing Cliff was right up front,' says Burns.

'I wanted him to be accepted in his own right even if he didn't sing "Move It" and have three guitarists backing him. When he reached that pinnacle it wouldn't matter whether he had seventy strings or the Shadows because you'd know they had come to see him.'

Says Hank Marvin, 'Tito probably hated the music anyway and he would much rather have seen Cliff with a group of professional musicians. I don't think he understood what we did or what was happening. He gave more than an impression that he was trying to drive a wedge between Cliff and ourselves.'

Cliff was as unhappy as they were. He'd fought hard to get them on the American tour and had persuaded Norrie Paramor to give them a recording deal in their own right. As far as he was concerned, they operated like a five-piece band for which he was the vocalist.

The Shadows' contract with Columbia had so far produced three singles, but none had made an impact. Then, after a show in Cannock in April 1960, they were played an instrumental which had been written by Jerry Lordan, who was in a band backing the other singers on the tour.

'I'd written this tune called "Apache",' says Lordan. 'It had been recorded by the guitarist Bert Weedon but I hadn't liked the result so I played it on my ukulele to the Shadows who I knew were looking for new material.'

Bruce Welch and Hank both liked it and took it to Norrie Paramor for their next single but Norrie wanted them to do a version of the traditional tune, 'Quartermasters Stores'. A compromise was reached with 'Apache' on one side and 'Quartermasters Stores' on the other.

For British teenagers the Shadows were the first home-grown group where names could be put to faces and characters to names. The simple Gretch drum kit and the solid-body guitars with tremolo arms completed the image of the archetypal rock 'n' roll outfit.

When the Beatles were still wearing leather jackets and jeans on stage, Brian Epstein took them to the Liverpool Empire to see a Cliff and the Shadows concert, pointing out their mohair suits, their choreographed footsteps and the way they bowed at the close of the show. Epstein told them that this was how big-time groups dressed and moved and the Beatles took his advice right down to the last bow of the head.

To maintain their separateness from Tito Burns, who never had any say in their career, the Shadows hired a young Irishman to be their tour manager. His name was Mike Conlin, and they had met him at the 2 I's. Within six months he found himself doing the same for Cliff and moved in to 2 Colne Road so that he could be on hand 24 hours a day.

When on tour Cliff would be eminently sociable during the daytime, eating with the group, going to the cinema and participating in such crazes as archery, pistol shooting and home movies.

'You have to remember that he was the idol of his day,' says Conlin. 'There had never been an English pop star of this magnitude and everywhere he went he was harassed. But when he wasn't constrained by the eyes of the world being on him he was one of the lads.

'If we went to a gig I would often drive him in my car and we would sing all the way down. It wasn't until we got within ten miles of where we were going that we'd have to pull our horns in and work out how to get in the theatre.'

It was at night that they tended to live separate lives. The Shadows' idea of a fun time was to surround themselves with drink and girls and to party into the night but Cliff – who didn't smoke or drink – would only make token appearances at these affairs before disappearing back to his room.

'The Shadows thought they had the world on a string and they really did give it some,' remembers Ronnie Ernstone who would often spend his weekends on the tours. 'Cliff was a bit removed. If he came to a party he wouldn't partake.

'He had great power at the time but he chose not to use it. In fact, rather than choosing not to use it I think he just didn't want the things that he could get with it.'

Sometimes he would take long drives in the night to clear his mind. He later told Royston Ellis, 'I just drive because it's rather a strain to be with people all the time. Even my mother doesn't know this. I'll just drive around for about an hour and a half and then I'll come back and I'll feel great. I go straight to sleep and wake up feeling great in the morning.'

In May, while in Derby to play a concert, he got back in touch with Diana Ward who he'd last seen in Stockton when they were in *Babes in the Wood*. It was to be their last date. When she came down to London a few weeks later he arranged to pick her up from her cousin's house in Waltham's Cross, but never arrived or called to cancel.

When she wrote to him to find out the state of their relationship she received a terse reply by return of post.

'You ask me to be frank, so I will be. I think it would be better if you were to stop writing or contacting me. I sincerely hope that what I write doesn't upset you. Maybe we'll meet again in the near future. I hope so.'

Diana suspected that Cliff's mother, who had only recently learned of the relationship, had stepped in. This, she feels, would explain Cliff's uncharacteristic failure to keep their date, and also the forced nature of the letter – in one breath it forbad contact, and in the next suggested that a meeting would be welcome.

'I think that he had raised his family's standard of living and they were frightened that if he became too involved with a girl and lost his popularity they would lose everything,' she says. 'He was very

170

loving and affectionate but I think that, ultimately, fame was more important to him than anything.'

Yet it wasn't long before he found himself being drawn back into a relationship with Carol Costa. She was now Mrs Jet Harris, and on 22 April had given birth to Ricky Brian Harris – Ricky after Ricky Nelson, and Brian after Brian Rankin (Hank Marvin).

Although they had been married for less than a year Jet and Carol's marriage was breaking up. The explosive arguments which had seemed colourful when they were young lovers were now becoming bitter and increasingly violent as Jet's drinking habit got worse. He was also starting to have affairs with other women.

One night Tony Meehan saw Jet attack Carol after returning drunk from a concert. He dragged her to the floor and knelt on her arms while punching her. Meehan had to dive in and knock Jet out by smashing his head against the wall before he could pull him away.

'It was awful stuff,' Meehan remembers. 'He was out for two or three minutes, enough time to stop him doing awful damage. That's the sort of relationship they had. It wasn't a happy marriage. They weren't suited.'

The more Jet deserted and abused Carol, the more Cliff found his sympathy aroused and he began to comfort and support her. When she was pregnant he'd bought her oranges to satisfy a craving, and when Ricky was born he was one of the first to visit the hospital, bearing a giant bunch of flowers.

'I think Cliff knew more about what was going on with Jet than I did,' says Carol. 'It was while lying in hospital with a fractured skull after the car crash in Stockton that I discovered he was having an affair with a dancer. That was the first one I found out about.

'Cliff tried to protect me. He was more attentive and more loving than Jet ever was. When I was pregnant and had a twinge in my back, Cliff would ask if I was alright but Jet wouldn't notice. Cliff was there for me and I think a lot of it was because he knew what was going on behind my back.'

'It bothered me that Jet and Carol weren't very happy together,' says Cliff, 'and that played a part in drawing me back to her again. I never saw Jet hit her but he was obviously a bit of a rough dog. Some people can drink really well but he can't. His problems domestically and artistically were all to do with drink. His problems with Carol were due to the fact that he was drunk most of the time.'

In June Cliff began the most extended engagement of his career: a six-month stint at the London Palladium. This was Tito Burns' biggest coup so far and show business magazines were buzzing with the story of the former office clerk who was now topping the bill at the London Palladium and taking in an estimated £24,000.

Burns had managed it by doing a deal with agent Leslie Grade who had exclusive booking rights for this period at the Palladium and who desperately wanted to be involved in Cliff's career.

Knowing the extent of his enthusiasm, Burns used Cliff as a bargaining tool to get other artists of his on at theatres that Grade controlled. 'I wanted to establish Cliff not just as a rock 'n' roller with a few hits but as a personality, somebody who would mean something in years to come,' says Burns.

'I left the rock 'n' roll side to Cliff while I devoted my energies to getting the right things that would further him as a stayer – like the various television shows, like the Palladium over which I battled for a month.'

Leslie Grade was one of three Winogradsky brothers who had emigrated to London's East End from Russia. Lew and Leslie Winogradsky changed their surname to Grade, Leslie becoming a top show business agent while Lew became managing director of ATV. Linking up with the Grade agency was a significant move for Cliff, for between them the Grades had enormous power to establish an act through film, television and theatre circuits.

The third brother, Bernard, changed his surname to Delfont and became a theatre impresario. 'Stars In Your Eyes', as the Palladium show was titled, was a variety performance with something for everyone. There was up-and-coming comedian Des O'Connor, television actor David Kossoff, pianist Russ Conway, Canadian singer Edmund Hockridge, a team of Palladium dancers, fall-about comedian Billy Dainty, and Joan Regan, a top recording star in the early fifties.

Cliff and the Shadows closed each show with a five-song set, which was interrupted every night by David Kossoff in character as the cockney Alf Larkin from the popular television series 'The

Larkins', who would scream abuse from the royal box before making his way on stage and doing a soft-shoe routine with Cliff.

'Almost nothing I said could be heard because of the screaming,' says Kossoff. 'This was to me an entirely new and frightening experience in that I was working with someone who, every time he moved his body, had the audience screaming in orgasmic delight.'

Seven weeks into the 26-week run the Shadows' 'Apache' was released and went into the top twenty. The group pushed to include it in the show but Tito Burns refused them. From his point of view it would detract from Cliff.

The Shadows were understandably resentful. It seemed to them petty to exclude one of the summer's biggest hits from a show where they were part of the headline entertainment. On 20 August 'Apache' actually knocked Cliff off the top of the hit parade when it replaced 'Please Don't Tease'.

Hank and Bruce Welch were now writing together for Cliff. The album *Me And My Shadows* was released in October, and was a prototypical beat record with over half the songs written by them or Jet, Samwell and their friend Pete Chester. It was the first time a British group had recorded so much self-written material and was an indication of the changes that would occur in the record industry after the Beatles. Like *Cliff Sings*, it went to number two in the LP charts.

'I'm still really proud of that album,' says Cliff. 'A lot of people like Eric Clapton and the guys in Fleetwood Mac were inspired by it because of Hank's guitar work; I think we invented our own English rock 'n' roll. It wasn't American, but neither was it "Rock With The Caveman".'

Committed to the Palladium for six days a week, there were still concerts out of London on Sundays. On one of these dates Jet had a brief fling with a hairdresser and word got back to Carol who threatened to leave him.

'I just went berserk that day,' remembers Carol. 'I was beside myself. I had a young child and I couldn't stand it any more. I spoke to him on the phone, told him I was leaving. Then as I was packing my car he and Cliff arrived. Jet begged me not to leave. Cliff went in the kitchen and Jet was with me in the lounge. I asked him how he could do this to me with a new baby and he just smacked me in the mouth. Cliff didn't see him do it but he saw the blood afterwards.'

Cliff drove Carol and Ricky back to her parents in Hounslow and promised to stay in touch. Within days he arrived to take her to the cinema. 'When he took me home,' says Carol, 'he kissed me goodnight and told me that he loved me. Things went on from there really.'

Over the next few weeks they met whenever they could and Cliff began to get more openly affectionate, telling her that he loved her.

The relationship had to be clandestine, not just because of Jet, but because of Cliff's career. They would meet up at the flats of trusted friends, in a central London car park close by the Palladium or they would drive out into the Essex countryside, always with Mike Conlin on hand as a lookout man.

Carol was the most sexually experienced and worldly girl he had ever dated. He had previously been attracted to shy and virginal girls who were guaranteed not to put any demands on him but Carol, already a wife and mother, was recognized as being streetwise and opinionated.

'She made a beeline for him in a very subtle way which, when you're young, you sometimes mistake for mutual attraction,' says Tony Meehan. 'You don't realize you are being pursued. She had all the allure of a woman and all the forcefulness of a man and she totally dominated him.'

After a Sunday night concert in Blackpool, Carol and Cliff saw a rare opportunity to be alone. They were travelling back on an overnight train and Meehan was booked to share a sleeper with Cliff but, just after boarding, he gave up his bed to Carol. During the night things became more passionate than they had ever been before, but Cliff seemed inhibited.

'I sensed there was something not quite right, and on the Wednesday of the next week he called me into his dressing room at the Palladium and explained to me that he was a virgin,' says Carol. 'It was then that I understood why he'd been like he had. I was quite shocked when he told me. I think I laughed – but with happiness because I was so relieved.

'I think he was frightened of going all the way because of who he was. That was the reason. He was telling me as though it was something to be ashamed of, but I told him that it was fine.'

Soon after, they did make love twice, at 52 Creighton Road, Ealing, the home of Vicky Marshall, a dancer who had appeared in *Serious Charge* and *Expresso Bongo*. Cliff told his parents that he needed to stay in London overnight for business but instead slept with Carol in an attic room.

The affair ended rather abruptly when an intimate letter sent by Carol to Cliff was opened by Cliff's mother who had assumed it was a piece of fan mail. According to Carol the letter was 'passionate' and expressed delight at the goings-on in Ealing.

'We got back from the Palladium late one night and Cliff's parents were waiting up for him,' remembers Mike Conlin. 'His mother had the letter in her hand. They asked me to go up to bed and then they talked to Cliff until the small hours.

'I never saw the letter but it more or less gave the game away. It was a hell of a lot more personal than a fan letter should have been and his mother and father talked to him all night about the evils of sin and I think that was what broke it off.'

His sister Jacqui was then only twelve but she can recall the night.

'I remember Cliff coming home and being yanked off to a room,' she says. 'I closed my bedroom door. I knew they were having a serious talk and I knew the subject was Carol. I don't know what was said but my dad would have been seeing it from a spiritual point of view.

'He wouldn't have been so concerned about the effect on Cliff's career or what the neighbours might think but the fact that what he'd done went against God's commandments. That's what would have been uppermost in his mind.

'I remember my mother telling me very bluntly that the Christian way was not to have sex before marriage. She said that sex was something given to married couples. That's all she said! I can remember being a bit taken aback because they didn't normally discuss things like that openly.'

Cliff couldn't bear to offend his mother and matters were made worse by the fact that his father had recently been taken ill. While playing a game of badminton at the club he had suddenly collapsed. The doctor diagnosed thrombosis. Cliff was worried that the news about Carol might kill him.

In desperation he asked Tony Meehan to make the call that would end the affair.

'He couldn't handle it so he asked me to do it and I said yes, because someone had to do it,' says Meehan. 'The relationship was destroying him and it was likely to destroy the group. It was getting too close.

'The way I looked at it was that there was no future in it because he really wasn't prepared. I asked him whether he would be willing to give up his career for this because that's what it amounted to in those days. That she was a married woman was quite a scandal in itself. I said that he would have to jack it all in for her and go away somewhere because the fans wouldn't put up with it.

'When I called up she was quite furious. Understandably so. I think he may have said a few words to her but he was definitely crying. It was a very romantic, child-like affair and it had been making a lot of demands on him.'

For Carol it was a bolt out of the blue. Only days before they had been looking through copies of *Country Life*, deciding on the home they would live in as soon as she was able to divorce Jet and marry Cliff. Now it was all over and he apparently didn't have the courage to tell her himself.

'We had been talking about getting married, we'd made love and now it was all over,' she says. 'I was devastated. I said, "What does he mean?" I insisted that I spoke to him. I wasn't going to have this from Tony Meehan.

'Cliff came on the line and told me that his mother had seen the letter and that he thought the whole thing might kill his father. They were his exact words. He said that he loved me and that he would never marry anyone else. That was it I just had to accept it.'

The episode is surprising not because a pop star had an affair with a married woman, but because it was so out of character for Cliff, who seemed so uninterested in sex and had gone into print celebrating chaste ideals.

'I suppose in my naïvety I thought no one would either know about it or believe it,' says Cliff. 'It didn't seem to matter at the time. It went against my principles but when you are experiencing these things your principles become unimportant.

'Looking back I can see that they weren't important to me because God wasn't important in my life. He was there, but what part did he really have to play? My parents instilled values into me but possibly if I hadn't have become a Christian they wouldn't have come into play any more.

'When you live a life outside of God you think well, even if there is a God he's there and I'm here. So what if I steal or commit adultery? I guess that was what was in my mind because I didn't really feel a great deal of guilt. I feel more guilt now over it.

'With Carol it was like the first full-blooded romance, I suppose. It was a love affair. It was one of those things people go through.'

Carol seemed an unlikely girl to have broken down his fabled resistance. She was nothing like the 'slightly shy', demure, plain-looking girl who knew 'when it was time to say good night' that Cliff had always claimed to be his ideal.

She harked back to the blonde bombshell fantasy of Brigitte Bardot but, more significantly, she happened to be around at a time when all the Shadows had married and he was beginning to feel lonely.

'Carol obviously got into the inner circle once she'd met Jet,' he says, 'and the next thing I realized was that she was there travelling around on tour. At the Palladium everyone would be there, Carol included, and we became a social unit. Brief encounter though it was, it was a growing-up experience for me.'

It didn't bring him the consolation he needed. Some of his friends felt that it pushed him further away from a fulfilling relationship.

'If you want to be blunt about it, Carol had sex with Cliff rather than the other way round,' says Tony Meehan. 'She was tough and determined and Cliff had always been timid with women.

'I think he had a very romantic notion of romance and sex. It was like a schoolboy view. As soon as he was confronted with the reality of it, the forbidding was too strong. So, he was never able to make the jump from schoolboy to man.'

Vicky Marshall disagrees. 'I was in at the beginning, and I was there at the end when the terrible break up took place over the phone in my home,' she says. 'I was on the extension trying to calm them both down while they were crying.

'If it had happened today it would have carried on. It was a beautiful and lovely relationship. It was no quick fling. I heard him say on the phone that he would never ever fall in love again with someone else like he'd fallen in love with her.

'Carol and he were soul mates. They knew each other so well. They were right for each other. Perhaps that was his love. That was it.'

Before the Christmas of 1960 Carol discovered she was pregnant. Rather than telling Cliff, she arranged for a back street abortion.

'He didn't know about the baby,' admits Vicky. 'She made a sacrifice for him. She could have used it to pressurize him into marriage but she didn't. Somebody that can do that isn't half bad.'

Cliff says that he now looks back on the affair with a different set of values. He doesn't deny that it happened but says he is not proud of his behaviour.

He continued to like female company but he would never again have sex with a woman even though, for the next four years at least, there was no religious reason to remain celibate. 'I never got round to it,' he explains. 'There was still a fairly old-fashioned bit left in me I suppose.'

To a lot of observers in show business such a muted interest in sex suggested latent homosexuality.

'There was much more speculation in those days because it was illegal,' says Mike Conlin. 'If someone was in the theatre and not going out with a girl it was assumed that they were gay.

'Cliff was a target for homosexuals because he was a sex symbol and he didn't have a girlfriend. The fact is that at the time Cliff was terrified of homosexuals. He never wanted to be left alone with them.'

The only time an aggressive homosexual did get close to Cliff was after a concert in Portsmouth when a man managed to get into his hotel room late at night.

'I can remember being nervous because the guy wouldn't leave,' says Cliff. 'I kept saying, "Look, this is my private time and this is my room," but he just kept advancing.

'Mike Conlin always slept in an adjoining room and I called out for him and he came and got rid of the guy.'

'Funnily enough,' says Conlin, 'at the same time that all these rumours were going around I knew that Cliff was having this affair with Carol that no one else knew about.

'Also, I spent 24 hours a day for months on end with him, travelling the world and sharing hotel bedrooms, and there was never a sniff of anything that you could even begin to raise an eyebrow at.

'I think that if he got burned over the affair with Carol it may have left a scar and made him loath to go into anything else.'

In November 1960 he was interviewed by Steve Race and Royston Ellis for the BBC Radio programme 'Frankly Speaking'. He emerged as an assured, if slightly naïve, young man who was much more in control of his career than his interviewers appeared to have given him credit for.

His image was already set. He spoke of his respect for his parents, his lack of interest in party politics and his belief that he needed to be single for the sake of his career.

'Because I am a male singer,' he confessed, 'my fans like to think that perhaps they have the chance of dating me. I have to stay this way as long as I possibly can. It's not always a good thing, because people then say, "Well, he's not really relying on his singing, he's relying on the fact that girls like him."'

Royston Ellis asked whether he'd ever felt like exploiting his position to go out with as many girls as he could.

'No, I haven't,' said Cliff. 'In fact I think I've only ever dated one fan. But I found the reaction from fans wasn't too good so I just gave up on it altogether.'

Steve Race then leapt in. 'Can I speak here as the elderly parent type?' he said. 'In this teenage world you have this image that regardless of the opposition you will marry the girl you love. "They try to tell us that we're too young, but we're not" and so on. Now you're saying that "love is all, but my teenage audience want me unmarried so I won't marry". Isn't that a betrayal of your attitude?'

'Oh sure, I'll marry her eventually,' Cliff answered. 'But I shan't make it public that I'm going out with a girl. It's a sly way of doing it but I haven't met the girl I love yet anyhow. I don't think I will because at the moment I've dated perhaps four or five girls, and none of them more than two or three times each.'

It was a fair point. There was an irony in the fact that the great icon of teenage romance had to deprive himself of romance to keep his position. But that's the way things were and Cliff would admit to no regrets.

'As far as I'm concerned, it [my career] may die out next week,' he said. 'Well, I've done everything I could possibly want to do and possibly everything anybody could want to do. I've got a gold disc, I've been to America, I've filmed, I've made records. So if it all ended for me, the one thing I could say is that I've lived a fuller life than most people will ever do.'

'HE'S THE PERSON
TO MAKE A FILM
WITH'

fourteen

Two days after Christmas 1960, Cliff's father's health took a turn for the worse and he was rushed into hospital where he stayed until 28 January. Over the autumn months he had got weaker. He was having difficulty in breathing and spent most of the days lying on a settee. During this time his relationship with Cliff slowly changed.

'Dad became helpless and I had to do everything,' says Cliff. 'I hadn't done anything before because he wouldn't let me but suddenly I had become the head of the house. Not only was I the breadwinner but I had to change the plugs.'

No one who saw Cliff and his father together ever thought there was the normal bond of familial affection. Most would say that there was no real love. Some go as far as to say that they believed Cliff resented his father. As one friend put it, 'Cliff always showed respect to his father but I don't think he ever really had respect for him.'

Cliff admits that he was always frightened of his father, but there was never any discussion of what might have gone wrong between them, even when his father was dying. 'We just didn't talk like that,' he says.

Because Cliff was still under the legal age of consent, all contracts, including those with EMI and his management, had to be approved and signed by his father, Rodger, who feared that his son could be exploited by those only interested in short-term gain. This fatherly concern naturally annoyed those who wanted a free hand in shaping Cliff's career.

He was given an office desk and a handsome salary of £100 a week. 'He felt that he had become beholden to his son,' says Cliff's aunt, Olive Queenie, 'and that was a terrible thing for him to feel. Instead of him supporting the family, his son was supporting the family. When Cliff gave him the job it made him feel he was doing something.'

Burns had to tolerate the arrangement because it had been he who had originally charmed Cliff's parents into giving him their boy, but privately he considered Rodger Webb the biggest drawback in Cliff's career and he resented his attempts to offer business advice.

'He was a very dogmatic man,' he says. 'He had his ideas but I thought they were all wrong. We ended up having arguments because he was quite ill and getting very edgy. He wanted my management contract with Cliff ended although he gave no specific reasons and, under the terms of the contract, there should have been.'

Burns suspected that the real reason was that agent Leslie Grade wanted to take over Cliff's career. Grade had just bought the option for his next film from Mickey Delamar for £7,500, and was courting Cliff's parents.

'I was involved in a dispute with Leslie Grade over what Cliff should be paid for the film,' says Burns, 'when in walks Cliff's father smoking a big cigar. I knew then that the only person who could have given him that was Grade.

'I think he was giving the old man money to make my severance pay. When it came within £1,000 of what I would have got if I had seen the three-year contract out, I said OK.'

When Burns' departure was announced in the press in February 1961 it was said to be 'amicable' and Rodger Webb claimed he was now 'looking after' his son. Neither statement was true.

Burns was furious to have been eased out in such circumstances and although Cliff's father may have momentarily held the reins that was only because he knew someone even more capable was coming in to take over.

Peter Gormley was a 41-year-old Australian who had served in the war and then worked in various media jobs which had prepared him for his real role in life, that of being a personal manager to show business stars.

He had been a journalist, a literary agent, a film director's assistant, the manager of a circuit of cinemas and, most recently, the manager of an Australian singer called Frank Ifield. It meant he not only knew about publicity and journalism but about making and screening films. Most importantly, he knew how to get bottoms on seats.

He'd arrived in Britain in 1959 to prepare the way for Frank Ifield. Ifield was a country-style singer with a trademark yodel and Gormley had a recording contract with Columbia waiting for him in England by early 1960.

Three top fifty hits followed that year and in the summer Norrie Paramor approached Gormley to look after the Shadows now that they were a pop act in their own right. He listened to 'Apache' and saw them in 'Stars In Your Eyes' at the Palladium before he agreed to become their manager.

Peter Gormley was as unlike Tito Burns as a manager could possibly be. Where Burns oozed showbiz patter and was still appearing on television as a performer while managing Cliff, Gormley was soft spoken, modest and keen to stay out of the limelight.

The Shadows were impressed with his quiet but thorough ways and it was natural that after Burns was dismissed by Rodger, Gormley would start to manage Cliff as well.

'The request came from Rodger and Cliff's lawyer,' says Gormley. 'I was already managing the Shadows, so first of all I had to satisfy myself that it was all clean and clear between Cliff and the Shadows, and then I had to meet with Rodger to make sure there was no conflict going on, no resentments or undertones.'

Most unusually for a show business manager, Peter Gormley didn't draw up a contract, preferring to do business on trust, and refused to take anything for the first year because the work hadn't been created by him.

Two months after Gormley had taken control, Rodger had a sudden relapse and was rushed into an intensive care unit at Highlands Hospital, Enfield, where he was immediately put into an oxygen tent.

'I don't know whether he knew he was dying but he was such a stubborn man,' says Cliff. 'They actually caught him once undoing the oxygen tent from the inside so that he could have a smoke. He managed to hide a safety pin so that he could pull the zip up from the inside. He was a dominant character right to the end.'

On 15 May, at the age of 56, he died. It was a shock to Cliff because he was just beginning to get close to him and felt that if he'd had the right treatment earlier he could have lived longer.

'At the funeral I can remember not being able to control my tears and it didn't bother me,' says Cliff. 'It was one of the first times I had ever cried publicly.'

By now he was in rehearsals for the first film set up by the Grade Organization's film department after the Delamar buy-out. For months rumours had been circulating. It was suggested that Cliff would star in *Hide My Eyes*, a murder thriller written by Margery Allingham. Several actresses were mentioned as being under consideration as his co-star – Carol Lynley, Heidi Bruhl, Helen Shapiro and Diana Dors among them.

Then came the announcement that Cliff's debut as a leading man was to be in an original musical produced by Kenneth Harper. None of the stars whose names had been bandied about were mentioned.

Kenneth Harper was a tall, well-spoken man in his 40s who had an apartment in Mayfair and offices in a Regency terrace off St Martin's Lane.

Since coming to London after the war he had worked for a theatrical agency and, for the past six years, as an independent film producer on films such as *For Better, For Worse* with Dirk Bogarde, *Yield To The Night* with Diana Dors and Sean Connery's debut film *Action Of The Tiger*.

Now, working from within the Grade Organization, Kenneth Harper was focusing his attention on Cliff Richard.

'I found that Cliff was filling cinemas on a Sunday when films were emptying them,' says Harper. 'I went to see him and he was knocking the audience out. I thought, if he can knock an audience out on a Sunday night in a cinema that is absolutely full, then he's the person to make a film with. We hadn't made proper musicals in the UK before and no one believed we could.'

Kenneth Harper and Leslie Grade took the idea of a Cliff Richard musical to Jimmy Wallis, Head of Production at ABC (Associated British Picture Corporation), who asked them to come up with a figure. Harper asked for £110,000 and got it. When Leslie Grade later asked him how he knew it would cost £110,000 he said, 'I haven't a clue. It'll probably cost more but let's just go for a nice round figure.' It was eventually to cost half as much again.

With the money in hand Harper set about gathering a creative team. To write the screenplay and the production numbers he called on lyricist Peter Myers and composer Ron Cass who had worked together on a number of popular West End revues including *Intimacy At Eight* (1952), *For Amusement Only* (1956) and *For Adults Only* (1958).

To direct it he chose Sid Furie, a 28-year-old Canadian who had made the well-received *A Dangerous Age* and *A Cool Sound From Hell* before coming to Britain in 1959 to make *The Snake Woman, Doctor Blood's Coffin* and *During One Night*.

The initial problem was finding a story strong enough to turn into a musical. The most obvious device was to do *The Cliff Richard Story* in the way that Tommy Steele had done *The Tommy Steele Story* but Harper had found Cliff's 1960 autobiography *It's Great To Be Young* so undramatic that he'd abandoned reading it after ten pages. He then gave to it to songwriter Herbie Kretzmer who had scolded him by saying, 'I don't know how you could conceivably make a film with any attraction at all when the only thing that has ever happened to this boy was when a microphone broke down at the Elephant and Castle when he was eighteen!'

The idea that eventually became *The Young Ones* emerged from an evening's brainstorming at Kenneth Harper's flat with Sid Furie, Peter Myers and Ron Cass. None of them wanted to make a rock 'n' roll movie but they all loved the old MGM musicals.

They talked about *Babes in Arms*, the Rodgers and Hart musical that starred Mickey Rooney and Judy Garland as the teenage children of retired vaudevillians who put on a show to raise money. The idea grew of a group of young people getting together to save their youth club from being torn down by a rich property developer – youth clubs and property developers being topical in 1961.

'We watched every old MGM film that Mickey Rooney ever

made,' says Harper. 'I didn't see anything wrong in pinching from things that have already been a huge success. Most people had forgotten them anyway. There was nothing enormously original about the plot we used but I don't believe there is anything wrong with making something which is pure entertainment. We didn't want to send a message.'

Because Cliff was inexperienced as an actor the plan was to surround him with talented actors and dancers who would draw attention away from his inadequacies. The property developer, Hamilton Black, was to be played by Robert Morley; Richard O'Sullivan, Teddy Green and Melvyn Hayes were to play the key members of the youth club gang and Cliff was to be Hamilton Black's son Nicky. The choreography would be by Broadway dance specialist Herb Ross.

Casting a female lead was difficult. If she was too beautiful the fans would resent her. If she was too plain she wouldn't be credible as Cliff's love interest. While Kenneth Harper was in New York he had been taken by Herb Ross to see a show featuring a talented Jewish girl he thought would be right for the part.

Harper wasn't as convinced and so didn't invite her to an audition. Her name was Barbra Streisand.

The girl who eventually got the role was Carole Gray, a young dancer from Rhodesia who had come to London and had appeared in West End stage versions of *The Boyfriend* and *West Side Story*. She had fleshy lips, a long nose and narrow eyes and was virtually unknown. After the publicity surrounding the film had subsided she would return to her anonymity in Africa. She was the perfect girl for Cliff.

Much to the annoyance of Peter Myers and Ron Cass, who were writing the soundtrack, it was decided to import half a dozen pop songs to hook the teenage audience.

'Basically we weren't given a chance to write any of the alleged pop numbers,' says Ron Cass. 'We were just the work horses who did the vital and more difficult work.'

For the songs that would hopefully be hits, Norrie Paramor, musical director for the film, turned to Sid Tepper and Roy Bennett, the writers of 'Travellin' Light'. He sent music publisher Cyril Simons to New York with a script and a commission for them to write three numbers.

186

'I arrived in New York in the morning, left the scripts with Tepper and Bennett and told them I wanted a song called "The Young Ones",' says Simons. 'I then went on to LA and when I returned 48 hours later they had produced three songs, one of which was "The Young Ones", one was "Outsider" and the other was "When The Girl In Your Arms Is The Girl In Your Heart", which they had already written but which no one had recorded.

'I flew back to London that day and played them to Norrie and he loved them and Cliff had two number ones from them. They recorded "Outsider" but eventually decided not to use it because nobody was 100 per cent sold on it.' (It was used on the album *21 Today*, along with another Tepper-Bennett song, 'Catch Me'.)

Most of the filming took place at the Elstree Studios during June and July 1961 except for the vaudeville finale which took place at the Finsbury Park Empire.

Although the period of 'Stars In Your Eyes' at the Palladium had been marred in Cliff's memory by the clandestine affair with Carol, it had also introduced him to the next girl in his life. She was an attractive 22-year-old blonde called Delia Wicks, one of the dancers in the show, who had been selected from the line-up to play a special scene with Cliff where he sang a medley of songs about the moon and then kissed her. The girls in the audience would all shriek at this point and Delia was paid an extra four pounds a week for her hard work.

She had come to London from Leeds at the age of fifteen to learn dancing at the John Tiller School and had been a Tiller Girl for five years before joining Billy Petch's dancers at the Palladium.

They hadn't dated during the Palladium run and then, early in 1961, while making a promotional appearance at the Queen's Hotel in Leeds, he phoned her at her mother's and came to the family home in Dewsbury Road for tea. It was the start of a brief romance which no one but their families, Mike Conlin and Delia's friend Eve Sewell ever knew about.

'Our romance was very secret,' says Delia. 'He never mentioned it afterwards and so, out of respect for Cliff, I never mentioned it either. It was a wonderful time in my life because, as you can imagine, I was absolutely overwhelmed by him.'

His arrival in Leeds was a bolt out of the blue for Delia who had assumed she would never see him again after the Palladium. 'He told me that he'd missed me,' she says. 'Then he started to call me up, often very late at night, while he was touring.'

Mike Conlin's memory is that during these early months 'he pursued her like a bat out of hell', driving back to her basement flat in Stockwell after one-night stands in the north of England and grabbing every available opportunity to be at her side.

'Once he drove all the way down from Newcastle after a show to see me and I remember he hadn't shaved and he was wearing a long leather coat,' says Delia. 'He parked his car outside and felt he couldn't stay too long because everyone would see his Thunderbird.'

'Another day he came running to my flat, saying "I'm so lonely, Delia. I've got to see you." He fell through the door and gave me a big kiss and I was just standing there dripping wet because I'd been washing my feet when the doorbell rang.

'We used to go out for drives in the country and I would visit him at his home. On Sundays he'd sometimes hire the whole swimming pool at Dolphin Square [London's largest complex of serviced apartments] and Mike Conlin, Cliff's mum and his sisters would come.'

It was a busy year for Cliff. A typical week would consist of several one-night stands, a couple of press interviews, a late-night recording session at Abbey Road, a promotional appearance and a radio show such as 'Saturday Club' or 'Parade Of The Pops'. Then there was the rehearsing and filming of *The Young Ones*.

In March he made his first tour of South Africa and encountered some of the most frenzied crowd scenes of his career. There were 3,000 fans at Salisbury airport (now Harare airport) when he flew in, and in Johannesburg a few days later 10,000 fans converged on the Carlton Hotel, where he was staying, bringing the city centre to a standstill. The police had to ask him to make an announcement from his balcony to pacify the crowds.

In Durban the local Indian population tried to claim him as one of their own, lining the route from the airport to the city and cheering him on. The Shadows noticed that he was disturbed by this response because it awakened the memories of the abuse he'd suffered over his racial identity when he first came to England.

Because of apartheid laws preventing mixed-race audiences

Cliff agreed to do two shows – one in Harare for whites only and one in Cape Town for Black Africans only, the profits for the latter show being given to the Salisbury Society for Handicapped Africans.

Once back home his secret relationship with Delia continued. She had to promise not to mention it to anyone and when in public they couldn't hold hands or kiss. At clubs and cinemas Delia had to make a separate entrance so that they wouldn't be perceived as a couple. In the street he would hide his face behind a handkerchief.

'I was prepared for the fact that these relationships would be difficult,' says Cliff. 'It was because of the kind of press I might get and what that might do. No one really knew whether it would damage your career, but I wasn't prepared to find out.

'It was hard to sustain anything that was going to have any meaning because we didn't see each other very often. I saw more of Delia during the Palladium run than I did when we later went out with each other.'

The impression Delia got was of a very harassed young man, denied a normal life, who just longed for some space in which to be himself.

'He hardly had any time to relax,' she says. 'He was always being pressured into doing things. He used to work so hard that sometimes when he came to see me he would just fall asleep in my arms.

'We were usually just so overwhelmed to see each other. You've no idea. It was such a relief for him. Everybody was always watching him and yet when he came to see me this was his big secret.'

He never mentioned his affair with Carol Costa to Delia and didn't seem about to repeat the experience. 'We kissed and cuddled but sleeping together was a bit taboo in those days,' she says. 'People didn't live together or anything like that.'

When his father died he seemed to change. Delia remembers him suddenly asking her out of the blue whether she was a Christian.

'He must have been thinking about it for a long time but it just came out like that,' she says. 'I don't think he would have carried on going out with me if I had said no.'

He also started to draw closer to his mother. Often when he came to Delia's flat he would call her to tell her where he was and he'd refuse to make decisions until she had been consulted.

'I used to ask him why he always had to ask his mother,' says

Delia. 'He used to say he was very concerned about her. I suppose he felt he was looking after his family.'

One night, when Delia went to Winchmore Hill before going out with Cliff to see the American singer Peggy Lee at the Pigalle nightclub, Cliff's mother drew her aside as she was getting herself ready in one of the bedrooms.

'I can visualize it now,' says Delia. 'I was wearing a white strapless dress. She had said something before when we were downstairs but now she was saying it again. She was telling me not to get too fond of Cliff because his career was going ahead. I just shrugged it off at the time. I thought Cliff could make his own mind up.'

In August he toured Scandinavia with the Shadows and sent Delia a series of postcards which indicated that all was still well. Some were written as soon as he settled in a new hotel and all of them started 'Hi Sweetie' and were signed 'Love, Cliff'. Then, on his 21st birthday, he left for his first tour of Australia, playing in Singapore and Kuala Lumpur on the way. After three sell-out concerts in Sydney he travelled to Melbourne where he sat in his hotel room and wrote a letter to Delia.

'Dear Delia

I know I haven't written for a long time, but I've been confused in my mind about you and about myself.

I have had to make, probably, one of the biggest decisions I'm ever going to make and I'm praying that I won't hurt you too much.

Delia, I want you to try and understand the position I'm in. Being a singer I'm going to have to give up many things in life.

But being a pop singer I have to give up one very priceless thing – the right to have any lasting relationship with any special girl.

Delia, you must find someone who is free to love you as you deserve to be loved, and is able to marry you.

I couldn't give up my career. Besides the fact that my mother and sisters, since my father's death, rely on me completely, I have show biz in my blood now and I would be lost without it.

"D" all I can say now is, goodbye and don't think too badly of me. Love, Cliff.'

The letter arrived at the basement flat of 41 West Cromwell Road on the morning of 26 October.

'I remember that day so well,' says Delia. 'My whole world changed. I was heartbroken. I thought, "Gosh, I'll never see him again." I remember having to be at the Motor Show in Earls Court and I walked around not really seeing anything. I was absolutely dumbstruck about it because I knew he was terribly fond of me at the time.

'I never contacted him after that because I thought there was no point. I felt, "That's it." I went into mourning for about two weeks and didn't speak to anyone. I wanted to tell the whole world but I realized that I couldn't because our romance had still to be kept a secret.

'He had obviously wanted to get involved with me but then he got frightened and that was it. It was all so confusing. I've never got to the bottom of it.'

'I was a coward there,' admits Cliff. 'I didn't want to face her and tell her – and I had been away a long time anyway – and I thought that if I saw her again I could confirm it but I'd rather get it off my chest. I thought it was unfair, once I'd decided that it wasn't for me, to leave someone at home thinking that when I came back it was all going to be hunky dory.'

A brief study of postmarks and diary dates reveals that another reason for breaking off with Delia must have been the fact that he had met someone new.

At the end of August he had done his first season at Blackpool, a six-week run at the Opera House, and he had been enamoured by a nineteen-year-old dancer called Jackie Irving who appeared earlier in the show. Cliff would go out and watch her each night and remembers thinking to himself, 'Gosh. She's beautiful.'

It was an opinion shared by the rest of the Shadows. Jet Harris fancied her madly and Tony Meehan felt that she was one of the most beautiful women he had ever seen. 'After Jackie Irving was made,' he says, 'they threw away the mould.'

'Cliff was a bit timid and he asked me if I'd do him a favour,' remembers Jet. 'He asked me to introduce her to him. I thought, "Dammit! I want to introduce myself to her!" So I got hold of her, took her to his dressing room, and I said, "Cliff, this is Jackie – Jackie, this is Cliff." And then I disappeared.'

Jackie was a local Blackpool girl whose mother ran a boarding house. She had large eyes, high cheek bones, long hair and a great sense of fun.

'We started going to all the after-show parties together and I found myself more attracted to her than anyone else and so I spent more time with her,' says Cliff.

'We went out dancing, we ate out and, of course, I went back and met her mum. It doesn't take that long to realize that something like that is happening.'

She soon moved down to London, taking a flat at 102 Hatherley Court in Hatherley Grove, Queensway, and Cliff and Jackie were seen as an inseparable couple. Everyone seemed to think they were perfect together and for the first time friends and family started whispering about marriage.

fifteen

'MY CAREER
HAD REACHED
A PLATEAU'

The Shadows' line-up had remained unchanged for almost three years, during which time they had enjoyed five top ten hits and had become the best-known beat group in Britain.

Hank had become a guitar hero inspiring thousands of boys to 'strum' their cricket bats in the mirror. It was the beginning of a lineage that would produce Eric Clapton, Peter Green, Pete Townshend, Jimmy Page, Jeff Beck, Mark Knopfler and Brian May.

Yet during 1961, friction between the four members was increasing. Hank was easy-going but Welch was an often tetchy perfectionist who prided himself on speaking his mind. One of the few occasions anyone can recall Cliff becoming violent was when he and Welch squared up at 100 Marylebone High Street after Welch returned one night to discover a dog sleeping in his bed.

'We always thought of Bruce as the moody guy,' says Cliff. 'If he couldn't tune his guitar he would sling it down and drive all the way back to London. He left the Shadows a number of times.'

In *The Shadows By Themselves* ('The Kings Of Beat Music Tell Their Own Fabulous Story') each Shadow was asked to comment on his colleagues. Tony Meehan said, 'He [Welch] is a great organizer and I often feel he would make a first-rate sergeant-major in the Guards.'

It was a thinly-veiled dig which Welch was quick to recognize, mentioning in his own comment that Meehan was 'quick tempered', a 'bit of a brain' who 'knows what he wants and he'll end up getting it'.

Meehan was a precocious teenager who, despite his lack of schooling, read voraciously, was a keen student of psychology and was a great lover of jazz and blues. Whereas the rest of the Shadows confessed to liking Agatha Christie and Dennis Wheatley (if they had time to read at all), Meehan put under 'Reading Matter' in the group's biography: *Mr Jelly Roll* by musicologist Alan Lomax and *Civilisation and its Discontents* by Sigmund Freud.

Other than drumming, his interests were philosophy and psychoanalysis. Says Royston Ellis, 'Tony was the most intelligent and analytical of the Shadows.'

But after three years of hard work Meehan was starting to slacken. 'He had no respect for time,' remembers Cliff. 'The coach would be leaving, we'd be telling him that he was five minutes late, and while you were telling him he would be sitting down and ordering fried eggs and bacon. There were many times when we just had to leave him behind.'

In October, shortly before the group was due to depart for Australia, Welch and Meehan got into a violent row which ended with Meehan walking out and suggesting they look for another drummer. Welch took him at his word and Brian Bennett, ex-Marty Wilde's Wildcats, was called up and offered the job.

'It was all getting too much for me,' says Meehan. 'We worked seven days a week, we never had any holidays and I had just started my first family. We had been worked into the ground because nobody thought it was going to last.

'When we were at the Palladium we used to work for six days a week, do three shows on a Saturday and were then put on a train to do a Sunday concert for which we would be paid five pounds extra.'

Jet was the next to go. The official leader of the Shadows, he had been causing concern for some time because of the effects of his drinking.

In *The Shadows By Themselves* he described his favourite drink as 'shandy' but it was really whisky. 'He was a lush,' says Meehan. 'He drank himself stupid. He was a totally self-destructive creature.' None of this was known to the fans at the time. They were told that Jet suffered from 'nerves' and was therefore 'taking the plunge to go solo'.

He has since blamed his descent into alcoholism on Cliff's dalliance with Carol, but those who knew him at the time say that the habit had been acquired long before. 'It wasn't so much that he drank a lot,' says Cliff, 'but that he couldn't drink well.'

He would be found in theatre bars when he was due to be on stage and often had to be rescued from fights that started when men called him 'queer' because he dyed his hair and wore fancy clothes. On tour in New Zealand he woke up one morning to find himself on the floor of a hut next to a Maori woman in full tribal costume. He had no idea how he came to be there.

When Bruce Welch broke the news to Jet on 15 April 1962 that he was no longer a member of the Shadows, his replacement had already been found. A month before, on 13 March, Peter Gormley had met with Brian 'Licorice' Locking, an unassuming young bass player who had played with Brian Bennett in bands for Vince Taylor and Tony Sheridan.

What no one except Bennett knew at the time was that Locking was an ardent Jehovah's Witness who, even when he was on tour, would carry out door-to-door evangelism. Bennett knew because he had introduced Locking to the teachings in 1958. Although not a member himself, he had been raised as a Witness by his mother. Locking studied the teachings for two years and then was baptized in 1961.

'He was just a nice guy,' says Bruce Welch. 'We were twenty or twenty-one years old and you don't ask a guy his religion when he plays bass guitar. The question was whether or not he was a good musician. And we liked him.'

Although his stay with the Shadows was brief his influence was profound because it was through him that Cliff began studying the Bible for the first time since his teens.

Previous biographies and autobiographies say that Locking talked with Cliff about religion while on tour in Australia, a story which can't be true because Locking never toured Australia with the Shadows. The discussion must have taken place in England and was almost certainly in 1962.

'I remember the conversation,' says Locking. 'I think it was in a hotel room and it wasn't with Cliff alone. There were one or two other people from another group that was on the same tour. We were having a bit of an argument and the subject of spiritualism came up and I just brought out what I believed. But my initial conversations on the subject had been with Hank who seemed to be the most interested.'

The only comments on religion made by Cliff in his early autobiography make interesting reading today.

'Whatever else becomes public,' he said, 'one's own beliefs should be private. Religion is something that is in one's heart. I don't go to church a lot. Leading my hectic sort of life it's often difficult.'

His change of view began with his father's death which produced a period of reflection. The satisfaction that he'd once gained from doing a successful concert diminished.

'I was quite enjoying myself in showbiz... but there was this "something" missing,' he wrote in 1968. 'I'd go on stage for half an hour... and I'd be quite excited and exhilarated. Then, after the show, we'd all sit about and "wind down", talking about the show, the audience and so on. Gradually, the excitement would wear off, and I'd find myself thinking, What a drag this all is! This was before I began even thinking about religion.'

During the Australian tour of 1961 he idly began to contemplate the possibility of contacting his father through a medium. Some of the girls in the Blackpool show had been playing with moving glasses and he told a Melody Maker journalist that this had prompted him to think of 'delving into spiritualism'.

'After enjoying this new closeness with my dad just before he died I was beginning to feel dissatisfied with my career,' he says.

'I thought that if it was possible I would get in touch to find out what was happening, to find out why I was feeling this way and to see what was ahead for me. My career was going well but it had reached a plateau. I wondered where I was going.'

It was when he talked openly about contacting a medium that Locking jumped in with what the Bible said about dabbling with the spirit world.

'He jolted back and said "You shouldn't do that. It's dangerous," Cliff remembers. 'He said the Bible prohibited it. I told him to show me. I wasn't prepared to accept his word for it.'

Locking got his Bible and read from the Old Testament book of Deuteronomy: 'There should not be found in you anyone who makes his son or his daughter pass through the fire, anyone who employs divination, a practitioner of magic or anyone who looks for omens or a sorcerer, or one who binds others with a spell or anyone who consults a spirit medium or a professional foreteller of events or anyone who inquires of the dead. For anybody doing these things is something detestable to Jehovah.'

Cliff was impressed with this seasoned musician who quoted the Bible with such assurance.

'I think it was a bit of a revelation to Cliff that this rocker should be involved with something so completely divorced from rock 'n' roll,' says Mike Conlin.

'I know that he used to talk to Licorice because he was trying to understand it. He was trying to put a finger on what it was that made this guy someone who one minute would be playing rock 'n' roll and the next would be putting pamphlets through people's doors.'

He already respected the Bible so it wasn't what Locking said that made the initial impact but the zeal with which he said it. He envied the fact that Locking had something more substantial than his career to be passionate about.

The Jehovah's Witnesses had started in America during the nineteenth century and came to be characterized by their vigorous proselytizing techniques, including 'doorstep evangelism'.

They used their translation of the Bible as a source book but diverged from historical Christian teaching on key doctrines such as the trinity (Father, Son and Holy Ghost), the eternal human soul and the incarnation (Jesus as God in the flesh).

'Christianity hadn't been relevant to me before,' says Cliff. 'I didn't even know that God had a name – Jehovah. I started to read more and more. I was impressed by the prophecies they mentioned and by the fact that God could be understood rationally.'

Locking's entry into the Shadows coincided with *Summer Holiday*, the second film put together by Leslie Grade. It was set in Greece because Kenneth Harper wanted to make a film which would capitalise on the British boom in foreign travel. He had toyed with the idea of setting a story in Spain, then untouched by mass tourism, but decided that it was too near and that Greece had more romantic connotations.

He kept the core of Cliff's gang from *The Young Ones*, Peter

Myers and Ron Cass as writers and Herb Ross as choreographer. He wanted to keep Sid Furie as director but he didn't want to make another musical so he hired 33-year-old Peter Yates.

The problem for the writers was to create a story that would get the characters from London to Athens.

'If they were basically classless, but without the money for expensive holidays, we needed a reason to get them abroad without them losing their identity as the Young Ones,' says Ron Cass.

'One day while travelling on a London bus it suddenly occurred to me that if we couldn't get them to Greece by air why not get them there on a London bus which we could convert into living quarters?'

Once the red double-decker bus had been cast in the lead role the screenplay fell into place. Cliff would be the leader of a gang of London Transport mechanics who decide to turn a bus into a hotel and drive it across Europe.

Interiors were shot at Elstree Studios but all the exteriors (except for a brief longshot in Paris) were shot on location in and around Athens starting in May 1962. Two London buses were bought for the film but the logistics of getting a double-decker from London to Athens were problematic in real life.

Kenneth Harper remembers, 'We needed two buses because we needed one as a back-up but when they were driven overland they came across so many bridges that they wouldn't fit under. One of them actually made it eventually by road but the other one had to turn back and be sent by sea.'

There were also problems getting in the guns needed for a scene where Yugoslavian border guards challenge the bus. 'There was a most almighty fuss,' says Harper. 'My assistant producer, Andy Mitchell, was almost put in jail because they thought he was starting a revolutionary cell.'

Cliff's leading lady was nineteen-year-old Lauri Peters, a classically-trained dancer who had spent the past two years in the Broadway production of *The Sound Of Music*. She had made one previous film, *Mr Hobbs Takes A Train* with James Stewart, and was recommended by Herb Ross as someone who might appeal to potential American distributors.

As with Carole Gray in *The Young Ones* she was not the

glamorous lead that might be expected, and looked unlikely as Cliff's romantic interest. Harper was furious that she had put on a lot of weight just prior to filming.

'The choice of Cliff's leading ladies was always strange,' says Tony Meehan. 'I think the notion was to pick girls who were quite plain and who wouldn't threaten the fans. I think the girls liked leading ladies who they could identify with.'

There was never any off-screen romance between the two leads. Three days after Cliff arrived in Athens he was joined by Jackie Irving, and Lauri had just got married to a young American actor called Jon Voight, later to star in *Midnight Cowboy* and later still to father Angelina Jolie.

Una Stubbs, who played one of the stranded singers, remembers, 'Like most people who have just fallen in love, Lauri was wrapped up in just one person. I think she was dreadfully homesick and pining for him. She couldn't wait for the film to finish.'

Although Jon Voight came out to Athens for one weekend he was mostly confined to New York where he was in a play. 'Lauri confided in me one day,' says Melvyn Hayes. 'She said, "Where do you think I go on a Saturday night? I must tell somebody." I told her I had no idea. She said, "I fly back to America and then come back on the Sunday night because it's costing me that much a week in phone calls home."'

She played the part of a genderless-looking stowaway who eventually melts Cliff's heart despite having been told by him, 'Girls are all very well but date them once and then run. Date them twice and they get serious... Next thing you know, you're hooked and wondering what's hit you. No. No girl is going to own me.'

This was remarkably close to Cliff's code of caution, a code reinforced by a song which he had written with Bruce Welch which was added after the location filming had been completed. Just as Tepper and Bennett's song 'The Young Ones' forever associated Cliff with youth, so 'Bachelor Boy' connected him with a permanent state of singleness.

'We started the song just with the title,' remembers Welch. 'I wrote it with Cliff because I thought it would be a great song for him. We both wrote words and music. It was an afterthought as far as *Summer Holiday* was concerned but it became a million-seller.'

Una Stubbs was the girl in the film who many thought should have taken the lead role. She was a vivacious young dancer with a flicked-up bob haircut whose innocent freshness matched Cliff's own uncomplicated image. When Cliff saw her being auditioned he singled her out, catching the eye of the casting director and making the sign of the haircut to indicate his preference.

'I definitely think they should have cast Una in the lead role,' says Melvyn Hayes. 'They never got Cliff the right leading ladies. In *The Young Ones* he had a girl who looked as if she could have been his mother and then in *Summer Holiday* they had Lauri Peters who was great and yet wrong.'

In preparation for the filming Cliff went on a crash diet and also had his pointed tooth capped (he'd worn a temporary cap for *The Young Ones*). He'd started putting on weight during the American tour in 1960 and by the time he arrived at the Palladium run he was up to twelve stone.

Comments about his weight had been cropping up in the press since 1959 when Donald Zec, in a *Daily Mirror* interview, described him as a 'well-set, meaty youth' and Maureen Cleave had referred to 'chubby Mr Richard's tautened muscles in bathing trunks' when she reviewed *It's Great To Be Young*.

In the BBC radio programme *Frankly Speaking* (November 1960), Royston Ellis had asked, 'Does your weight worry you at all? People say that you're getting too plump. Does this worry you?'

Cliff had replied that it did. 'But I don't know what to do about it. It does worry me because I should keep up my appearance. But how does one get rid of fat except by starving oneself?'

It was a comment of Minnie Caldwell, one of the original characters in *Coronation Street*, that finally prompted him to do something about it.

Transmitted in April 1962 and scripted by Tony Warren, the episode featured Minnie sitting in a park with Ena Sharples and Martha Longhurst listening to a brass band playing.

Ena Sharples: 'I'll have you know, I've got perfect pitch. To hear folks talk now you'd think everything began and ended with *Annie Get Your Gun*.'
Martha Longhurst: 'You can't beat the old tunes though can you?'

Ena Sharples: 'Oh I don't know. Have you ever heard *West Side Story* on *Sandy McPherson*?'
Martha Longhurst: 'Aye. But it doesn't seem the same thing somehow.'
Minnie Caldwell: 'Isn't Cliff Richard a lovely chubby lad?'

'He used to go to a store just off Tottenham Court Road and buy Indian sweetmeats called Jelabis,' recalls Ray Mackender.

'They had more calories in them than you can possibly imagine and the result didn't exactly enhance his photographs. The comment about him being a "chubby lad" on "Coronation Street" hurt him and from then on Jelabis were out and he became an absolute addict at keeping fit.'

By the time he started shooting *Summer Holiday* on 25 May he was down to eleven stone, the same weight that he maintains today.

Already conscious of the value of the youthfulness which he had feared was skipping away the day he left his teens, he was now, at 21, becoming aware that the lean physique and the wide smile had to be worked for.

In October 1962 Cliff and the restructured Shadows toured America for the second time, this time to promote *The Young Ones* (retitled *It's Wonderful To Be Young* by Paramount and disastrously re-edited). The idea was great. The first half of the evening would be a screening of the film and the second half would be a concert.

What no one could have imagined when planning the tour was that America and Russia were to teeter on the brink of nuclear warfare that month over the issue of Soviet missiles being set up in Cuba. It wasn't until 28 October that President Kennedy called the bluff of Russian premier Khrushchev, and Khrushchev promised to remove the weapons.

The Cuban Missile Crisis was the closest that the superpowers came to conflict during the Cold War years and it meant that during Cliff's tour America was in a state of panic, with few people venturing out. As a result the concerts were poorly attended, sometimes half empty.

While in Memphis another attempt was made to see Elvis but again the meeting didn't work out. 'It was arranged that we should go to his home, Graceland,' remembers Locking.

'When we got there we realized he was out of town and so his father, Vernon, met us and took us on a guided tour of the mansion. He didn't say much to us and all I can remember was seeing piles of teddy bears in his bedroom upstairs.'

It may seem surprising today that Britain's biggest chart act was met with such disinterest yet the American fascination with British groups was only established with the Beatles. In 1962 the idea of a group of Englishmen playing rock 'n' roll appeared to have as much potential as Americans playing cricket or the French playing baseball.

The only real success to date had been Lonnie Donegan's version of 'Rock Island Line', which had reached number eight in the charts during 1956 and had been backed up with a four-month tour. Marty Wilde reached number 45 with 'Bad Boy' in March 1960, but wasn't able to follow it up.

Although other acts, such as Billy Fury, had released singles in America, nothing had come of them. The only British acts to reach the number one slot at the time were Acker Bilk with 'Stranger On The Shore' in 1961, and Vera Lynn with 'Auf Wiedersehen' in 1952. (The Tornadoes were to have a surprise number one with their instrumental, 'Telstar', in December 1962.)

When Cliff arrived back in London on 13 November he told *Melody Maker* that despite the month-long tour and appearances on the 'Ed Sullivan Show' and 'Dick Clark's Bandstand' he was still very much an unknown in America. 'You've got to fight to make yourself known there,' he said. 'You're up against so much.'

But the tour had personal significance for Cliff in that it gave him more opportunities to question Locking about his faith and marked the first time he'd attended a religious meeting since his teens.

'We were swimming in the hotel pool one day and someone came through and asked for me,' says Locking. 'I wondered who it could be because I knew no one in Miami.

'Apparently a room maid had seen my JW Bible, which in those days had a green-coloured cover, and she'd taken a look inside to see who it belonged to because she was a Witness. She then invited me to a local meeting and Cliff and Hank joined me.'

Again for Cliff it was the enthusiasm that swept him up. 'I was just so overwhelmed,' he says. 'Everyone was just so friendly. We got big hugs and everything. It was incredible. It was the feeling of being in a charismatic [Pentecostal-style] meeting long before I knew the word charismatic. When I came back to England I introduced it to all the family.'

What Cliff didn't know was that his mother was separately considering the claims of the Jehovah's Witnesses because her Uncle Vincent (Vincent Bridgwater) and his wife May, who had come to England in the early fifties, had been converted by doorstep evangelists and she had seen a lot of them after Rodger's death. One day May noticed a Bible by Dorothy Marie's bedside and talk turned to religion, beginning a conversation that went on until four o'clock the next morning.

'She then gave me a couple of magazines and asked me to read them,' says Dorothy Marie. 'She told me that she had been a very strong Roman Catholic and that nothing would move her. But she had decided that the church was doing nothing for her and she became a Witness.

'So I had the magazines, Cliff was on tour in America and when he came back he'd got copies of the same ones. He said he was interested in the Jehovah's Witnesses. So we all started studying together.'

Studying was necessarily spasmodic for Cliff, who was hardly ever in the same town two nights running. In January 1963 he returned to South Africa in shows that featured Jackie Irving and Carole Gray.

In Salisbury, Rhodesia (now Harare, Zimbabwe), Cliff and Jackie went along with Licorice Locking to a local meeting house. That June they were back in Blackpool for a long summer season at the ABC with Dailey and Wayne and Arthur Worsley. Cliff attended JW meetings in nearby Thornton Clevelys as well as meeting twice a week with Locking and a local JW to discuss Witnesses' view of the Bible.

Locking was perplexed as to why Cliff wanted to study in such depth without ever committing himself, or describing himself as a Jehovah's Witness. 'I just got the impression that he was interested,' says Locking. 'He was looking for something to commit himself to.'

When *Summer Holiday* was released at the close of 1962 it broke all previous box office records for a British film. Kenneth Harper had deliberately scheduled a winter premiére to increase the impact of the film.

'I had told Leslie Grade to pray for snow the week that the film came out,' he says. 'We were lucky. It did snow. Everybody was frozen and they went into the cinema and it was like having a summer holiday.'

By this time Cliff had been a major star for four years in a business where success runs were typically counted in months if not weeks.

His original opposition had by now disappeared. Tommy Steele, Marty Wilde and Terry Dene were never again to appear in the charts. Vince Eager, Duffy Power and Johnny Gentle, the great hopes of manager Larry Parnes, never had a hit single between them.

The only serious competition was from Adam Faith and Billy Fury, who had started in the business around the same time as Cliff but whose chart careers hadn't started until 1959. By 1962 they'd both had over a dozen hits but neither of them had developed the family appeal that helped Cliff reach out beyond the original teenage audience.

Fury had a great voice – perhaps the best rock 'n' roll voice of his generation – but he was painfully shy and compensated for this by developing a writhing stage act which newspapers reported as 'suggestive'. The management of Dublin's Theatre Royal once dropped the curtain on the act because it was considered too 'offensive'.

Adam Faith was less of a threat. He suffered from stage nerves and didn't have the voice to sustain a long career. He imitated Buddy Holly, and his vocal deficiencies were expertly covered up by John Barry's string arrangements.

'I suppose I felt a certain amount of competition from Cliff,' says Faith, 'but, amazingly enough, we never got to know each other well in those days because we were both so busy. The only times we would meet would be at a transport cafe and he'd say, "I've just been to Grantham. Where are you going?" and I'd say, "Well, I'm off to Southampton." Then we'd meet at the *New Musical Express* Poll Winners concerts at Wembley Pool and we'd sit and chat. He was a nice lad, but there was a big enough audience for all of us.'

The real threat to Cliff's standing as Britain's number one pop idol was to come from the Beatles, who had their first hit single in October 1962. With their floppy haircuts and collarless jackets, they appeared to be the challenge of a new generation but were actually contemporaries of Cliff who had started playing skiffle at the same time. John Lennon was five days older than Cliff.

The Beatles first met Cliff at a party thrown by Bruce Welch after they had played the Lewisham Odeon on 29 March 1963. Although they had never bought Cliff's records they were impressed to meet the man they knew they had to beat to be Britain's best.

They gathered in Welch's kitchen and John Lennon made jokes about Cliff holding off his next release so that the Beatles could stand a chance of getting to number one with their follow-up to 'Please Please Me'.

Then they got out their guitars. Cliff and the Shadows played 'Lucky Lips' while the Beatles sang 'From Me To You', which they had recorded three weeks previously.

The one exchange of the evening that Cliff still remembers came when he expressed an interest in Ray Charles and Lennon said, 'I used to like him until everybody else started to like him.' The elitism of the comment perplexed Cliff.

'The Beatles were fairly small at the time but I remember we spent the whole night talking,' says Mike Conlin. 'They were very worried about the effect of Cliff's next release.

'We all got on very well and when we played the Blackpool season later that year I would meet up with Paul when they were doing Sunday concerts up there and he always made me feel welcome. He never made any snide remarks about Cliff.'

In April 1963, shortly after the birth of Julian Lennon, John took off to Spain for a private holiday with manager Brian Epstein. They booked into a hotel in Sitges where Cliff and the Shadows were staying while recording the album *When In Spain* in Barcelona. Mike Conlin remembers Lennon being a bit distant, as though he wanted to get into a conversation but felt it was a bit beneath him.

'It was winter time and there were no other English people around,' says Conlin. 'We used to see Brian and John every day in the street and you could see John half thinking that he'd spend some time with us but then sniffing and turning away. I never knew what effect that had but it was after that that Lennon began sounding off about Cliff.'

In a conversation which took place the following month,

recorded in Michael Braun's book *Love Me Do*, Lennon said, 'We've always hated Cliff. He was everything we hated in pop. But when we met him we didn't mind him at all. He was very nice. Now when people ask us if he's a bit soft we say "no". We still hate his records but he's really very nice.'

What they hated was his 'niceness' when singing rock 'n' roll. They had spent years in sweaty cellars learning how to rock audiences until they dropped from exhaustion. To the boys from Liverpool, Cliff was a British Frankie Avalon, a house-trained rock star for the family audience.

'From Me To You' went to number one, and 1963 belonged to the Beatles who had three number ones in a row. It wasn't as if Cliff had a bad year. His next three singles were all top five but it was enough to suggest that his reign as the undisputed king of British pop might be coming to an end.

It unnerved him that 'Lucky Lips' was not only beaten by 'From Me To You' but by 'Scarlett O'Hara', the second single by Jet Harris and Tony Meehan who'd teamed up after leaving the Shadows. For someone who has always been concerned with his showing in the singles charts this was a public humiliation.

He told *Melody Maker* that he became quite agitated when 'Lucky Lips' stalled at number four.

'I went home and poured my heart out to Mum and shouted, "'Lucky Lips' isn't getting to the top." You need someone to talk to. People think the showbiz life is cushy. But Jet's right in saying that you need nerves of steel. You go to bed at night wondering if things will still be the same tomorrow, if you'll still be at the top.'

In another interview he was asked whether he was buckling under the challenge of the new groups from Liverpool. 'I don't think it's that that has stopped me,' said Cliff.

'The record of mine just wasn't strong enough. Perhaps we have slipped into a rut, but it's not just a sound that sells records. They have to be good. We will just have to be more selective in choosing material. I'm certainly not going to be "Beatled" into making a disc for the sake of it.'

Getting in the lower half of the top five was hardly a disaster and the song became his best-selling single ever in Germany. But it was the start of press speculation about his future, particularly as the beat group boom was throwing up new acts every week.

After years of 'Cliff Is Tops Again' headlines, they were writing 'Is Cliff Slipping?', 'Cliff At The Crossroads' and "We're Not Has Beens" Says Cliff'.

'These are dangerous days for Cliff Richard and he is facing them with zest, honesty and fervour,' wrote Ray Coleman in *Melody Maker*.

'After five years of glory during which he has established himself as Britain's top solo pop idol, it has been said that the route from now on can only be downhill.'

'I'M *sixteen* THINKING ABOUT GOD'

In October 1963 Licorice Locking made the surprise announcement that he would be leaving the Shadows in order to devote more time to his religious activities.

'I love being with the group,' he told the *Daily Mail*, 'but the constant touring doesn't allow me to fulfil my promise to life. I have thought about this step for a long time. It has become a strain dividing myself into two – being loyal to the show and being loyal to my beliefs. I feel I must stay in one place and do my work there.'

Locking completed his recording commitments and was then replaced by John Rostill, a handsome young bass player the Shadows had met in Blackpool.

On 2 December, with the Beatles at the top of the hit parade with 'She Loves You', Cliff left for the Canary Islands and *Wonderful Life*, the third of his films with the Harper, Cass and Myers team and the second to be directed by Sid Furie.

Just as *Summer Holiday* had been the best received and most lucrative of Cliff's films, *Wonderful Life* was to be the worst received and least lucrative.

There were problems from the start. To sustain the rhythm started with *The Young Ones*, filming should have been the previous summer with a release date in early 1964 but because of the interruption of the Blackpool summer season the momentum was lost.

Then there was a problem with Ron Cass and Peter Myers' story. Originally Cliff was to have played the role of a dashing guardsman mysteriously called out to Mexico after the death of an uncle. While travelling through the dry Mexican countryside his train is ambushed and he is taken prisoner by a gang of bandits who blindfold him and take him to the uncle's village. When the blindfold is taken off it is revealed that the uncle was the leader of the bandits and that as his only living relative the guardsman must now adopt his mantle.

The rest of the film was to have shown him desperately assuming the bandit leadership while simultaneously trying to ensure that those under his control committed no real crimes. 'It would have been a very different film for Cliff,' argues Ron Cass, 'and very, very funny.'

After a costing of the film based on this script Kenneth Harper broke the news that it would be impossible to do something set in Mexico.

'Andy Mitchell went out to research the possibility and found that it was absolutely out of court,' says Harper. 'So we went out looking for islands that were closer, and finally decided on the Canary Islands. That's when we realized we were going to have to change the story.'

Through changing the screenplay to fit a new location the heart was taken out of the film. Much of the final script was written on location with scenes changing day by day as the weather affected the contours and colour of the sand and made continuity a nightmare.

'I can't really take the same pride in the result as I did in *The Young Ones* and *Summer Holiday* because it was all over the place,' admits Ron Cass.

'I've always said that a musical should be fanciful but the idea we used of a group of young kids making a film was too fanciful. There comes a certain point where people reject "fanciful" and say "impossible". The screenplay grew rather than arrived.'

The problems didn't end when they reached the Canary Islands. Filming was held up by rainstorms, Melvyn Hayes broke his leg falling down a flight of steps and one of the leading actors, Dennis Price, had to be replaced.

'There was no excitement at all on that set,' remembers Royston Ellis, who was flown out to research a book of the film that was never written. 'There was this scandal because Dennis Price was totally drunk and incapable of filming. Cliff asked me to try and straighten him out so they could get the film done but it didn't work out. He had to be flown home and his part was taken over by Derek Bond.

'By that time Cliff was keeping very much to himself and was very into discussing religion with Una Stubbs and Hank Marvin. That was when a lot of us became aware that Cliff had got religion and word got out.'

The lack of excitement is confirmed by Melvyn Hayes, reckoned by most to be the liveliest of the cast.

He remembers a journalist from a national paper flying in to write a story along the lines of 'High Jinks On Cliff Film' and asking him what really went on. Hayes remembers, 'I turned to him conspiratorially and said, "I'll tell you what really happens. We have a wake-up call at 6.30. We do make-up. We then get into a terrible jeep which takes us forty miles to Las Palmas which is like an oven. Then we work until lunch time.

"The sun is so hot we don't enjoy our food. Then we film all afternoon until the winds start getting up at four o'clock and it starts turning cold. The sand whips into our faces and cuts us like sandpaper. But we haven't finished yet.

"We go on until the light drops and then we get back into the bus and feel sick and rough from the heat. We eventually get back to the hotel, have a bath, go to the restaurant and fall asleep."

'This wasn't good enough for the journalist so he found Richard O'Sullivan and pushed him into the swimming pool. Richard pulled the journalist in with him and when the story came out it was all about the things we all got up to at night, like throwing one another into the swimming pool.'

It was during the making of *Wonderful Life* that Cliff's relationship with Jackie Irving reached crunch point. He had now been seeing her for almost two and a half years but whereas he seemed content to have her as his permanent high school date, Jackie wanted the relationship to deepen.

'I think that for Cliff it was a very platonic relationship,' says one friend of the period. 'I don't know what Jackie would have called it. It wasn't physical. She was just the girl that he would take to things.'

His physical restraint was accompanied by a refusal to discuss where they were headed. Newspapers had been speculating on their likely marriage since September 1963 but Cliff never raised the topic with Jackie.

'All this week, since these rumours that we were getting married started, people have tried to ask me about it,' Jackie told the *Daily Mirror*. 'I have just kept away from them. That kind of thing is embarrassing for both Cliff and myself.

'Obviously I like him a lot. So does my mother... but neither of us is planning to get married. There's nothing like that.'

Cliff's response was to say, 'Jackie is my only girlfriend.'

But although they never spoke of marriage to each other they both pondered on it when alone. Jackie assumed that Cliff's reluctance to put the relationship into a higher gear was because his mother was restraining him. One evening, while on tour in Birmingham, she came to Dorothy Marie's hotel room and tried to sort the matter out.

'She thought I was putting a spoke in his wheel,' says Dorothy Marie. 'I said, "My dear girl, I'm nothing to do with him. Cliff is grown up. He's a man. If he wants to get married he'll get married. If he doesn't, he won't. There's nothing that you and I can do that will change him."'

The 'forbidding' that Tony Meehan had noticed was still operating. He was comfortable with a schoolboyish friendship but balked at the idea of what an adult relationship might entail.

'Jackie Irving was the first girl that I thought I might marry,' Cliff says. 'I thought that if I was going to get married at all it would be to Jackie.

'I went to Peter Gormley and said, "Supposing I wanted to get married..." and Peter said, "Well, you might lose 10 per cent of your fans but that doesn't mean too much." He was saying that if I got married I'd still keep 90 per cent of my fans.

'That's when I decided not to get married because as soon as the cards were dealt out and I had the OK I thought, "Ooh, I don't know if I want this anyway."'

The bottom line was that he loved being Cliff Richard so much that commitment to anyone else would be second best. There was no room in his life for a Mrs Cliff Richard. The fires of sexual passion, which could have prompted him to marry, were never as strong as his determination to enjoy his career.

'I don't think I'm cut out for marriage. Even though I have enjoyed the relationships I've had I have always felt fairly dispassionate afterwards and able to say I'm glad I didn't get married,' he admits. 'I obviously haven't been hit by the same bug that has hit others.'

Jackie had joined Cliff in the Canaries and it was here that he broke the news that he had decided not to see her any more.

'Obviously it takes one person to bring up the subject and I was the one to bring it up,' says Cliff. 'I said, "Look, I don't want to get married." So we called it off.

'What she felt like when I told her I don't know. I can't speak for her. I don't think she was hysterically happy but I've always felt it's best to get things said. I've never wanted to live a lie. At least I have been upfront with everybody and told them I couldn't do it.'

A brief flirtation with Una Stubbs followed but Cliff felt inhibited by the fact that although her relationship with actor Peter Gilmore was breaking up, she was still married to him.

'We had been keen on each other for quite a while,' says Una. 'Then, during *Wonderful Life*, it turned into a romance although I always kept very quiet about it. Even my closest friends didn't know.'

Cliff was still in Las Palmas when the news came that the Beatles had arrived in America to be greeted by 4,000 screaming fans in an unprecedented display of pop devotion. Like Cliff they had then appeared live on the 'Ed Sullivan Show', the difference being that they had drawn the largest audience in the history of entertainment television. To cap it all, 'I Want To Hold Your Hand' had gone to number one in the US charts.

All this must have been galling to someone who had spent five years struggling for American recognition. *It's Wonderful To Be Young* hadn't done great business, none of his ten singles since 'Living Doll' had made a mark ('Lucky Lips' had hovered around the bottom end of the top one hundred) and his new American label, Epic, was just starting to have some success with 'It's All In The Game' after having launched what it called 'one of the greatest introductory campaigns in our history.'

Now the Beatles, with a recording career of just over twelve months, were causing a sensation on their very first trip. In fact, it had been the failure of Cliff's career in America that had determined the nature of the Beatles' conquest.

'Cliff went there and he died,' John Lennon told author Michael Braun on the eve of their visit. 'He was fourteenth on a bill with Frankie Avalon and George [Harrison] said that *Summer Holiday* was second feature at a drive-in in St Louis.'

To avoid such indignities the Beatles waited to take America until they could be guaranteed top billing and maximum exposure. The airport welcome was part of a well-orchestrated campaign by Capitol Records.

There were major features in the trade press, DJs were primed to announce the arrival time of the plane, Beatle souvenirs were being mass marketed and five million posters saying 'The Beatles Are Coming' were posted all over America in December 1963.

But success on such a grand scale cannot be explained by marketing techniques alone. The Beatles captured the mood of international cultural change in a way in which Cliff never had and never would.

They were the first of a better-educated, more sophisticated generation of rock musicians who wrote their own songs and guided their own careers.

Cliff took the news philosophically. He was still Britain's most popular male singer even though, in the *New Musical Express* annual points survey, which reflected the number of weeks an act was in the charts, he was now eleventh in a list that he had topped the year before.

'We're not going to contest the beat groups,' he said. 'We won't follow trends. We will continue doing what we do until the public stops buying our records.'

There was premature talk of him retiring. At the end of 1963 he had bought Rookswood, a six-bedroom Tudor-style mansion in Upper Nazeing, Essex, where he would live with his mother and sisters. He also bought a holiday home in Portugal.

At that time the Algarve coast was completely undeveloped. There was no airport at Faro and the only way to travel there was to fly to Lisbon and drive the rest of the way. Peter Gormley heard of it through Muriel Young, then a disc jockey on Radio Luxembourg, who had built a house in Albufeira at a time when only two other British people had homes in the region.

'It was completely undiscovered,' she says. 'Peter came down initially because he was a deep-sea fisherman and he ended up buying six houses – two for Leslie Grade and one each for himself, Cliff, Frank Ifield and Bruce Welch.

'It was because these people were all so famous that the place got written about. The Algarve burst wide open six or seven years before it might have done because of the attention it got through stars such as Cliff.'

Mike Conlin remembers him being at his happiest when he was able to disappear to Portugal.

'He liked being able to get away completely from the show-business scene,' says Conlin. 'We used to go down for a month at a time. There was a fellow we knew who was at university near Lisbon and he used to take us to restaurants and introduce us to the local fishermen.

'We used to go out on the boats all night sardine fishing, things like that, and Cliff would sometimes come back and sing to the fishermen in their homes. None of them had any idea who he was and that's what he liked about it. He could go anywhere and not be recognized.'

The retirement talk had started when he had casually remarked that Portugal seemed to be the ideal place to retire. It took on added significance because Cliff was known to be deeply involved in the teaching of the Jehovah's Witnesses and some thought he might eventually follow Licorice Locking's example and quit the business.

One of those disturbed by his new obsession was Jay Norris, his old form mistress from Cheshunt, with whom he had stayed in touch over the years. Educated in a convent school, she knew enough of the Bible to know he was flirting with a quasi-Christian group, but not enough to correct his theology.

For help she turned to the school's religious education master, Bill Latham, a 26-year-old evangelical Christian who had an easy-going manner and an exceptional gift for communicating his beliefs.

She also entertained the idea that Bill would make an ideal friend for Cliff.

'I'm a natural organizer of other people's lives and I thought they would have a lot to offer each other,' she explains.

'Cliff had no nice ordinary friends. He was stuck in the pop world where the people were often second-rate and Bill had a lot of Christian friends. Actually I thought that Bill had much more to offer Cliff than Cliff had to offer Bill. Being a pop star could be lonely and dull.'

On the surface of things Bill Latham was an unusual match for anyone to make for Cliff. The only things they appeared to have in common were a lower middle-class background (Latham was born and raised in Finchley), a father who worked in the catering business (Latham's father had worked in a Camden bakery) and an interest in religion.

Latham was not a rock 'n' roll fan and dressed comfortably rather than fashionably. He spent a lot of his evenings and weekends as a leader in an interdenominational Christian youth organization called Crusaders which arranged Bible studies and outdoor activities for teenage boys.

His own conversion, in 1952, had been through this group which happened to hold their weekend meetings in a room of the school he attended. He went with them to a summer camp in Norfolk where he understood the Christian message for the first time.

'Crusaders influenced my life very significantly, both directly and indirectly, after that,' Latham says. 'I began to be trained as a leader and that had one of the most profound shaping effects I have ever known. At the age of seventeen I was being put into positions of authority and the experience got me out of a fairly introverted life.'

Each July Jay Norris celebrated her birthday with a car rally which met at her house and then dispersed into the Hertfordshire countryside with sheets of clues imaginatively written out in rhyming couplets. In July 1964 her plan was to assign Cliff to Bill Latham's car.

'I wasn't intimidated when I met him that day at Jay's house but I was certainly curious,' remembers Latham. 'I was slightly apprehensive as to how we would get on because it was an interesting set-up. I was almost working to a brief. I was under strict instructions to get him into a spiritual discussion and this was a tall order in the context of a car rally.'

Cliff's recollection is that they 'spent the whole time arguing'. Latham thinks they were too busy. 'The car was full of people so there wasn't really a chance,' he says.

'I talked to him more when we got back to Jay's house but I don't think the JW thing came up. But something must have been sown because sometime later there came an invitation to go to Rookswood to talk about JWs with him and his family.'

Remembers Jay, 'I had to do it all again after the car rally because they didn't see each other. The next thing was that Cliff came to supper with me alone and talked about the JWs and I said, "I can't answer these questions but Bill can." So he asked me to bring Bill along to his home.'

After this meeting Latham felt he needed theological support as the questions were now quite specialized, focusing on differences between the teachings of Jehovah's Witnesses and those of historical Christianity. Having a fastidious mind, Cliff wanted to be absolutely sure of all the possible interpretations of the key passages in the Bible.

'None of the family were actually paid-up members at the time but they were all quite in favour and arguing from a Jehovah's Witness position,' remembers Latham.

'The discussions were very high-powered right from the word go and with my somewhat limited Crusader theology I found myself on pretty thin ice. I thought I was floundering and was aware that I needed to bring in people who had more authority than I had.'

Graham Disbrey, a friend from Finchley who was also involved with the Crusaders, was recruited for the next meeting. It took place in December 1964, while Cliff was appearing at the Palladium in the pantomime *Aladdin and His Wonderful Lamp* (for which the Shadows had written the entire score). They arrived at around eleven o'clock at night and Cliff's mother served them coffee as they waited for Cliff to return.

'It must have been after midnight when he finally got back,' says Disbrey. I remember him saying, "Right, where are your Bibles? Let's get down to it!" He wanted to get on with things straight away.

He went out of the room, came back armed with a Bible and we started discussing.

'I can't remember exactly what we talked about. Bill and I were very young, very naïve and terribly conservative in our views and we just fired everything we had at him and he fired everything he had at us.

'It was a heavy time and I think we were basically trying to score points off each other. The core of the discussion was about whether Jesus was alive today, whether you could enjoy a personal relationship with a loving God, and how it affected our daily lives.

'This went on for most of the night. When Bill and I got back to Finchley the dawn was breaking.'

The next person brought in to bolster the cause was David Winter, a layreader at Latham's local church, St Paul's in Finchley, and editor of the magazine *Crusade*. Winter had a keen intellect, a good grasp of theology and an ability to discuss it in non-specialist language.

The surprise for Winter was to find that Cliff's questions weren't those typical of an unbeliever, but of someone who respected the Bible but was unsure of the correct interpretation.

'Most people searching for Christianity have moral objections and questions,' says Winter. 'They want to know whether their lives will have to change. They don't want to be seen as nuts or religious maniacs. They can't stand church. They think Christians are weirdos. But with Cliff there was none of that.

'He would say, "I can't see how you can believe that Christ is the Son of God. The Bible doesn't teach that." What his experience with the Jehovah's Witnesses had done for him was to convince him of the authority of the Bible. He didn't want any other arguments. Arguing with him like this drove me back to the Bible and I know it drove Bill and a few others back to the same place to find the answers.'

Graham Disbrey was Latham's closest friend at the time. They had known each other since they were boys, had been Crusaders together and were now both teaching at the same school. But, following the meeting at Rookswood, Disbrey noticed that Cliff was taking his place in Latham's life.

'It was actually quite difficult for me,' he admits. 'Bill and I used to do things together and suddenly his time was taken up and he couldn't exactly say why. He was very discreet and wouldn't tell me what was happening but I would know that the big car was outside his house which meant that Cliff was there.

'I suppose I was a little envious. My nose was put out of joint. Bill used to collect me in the morning to take me to work and it was a bit difficult to know how to start a conversation at the beginning of the day. Bill wouldn't always say whether Cliff had been around the previous evening or exactly what was going on.'

Clearly Latham was becoming more than a religious adviser. Despite the gulf in their interests and in their experiences of adulthood the friendship was obviously fulfilling a deep emotional need in Cliff's life.

It wasn't as though Latham was replacing any close friends in Cliff's life. All his friends since leaving school had been business associates of one sort or another. There were no ties to cut because no ties had been made.

'I think Cliff desperately needed somebody who was wholly trustworthy and that he could look up to because everyone was looking up to him,' says Disbrey. 'He needed somebody to spend time with who was utterly reliable, absolutely confidential and I think he found that in Bill.'

It was this friendship and the wider circle of Latham's friends as much as the theological arguments that attracted Cliff to Christianity.

'I was so much into my Christian circle of church fellowship, youth fellowship and Crusader classes,' says Latham, 'that I thought the best exposure I could give Cliff was to meet Christians and introduce him to a Christian lifestyle.'

When Bill taught his Crusader class in Finchley, Cliff would sit quietly at the back listening. At first the young people were impressed to be joined by a pop singer but after a few weeks they just accepted him as one of them. He even attended church services at St Paul's, finding himself attracted to the sheer ordinariness of the people.

He was now arguing far less from the Jehovah's Witness viewpoint and was beginning to absorb the outlook of those around him. David Winter remembers that the most significant change came when he shifted to arguing from an evangelical Christian point of view.

Wonderful Life was premiered in July, the same month that the Beatles made their film debut in *A Hard Day's Night*. Whereas *Wonderful Life* had a contrived madness about it, *A Hard Day's Night* managed to communicate a refreshing irreverence, and, whereas Cliff had adopted a middle-class accent and had middle-class values, the Beatles rejoiced in their working-class roots.

Cliff was beginning to look dated. Almost all the new groups had long hair brushed over their foreheads. They dressed in Cuban-heeled boots, leather waistcoats and high-collared shirts. Cliff was still neat and Brylcreemed with well-polished shoes and mohair suits.

The music too was changing. The Shadows sounded clean and clinical in contrast with the raunchy, often distorted, sounds of those who had schooled themselves in primitive rock 'n' roll and the electric blues of Chicago.

Cliff was sometimes heard commenting on the 'noise' of the Rolling Stones, or saying that the Beatles played out of tune. He failed to realize that part of the appeal of the new music was its unpolished nature. The point wasn't to play and dress with precision, but with feeling.

The subject matter of pop was also becoming more adult. Sparkling innocence and obedience were giving way to expressions of anger, boredom and restlessness and a desire for social change. It was also no longer taken for granted that teenagers were sexually inexperienced.

A twenty-year-old 'beat fan' interviewed by *Melody Maker* in a feature which looked at shifting tastes said, 'I grew out of my Cliff Richard days a couple of years ago. When I look back I think how soppy I must have been. Groups now like the Beatles and the Stones have really got something and I can't see me getting tired of them. Not until I'm old anyway.'

It was just before Christmas 1964 that the press finally caught on to the fact that Cliff was becoming increasingly serious about religion. A *Daily Express* reporter approached him outside Rookswood and asked him about the rumours that he was a Jehovah's Witness.

'I am thinking about God,' he admitted. 'This is a very personal thing. It was Licorice Locking who set me thinking. I am not considering joining the Jehovah's Witnesses... I'm just thinking a lot about God. That's all. It's very important to me.'

Left July 1962: Cliff with his leading lady, Lauri Peters (far right), and other members of the cast of *Summer Holiday*

Right Cliff with the Shadows in their new line-up which included bass player Licorice Locking (rear) and drummer Brian Bennett (centre)

Below Cliff with girlfriend Jackie Irving. Taken while on tour in South Africa

Above 1962: Listening to a playback of the sound track for *Summer Holiday* – (from left to right) producer Norrie Paramor, engineer Malcolm Addey, Licorice Locking, Cliff, Hank Marvin, manager Peter Gormley

Above October 1963: Rehearsing with Susan Hampshire for dance scenes in *Wonderful Life*

Right Mobbed by British fans

Left July 1964: Hunting for clues during a car rally – Bill Latham and Cliff on the day of their first meeting

Right April 1965: Graham Disbrey (third from left) with Cliff on his first Crusader holiday on the Norfolk Broads

Left Bill Latham (left) and Cliff on board one of the Crusader holiday boats

Above 16 June, 1966: Cliff addresses the crowd of 5,000 that couldn't get into Billy Graham's Earls Court rally. This was the day Cliff's Christian faith became public

Below Cliff with Norrie Paramor – producer, arranger and father figure

Left California, July 1968: (from left to right) John Davey, Graham Disbrey, Cliff, Bill Latham, Peter Graves and Peter Hutt

Above April 1968: Cliff with the Settlers – (from left to right) John Fyffe, Cindy Kent, Mike Jones, Cliff and Geoff Srodzinski

Right 1968: Cliff and the Settlers returning to Britain after playing a groundbreaking gospel concert tour in Croatia (then Yugoslavia)

Above Cliff sings 'Congratulations', Britain's entry in the 1968 Eurovision Song Contest

Above April 1970: Cliff speaks and sings at Kingsway Hall, London, as part of his Christian work

Above May 1970: Cliff plays student Clive Harrington alongside actress Pamela Denton in Peter Schaffer's stage play *Five Finger Exercise*

Left Cliff and Una Stubbs in his early seventies BBC TV series 'It's Cliff Richard'

Below Cliff with the beard he grew for the part of James Callifer in Graham Greene's *The Potting Shed*

Right October 1971: Cliff with his long-standing friend Olivia Newton-John

Above On stage in the mid seventies: (from left to right) Terry Britten, Cliff, Alan Tarney, Olivia Newton-John and Trevor Spencer

'THE *seventeen* CLOSING OF ONE DOOR AND THE OPENING OF ANOTHER'

To his colleagues in the music business it seemed quite bizarre that Cliff's social life was now centred on a group of young North London schoolteachers. Who else, given unprecedented fame, money and female attention would eschew it all for teenage Bible classes in the leafy suburbs and the occasional drink in a Hertfordshire pub?

'What on earth do they find to talk about?' asked an incredulous Bruce Welch at the time.

Yet it was in the company of these Crusaders, none of whom knew much about pop music, that Cliff was to negotiate his re-entry into normal life.

For six years he had been living in a world where he was overprotected, overpraised and overpaid. In Finchley he could almost be Harry Webb again. No one wanted anything from him and no one appeared to be overawed by his status.

'He gave the impression of being very happy to join in my lifestyle,' says Bill Latham. 'He seemed to be glad to be doing ordinary things again. He'd had all those years of a pop star's lifestyle and now he was mixing with people who had nothing to do with show business.'

Because of the Christian ethos it was also a sexually unthreatening environment. There was no pressure to pair off because singleness didn't have the stigma it had elsewhere, and none of the group believed that masculinity was proven by sexual conquest.

Peter Graves met Cliff in September 1965 while waiting to take a diploma in education at Oxford.

'I think that one of the things that attracted him to our group was the fact that there were no girls to bother him,' says Graves. 'We were an all-male group. If girls did join us they were always on the fringe.'

During Easter of that year he joined 24 young Crusaders for an eight-day boat trip on the Norfolk Broads and was relieved to find himself treated as just another crew member. He played guitar for their sing-songs, cooked shepherd's pies and was subjected to pillow fights before lights-out.

The interviews he gave around this time show that these simple activities were making an impression. He wistfully envied the less-pressured lives of his new friends and could see that a great schoolteacher probably did more for the world than a celebrated pop star.

'Records don't mean all that much any more,' he told the music weekly *Disc*. 'Sometimes I'd love to have a job where I could work regular office hours and have weekends off.'

To the *Daily Express* he admitted that he was catching up with the life he had missed out on as a teenager.

'I feel I could do a lot more with my life. If this feeling continues for another year I will make a decision about my future. I could probably work in show business for the next twenty years. But if the day comes when I don't feel satisfied, I'll get out.'

For the first time in his career, Cliff was clearly out of sync with the times and apparently unconcerned. While he played cabaret at the London Palladium and put out singles like 'Wind Me Up' and 'The Time In Between', the sounds that would eventually define the decade were being produced – such songs as 'Help' by the Beatles, 'Satisfaction' by the Rolling Stones and 'My Generation' by the Who.

'Christianity had become pre-eminent in everything I did,' says Cliff. 'It changed my priorities. I had been rejuvenated and my career seemed uninteresting. At the same time the success of the Beatles and the Stones had shelved me and the Shadows. We were now the oldsters.'

He was also spending a lot less time with his mother, a situation which profoundly affected the still-young widow.

After Rodger had died in 1961 Dorothy Marie had seemed to blossom. No longer burdened with the problems of financing a home or being under the rule of a much older man she was enjoying the perks of being a pop star's mum.

'She was a totally different person after Cliff's father died,' remembers Pete Bush. 'She seemed to come out of her shell and want to be with Cliff. I don't know if it was out of wanting to be protected because of the loss of a husband but she seemed to be with him a lot more.'

Olive Queenie remembers it as a time of high excitement, 'All of these things were happening to Cliff and she was enjoying life for the first time. Instead of having to slave away to get things for people it was all coming to her easily and she was going overboard with it.

'She married her first boyfriend more or less straight from school and never knew what it was like to be adventurous and flirt and do all the things that girls do.'

She had become Cliff's constant companion as he attended film premiéres and ate out at fashionable restaurants. But with Cliff's involvement in the Crusaders, that began to change. Cliff no longer required her company as much as before and he was frequently absent from Rookswood for days while he stayed with Bill Latham and his mother Mamie.

'It was difficult for Cliff's mum to see him leave her and join another family,' Latham admits. 'It was compounded by the Christian dimension because she was getting more involved with the Jehovah's Witnesses. In the early days I think she thought that I had poached him and I know that she voiced this apprehension to other people.'

She began to feel lonely and it was in this state that she drew close to Derek Bodkin, a chauffeur hired for her by Cliff as she didn't drive and felt cut off living in a country house. Bodkin would take her shopping in London and to visit relatives. He would play badminton with her at a local club and later moved into a lodge at the entrance to Rookswood.

Out of this close association developed an unlikely romance between a 45-year-old mother of four children and a 23-year-old driver. At first, no one suspected anything because the two had so little in common. He wasn't a Jehovah's Witness, didn't have an interest in pop music, and admitted to being clumsy around women. Their continuing closeness was excused on the grounds that it was Bodkin's job to be at her beck and call.

'She came to see me when I was living in Manchester,' remembers Olive Queenie. 'Derek had driven her up. He was introduced to me as the chauffeur. I had never met him before. I was a little bit worried because by certain things that were said you could tell something was going on. I was thinking, "Surely not! He's younger than her son!"'

By February 1965 Cliff had become so integrated into the Crusaders set that he considered himself a Christian. When Ray Coleman of *Melody Maker* asked him what he thought of John Lennon's stinging comment that he found his singing voice 'too Christian' he responded, 'I'm glad it shows because I am a Christian and I don't want anyone to get any other idea. That's the way I am and I have no intention of covering up the fact.'

Yet his Crusader friends felt that even though he was becoming more 'Christian' by imitation he had not yet become a Christian by conviction. He appeared to regard Christianity as the highest level of decent living rather than as a change of heart.

'He was doing all the right things with all the right people in all the right places but I think that in his inner self he knew he hadn't reached the point of commitment,' says John Davey, a Crusader leader in Sussex.

'I think we all sensed that he was very close and there was a great deal of speculation between us about what would happen if he did make a public announcement.'

During a Crusader camp at Lewes, Graham Disbrey posed him the simple question: 'How can you be sure that you are a Christian?' Cliff later confessed that this was the provocation he had needed on the final stretch of his spiritual search. It bothered him that he had no answer other than to say he was British, he didn't think himself particularly evil and he believed in the existence of God.

Neither Cliff nor Bill Latham is now sure exactly when he made the decision that removed all doubt. In interviews of the period he refers back to 1965 and on 20 March 1966 he gave a talk on 'Christian Maturity' at Lewes YMCA, yet in his biography *Which One's Cliff?* he pinpoints May 1966 when he was making *Finders Keepers*, the last of his youth-orientated films.

What isn't disputed is the fact that it was in his bedroom at the Lathams' at 124 Etchingham Park Road, Finchley, that he prayed the prayer that ended the search.

A Crusader friend, Roger Stacey, had recommended that he check out verse twenty of Revelation chapter three, the last book in the New Testament. He told him that there he would find the key to his questions.

Before going to sleep that night Cliff opened his Bible and read the words of Jesus: 'Here I am! I stand at the door and knock. If anyone hears my voice and opens the door, I will go in and eat with him, and he with me.'

'I thought that this was it,' he remembers. 'I thought that if this was true I wanted to become a Christian. I didn't know how to do it though. I knew that the door was, figuratively speaking, the door of my life but I thought – how do you open it?

'I just remember saying the words, "Come on in. I want you in my life." Then I went to sleep. I didn't feel very religious the next day but, when I look back, that's when things started to change.'

June 1966 was an important month for British evangelical Christians. Billy Graham, the best-known preacher of his generation, was coming to London for a four-week crusade at Earls Court, his first in Britain since 1954.

There had been no public announcement, but word of Cliff's conversion had spread and an invitation came from the Greater London Crusade asking him to appear as a guest on the night of 16 June, a youth evening at which England cricketer Colin Cowdrey would be reading the lesson.

His career, he knew, would be on the line. If it was seen as a gimmick, it would backfire, and even if he was believed to be sincere there was no guarantee that his fans would continue to support him. In the era of drugs and mysticism Christianity was not a cool religion for a pop star to embrace.

His management were naturally concerned that Cliff could be

exploited by the American evangelist, whom they knew little about, or that he could become so absorbed by religion that he would let his career slide.

'They were worried about it,' admits Mike Conlin. 'They had already had the trouble with Licorice Locking. But it was a vague worry rather than a fretful worry. They thought, "If he gets into that kind of rubbish we'll have to watch him like a hawk otherwise he'll be knocking on doors."'

The night of the appearance there were 25,000 people packed into the Earls Court arena with an additional 5,000 outside listening to the service on a sound-only relay. Cliff, who had been seated on the platform along with churchmen and dignitaries, made his way forward to the lectern, dressed in a corduroy jacket and horn-rimmed spectacles.

In a brief statement he credited his parents for rearing him on the Bible and ended by saying, 'I can only say to people who are not Christians that until you have taken the step of asking Christ into your life, your life is not worthwhile. It works. It works for me.'

He then sang 'It Is No Secret', a gospel song which Elvis had recorded, and when he walked away from the lectern he found he was so nervous that his arms remained in their outstretched position. When the meeting ended, Cliff went outside and addressed the crowd of 5,000 who hadn't been able to get into the arena.

Two days after Earls Court his mother married Derek Bodkin at Epping Register Office. The first Cliff knew of the impending wedding was a call from someone in a public phone inviting him to the reception at Rookswood. He went and filmed the couple as they were showered with rose petals from a balcony over the front door and then they drove off for their honeymoon in an E-type Jaguar.

Confronted by the press at Pinewood Film Studios where he was shooting *Finders Keepers*, Cliff kept up his usual jaunty exterior, admitting that he hadn't known of the wedding until that morning but saying that he hoped his mother and Derek would be very happy. 'I'll be buying them a house as a wedding present and they'll be going to my place in Portugal.'

The pleasant chatter concealed his real feelings. He was disturbed by the relationship, not because he disliked Bodkin, but because he thought that the age difference problem would be insurmountable.

Having lost Cliff to Bill Latham had she, in effect, married on the rebound? Bodkin himself may have unwittingly put his finger on the problem when he later said in an interview with the *Sunday Express*: 'I suppose I have taken over Cliff's place in Dorothy's life.'

Cliff's old way of life was fast disappearing. His mother was gone, Jackie Irving was dating his old rival Adam Faith and for the first time in six years (since 1960) he didn't appear in *NME*'s annual points list of best-selling singles.

Whatever was left standing he dismantled himself. His highly successful official fan club which Jan Vane had been running since 1958 was wound down, Rookswood was put on the market and in November 1966 he announced that he would be making no personal appearances during 1967.

'It was the closing of one door and the opening of another,' says Cliff. 'Up until that time I had felt responsible for my family. When my mother married I knew I could do what I wanted – which I did. I moved in with Bill and his mother. I wanted a different scene.'

For his fans, the most staggering news was that Cliff was considering becoming a schoolteacher. The notion had been floated a few times before, usually out of admiration for friends such as Bill Latham and Graham Disbrey, but now he appeared to be serious.

Through John Davey, a teacher at Lewes County Grammar School in Sussex, he arranged to take an O level in Religious Education and by sitting in on lessons at the school he was able to test the response of ordinary pupils to his presence in the classroom.

He also spent two months at Oak Hill, an Anglican theological college, where he studied the Bible and learned how to articulate his faith.

'I was the one who tried to get him to be a teacher,' admits Jay Norris. 'I believed that he would make a good teacher. I took him to meet the principal of Trent Park Training College in Cockfosters who said that if he got a couple of O levels they would take him.'

He was now so surrounded by schoolteachers and lecturers that it wasn't surprising that education should become his chosen alternative profession. Of his Crusader circle of friends Graham Disbrey taught art and design, Bill Latham taught religious education, John Davey taught chemistry, Peter Graves became a professor of German and John Harvey was a lecturer in aeronautics.

At the same time he was questioning whether show business was a worthy occupation for a Christian. Could he be guilty of setting himself up as a 'false idol' for teenagers? A recurring theme in interviews of the time was his desire to 'do something' with his life.

These misgivings, which had been building up long before his conversion, were confirmed by those Christians who thought that the entertainment industry was ungodly anyway. Some of them didn't own televisions on principle, never went to the cinema and maintained a Puritan attitude towards the theatre.

Coupled with a disapproval of smoking, drinking, dancing, swearing and make-up, it meant that a life on the stage was unthinkable for the thoroughly evangelical Christian because even if you weren't doing bad things you would surely be rubbing up against those who were.

The prohibition was rarely spelt out but anyone new to church circles would be quick to notice that there were no role models for committed Christians in show business. There had been actors and pop singers who had converted but the happy ending was almost always that they abandoned their worldly trappings and were now happier than they had ever been in what was known as 'full-time Christian world'. When Terry Dene had become a Christian, in September 1964, he got rid of his guitar and his records, and changed his name back to Terry Williams.

The implication was that show business, like sin itself, was something to be spurned and that anyone who secretly enjoyed the goings on at the London Palladium more than chorus singing at the church hall was spiritually suspect.

'The evangelical world had its own pressures which operated without a word ever being said,' says Cliff. 'I felt that I ought to leave show business. The majority of my friends hadn't actually said anything to that effect. They hadn't said, "Get thee out", but the pressures were vaguely there. I thought I'd move before it got any hotter and so I made my plans to leave.'

He talked it over with Peter Gormley who agreed to support him whatever decision he came to.

'I thought that was up to him,' says Gormley. 'It was his life. At one stage he asked me how much notice he would have to give to fulfil all his commitments and I can remember telling him that it would probably take twelve months.'

John Davey admits that initially his circle of friends did little to persuade him otherwise. They argued he could probably live comfortably on his earnings to date and could devote the rest of his life to worthier causes.

'He was at my parents' home in Lewes one day when the issue of him going to teacher training college came up,' Davey recalls. 'He actually rang his accountant up right there and then to find out what would happen if he didn't do any more show business work.

'He came off the phone looking quite shaken because he'd been given the news that even if he didn't do another day's work in his life he would be happily secure. He couldn't believe that he could safely sit back.'

The eventual decision to stick with pop was helped by a shift in attitude among some younger Christians who argued that evangelicals had been misguided in their rejection of the arts, media and entertainment. Even his normally conservative Crusader friends conceded that no area of culture was beyond redemption.

'I think we came to see that it would be a loss to show business if he stopped and a loss to Christianity if he didn't take advantage of the opportunities,' says John Davey. 'We realized that there was a definite job for him to do as a Christian believer within show business.'

The most encouraging discovery was a group who were meeting informally to discuss how Christians could become more actively involved in the arts. One of the group was actor Nigel Goodwin.

'We were discussing how it was possible to be a Christian and also to earn our wages as artists,' says Goodwin. 'I had this vision of a centre being created in London where Christian artists could meet and debate with their peers. Cliff started to come along to these meetings.'

David Winter was another group member, and in his role as editor of *Crusade* he chided those who withdrew from the arts and then became dismayed when other world views came to predominate. He encouraged his readers to listen to what non-Christian artists had to say about the human condition.

Winter helped to persuade Cliff that he had two valuable assets which he shouldn't waste: his performing talent and his audience.

Independent of these discussions, Winter was involved with American film director Jim Collier in developing the story for a Billy Graham movie which would be set in contemporary London. Although Cliff wasn't under consideration at the beginning, this was to be the project which confirmed him in his growing belief that he could marry his faith to his work.

The result, *Two A Penny*, with a screenplay by Stella Linden would not have merited much attention outside the Christian community had it not been for Cliff's involvement. The brief review in *Halliwell's Film Guide* called it 'Naïve religious propaganda sponsored by the Billy Graham movement and featuring the evangelist in a cameo. A curiosity.'

Yet for the Billy Graham Organization it was a departure from the conversion stories disguised as dramas which it had been making since the fifties. The main differences were that *Two A Penny* was marginally more realistic and the hero of the film, played by Cliff, didn't get 'saved' on camera. The puzzle was left with the audience rather than solved by the film maker.

Cast as a drug-dealing art student called Jamie, Cliff at least tackled the role of someone less virtuous than the squeaky-clean hero of *The Young Ones* and *Wonderful Life*. He got to fight, swear, shout and wear stubble on his chin.

'Among Cliff's Christian friends there were people who were quite pleased that he was thinking of giving it all up,' says Winter. 'But Jim Collier was the person who tipped the balance. He said, "Look what you can do! You can't throw all this away."'

Because Cliff had never been someone to whom people looked for guidance on daily living it was harder for him to find a natural way of expressing his new-found beliefs through his work. His songs didn't articulate his inner anxieties.

Entertainment, to be successful, had to reassure rather than disturb, to sweep people off to a fantasy world of sweetness and light rather than plunge them into debates about the security of their souls.

It was easier for novelists, poets or those in the fine arts to incorporate spiritual discovery into their creations than it was for a man who performed other people's songs. During 1967 Cliff struggled with the issue of whether it was possible to Christianize his brand of entertainment.

His first steps towards working out an answer were necessarily faltering. There were no examples to follow. Norrie Paramor suggested that he might like to do a gospel album. After all, Elvis had recorded gospel material and it hadn't adversely affected his career.

Cliff acted on the suggestion and in February 1967 he went into Abbey Road Studios to begin recording *Good News*, a collection of spirituals, hymns and gospel songs, while the Beatles recorded their 'Magical Mystery Tour' EP in the studio next door.

Yet while the Beatles' lyrics were dissected by those keen to understand the group's shifting point of view, and only rarely were the group interviewed in depth, Cliff was increasingly being drawn into debate and argument about his faith. For producers of religious radio and television programmes he was a welcome alternative from the parade of vicars and bishops who dominated the 'God slots'. For Cliff it was an opportunity to say what he could never say in his singles.

In the 'love and peace' summer of 1967 Cliff was to be found on British television discussing his faith with Billy Graham and 'Ready Steady Go' presenter Cathy McGowan. In July he was brought into ABC's studios to face a roasting by ex-Manfred Mann singer Paul Jones, who had just starred in *Privilege*, Peter Watkins' futuristic film of a pop singer who is tamed by the church and then used to curb teenage behaviour by making young rebels subservient to the state.

The programme, 'Looking For An Answer', began by showing a clip from the film contrasted with shots of Cliff at Earls Court with Billy Graham. Jones, then an outspoken atheist, accused Cliff of being an instrument of the established church.

Cliff denied that he was being used in this way. 'I put myself in God's hands and say, "Look if this is the thing I ought to do I shall do it,"' he said. 'The church is just, I think, a front. You know, it's a name. We are always fooled by words and names and things.'

Jones: 'Well, one of the bishops in *Privilege* says, when he is accused of using the pop singer to further the ends of the church, "Once they used a Spanish Inquisition and this is less painful." You know, it's exactly what you have just said, really.'

Cliff: 'Before I came on the scene Graham packed out places like Earls Court. He doesn't need me.'

Jones: 'But people don't know what they're coming for. Billy Graham knows why people go to his meetings is the same reason people in American spent $125 million in one year going to fortune tellers. They are insecure; they're unsure. They don't know what they're going for. Right, so you say: "We are giving them Christ." I say you're not. You're giving them a show...'

What Cliff offered was not a dazzling display of Christian apologetics – in fact his statements were often extremely unsophisticated – but a simple admission that he had 'accepted a thing called salvation which means that if I die I can look forward to an eternal life of peace and joy and no pain'. (Interestingly, Jones went on to become a Christian himself.)

Within the next few years Cliff was to become one of the most visible defenders of the Christian faith. Just when the trend among rock musicians was to 'let the music do the talking' Cliff was pouring out the first of millions of words which would attempt to answer the public's questions on everything from Bible reading to nuclear warfare. Never before had a pop star committed so many opinions to print on behalf of something other than his own career.

With David Winter he collaborated on Christian books. The first of these was *New Singer, New Song*, a biography which had his conversion as a convenient last chapter and his confirmation by Graham Leonard (later to be Bishop of London) in December 1967 as the final page: 'It was another great turning point, in its way: like Hoddesdon, and Butlin's, and "Oh Boy!" and Earls Court, and yet so natural, so easy, that it seemed that all his life up to this moment had merely been a preparation for it. It was – and no simile could possibly please Cliff more – just like coming home.'

The next, *The Way I See It*, was a collection of answers to the sort of questions he had been bombarded with since becoming a Christian.

'We sat down with the questions and Cliff just spoke his answers into a tape recorder,' says David Winter. 'I often didn't agree with what he said but it all went in the way that he said it.'

It was a hard time to be saying the things that Cliff was saying. Although the sixties' search for alternative lifestyles was a rejection of materialistic culture, Christianity was too closely associated with the old order to merit much serious consideration.

At a time when, in the wake of the more widely available contraceptive pill for women, 'free love' was being advocated, Cliff was having to say, for instance, 'Sex outside marriage is always wrong.' At a time when recreational drugs were all the rage Cliff was saying, 'Drugs ruin your health, turn you into a sort of zombie and, in many cases, finally cause death.'

To the hippie generation, listening to Cliff was like listening to their parents who were always advising moderation or abstention and who always seemed to think that the government knew best.

One of the questions asked in *The Way I See It* was 'Do you see yourself as a conformist?' Cliff answered that he was not a conformist because conformism is a result of peer pressure and he has never altered his views in order to gain the approval of his peers.

This is one of the paradoxes of Cliff's life, that while he always seems eager to please and his show business career is built on giving people what they want, he is determined to do things his way and never acts against his conscience.

His decision to go public as a Christian was an example of this. Faced with the option of staying quiet and continuing to fulfil audience expectations or speaking out and risking rejection he hadn't hesitated to take the more dangerous route.

'I don't think I've ever met anybody who is as sure of himself as Cliff is,' observes Tony Meehan. 'I don't think I've met anyone who was integrated in the sense that he believes he's right and that's it. He was always like that.

'The public often think of him as being soft. He's a very charming and personable man but beneath that I think it's sheer metal and that doesn't come across to the public.'

DROPPING BACK
INTO SUBURBIA

Approaching the end of his first decade in show business, Cliff was virtually unscathed by trauma or scandal. Many of those who had shared in his success had already buckled under the pressure.

Jet Harris was an alcoholic and had suffered a nervous breakdown, Bruce Welch was on the brink of a divorce and, during a run at the Talk Of The Town in January 1968, bass player John Rostill collapsed with mental exhaustion and Licorice Locking had to be brought back as his temporary replacement.

Yet while Cliff's level of personal contentment had risen, his creative stock had fallen. No longer 'too sexy for TV', he was beginning to dress like his schoolteacher friends, suppressing the instinct he'd once had to be sensuous and exciting.

While the younger generation indulged in a riot of kaftans and afro hairstyles Cliff was sporting a Beatles (circa 1962) fringe, tortoiseshell-framed spectacles and elephant-cord slacks. In a perverse way he seemed to be toying with the power of his fame; seeing how far from the sex idol he could move without losing the bulk of his fans.

The middle years of the sixties were a golden age for the pop single. You could take the top thirty for almost any week during 1966 and find it jammed with songs now regarded as classics.

In June, for example, as Cliff was performing for Billy Graham, the following singles were in the top thirty: 'Strangers In The Night', 'Wild Thing', 'Sorrow', 'Monday, Monday', 'Sloop John B.', 'When A Man Loves A Woman', 'Pretty Flamingo', 'You Don't Have To Say

You Love Me', 'Paperback Writer', 'River Deep, Mountain High', and 'Sunny Afternoon'.

Cliff, however, wasn't carried along on this wave of creativity. He was too busy developing his spiritual life and dropping back into suburbia.

In the years before his interest in religion he had enjoyed phenomenal chart success. Between 'Living Doll' in 1959 and 'Don't Talk To Him' at the end of 1963 he had had an unbroken run of twenty hit singles each of which sold over one million copies. Yet of the seventeen singles released between then and the end of 1967 only three had topped a million.

His domination of British pop was over. Cliff's high point had come in that dull period between Elvis' induction into the army and the Beatles' conquest of America when he pretty much had the show to himself in Britain. Now he was facing massive competition in a proliferating music market.

But the relative decline in his fortunes was also partly self-inflicted. His career had been his religion. He had worshipped it and forsaken all else for it. Now it had been toppled from this pre-eminent position in his life. 'God became more important than his career,' says Bruce Welch.

In 1966 he told journalist George Tremlett, 'I could leave show business tomorrow. It wouldn't bother me one bit. I'm sure of that. I know now that if someone was to tell me that I couldn't sing any more it wouldn't worry me at all. It's just the way I've changed. If someone had told me that four years ago I would probably have hanged myself. But I've changed a lot.'

It was a confused signal to send out to his fans. It suggested that he was half-hearted about recording and performing. Why should the public respond with passion to material that was no longer created with passion?

'That's what he wanted to do at the time and there was nothing wrong with that,' says Hank Marvin. 'The problem that resulted though was that he still wanted a career and still expected the same results while he wasn't putting the same sort of effort in. It was as though he expected things to happen by accident.'

Tony Meehan was hired to try to give him direction by introducing him to contemporary songs. Cliff had already hooked up with country producer Billy Sherrill who had taken him to Nashville and produced 'The Minute You're Gone' and 'Wind Me Up', both of which became big hits. Cliff then recorded 'Blue Turns To Grey', a song written by Mick Jagger and Keith Richards, which reached number fifteen.

'Norrie Paramor seemed to have lost direction completely at that point,' says Meehan. 'I was brought in to try and bring Cliff up to date. Norrie was very threatened by it. I was supposed to carve myself a place in the office but I didn't fit in. It was hard having been one thing in an organization and then coming back as something else.'

At the age of 54 Paramor, who had overseen Cliff's recording career brilliantly from teenage rock 'n' roll star to show business legend, seemed to be losing touch with a market that was being flooded with new musical influences and technology. While such bands as Cream and the Jimi Hendrix Experience spent days over one song, experimented with new sounds and pushed recording techniques as far as they would then go, Cliff was still only turning up to add his vocals and expected to get at least five numbers completed in a session.

After the watershed year of 1966 the only million-seller Paramor was to enjoy with Cliff was 'Congratulations', written by Bill Martin and Phil Coulter. It was a massive hit, selling over two and a quarter million copies, but it identified Cliff with a jaunty Eurovision sound at a time when rock was actually returning to its roots with the re-release of Bill Haley's 'Rock Around The Clock', 'Lady Madonna' from the Beatles and the Rolling Stones' 'Jumping Jack Flash'.

Phil Coulter had sketched out a song called 'I Think I Love You' with a lyric that went: 'I think I love you/ I think I love you/ I think the world is fine/ When you say that you're mine'. He played it to his song-writing partner in their small Denmark Street office but Bill Martin found the sentiment risible.

'It was terrible,' says Martin. 'I explained to Phil, "You don't say to anyone, 'I think I love you.' You either say 'I love you' or 'I don't love you' – it's either a negative or a positive. It can't be a nebulous thing. It's got five syllables, why don't we try 'congratulations and celebrations'?"'

Martin had nursed the idea of writing a song around the word 'congratulations', thinking it might be possible to write another

'Happy Birthday' or 'White Christmas' – a jingle for any cork-popping occasion.

'Congratulations' is now one of the most recorded songs in Britain with over one thousand versions. It was played outside Buckingham Palace after the wedding of Charles and Diana, and on the dockside at Southampton when British troop ships returned from the Falklands War.

However, in 1968 when it was Britain's Eurovision entry, it lost by one vote to Spain's long-forgotten 'La La La'. It was a bemusing decision which came about in the final seconds of voting when Germany awarded Spain six points, bringing its total up to 29 against Britain's 28.

'I remember that we were taken back stage to get ready to receive the award and then we were given the news that it had lost,' says Bill Martin. 'We were sure that Cliff had walked it and of course after that it became number one in all the main markets outside America.'

Under Norrie Paramor's direction Cliff had moved away from the rock 'n' roll group sound and was now almost always backed by an orchestra. By 1967, less than a fifth of all Cliff's sessions were recorded with the Shadows and in the summer of 1968 he went in the studio with the Shadows for the last time. The title of the track was 'Not The Way it Should Be'.

On 19 December 1968 Hank Marvin, Bruce Welch, John Rostill and Brian Bennett broke up and went their separate ways. The Shadows did not reform until 1974 when the line-up was Hank, Bruce, Brian and John Farrar.

In ten years the Shadows had come from being Cliff's backing group to an internationally recognized group in their own right. They had had thirteen top ten hits but there had been a gap of almost three years since 'Don't Make My Baby Blue' reached number ten.

Like any group that had been together for so long and toured so hard they were beginning to irritate each other. John Rostill and Hank Marvin were constantly arguing, Bruce Welch had met Olivia Newton-John and wanted to spend more time with her and Brian Bennett had recorded a solo album titled, tellingly, *Change Of Direction*.

'We worked too hard and we saw each other too often,' says Bennett. 'If we weren't touring we were recording and if we weren't recording we were doing a film, a pantomime or television.

'In your late teens and early twenties you accept all those things as new experiences, but as you start to mature you realize that there are things that you are not going to put up with about one another.'

Cliff by now had bought a house with Bill Latham in Northcliffe Drive, Totteridge, where they lived with Latham's mother Mamie who looked after them as if they were both her sons.

For someone of his status, his lifestyle wasn't extravagant. His biggest luxuries were the houses, a six-berth boat on the Norfolk Broads and his two cars – an MG and an E-type Jaguar. He followed the Christian practice of tithing, which meant giving 10 per cent of his income to charity, and continued to take only 15 pounds spending money in cash each week from the office.

His holidays were now taken in August with his Crusader friends. The group was always exclusively male and bachelor, and became known as the 'holiday gang'. If any of them married – as John Davey, David Rivett and Peter Graves subsequently did – they inevitably dropped out, though they stayed close friends.

For the first two years they went to Portugal, driving down through France in 1966 in Cliff's E-type Jaguar and John Davey's Vauxhall Victor Estate.

'Cliff identified with the style in which we did things, which was very much on the cheap,' remembers Peter Graves.

'On the way down through France we camped and this was an entirely new experience for him. To him we were all extremely normal and he found that he wasn't put on a pedestal. There are a lot of insults flying between us, a lot of banter, and he soon got caught up in it. Once we'd all got over the initial excitement of meeting him he became an ordinary friend and that appealed to him.'

In 1968 the holiday gang – Bill, Cliff, Graham, Peter and John – met up in Los Angeles where World Wide Films had given Cliff the use of a plush apartment in Burbank and a large estate car in lieu of his fee for *Two A Penny*.

For a month they became tourists, taking VIP trips of Universal Studios and Disneyland, going to an Animals' concert at the

Hollywood Bowl, seeing Tony Bennett play in San Francisco and staying at the Dunes Hotel in Las Vegas.

Neither Cliff nor Bill Latham had much time for the more traditional sightseeing. When John Davey arranged a trip to the Grand Canyon neither of them were interested in going. Similarly, a few years later, when they were all in Israel, Latham preferred to spend his time poolside at Jerusalem's Diplomat Hotel rather than visit the sites.

The Shadows couldn't wholeheartedly get behind the Christian side of Cliff's career, and he didn't expect them to feel as much a part of this work.

Bruce Welch in particular had no time for his religious beliefs and hot-footed it out of the dressing room whenever Bible studies were mentioned. This lack of empathy, plus the fact that the Shadows were suffering internal strife, gave Cliff the freedom to work with other musicians.

The first of these were the folk-rock group the Settlers. Early in 1968 he met the group's singer Cindy Kent, one of the few evangelical Christians in the business. Feeling isolated from the church after six years on the road, a friend had suggested that she turn up at one of Cliff's meetings at St Paul's church in Barnet. Afterwards, in the vestry, they were introduced.

'It was then that I mentioned to him that I was looking for a church,' remembers Cindy. 'I wanted to find somewhere where they would understand my lifestyle and the fact that I couldn't be there every week. He immediately understood my problem and suggested his church. I started going and we became good friends.'

A group from St Paul's, including Cliff and Bill Latham, later saw the Settlers at the Festival Hall. Cliff was impressed enough to ask them to be part of a special gospel tour he was planning to do on behalf of Eurovangelism, a Christian charity which sent aid to European nationals.

The international director of Eurovangelism was Dave Foster, who had met Cliff for the first time on location during the filming of *Two A Penny*. The two men had sat in the back of a van in Shepherd's Bush eating lunch and Cliff had again talked about the possibility of leaving music.

'Cliff said, "Well, what on earth can you do in the business I'm in?",' says Dave Foster. 'So off the top of my head I said, "Why not gospel concerts?" He went away and thought about it and at first he couldn't find any good Christian musicians to work with him because there was virtually no gospel scene at the time. Then one day he called and said he thought he'd found them. I hadn't heard of them but they were called the Settlers.'

Cliff hadn't done a gospel tour before but was intrigued with the possibility of creating a show that would promote his beliefs. With David Winter he discussed whether it should be a programme of hymns or whether new material should be commissioned. David suggested a concert arranged in three sections on the theme of 'Help, Hope and Hallelujah' which would involve gospel songs, spirituals and hymns alongside some thought-provoking secular material.

'The Help section consisted of songs like "Nowhere Man" which were about the longings that people have,' says Dave Foster. 'The Hope section began with "In The Bleak Mid-Winter" and concentrated on the life of Christ through to the crucifixion and resurrection. Hallelujah was a rip-roaring gospel celebration at the end.'

Peter Gormley was uncertain about this new direction and didn't want the show launched in Britain in case it failed and damaged Cliff's primary market. As a result of this Dave Foster set up the first mini-tour with dates in Stockholm, The Hague and Zagreb.

'Cliff very much became a part of us on that tour,' says Cindy Kent. 'There was no feeling of him being the star and us the humble group of backing musicians. Looking back I can see that it was a time when he was sorting himself out, trying to discover what it was he should be doing with his music and his life.'

Even though 'Congratulations' was the biggest hit in Europe that month, Cliff had decided that this was to be his first show without hits.

'I have sung pop songs in Stockholm before,' he told the crowd of 3,000 on his opening night. 'But this evening we want to sing only gospel songs because of the special purpose of this concert.'

No one complained in Sweden but the next day in Holland they found the venue half empty despite the success of 'Congratulations' and prominent national publicity. In a confidential Eurovangelism report after the tour it was noted that this could have been because: 'Some Christians steered clear of what they expected to be an irreverent fiasco and some secular fans shunned what they thought would be a sort of staid hymn singing session.'

Says Dave Foster: 'It was an unusual experience for Cliff to see a half-empty hall. I think the analysis we came up with at the time was probably true. Something like this may have been what Peter Gormley foresaw when he was less than enthusiastic at the beginning.'

The show in Croatia, then Yugoslavia with Tito as president, was a boost for local Christians who were harassed at every turn and refused access to the media. Cliff not only used a secular venue to tell the Christian story but was also allowed to appear live on national television for three minutes before their ten o'clock news.

'We were backstage synchronizing our watches, and even changed the running order that night so that when we went live Cliff would be speaking about his faith and how he became a Christian,' remembers Dave Foster.

'At about a minute before ten he launched into "What A Friend We Have In Jesus" which then faded into the news. Yugoslav Christians, some of whom were really suffering for sharing their faith, were ecstatic that someone had got away with it on national television!'

The head of the country's Baptist Union, Dr Horak, was later called in by the head of Zagreb's secret police. Expecting a reprimand he was surprised to be offered a coffee and some mild compliments about the concert. It emerged that the police chief's teenage daughters had been there and had loved it.

'That was really a turning point for the church in Yugoslavia,' says Dave Foster. 'The money raised was given to local Christians to help with a home for destitute children. This action helped raise their image.

'Two weeks later Dr Horak was asked to meet President Tito which was really something. Then, in 1970, Billy Graham was allowed to do his first visual relays by land line to Zagreb. I don't think any of that would have happened without Cliff.'

While his secular career entered a period of stasis, allowing challengers such as Tom Jones and Engelbert Humperdinck to snatch his crown as Britain's most popular male vocalist, Cliff was learning how to craft a show with a message, not such an easy task for someone whose success had been built on orchestrating female frenzy.

Although he had toyed with song-writing over the years, usually with Hank or Bruce Welch, it was only on becoming a Christian that he had taken it seriously, providing the title track of *Two A Penny* and, late in 1968, writing songs with David Winter for a Tyne Tees television series, 'Life With Johnny'.

Based on the parables of Jesus but set in the contemporary world, the half-hour mini-musicals were the idea of religious television adviser Maxwell Dees and David Winter, and just as 'Help, Hope and Hallelujah' was an innovation for Christian music in Britain, so 'Life With Johnny' was a breakthrough for God-slot television.

Cliff was Johnny while Cindy Kent, Una Stubbs and Lynda Marchal (now known as the television writer and novelist Lynda La Plante) played his girlfriends. Twenty songs, some written by Cliff, others by David Winter and Mike Jones of the Settlers, were recorded at Abbey Road for the soundtrack.

'It was recommended at the time by the *ITV Yearbook* as one of the most imaginative bits of religious broadcasting,' says David Winter.

'There were very strong character actors in it and Tyne Tees spent a lot of money on it. Every company showed it except the four majors – Granada, Yorkshire, LWT and Anglia – who were upset that a small company had muscled in and made a programme for the main evening show.'

It was rumoured around this time that Cliff was dating Cindy Kent. After all, she seemed to fit the bill: she was wholesome, she had long hair, she liked music, she didn't wear too much make-up and she shared his Christian faith.

The *TV Times* approached her, ostensibly to write a profile, and during the interview asked what sort of man she would like to marry. She outlined her preferences and the interviewer casually suggested that it sounded as though she was describing someone like Cliff Richard. 'I suppose so,' said Cindy, and that was that.

'When the story came out it was run as part of a series titled "The Men In My Life",' says Cindy. 'They had rung Cliff's mum up to see what she thought of me.

'It was absolutely awful. Girls turned up at Cliff's house weeping, saying "It's not true, is it? He's not planning to marry Cindy, is he?" I rang him up straight away. I was so upset. He just told me not to worry.'

By the end of the sixties Cliff's secular career had settled into a dull and unadventurous rut. The only thing the singles had going for them was that they were 'catchy', in the sense that they could be whistled.

They certainly didn't have soul or musical innovation. Was it really possible to be moved by 'Good Times'? Did anyone care who played guitar on 'Big Ship' or what the lyric of 'Goodbye Sam, Hello Samantha' was attempting to describe?

A similar emptiness could be experienced by watching his television series 'It's Cliff Richard' in 1970 and 1971 where he played some of the same songs and indulged in safe humour with Una Stubbs, Olivia Newton-John and Hank Marvin (who was now one third of the group Marvin, Welch and Farrar).

Olivia seemed wonderfully suited to Cliff. With her attractive white smile and innocent beauty she looked like his female counterpart. The image of togetherness was enhanced by the duets they sang together during the series and a sketch in which they played bride and bridegroom. The public wished them on each other.

Cliff helped launch her career in Britain and Peter Gormley became her manager. After the debut on television he introduced her into his concerts and she and her friend Pat Farrar began singing backing vocals.

There was never any romance. From the time of her arrival in England in 1967 she was involved with Bruce Welch, eventually setting up home with him and getting engaged. When they split up in 1972 she had a relationship with her new manager Lee Kramer before meeting dancer Matt Lattanzi on the set of *Xanadu* in 1980 and marrying him five years later. (They were to divorce in 1995.)

But they were extremely close. Cliff kept framed photos of her at home and at the office and whenever she was in town they would end up going out together. Once they even called a radio station late at night from a hotel room and requested a song.

'I think that it was Capital Radio in London,' says Olivia. 'Cliff called up and said, "Hello, this is Cliff Richard." The DJ said, "Yes, and I'm Elvis Presley." He didn't believe Cliff! Then I called up and said, "Hello, this is Olivia Newton-John." From then on it became a running gag.

'Every DJ that took over would say, "Cliff and Olivia, are you still there? Are you having your breakfast yet?" It was all quite innocent, but that's how rumours start!'

'There was only one girl we thought had a chance with Cliff,' his mother admits. 'That was Olivia. Knowing all the girls he's been out with and knowing him I think that was his chance. If he was going to marry, she would have been the girl.'

Yet, according to Cliff, it wasn't just the fact of her boyfriends that kept them apart.

'I don't think we would have got involved anyway,' he says. 'I'm very fond of her and I guess it's because we never got involved that we can remain such good friends. I feel totally comfortable with her and would like to think she feels comfortable with me. When we see each other we hug each other to death for about ten minutes.

'We feel that close and yet I know there was no romantic thing from my point of view and I never got the romantic vibe from her. Yet, having said that, I never felt put down by it.'

In 1971 Cliff was drawn into the then-lively pornography debate which saw him side with Mary Whitehouse, Malcolm Muggeridge and Lord Longford against the massed ranks of the various liberation 'fronts' and Marxist-Leninist splinter groups which had emerged from Britain's alternative culture.

The Nationwide Festival of Light had been founded by Peter Hill, a young missionary who had returned home to England and been shocked by what he saw as a sharp moral decline. In a very short time he motivated thousands of Christians to register their protest in marches and rallies throughout the country. It was to be a display of solidarity and a reassertion of Christian values.

Cliff was invited to perform at the opening rally on 9 September at Westminster Central Hall in London. The Gay Liberation Front, who saw the Festival of Light as an establishment plan to curb the freedoms they had gained in the sixties, planned to disrupt the event.

Operation Rupert Bear, as it was code-named, was organized by Dennis Lemon (later to be taken to court by Mary Whitehouse in a well-known blasphemy case when he became editor of *Gay News*) and financed by Graham Chapman of Monty Python. It involved a group of GLF members who infiltrated the crowd dressed as nuns and then, as things got going, began shouting 'Glory Hallelujah!' and 'Praise the Lord!' while releasing bagfuls of white mice.

From that point on Cliff became a particular target of left-wing groups, anarchist groups and gay liberation organizations. The homosexual activists suspected that Cliff was a repressed homosexual dealing with his repression by attacking those who had 'come out'.

When he played a 35-minute set at the Festival of Light's final rally in Hyde Park on 25 September he was jeered and pelted with eggs.

'It was early days for Cliff as a Christian and here he was being pitched into public opposition that most of us never have to confront in a lifetime,' says Bill Latham. 'But he took it all without flinching. There was never any question of him retreating!'

nineteen
'A TIME OF GROWTH'

Between 1972 and 1975 Cliff's career slumped to an all-time low. He was out of fashion, out of touch and, for long periods, out of the charts. He was a figure of ridicule to the new rock aristocracy who derided his music as too bland and innocuous.

Just as he had grown his hair, worn chunky crucifixes and started singing songs of love, peace and freedom, the rock culture he must have hoped to relate to had abandoned the good vibes of the sixties for a taste of decadence.

David Bowie, who had appeared on one album cover in a full-length dress, had become the first rock singer to confess to homosexual experience. The American rock star Alice Cooper was grabbing headlines by attacking blood-filled baby dolls on stage with a sharpened axe, and Marc Bolan was draping himself with feather boas and liberally applying mascara.

With hippie culture Cliff had been able to take the buzz words of love, peace, freedom and harmony and invest them with Christian meaning. The new mood of hard drugs, violence and sexual explicitness couldn't be given the same sort of spin. You could possibly interest a hippy in discovering 'real peace' or 'real freedom' but you couldn't honestly claim that Jesus offered the tops in decadence.

Cliff was disturbed by Bowie's use of bisexual imagery and by the mock horror of Alice Cooper. It not only offended his Christian sensitivity but it went against his natural conservativism. His acid test was always whether it would embarrass or shock his mother. If he thought it would then, in his opinion, it had gone too far. It was indecent.

He spoke out against homosexual practice and began to identify himself more with Mary Whitehouse who, as President of the Viewers and Listeners Association, had been fighting a long battle against what she saw as declining moral standards in the media. She vigilantly monitored radio and television output and encouraged her followers to complain about obscene language or scenes of violence and nudity.

'What is this Bowie man/woman image on the stage doing to young people?' Cliff asked at the time. 'He upsets me as a man. There's a great responsibility all of us singers have to the ten year olds and some of us aren't living up to it.'

New Musical Express, which in 1958 had questioned his own suitability for television, was by now on the side of those who offended respectable opinion. It gloried in tales of sleaze, debauchery and drug-taking and saw in Cliff an appropriate figure of hate.

The paper repeatedly pilloried him for his celibacy, his Christian faith and his consummate 'cleanness'. Nick Kent, whose hero of the moment was Rolling Stone Keith Richards, was sent to report on Cliff's appearance at Spre-e '73, a Christian event at Wembley Stadium at which Billy Graham was preaching.

There was no mention of the music. Cliff, he said, 'bounced around flashing his teeth' and looked as though 'he'd just come out of rigorous training for the John Denver "Wimp of the Week" sweepstakes'.

There were feeble attempts to be relevant but they only served to show how out of tune he was. 'Power To All Our Friends' sounded like a belated response to 'Power To The People', but whereas John Lennon sang left-wing orthodoxy with passion and soul, Cliff sang candy-floss lyrics to a Eurovision beat.

'Take Me High' nodded in the direction of the coded drugs songs of the mid-sixties, 'Honky Tonk Angel' mined the same territory as the Rolling Stones' 1969 song 'Honky Tonk Woman' and 'Sing A Song Of Freedom' was an all-purpose anthem with no real message which drew on the popular banner-waving slogans of campus politics.

What was more worrying, for Cliff and his management, was that the fans were no longer buying the singles in such huge numbers. His entire singles sales between 1970 and 1975 were easily beaten by the combined sales of 'Living Doll' and 'Travellin' Light' back in the early days of his career.

His first attempt to put out a religious song as a single was a resounding flop. 'Jesus', released in 1972, was his worst-selling record to date and didn't even make the top thirty. Later the same year he lost Norrie Paramor, who retired from EMI and moved to Birmingham to conduct the Midland Light Orchestra.

Paramor might have lost his magic touch but he'd been in the studio with Cliff for almost every session since 1958, and had become an important father figure. The first single he recorded without Paramor, 'A Brand New Song', was also the first of his career not to enter the top fifty. It seemed to be a bad omen.

The challenge apparently gone from his music, his desire to act was rekindled. He was approached in 1970 by the New Theatre in Bromley to take on the part of Clive Harrington in *Five Finger Exercise*, Peter Shaffer's play about the 'deep friendship' between an artistic student and a tutor.

Controversial when first produced in 1958 because of its veiled treatment of homosexual affection, it was a strange choice of subject matter for Cliff's stage debut in a dramatic role.

'It was about a young fellow discovering his sexual identity,' explains William Gaunt, who played the part of the tutor.

'We discussed the play as a cast but Cliff never related any of the emotions to himself. It was all very much, "Yes, that's interesting – let's get on with it." He didn't flinch from the subject, and he acted very capably, but at the same time I don't think he really put himself into it.

'When I visited his dressing room during the interval on the opening night I found him sitting there signing a pile of photographs. That was indicative of his attitude. It was a job he wanted to do in order to prove that he could do it.'

The local newspaper, the *Kentish Times*, felt that he couldn't ultimately master the role because of his natural niceness and his inexperience. The years hoofing it around in pantomimes and doing cute television sketches for tea-time audiences weren't an adequate training ground for serious acting.

'But within those limitations,' the theatre critic conceded, 'Cliff Richard's straight acting debut at the New Theatre Bromley was a success and a triumph for his determination to make his way in the theatre.'

Emboldened by the experience he returned a year later having grown his first beard to rehearse for a part in Graham Greene's 1958 play *The Potting Shed* but two days before opening night the theatre burned down and the production had to be transferred to Sadler's Wells Theatre in North London.

This time the *Kentish Times* saw an improvement. 'As the obsessed James Callifer he gives a nicely restrained performance that nevertheless has the undercurrent of poignancy and despairing drive.' Cliff has since said that this remains one of his proudest achievements.

The next year he took a part in a television drama, 'The Case', and then in 1974 he renewed his relationship with Kenneth Harper to star in *Take Me High*, with Anthony Andrews and Deborah Watling.

The story of a young merchant banker who goes to Birmingham and revives a restaurant's flagging trade by inventing the Brumburger, *Take Me High* was an artistic and commercial flop.

'We all wanted to prove that we could do a musical film without dances, and the answer is that you can't,' says Kenneth Harper.

'It was rushed into scripting and then rushed into filming. When you get to a point in the script and you think you're up a gum tree a great director can generally invent something but it just didn't happen this time. It didn't make its money back.'

Kenneth Harper and his director David Askey had made the film as if nothing had changed in the world since *Wonderful Life*. There was the same attempt at innocent joviality and coy flirtatiousness but cinema audiences no longer found the immaturity believable.

'As soon as I saw it I realized how old-fashioned it was,' says Anthony Andrews, who was then at the beginning of his film career. 'It was a hangover from a previous era. That was a slightly disappointing realization because during the making of it we'd had such fun. It was like being in *The Young Ones*.'

That year, 1974, Cliff released only one single, '(You Keep Me) Hanging On', and 1975 was his first year without a hit single. 'Honky Tonk Angel' was withdrawn after only a thousand copies had been pressed because it was brought to Cliff's attention that a honky tonk angel is not an attractive piano player but an American prostitute.

'I was at a Christian conference centre with Bill and I was taking questions from the audience when a girl asked me why my new record was about a prostitute,' says Cliff. 'It shook me rigid. I said, "You're joking, aren't you?" I promised to check it out and when I got back home I called Peter Gormley.'

Gormley wasn't sure but called some friends in Los Angeles, and confirmed that a honky tonk angel was at least a 'loose woman' who frequented honky tonk bars, if not a whore. Cliff ordered the record's production to be stopped, and he even went on a pre-booked 'Russell Harty Show' to explain why he wouldn't be performing his latest single.

'I had already sent copies out to the DJs on Radio 1,' says Eric Hall, then Head of Promotion for EMI. 'To make sure the record was completely withdrawn I had to go round personally and take them back because I knew that if I just told them not to play it the records would end up as collectors' items.'

Yet while the first half of the seventies was an artistic and commercial failure it was a time of great spiritual growth. The let-up of pressure gave him the time to work out how the demands of his faith should affect his work.

'It was my growth time as a Christian,' he admits. 'It wasn't planned that way but it gave me time to get my Christian life to a point where I was totally comfortable with it.'

Having moved from Totteridge into a £70,000 house in the exclusive St George's Hill estate in Weybridge, he and Bill Latham regularly began to attend Sunday evening services at Guildford Baptist Church. David Pawson, a noted Bible teacher, would preach 50-minute sermons to a congregation that was over seven hundred strong. Often the church was so packed that the service had to be relayed to ante-rooms on closed circuit television.

Although Cliff never became a member of the church he went as often as his job would allow and a small group was organized to pray with him when he was around and for him when he wasn't.

'When Cliff came to our church I made him a two-fold promise,' says David Pawson. 'One part of it was that I would never ask him to do anything unless he wanted to do it, and the other was that I would never pass on any requests I got for his services.

'I wanted him to have one place where he could come and be himself and not be bothered by anyone else. He usually came in at the last minute and because there were no seats left he would sit on the floor with most of the young people. He was accepted as one of the congregation and the lack of special attention was quite noticeable.'

The move to Weybridge in 1973 had been made possible when Bill Latham gave up his job as a teacher to work with a fledgling relief agency attached to the Evangelical Alliance, an umbrella organization which looked after the concerns of evangelical Christians in all denominations.

A dynamic young vicar in his thirties, George Hoffman, had been hired by them to organize a series of social action projects, one of which was a fund for overseas aid which had been started in 1968 from money sent in by Christians who wanted to see something done in the world's disaster areas. It became known as The Evangelical Alliance Relief Fund, Tear Fund for short.

'The work grew rapidly,' says Hoffman. 'David Winter, who was editing *Crusade* magazine in the same building, said he knew the right person to help me. That was how Bill Latham came to be my assistant. He did what I didn't do and I did what he didn't do.'

Tear Fund bought food and equipment and also sponsored workers to help on existing relief projects. Cliff had made his first donation in 1968 when the £2,000 profit from his first British gospel concert bought a Land Rover for a group in northern Argentina.

'It was very much a venture of faith on Cliff's part,' says Hoffman, 'because there was no way that he was identifying with an established or a prestigious organization. There was only me, Bill Latham, a secretary and a lot of enthusiasm.'

In 1973, more than a decade before Bob Geldof's celebrated visit to the refugee camps of Ethiopia, Cliff became the first major British pop star to visit the sick and dying in the Third World.

He had wanted to experience Tear Fund's work first hand and in November he set off for Bangladesh, the independent republic created in the aftermath of the Indo-Pakistan War, where refugees were flooding in from North India to avoid persecution. The camps were overcrowded and filthy, the refugees sick and undernourished.

He arrived in Dacca with Bill Latham, George Hoffman, and photographer Clifford Shirley and was introduced to the local team supported by Tear Fund. On the first day he was escorted by Liz Hutchison, a young nurse from Devon, who was working with children in a cluster of bombed-out buildings and makeshift shacks that was known as Mirpur Camp.

She picked him up in a Volkswagen minibus which then collected a group of severely malnourished children who needed to be bathed, fed and given medicine at a compound run by the Southern Baptist Mission.

'I don't think he'd ever seen anything like it before,' remembers Hutchison. 'Its very difficult to explain. You can see pictures but to physically touch and smell... it's very different.

'The children he saw were terribly underweight. Their emotional development was stunted. Some were very sick. I can remember going back with him that afternoon in the van and he couldn't say a thing. He was just staring out of the window and you knew it wasn't appropriate to talk. He was obviously trying to cope with all the impressions and emotions.'

During the rest of the stay he visited other camps dealing with similar problems. He saw adults with bullet wounds and burns and saw children dying of starvation. He began to feel a sense of shame about his own life of riches and glamour. What benefit was he to a sick and starving world? Wouldn't one month spent as a relief worker be better than all his years at the top of the charts?

At the end of each day workers and visitors met at the nurses' quarters for prayer and a Bible study led by George Hoffman. In one of the discussions that followed, Cliff expressed his longing to be of more practical use.

'He said, "You know, what I've seen today makes me feel as though I want to give it all up and come out here and work,"' remembers Hoffman. 'Liz Hutchison turned to him very quietly and said, "Can you give an injection or put a person on a drip?" He said, "No, I'd be horrified." She said, "Well you go back home and raise money for us to do it. That's what you can do and this is what we do. That's what it's all about."'

This comment, made without reflection, was to mark a turning point in his life. His songs might not be the sort to change the world but the money they earned could be used to bring about change.

'THE BEST *twenty* THING
I'VE DONE FOR
YEARS'

Cliff was still approaching his career with the attitudes of the fifties when singles mattered and albums didn't; when singers weren't expected to write or even choose their own material and when concerts involved singing a string of hits for twenty minutes.

He had always relied on Norrie Paramor to organize his recordings. After choosing the songs with Paramor and discussing possible musical arrangements, Cliff's only task was to drop by the studio and add his vocals – sometimes five or six in a day. Bruce Welch once said that if Cliff didn't have three hits completed by half past ten in the evening he would think it had been a bad night.

The practice harked back to the days when record companies and music publishers controlled the business and used singers to promote their product. But all this had been broken down in the era ushered in by the Beatles. Power began to return to the artists.

After Paramor's fourteen-year reign, Peter Gormley wanted to try different producers; to move the work around between more people. His first choice was Dave Mackay, a former house producer for EMI Australia, who had come to London to work with the New Seekers.

Mackay knew that Cliff's recording career needed turning round. It had lost momentum. He sat down and talked to him about contemporary music, played him tracks he liked and listened to some of the gospel material that Cliff found interesting.

One of the artists Cliff told Mackay about was Larry Norman, a Californian with shoulder-length blond hair and an acoustic guitar who was writing what the media called 'Jesus Rock'. This was a new type of Christian music that owed more to Bob Dylan and the Rolling Stones than it did to the sort of gospel music that Elvis Presley used to record.

Norman was a mesmerizing stage performer who planned every gesture for maximum effect. He often chided audiences for clapping during his concerts and developed the 'one way sign' (an index finger pointing heavenwards) to indicate where the appreciation should be directed.

Cliff went to see Larry Norman in concert at the Albert Hall and later they met up to talk.

'As soon as we met we started talking about the songs and the reasons I had for writing them,' says Norman. 'He explained the dilemma he was in having to sing music from his past, music for the future and also gospel music.

'He wasn't sure what was the most dignified or credible way to present the songs he really cared about. He seemed very wise and thoughtful about it all.'

Dave Mackay encouraged Cliff to write more of his own material and to work on his playing technique as a way of getting back in touch with the music.

'We had to break down the old routine,' says Mackay. 'I had to tell him that things had changed and that he needed to come in and work with the band. We needed to listen to songs, to work them out and to discuss the strengths and weaknesses. In the past he had only needed to decide what key to sing it in and the next time he heard the song it was already out as a record.'

Through Mackay he met a rhythm section known as Quartet, two of whose members were later to play a major part in reshaping his career.

Guitarist Terry Britten had come to England in 1969 when his band the Twilights, which had been one of Australia's top acts, broke up. Here Britten had joined up again with Alan Tarney (bass), Kevin Peek (guitar) and Trevor Spencer (drums) who had played in the James Taylor Move (nothing to do with the American singer of the same name), an Adelaide band which rivalled the Twilights.

'In those days you had to sing cover versions of pop hits in order to make a living,' says Trevor Spencer. 'But the cover bands in Australia were very good, a bit like the Irish cover bands but not as cabaret-orientated. The James Taylor Move – the singer's name was James and Kevin Peek's middle name was Taylor – played Jimi Hendrix and the Cream. The Twilights played the Hollies and the Beatles.'

Living in flats in West Kensington they had formed Quartet and signed to Decca Records. Fame though was not to come under this name but through working with Dave Mackay as session musicians and later as a working band with Cliff.

'Kevin Peek was the first to play on a Cliff session,' Trevor Spencer recalls. 'He replaced an Australian called Tweed Harris on a tour. When that tour finished they wanted Alan Tarney to join. Then Brian Bennett, who'd been playing drums, left to concentrate on the Shadows and I was brought in.'

Touring with Cliff at this point was a mixed blessing. The up-side was getting well paid for playing some of the chart hits of their youth. The down-side was the brain-deadening experience of playing songs such as 'Goodbye Sam, Hello Samantha' and 'Flying Machine' in northern night clubs where they often had to enter the stage from kitchens slippery with cooking oil.

Tales abound of musicians falling asleep on stage and losing their places in the music. There were times during runs at the Palladium when they would forget whether they were playing the matinée or the evening show. They called themselves the 'scumbags', a derogatory term for pick-up musicians, and planned to turn up wearing T-shirts reading 'Scumbag World Tour'.

'A lot of the musicians just didn't feel involved in what Cliff was doing,' says Trevor Spencer. 'They were more interested in getting drunk than playing. These were tours where we had to dress completely in black and there would be a black backdrop so that we would all merge into the background. They just about nailed the backing singers' feet to the floor so that they wouldn't detract from Cliff.'

'I found this period quite depressing,' agrees Terry Britten. 'I remember Batley Variety Club and these bleak Yorkshire days. You'd go to do the show and there'd be "Congratulations", "Living Doll" and all this stuff and you'd be sitting on a chair stuck behind a music stand, and it had the feeling of being a hired help.

'You'd do the show and there would be the clanging of knives and forks and the smell of scampi and chips everywhere. My heart wasn't in it. It was just a job. But Cliff always gave his best wherever he was.'

Some of his musicians hated the club work so much that they welcomed the annual gospel tours where, with songs like those of Larry Norman's, there would at least be a bit of speed and aggression.

Dave Mackay came into Cliff's career at its most crucial juncture. Without any more hits, Cliff was obviously destined to become a Tommy Steele or Frankie Vaughan type of entertainer who could always sell out a show but who no longer belonged on the top table.

It wasn't only Cliff who had lost his way. Rock music was suffering fatigue after the great party of the sixties. The Beatles, who had led so many of the changes, had broken up acrimoniously. Both Brian Jones of the Rolling Stones and Jim Morrison of the Doors were now dead. The British charts, which had such a short time ago been full of classics, were now laden with acts such as Chicory Tip, Donny Osmond, Lieutenant Pigeon and Terry Dactyl and the Dinosaurs.

Acts which had survived the sixties were no longer sure where they belonged. There wasn't a movement to be part of, and none of them were willing to compete with the likes of Slade, Mud and Sweet by becoming 'glam rockers' – it seemed like such a retrogressive step.

Mackay could see clearly the changes that would need to be made, but initially he wasn't in a position to make them. He had inherited the responsibility of producing a soundtrack to *Take Me High*. The songs, written by Australian Tony Cole, were vacuous and instantly forgettable. Mackay then produced the gospel album *Help It Along*.

Other than the Eurovision entry, 'Power To All Our Friends', which sold over one million worldwide, Mackay's singles were a commercial disappointment with one complete failure and three low-ranking hits.

The project which introduced the changes he had talked about was *31st of February Street*, Cliff's first proper album since 1970. Released in November 1974 it didn't get great reviews, didn't produce any singles and wasn't a best-seller but, with its softer, more introspective mood it at least helped drag Cliff into the seventies and almost half the songs were self-written.

'The recording coincided with my renewed interest in my own career,' says Cliff. 'I suddenly started getting involved in the production side. I started writing.

'Dave would sit down with me and I would play him bits that I had written and he'd tell me what he thought was good and what he thought I should finish. Other than Bill and Tear Fund he was the only person ever to encourage me to write.

'That album was, to me, the turning point of my career.'

But it was Bruce Welch who was to take full advantage of Cliff's new attitude towards his music by laying the groundwork for one of the most durable comebacks in show business history. In one 48-hour period in September 1975, Welch produced 'Devil Woman' and 'Miss You Nights'. These two records, more than any others, were to set the tone for the rest of his career.

There was some irony in that it was Welch who was to help relaunch Cliff's career because the two men had never been close. Privately Welch scoffed at Cliff's religious views and considered himself too down to earth and plain speaking for Cliff's liking.

'Cliff doesn't like my lifestyle and I can't believe his' was how he once put it. 'We don't have anything in common but our love of music.'

He'd come back into the picture through an off-hand remark made by Peter Gormley who was by now quite worried about the state of Cliff's record sales.

'Cliff was putting out records and they weren't becoming hits,' says Welch. 'He was making boring, bland records and he didn't seem to care. The only thing in his life was religion. Peter Gormley, who was still managing me as a member of the Shadows, happened to mention that whoever found the right songs for Cliff would have a strong chance of producing him.'

Since his successes with Olivia Newton-John (he had co-written and co-produced three of her American top ten hits), Welch was keen to do more production. He had good contacts among music publishers and songwriters and began to trawl for new songs, putting the word out that Cliff Richard was ready to shed his middle-of-the-road image. The 'Congratulations' era was over.

On a material-gathering trip to Los Angeles he met Lionel Conway, British-born head of Island Music in Los Angeles, who played him songs by his writers.

'I wasn't really struck by any of them but I said I'd take the tapes away and listen to them again,' says Welch. 'I came back to London and I was in my music room when I played them through again. I still didn't like them but I turned one of the cassettes over and there on the other side was "Miss You Nights" – a song Lionel hadn't even bothered to play me. I knew instantly that it was a smash hit.'

What he was hearing was the work of Dave Townsend, a 26-year-old writer from England, who'd recorded the song not as a publisher's demo but as a track for an Island Records album. Produced at a cost of £20,000, the album had been shelved as uncommercial. The only chance of recouping the production cost was through cover versions of the songs.

Dave Townsend had written 'Miss You Nights' while living in Somerset the year before. His girlfriend, Sally, had taken off for a solo holiday in Majorca and he had turned his feelings of longing and loneliness into a beautiful ballad with hauntingly fresh images. A swelling string arrangement by Andrew Powell on the recording had endowed it with an ethereal quality.

It was this version of the song that Welch took down to Cliff's home in Weybridge one summer evening along with 'Devil Woman' written by Terry Britten and 'I Can't Ask For Any More Than You' by Ken Gold and Michael Denne.

'Cliff put the cassette of "Miss You Nights" on in his music room and the hairs stood up on his arms,' remembers Welch. 'He'd already been given "Devil Woman" some months before but he hadn't done anything with it. I pushed him. I said, "Why on earth haven't you recorded this song?" '

'Devil Woman' had started off as a riff which Terry Britten couldn't find words for and then he linked up with Christine Holmes, a singer and children's television presenter who had been produced by Dave Mackay, and she gave it a title and wrote the story of a seductive fortune teller.

'I had my ideas about this fortune teller song in my notebook and Terry had this guitar riff and we just put them together,' says Holmes. 'We wrote it together at my flat.'

'I knew it had to be a rock number. Helen Reddy had done a song called "Angie Baby" which was a really spooky song and used sounds in the mix that hadn't been used too much in pop music. In my mind I knew that I wanted "Devil Woman" to sound similarly spooky. We both very much knew what we wanted and Cliff copied the demo exactly.'

When Cliff went into Abbey Road to record the three songs, Welch, as producer, retained Alan Tarney and Terry Britten from Dave Mackay's rhythm section but added Graham Todd on keyboards and Tony Rivers, John Perry and Ken Gold on backing vocals.

'It was a great session the day we did "Devil Woman",' remembers Terry Britten. 'The engineer Tony Clark was standing in front of the speakers as it was played back and as quick as a flash he said, "America! This is gonna be a smash in America!"'

Tony Clark remembers the emotion of the session. 'You could feel something was happening,' he says. 'The actual groove of the track was something instant. When I said it was made for America I was probably more excited than anyone else. In those days it wasn't normal to stand up in the control room and shout out loud.'

Three months later, with 'Devil Woman' and 'Miss You Nights' still unreleased as singles, the same team returned to the studio to complete an album of the songs that Welch had gathered.

'I knew what I was capable of but I'd happily got into doing family shows,' says Cliff. 'For this album I was getting songs that publishers would never normally give me because they would insist on sending me material that sounded like "Congratulations". So it was the first time in years that I'd had the chance to stretch my voice and do some rock.'

It now sounded as though Cliff was working with a band rather than dubbing his vocals over one. Although there were still ballads there was a looser, funkier feel to the tracks and a spirit of exploration that had long been missing in his music.

'I had told him that he needed to change the way he recorded,' says Welch. 'I told him I wanted rehearsals, that I wanted to make sure we got the right keys on every song. I changed the way he sang.

He had never sung falsetto. He said he couldn't sing like that. I told him he could. He had just never tried it. Now he does it all the time.'

'Miss You Nights' was the first single to be released, in February 1976, because there was some concern that 'Devil Woman' might get confused with the Electric Light Orchestra's 'Evil Woman' which had entered the charts in January. It sold impressively and returned Cliff to the top twenty for the first time in two years, but it was 'Devil Woman', released two months later, which re-established him as a chart force.

'I was sitting in my kitchen in Epsom and the DJ said he was going to play a record and we should try and guess who it was,' remembers Terry Britten of the first radio play he heard. 'He played this record and my ears went up when I heard the first couple of bars.

'Then everyone started ringing in and getting it wrong and he played it again and there was this tremendous excitement that this was Cliff Richard. No one could believe that Cliff could make a record like this.'

'Devil Woman' sounded like something that the Rolling Stones or at least Elton John would record. The voice was as clean as ever but the sound of the track was dirty and swampy. Cliff had never worked around a riff like this before and this story of seduction conjured up images of dark backstreets in New Orleans; of a world a million miles away from 'Take Me High'.

The writer, Christine Holmes, says that the song is about a man who is seduced by a fortune teller.

'It's a very rude song actually,' admits Holmes. 'But I'm not sure that Cliff was aware how rude it was. My whole thing was to convey that women can be very spooky and clever when they try to snare a guy. They can force a guy into doing things he wouldn't normally do. They can be witches when they want to be.'

Cliff has indeed interpreted the lyric in a different way, believing it to be a warning against dabbling in the occult. This view was endorsed for him when a young woman from Australia wrote to him to say that the song had been instrumental in her Christian conversion. 'I heeded the warning,' she told him.

The music press was enthusiastic about the single, seeing it as a definite return to form. There was talk of the Cliff Richard Renaissance. The record climbed into the top ten, eventually becoming his biggest international seller since 'The Young Ones'.

The album, *I'm Nearly Famous*, released a month later, featured Cliff on the cover lying on a single bed with a notepad and pen transcribing the lyrics of Eddie Cochran's 'C'Mon Everybody' which is spinning on an old-fashioned monophonic turntable beside him.

On the walls are photographs of Elvis Presley, Little Richard, Chuck Berry and Ricky Nelson. Although it was hardly a return to fifties rock 'n' roll it was a return to his own roots as a working musician with band members who could write.

EMI was excited by the album and promoted it heavily, printing 'I'm Nearly Famous' T-shirts and badges which were sported by celebrities such as Elton John, Jeff Beck, Pete Townshend and Elizabeth Taylor. Although he would never be taken up by the emerging punk generation, it was suddenly OK to admit to liking Cliff.

Bruce Welch says that *I'm Nearly Famous* was the album which gave Cliff his credibility back. 'He got great reviews and he had big hits. Since that moment he's just developed and developed. His concerts have got bigger and his money has got bigger.'

Reviewing the album in *Melody Maker*, Geoff Brown wrote, 'Cliff Richard has at last made the sort of album he could, and should, have been making for years. It is with some incredulity I have to say that for the past ten days I've been playing two albums consistently. One is Marvin Gaye's *I Want You*. The other is *I'm Nearly Famous*. The renaissance of Richard, for that is what I believe this album heralds, is long overdue...

'I doubt whether *I'm Nearly Famous* will rid Cliff at a stroke of his straitlaced image as Mary Whitehouse's favourite son, nor, I suspect, would he want it to; for that is what he most likely is. Neither will it win him a whole new concert audience overnight.

'However, it is the best album of new songs ever and, if there are enough unprejudiced ears around, could well mark the start of a fresh Cliff Richard record-buying public. Closet Cliff Richard rock fans? Why not? *I'm Nearly Famous* is, in its way, the most surprising album for many years. Hear it.'

Brown interviewed Cliff in the next issue for a major feature which struck a similarly positive note. Cliff spoke of the forty songs that Bruce Welch had collected and how they whittled the list down to the fourteen or fifteen that were recorded.

'I think it's the best thing I've done for years,' Cliff said. 'It may be the only hit album I'll have had in years. I had more to say about how I would sing, and vocal harmonies and all that. We didn't go into the studio and say we were going to do a certain thing. What we did say was that we weren't going to record anything that sounded like "Congratulations".'

Elton John's manager, John Reid, heard 'Miss You Nights' and wanted to release it in America on his three-year-old record label, Rocket. Elton had long been a fan (he could remember seeing him in pantomime at the Palladium) and it was thought that maybe Rocket could launch Cliff in America in the way that it had recently reversed the fortunes of Neil Sedaka in his home country.

Rocket's Executive Vice President in America was Tony King, a flamboyant English bachelor who had once worked for the Beatles' Apple label, and was closely acquainted with almost everyone who mattered in the rock industry.

He listened to the album and concluded that although 'Miss You Nights' was a good song, it was 'Devil Woman' that stood the better chance of becoming a hit. He had the track remastered to match the sound quality of American radio and it was released in June.

'We cut it really hot,' says King. 'Then I brought in publicist Sharon Lawrence who said that if we really wanted to crack America, Cliff would have to be brought over for a month to do press and radio. Peter Gormley agreed and so I went on the road with Cliff.

'Whenever I had met him before I had been in awe of him and very much on my best behaviour. The thought of spending four weeks with him made me feel a bit nervous.'

The tour party, which consisted of Tony King, Cliff, Sharon Lawrence and Peter Hebbes from Gormley Management, flew from coast to coast taking in major cities such as New York, Chicago, Boston, Memphis, Detroit, San Francisco and Los Angeles. In each city there would be a party for the media and then Cliff would spend hours being interviewed.

For Tony King it was a revelation. He had expected to wilt under withering Puritan scrutiny but instead found himself totally accepted by Cliff. The two became firm friends.

'I was pleased to find that he wasn't quite as abstemious as I had thought,' King says. 'He never got drunk but he liked a glass of wine and enjoyed getting jolly. In fact we ended up calling it the White Wine Tour of America because there would always be white wine at these receptions and by the end of the tour Cliff was getting to the wine waiter before me.

'I had always thought he might be offended if I swore and yet he just shrugged it off. I don't think he minded bad language or a clever *double entendre*. If it was clever then he was one to laugh but what he didn't like was coarseness.

'People imagine he looks down his nose at everyone because of his Christian faith but I found him a really relaxing person to be with. He wasn't at all judgmental. We had a lot of personal talks about our lives and about religion.'

In Atlanta they caught up with Elton John and went to his show at the Omni auditorium. In Los Angeles Olivia Newton-John threw a party for them at her new home. In New York, King, who was a close friend of John Lennon and had been responsible for bringing him together with Elton John, almost managed to arrange a reunion between Cliff and the former Beatle.

'Cliff was fascinated by the fact that I was close to John,' says King. 'He would ask me lots of questions because he always wanted to know what other people were like. I think the John Lennon of that period would have got on very well with Cliff. He was a much softer character and I had told him that I thought he would find Cliff quite interesting. John was up for it.'

He was even given his third and final opportunity to fulfil his earliest rock 'n' roll ambition of meeting Elvis. A magazine journalist, who said he was a personal friend, was ready to bring them together but when he then suggested bringing a photographer along Cliff changed his mind.

'The Elvis I wanted to remember was the one whose door I knocked on in 1959,' Cliff says. 'I didn't want to meet the big fat Elvis. I thought I'd wait until he got himself together.'

Cliff's career in America up to this point had been undistinguished. He'd scored a hit with 'Living Doll' and had twice been on tour but the films had flopped and Rocket was the ninth label to try to do something for him.

It was a source of frustration to him that while he'd conquered Europe, the Far East and all other English-speaking countries he had never become a household name in the country that had given rock 'n' roll to the world.

In America it was possible to have a regional hit but never to be known nationwide. The only realistic way to become a household name was to tour extensively and repeatedly and to spend at least half of each year there.

'I don't think Cliff was willing to give up his life here in England in order to make it in America,' says Peter Gormley.

'We had offers in television that would have meant staying there for up to a year compèring shows and being a part of other shows. He was offered a six-month contract with "Solid Gold" which Dionne Warwick was presenting. We toyed with the idea of flying over every week but then threw it out.'

Sharon Lawrence's game plan in 1976 was not to concentrate on Cliff's past achievements, great though they had been in Britain, nor his standing as a Christian spokesman, but to launch him as if he was a new artist. To have concentrated on his string of British hits would have projected him as a failure.

'We had to promote him as someone fresh,' says Tony King. '"Devil Woman" started picking up interest and getting added to secondary stations in each area but we still needed to crack a primary station. Within a month it began to edge in at the lower end of the charts and then we knew there was a chance it could make it.

'The most important radio stations to get on were those controlled by RKO. If you got on an RKO station it looked as though you were going to make it. The chain was run by a man called Paul Drew who was a friend of mine and of Elton John and of John Lennon but he was a tough guy and he wouldn't do anything to give me a break.

'However, because he was a friend, if he saw that I had something that looked as if it had "legs" he would maybe tip it a little in my direction. But only if the evidence was that he couldn't be accused of helping out a friend.

'When "Devil Woman" looked as though it was really happening he gave us the break that really cracked it. He gave us the number one station in Boston and that gave us a good chart position the next week. Once it performed well on that station the rest fell like dominoes.' The record entered the US charts at number 88 at the end of June and slowly began to climb through July and August.

When it finally broke into the top ten Cliff was playing in Leningrad and Moscow on a ground-breaking Russian visit – the first by a Western rock artist. It was a strange experience of playing to a mixture of sober-suited party officials and excited teenagers, with security guards leaping into action every time anyone showed any physical signs of appreciation.

'We were calling back home to get the *Billboard* chart positions all the time,' remembers Terry Britten. 'The news that it was going up really kept us going out there.'

'Devil Woman' went on to reach number five in the *Billboard* charts and to become an American million-seller. *I'm Nearly Famous* became his first album to make the British charts in a decade.

twenty one
'AGE HAS NOTHING TO DO WITH IT'

In September 1976 Cliff went back into the studios with Bruce Welch to record a follow-up to *I'm Nearly Famous* that would build on its success. This time there were over fifty songs to choose from because publishers no longer had him pegged as a Eurovision singer.

'I think this album is much better,' he said as he recorded what would later be called *Every Face Tells A Story*. 'I think it's more positive. With *I'm Nearly Famous* we accidentally found a new way of doing things. This one says, "Now we know what to do, let's do it!" Everything seems more confident, there's a greater sense of continuity and it's just better.'

It's part of Cliff's optimistic outlook to believe that his current project is the best thing he has ever done. In the case of *Every Face* the truth was that there had been little advance. He had hits with 'My Kinda Life' and 'When Two Worlds Drift Apart' but nothing that reached the top ten. The initial American success was never built on.

'It offers no radical departure or development from *I'm Nearly Famous*,' commented *Melody Maker*. 'Bruce Welch's production is clean and powerful, the songs are, once again, attractive and the musicianship is precise if occasionally verging on the coldly clinical.'

Despite the change in the fortunes of his career, Cliff stuck resolutely to the mix of charity work and show business that had been his lifestyle since 1966 – over a decade. For his first British tour since the comeback he went out for a twenty-concert gospel tour, often staying in the homes of local Tear Fund supporters rather than hotels. He even played to an audience of 1,200 in the centre of Belfast at a time when almost no English acts would take the risk.

His Christian vision remained undimmed. He told concert audiences that his Christian faith was by far the most important factor in his life and that everything else had to take second place. Quizzed by a reporter one evening as to why he divided his career into 'pop' and 'gospel', he answered that it was out of fairness to people who didn't want to sit through an evening of gospel songs. He wanted to be fair in letting the public know what they were getting.

'I'm not misusing my platform. I still have a responsibility to those who don't want to come to a gospel concert so I do a secular tour. I still do a smattering of gospel in that, but I choose music that I think is valid musically, so nobody minds that. There's no other real reason for separating them because I think that musically all of it stands up.'

Coming off this gospel tour (which raised £37,000 for Tear Fund) he went straight into his first secular tour of Britain in two years and then in 1976 paid a return visit to Bangladesh and India.

'We thought it would be a good idea to go back and see how things had changed in three years,' Cliff said. 'And the thing was, it had changed. Things were so much better than they were. We made a film strip to encourage Christians in the West and to show them what can be done in three years.

'There weren't as many beggars in Dacca. Twenty thousand of them had been given housing in this great encampment with thatched huts and gardens. They've had a couple of good harvests as well.'

In India he performed gospel concerts in Delhi, Bombay and Calcutta, seeing the city of his childhood for the first time since his family boarded a train at Howrah station in August 1948.

It was a very different Calcutta that he returned to. He recognized the old landmarks such as Howrah Station, Chowringhee Road and the Victoria monument but was shocked at the sight of people sleeping in the streets. With George Hoffman and Bill Latham he visited Mother Teresa at her hospice and spent a day watching her care for the sick and dying, later praying with her and reading from the Bible.

Because he was performing a gospel concert in Calcutta his visit was well publicized, and the Bengali community welcomed him like a local boy who'd done well and was on a quick visit home. George Hoffman had notified the British Embassy in Calcutta of Cliff's visit and the party was assigned a security guard.

'He was mobbed everywhere he went,' says Hoffman. 'We could never leave the watch of the security. The crowds were just flocking around and Cliff was signing autographs all the time.'

Once back in England, he set about recording his third gospel album, *Small Corners*. It had been natural to offer the project to Bruce Welch after the success of *I'm Nearly Famous* and *Every Face Tells A Story*, but Welch wasn't interested in being involved in this side of Cliff's life.

Remembers Tony Clark: 'He was asked but said he didn't have anything to offer a spiritual album with God lyrics. Cliff was obviously determined to do it and so he chose to produce it himself using me as his engineer because by then our working relationship was very strong.'

It was harder for him to come up with good material for his gospel albums because the pool of writers available to draw on was necessarily smaller. Most of the songs on *Small Corners* were written by American writers of what was becoming known as 'Contemporary Christian Music', which was really Jesus Rock under a different name.

'The problem is that I don't write,' said Cliff during the recording sessions. 'If I was a writer I would probably have done more gospel albums. So I rely on the fact that I listen to a whole lot of albums and then use the best songs in my stage act. This album is full of stuff I've sung in concert for a long time but never recorded.'

While he was preparing to record *Small Corners,* the Sex Pistols had become Britain's latest controversial group, mostly through swearing on live early evening television and being dropped by EMI for courting too much controversy. If there were two polar opposites in the music business it would have to be Cliff Richard and Johnny Rotten, who projected an arrogant petulance on stage and professed not to care about anything.

277

Cliff was bemused and angry about punk. It broke all the cardinal rules of show business. It was too loud, it was out of tune, it was irresponsible, it appeared to glory in images of destruction and its proponents showed neither love nor respect for their audience.

'The Sex Pistols are probably the worst band ever,' he said. 'Johnny Rotten can't sing and the band can't play. The fact that they can have any sort of a career is an indictment on the record-buying public. I know that I was criticized for being wild when I launched my career but that was by people who were relating what I did to a previous form of music. The Sex Pistols are trying to play rock 'n' roll and they're doing it badly.'

Not that the notoriety of the Sex Pistols had the remotest effect on Cliff's new rise. He was now committing himself to bigger and better tours and had left behind the club and cabaret scene.

In 1977 he went to South Africa, Australia, New Zealand and Europe. The day he returned from his summer holidays in Portugal he saw a television news flash that Elvis had been taken to hospital. He went to bed thinking it was a hoax, but at three o'clock in the morning he was woken by a call from L.B.C. Radio asking him to comment on Elvis' death.

'I couldn't think straight,' he remembers. 'I started arguing with the guy and telling him not to be ridiculous because they had said he was alright on the television news. He then said, "I hate to tell you this but it's true."'

At the age of 42 the one-time king of rock 'n' roll was dead from a heart attack, a bloated victim of self-indulgence. Although Cliff had never met Elvis the loss he felt was deeply personal because he knew that if it hadn't been for Elvis he would still be Harry Webb.

In January 1978 Cliff went back into the studios to record *Green Light*, his third album with Bruce Welch. By now Terry Britten was becoming Cliff's major songwriter. On *Green Light* he was involved as writer on half the album's songs.

One day during the recording, when Peter Gormley was discussing with Cliff the need to penetrate the American market, Bruce Welch suggested that the next album should have a consistent style of music.

'I had said that America was much different to Britain and

Europe in that they tend to pigeon-hole you,' says Welch. 'The songs in the album have to be in a similar vein. You can't do "Miss You Nights" and then "Devil Woman", because it's wrong for America.

'I suggested that what we should do is to get the same writer, perhaps someone like Terry Britten, to write the whole album. Now this was said to my manager, Peter Gormley, and to Cliff. I didn't hear any more about it.'

Assuming that he would be producing the next album, Welch spent the following months collecting new songs. Then, in July 1978, just as he was leaving Abbey Road Studios, Welch bumped into engineer Tony Clark who supposed he would be seeing him next week in Paris. 'What do you mean, Paris?' asked Welch. 'For the new Cliff album,' said Clark.

Welch had not been told that Cliff's new album, *Rock 'n' Roll Juvenile*, was scheduled to start recording at Pathe Marconi Studios in Paris on 18 July. Not only had his advice been heeded in that Terry Britten had authored almost all the songs, but Britten had been made co-producer with Cliff.

Welch fumed at the news. It wasn't the fact that he'd been replaced as producer after playing a key role in the launch of Cliff's recording career but that he hadn't been told, even though Peter Gormley was his manager. It opened up a rift between Welch, Gormley and Cliff that never healed.

'Our relationship after that could be described as strained,' says Welch. 'No one could call us close and I still think that someone like myself, who has been with him through thick and thin, deserved better than that.'

'I can understand him being disappointed, but not angry,' says Cliff in response. 'I wasn't tied to anybody anymore. Bruce may have assumed he was doing my next album, but I didn't.'

The words to half the songs on *Rock 'n' Roll Juvenile* were written by B.A. Robertson, a tall lantern-jawed Scot who was to enjoy his own pop career the following year beginning with the hit singles 'Bang Bang' and 'Knocked It Off'.

He'd been introduced to Terry Britten by bass guitarist Herbie Flowers who had played on Robertson's debut album *Shadow Of A Thin Man* in 1976 and the two had started writing songs together.

The most successful song from the partnership was 'Carrie',

which was to make number four in the charts. The riff and the title came from Terry Britten. The story was told by Robertson.

'The strength of the song comes from the fact that you're never quite sure what it's about,' says Robertson. 'You don't know whether Carrie is homeless or whether she's squatting or what.

'You don't know whether Cliff, as the narrator, is the husband, boyfriend, lover, brother or father. Nowhere does the song say what his relationship with Carrie is. It's very mysterious and musically it falls in the same groove as "I Heard It Through The Grapevine".'

Rock 'n' Roll Juvenile was an attempt to explore fresh subject matter but Terry Britten doesn't believe it worked.

'I think his fans want to hear him sing love songs,' he says. 'We did a lot of songs on that album that had very little to do with love and I honestly don't think they're liked by his fans.'

Much to Cliff and Terry Britten's chagrin the album's hit song was the one track that they hadn't produced. 'We Don't Talk Any More' was a last-minute addition, produced by Bruce Welch and surrounded in controversy.

In May 1979 Welch and Alan Tarney were producing an album for Island Records' artist Charlie Dore, and during a recording break Tarney played a cassette of 'We Don't Talk Any More' which he had written for his next album with Trevor Spencer. (The duo were signed to A&M as Tarney-Spencer.) When Welch heard it he immediately wanted to play it to Peter Gormley.

'I wasn't keen to lose the song but he pleaded and pleaded,' says Tarney. 'When he came in the next day he had played it to Peter and Cliff and they said they wanted to record it as soon as possible. We finished up the Charlie Dore album on the Friday and on the Saturday, which was Cup Final day, we recorded it with Cliff.'

Trevor Spencer remembers the session at R.G. Jones Studios.

'I don't think Cliff was all that keen on recording it at the time. He was so locked in to the *Rock 'n' Roll Juvenile* album. But all that was needed really was for us to remake the demo. Bruce then took the tapes to Abbey Road and popped Cliff's vocal on it.

'Alan felt sure that Cliff didn't want to do the song as he started it but then the vocal got better and better as it went on. There were only three or four takes. You can still hear him come in at the wrong point on part of the chorus. Bruce wanted to wipe that but Alan asked him not to so it remained part of the record.'

'We Don't Talk Any More' was released in July 1979 and its success meant that EMI felt it should be included on *Rock 'n' Roll Juvenile* which was scheduled to be released in September.

'Cliff and Terry didn't want it included,' says Welch. 'They said it was their album. EMI said, "But this is a monster single", I think in the end they had to half force Cliff to put it on the album.'

'We Don't Talk Any More' went to number one and sold two and three-quarter million copies. It was the best-selling single of his career, and Alan Tarney was brought in to produce his next album, *I'm No Hero*, which was recorded at Riverside Studios during May and June 1980.

It was a Tarney *tour de force*. No longer limited to being session bass player or occasional songwriter he dominated the whole project, playing and arranging almost all the music, writing or co-writing all but two of the songs and producing everything.

From his love of the Eagles' harmonies, Todd Rundgren's synthesizer wizardry and the chord changes of Steely Dan, Tarney was creating Cliff's first identifiable 'sound' since his days with the Shadows when the twang of Hank's Stratocaster announced the arrival of a Cliff disc.

One of his great strengths was that he could produce demo tapes that were so polished that Cliff could instantly imagine the finished result. The margin for error was reduced drastically because all that was normally required was for the engineer to remove Tarney's vocals and replace them with Cliff's. The backing tracks never needed re-recording.

'He was a dream to produce,' says Tarney. The first thing I noticed was his voice which sounded so huge. Then I noticed that he had a good sense of the person who would be listening to the song. He doesn't need to put on a great performance, he just needs to sing the song. He'll try it out two or three times and then that's it.'

Five weeks after completing the album Cliff went to Buckingham Palace to receive an OBE, the first time a pop star had been honoured since the Beatles were awarded MBEs in 1965. He arrived in his Rolls Royce, and was dressed in a black suit, red tie and red shoes.

'I've been to the palace before,' he explained. 'I know there's a lot of red about the place.'

I'm No Hero was released in September 1980 and the next month, during a five-concert run at the Apollo Theatre in London, Cliff turned forty. Just as had happened when he turned twenty and twenty-one and thirty, and when he'd been in the business for ten years and twenty years, a media hoopla ensued. How long could he go on? Did he ever think at eighteen that he would still be around at forty? Was he planning to retire?

What was extraordinary about this milestone, as he slipped into middle age, was that his career was in better shape than at any other time since the very early sixties.

Sitting in his dressing room at the Apollo the night before his birthday he said he was 'grateful and amazed' to arrive at middle age. His telephone had been ringing so much all day that he'd eventually had to take it off the hook.

'The two things that determine how well I will carry on are the quality of my voice and my own taste in music,' he said.

'If my taste in music continues to coincide with public taste then there's no reason why I shouldn't have a hit when I'm 50. No reason at all. I've had my biggest ever single at 39!'

'I never thought I'd top "The Young Ones", "Living Doll" and "Bachelor Boy" but I have. So age has nothing to do with it. I've just got to use my integrity and hope that my voice stays intact. If it breaks down, I'll have to think of doing something else.'

The success of 'We Don't Talk Any More' around the world raised the prospect of another assault on North America and so it was that in January 1981 Cliff went on a ten-day promotional tour to Los Angeles, Toronto and New York, appearing on the Merv Griffin and Dionne Warwick shows and facing two solid days of magazine and newspaper interviews.

Interest in America was still high. 'Suddenly', his duet with Olivia Newton-John, was at number twenty in the *Billboard* charts. Publications requesting interviews with him ranged from *People* magazine and the *New York Times* to rock magazines such as *Circus*, *Rock* and *New York Rocker*. He did a live interview on NBC's five o'clock news. He even found he was being played on some New Wave stations alongside the Police and Joe Jackson.

Cliff now had his most enduring band since the Shadows. Backing singers Tony Rivers and John Perry had recorded with him since 'Miss You Nights' and they were joined by Stu Calver. Drummer Graham Jarvis was musical director. There were two keyboard players, Alan Park and Graham Todd, lead guitarist John Clark, bass player Mark Griffiths and rhythm guitarist Mart Jenner.

Part of the tour was filmed by a television crew putting together a four-part documentary series for the BBC. Cliff had been approached by the light entertainment department, who were keen on an eighties follow-up to 'It's Cliff Richard', but he wanted to do something other than a song-and-dance show with special guests and so suggested the documentary approach.

Nineteen years since his last American tour, Cliff flew back. It was an unambitious tour of 2,000–3,000 capacity theatres in cities where his singles had been getting heavy airplay, but the idea was to gain a foothold.

The opening night of the tour was in Seattle but that weekend before the Monday show, while the band were still in Los Angeles, the trailer containing all their equipment was stolen from outside their motel. They were left with no lighting, no sound and no instruments.

'It was horrific,' remembers David Bryce, Cliff's professional manager. 'I just had to call all the music stores around LA and ask them to stay open late for us, which they did. It was hard for the musicians because they'd lost instruments that they were familiar with and which they'd modified in little ways.'

The tour arrived in New York on 2 April to play the opening night at a new club, the Ritz, with Jack Good and Olivia Newton-John in attendance. Cliff was still expressing his disappointment at the loss of equipment.

'At the moment we're only showing half of what we can do,' he explained. 'I came here to give them our current show but we haven't been able to do it. The fact that the fans like it means that when we come back they won't know what's hit them.'

The next day there was a smaller disaster when the tour bus arrived in Baltimore, and no one knew where the venue was.

'When we got to Baltimore the tour manager realized he had left his briefcase back in the hotel in New York and that the schedule was in it,' remembered Graham Todd.

'We were driving around looking for posters to find out where we were supposed to be and when we finally got there, half an hour before show time, we discovered that the revolving stage wasn't working.'

Cliff's longest-ever American tour finished on 20 April with much the same result as the others. He had been well received but by a very small group of people and, judging by the Union Jack flags waved in some of the auditoriums, a good proportion of these may have been Brits anyway.

Once back in London he started rehearsing for a rock 'n' roll special which was to form the basis of one of the documentary programmes. The idea was to fit him up with a pink jacket, get him to sing his favourite songs from the fifties and reunite him with one of his musical heroes.

Cliff's choice of heroes for the Hammersmith Odeon concert was either Elvis' original guitarist Scotty Moore, Ricky Nelson's guitarist James Burton or Phil Everly of the Everly Brothers.

James Burton asked for too much money and Scotty Moore, who hadn't picked up a guitar since playing on Elvis' comeback TV special in 1968, couldn't be coaxed from his tape-duplicating plant in Nashville. But Phil Everly, who had become familiar with Cliff's work when touring Britain in 1959, jumped at the opportunity.

'To step on a stage and sing with Cliff reminded me so much of singing with my brother,' he said. 'It was great to be able to sing Everly Brothers songs with someone I had tremendous respect for. That was really the reason I came over.'

The concert took place on 1 May and was a precursor of the 'Oh Boy!' section of 'The Event' in that Cliff sang rock 'n' roll songs, dressed in period costume, employed a troupe of dancers and sang duets with a star of the period. In the audience was John Foster, now a rotund man with spectacles, back home living with his mother, and the three original Drifters – Sammy Samwell, Norman Mitham and Terry Smart. They hadn't been together since Smart left to join the Navy in 1959.

At the end of the month he returned to the studios to record *Wired For Sound*, again with Alan Tarney producing and arranging. The title track was the most contemporary sounding single of his renaissance, showing that he was every bit a contender in the battle of such new techno-pop artists as Soft Cell and Human League.

The lyric, written by B.A. Robertson, was a departure from Cliff's romantic subject matter. It was a love song but this time expressing his love for the Sony Walkman and the new portable music that was revolutionizing listening habits.

'I'd never written with Alan Tarney but he called me up one night and asked me if I'd like to write a song with him,' says Robertson. 'Mickey Dolenz, who used to be in the Monkees, was coming for a meal that night so I stayed in for the starters and then drove down to Hammersmith to listen to the backing track during the main course and then arrived back home with a cassette in time for the dessert.

'I got up the next morning, put the kettle on, put the cassette in and the title came to me straight away as I listened to it. A couple of hours later, I had written the whole song and I just read the lyrics to him down the phone.'

Cliff had for some time attempted to use his position to raise the profile of various British gospel artists but although he had been able to give them exposure by producing them and inviting them on his tours, none of the acts had ever achieved general market success. The most positive outcome of his involvement was reflected in his use, for the first time, of gospel writers on a secular album.

'Better Than I Know Myself', a gospel song disguised as a love song, was written by Dave Cooke and his songwriting partner Judy McKenzie, who had been one of the pioneer Christian folk singers in the late sixties.

'Lost In A Lonely World' and 'Summer Rain' were both by Chris Eaton, a 20-year-old writer Cliff had met at a Christian convention in 1979 when Eaton was playing in a band for Dave Pope, an evangelist and singer whose album *Sail Away* Cliff had produced.

'I'd written the title track for Dave's album and Cliff said he liked it and would like to hear more,' says Eaton. 'I sent him five songs on a tape but didn't hear anything for eighteen months. Then I got a call from Gill Snow at his office saying that Cliff wanted to do four of the songs, two of them on *Wired For Sound*.'

Wired For Sound went on to be Cliff's best-selling album since *I'm Nearly Famous*, with sales of over one million. Chris Eaton was able to give up driving taxis and beer lorries and was signed up as a songwriter to Patch Music, a music publishing company run from the Cliff Richard Organization by Stuart Ongley.

Cliff was particularly pleased with his inclusion of Christian writers in this way. In 1965, even if he had decided it was possible, there were no Christian writers of high calibre who could have contributed to his albums or singles. Now there were, and it had a lot to do with the change in attitude which Cliff and his generation had created in the church that young people were growing up considering commercial songwriting as a career possibility. He had never felt that his faith was something stuck on to his life although, at times, his two-tier career seemed to suggest that.

'Interviewers tend to ask me certain questions and then suddenly switch to discussing Christianity,' he said. 'They don't realize that the first part of the interview was also coloured by my Christian faith. I can't separate me from me.'

twenty two
'WE'RE THE NEW CHARLES AND DI'

Since becoming a Christian in 1966 there had been no obvious romantic interest in Cliff's life. There had been girls who had adorned his arms when he arrived at film premiéres and charity functions but there had been no girlfriends.

The fact that this apparently abstemious period had coincided with his close relationship with Bill Latham didn't go unnoticed by the press.

Roderick Gilchrist, Entertainments Editor of the *Daily Mail*, observing that Jackie Irving had been his last serious date noted that: 'He now lives with a male friend in the show business shelter of Weybridge, with his friend's mother. Inevitably this has led to suggestions that he is "gay" – a word that had not been used in this way when he first entered show business.'

Cliff denied that he was homosexual and explained that his reasons for not bed-hopping with women were spiritual rather than psycho-sexual.

'As a Christian I don't believe in extramarital sex because God says it's wrong and I have to assume that he knows better,' he said. 'I don't sleep with women at all now. Not since my Christian conversion.'

Three years earlier he'd broken this news to pop writer John Blake, then of the *Evening News*, who commented: 'Since Cliff became an ardent Christian more than ten years ago, I am slightly stunned by this revelation.'

The story was headlined 'My Ten Years Without Sex... by Cliff Richard', as though celibacy was an outrageous perversion.

Cliff's fidelity to Christian teaching seemed beyond doubt. The deeper question was whether his celibacy was solely a matter of obedience or whether he was a celibate by nature.

If he was unmoved by sex his chastity was an acceptance of his natural condition rather than a victory over desire. In the days before religion his lack of interest appeared eccentric but, as a Christian, there was an explanation which non-believers could understand and accept even if they didn't approve.

'I don't particularly have any great sexual urges or needs,' he confessed to David Wigg of the *Daily Express*. 'I don't feel I have to spend my life with someone special for sexual favours. But that's my good fortune, isn't it, really?'

The implied good fortune was that he was free to devote his energies to his career. There were no distractions. There were no emotional entanglements. He was responsible to nobody but himself. His only marriage, as anyone who knows him well will say, was to his work.

This is why it was so out of character to see Cliff Richard going out with tennis star Sue Barker in the autumn of 1982. Ever since entering show business he had avoided being seen with the women he took out and avoided mentioning them by name to the press.

Jackie Irving, his longest-standing girlfriend, was rarely photographed with Cliff. Delia Wicks was sworn to secrecy. His romance with Una Stubbs was unknown even to his closest friends and colleagues. But on 23 March 1982 Cliff flew out to Denmark with Sue Barker to see her play an exhibition match and the next day's tabloids were full of it: 'Sue And Cliff In Love Riddle' (*The Sun*), 'Sue And Cliff Set Up A Love Riddle' (*Daily Mirror*), 'Cliff And Sue Take Off And Say There's No Love Match Blooming' (*Daily Mail*), 'Cliff, Love And Me by Sue Barker' (*Daily Star*).

The bare bones of the story were that Cliff had been spotted with Sue in a departure lounge at Heathrow Airport awaiting a flight to Copenhagen. What the press immediately wanted to know was whether this was love and whether a wedding was in the offing.

'I think he's a super person but to talk of marriage is wrong,' Sue told James Whitaker of the *Daily Star*. 'There's nothing nasty in the rumour. It just isn't accurate.'

When the couple flew back after an overnight stay Cliff was

asked whether he loved her. 'I'm not going to say that,' he said. 'I don't want to embarrass her. She says she doesn't mind, but it's not fair. I've only met her four times. We'll be seeing a lot more of each other, but it's early days. Who knows what we'll feel in a year's time?'

Within three months they were a hot item. Neither of them was now pretending it was still a case of 'just good friends'. They were spotted at Wimbledon where Sue openly nibbled his ear, kissed his neck and stroked his hair while watching a game. At a pre-Wimbledon party thrown by veteran tennis designer Teddy Tinling they allowed themselves to be photographed cuddling and holding hands.

Cliff even proudly announced to reporters that he and Sue were the new Charles and Di. 'There had to be someone to take over once they got married,' he boasted. Asked if they would be following the royal example Cliff said, 'I don't know. It's early days yet. We are taking it from day to day. If we decide to get married there will be an announcement.'

Cliff and Sue's relationship had all started with Alan Godson, a Church of England vicar with a parish in Liverpool. He had helped found an organization called Christians in Sport to bring together sports people with a shared faith and to help evangelize their peers.

Godson himself was a tough-looking ex-rugby-football player renowned for his fearlessness in presenting the Christian message in dressing rooms and on playing fields. It was not unknown for him to suddenly pull up in his car and start preaching to someone in the street if he felt called to do so.

He had been introduced to Sue Barker by sports commentator Gerald Williams, a personal friend and a supporter of Christians in Sport. At 25 Sue was then Britain's rising female tennis star and although she had been baptized at the age of 21 her Christian faith had been dormant until she met Godson. For the past few years she had been involved in two intense relationships with fellow sportsmen. Now she wanted to rededicate her life as a Christian.

Alan Godson was aware that life as a Christian was going to be tough for her on the tennis court. Not only would she find it hard to be in regular contact with a church but there would be ridicule from fellow players and grillings from the press. The only person that he could think of who had triumphed in a similar situation was Cliff. So he called him and gave him Sue's telephone number.

'I thought that because they lived in the same area and faced similar problems he could coach her into handling the gospel publicly without getting destroyed,' says Godson. 'I thought that he was the only one with the *nous* to be useful as a servant to her.'

While this was happening (September 1981), Sue was playing in the Brighton Indoor tournament and coincidentally had met the Shadows who were staying at the same hotel while playing concerts on the south coast.

'Hank was the tennis nut and he came and watched me playing doubles with Virginia Wade,' says Sue. 'The next day I was due to play against Tracey Austin in the finals and Hank, Bruce and Brian came and they all got hooked. Apparently Cliff was watching the match on his television at home, and when I won I went straight over and hugged Hank. Cliff wondered what on earth was going on!

'That night, when I got home to Wimbledon, he called me. At first I thought it was a joke. I had been having this running joke with some engineers from British Telecom and I thought it was one of them playing a prank. So I just played along. I said, "Oh really!" I didn't think it was him. But then he told me that Alan had given him my number and he thought it would be good if we got together to chat.

'I was flying off to Japan at the end of that week and we had to get together on the only free night I had which was when I was actually going to see the Shadows in London.'

Sue was going to the concert at the Dominion Theatre with fellow tennis player Sue Mappin, and they were joined in their box on the night by Cliff and Bill Latham. After the show they all went out to eat together and discussion turned to the problems of British tennis. Cliff wanted to know why tennis was such a privileged sport in this country and what needed to be done to find the tennis stars of tomorrow. Out of this first meeting grew the idea of what, in ten years' time, would be the Cliff Richard Tennis Trail – a charity which helps school-age children to develop a love for the game.

At the time Cliff was not known for his love of tennis. He was what Sue now refers to as a 'pat-a-cake' tennis player, someone who liked to knock a ball around a court but for whom 'the ball wasn't coming back very much and it wasn't much fun'.

It was Sue who stimulated his interest in playing tennis. 'He used to come and watch me train,' she says. 'I gave him a hit and he found he was getting absolutely exhausted in half an hour and he saw that if he learned to play well it would be a means of keeping fit. I think he'd played with his friends for hours but with me he was getting tired. He saw tennis as a challenge.'

From Japan Sue went down to Australia and then on to America where she lived as a tax exile. It was while she was away that the *Daily Star* broke the story that had been kept a secret for over 21 years. Beneath the headline 'Cliff – My Secret Lover' Carol Costa told all about her brief affair in the first of a three-part series.

The tone of the story was set in the first paragraphs. 'I loved Cliff Richard, and I suppose I always will. But over the years I have come to realise that he isn't perfect.

'And that's why I have decided to tell the truth... after keeping quiet for so long.'

On tour in the Far East at the time, Cliff had already got wind of the imminent publication because he had been called and asked for his comment on the story. He would say only that, 'Carol must have her reasons for publicizing what was very personal. She has the freedom to do that. But I also have my freedom and I don't wish to publicize anything that personal.'

He never discussed the relationship with Sue, but he did get together with Stu Calver and John Perry to pray about the situation and then he called his mother in Broxbourne and warned her what was about to happen.

'I'm sensitive about anything bad that is written in the papers,' says Cliff's mother, Dorothy Marie. 'Cliff told me not to worry. He said that if she wants to write that it's entirely up to her. I was quite upset but he wasn't.'

The story had come about because Carol had been approached by Jet Harris and Tony Meehan to collaborate on a book. The three met in London with freelance book editor Carol Illingworth, journalist Sharon Ring and some media executives who promised radio and television spin-offs from the project.

Carol became uneasy with some of the angles under discussion. 'It wasn't nice at all,' she says. 'I just didn't want to know. I made my objections clear and then I was approached by people who said that if I was to tell my story it would put the record straight and squash a lot of the rumours going around about Cliff. So I pulled away from this book project and did my own thing.'

Carol was paid £12,000 for the story but insists that she did it to defend Cliff's reputation. 'If I was only interested in the money I wouldn't have sat on it for 21 years,' she argues. 'I would have got myself a fortune when I was going through really hard times with my young family.'

With Cliff still touring the Far East and Sue in America, the pair exchanged a couple of letters and then, in February 1982, while playing in the Dallas Tournament, Sue received a phone call from him.

'It was totally out of the blue,' she says. 'He asked me what I was doing and I told him that I was only due back in England for a long weekend and I was going to Denmark with my brother to play an exhibition match. He said, "Well, I'm not doing anything. Do you mind if I come along?" I said, "No. Of course not." We met up in London in March and flew off to Copenhagen together, and I couldn't believe what happened after that.

'It was only the second time we had met. When we got off the plane people were asking us when we were going to get married and I thought this was absolutely bizarre.

'As far as I was concerned we had been to a concert, had a dinner, written two letters... and I was thinking, "Blimey, I don't think we're even going out!" I didn't count it as a date. I thought, "Gosh, I'm going to put my foot in it so badly." By saying nothing you make it worse. If you say, "Of course not," you insult the other person.

'In some ways it drew us closer together. Although the press tried to make out that we were upset, we just laughed at a lot of it. We used to phone each other up and say, "Did you read that article? I didn't say any of that. I haven't spoken to them."'

Press speculation increased over the following months. Sue was playing on the European circuit and Cliff was recording his new album *Now You See Me... Now You Don't* at Strawberry South Studios in Dorking. It was during this recording that the friendship changed into something recognizably different.

'After we returned from Denmark my parents stayed with me at my flat for the few days I was in England and Cliff was doing the album and he just phoned up and said, "Look, I'd really like to see you again. Will you come down to the studio tomorrow because I'm stuck down here."

'It was then that I sussed that something was up because we had arranged to meet in a week's time when he'd finished and my parents were gone, but he was saying "I don't want to wait a week. I want to see you tomorrow." So we did meet then. I felt the same way but I certainly wasn't going to make the phone call. I was very pleased that he had called.'

Now You See Me... Now You Don't was a further attempt to introduce the writing of his Christian friends to a wider audience, this time with an album which although regarded by EMI as a gospel project would get the same commercial push as any other release.

His choice of producer was Craig Pruess, a young American who'd been a child prodigy as a musician and had studied physics, philosophy and comparative religion at the Massachusetts Institute of Technology before arriving in England in 1973.

'He wanted this album to be more heavyweight and to break away from the pop sound,' says Pruess. 'He approached it to prove a point and he did have a point to prove. He didn't want his gospel albums to be regarded as inferior to his other albums. He felt they could be as good as anything else he did. He wanted to fuse his beliefs and his enthusiasm with his professional life.'

Pruess also noticed that Cliff was remarkably content during the period of recording. 'Of all the time I spent with Cliff I felt closest to him around that period,' he says. 'It was balanced. He could relate to couples and with my wife Jenny we went out a lot for meals as a foursome.

'I remember mixing the album at the Townhouse and Sue and Cliff were cuddling on the couch behind us. It was great. It was the happiest I had ever seen him. It helped him to loosen up. Sometimes around his band and all the people he works with he has to keep a distance for professional reasons.'

During the summer, Cliff and Sue began spending every available moment together, visiting the theatre, seeing films, playing tennis, but more often than not staying at home in Weybridge where Sue would cook a meal and they'd both watch a video. They were affectionate towards each other, they laughed a lot and there was the bonding of their Christian faith.

What was particularly refreshing about the relationship was that it took Cliff temporarily away from show business and Sue away from sport. They found they could relax and drop their guards.

'She enjoyed being with him and I think that she shook him up,' says Alan Godson. 'She brought the champagne back to his spiritual life.'

In August, Cliff and his mother left England for a three-week holiday in Bermuda. Her marriage to Derek Bodkin had recently ended in divorce after he had found another woman. Bill Latham and his mother Mamie, Graham Disbrey, Glyn MacAulay and David Rivett accompanied them on the trip. MacAulay and Rivett, both accountants with Crusader backgrounds, were the latest additions to the summer holiday gang. They stayed in a private villa in a secluded bay.

Sue went off to Marbella and when she returned on 26 August she broke down in tears at Heathrow when reporters surrounded her and surprised her by informing her that in her absence Cliff had said it was now 'Marry or break up time'. When Cliff flew back two days later Sue was not at the airport to meet him.

It was these incidents that prompted the *Daily Star* to publish its front-page headline story challenging Cliff to make his mind up.

'Cliff Richard, you are fast becoming a CAD!', wrote Sandra White on 28 August. 'You flew back from your holidays yesterday and kept quiet about your intentions. As Britain's Number One Bachelor Boy, you are too old to be coy. Do the decent thing. Make your mind up: Do you want to marry Sue Barker? Or not?'

The story went on in much the same vein and ended with a coupon 'What should Sue do?' with three boxes marked 'Marry Him Now', 'Wait a While' and 'Give Him the Elbow'.

Cliff read the story and told Sue about it. She told him not to worry and a few days later left for the US Open and didn't return until late in September. When they linked up again Sue realized that something was different. The physical affection was now gone. Whatever romance had been there had turned into friendship.

'We were still boyfriend and girlfriend but it wasn't the same,' says Sue. 'I think during that time away we had had a lot of time to sit back and think about what we wanted to do and I think we both realized that we were spending too much time together. It certainly still felt like a strong relationship but certainly not as fast and furious as it had been.

'I think that during the summer we had probably seen too much of each other. It certainly affected my tennis in that I was so busy working out how we could see each other that I wasn't getting on with what I should be doing. I don't think it was particularly good for him either because he was dashing out to watch tournament after tournament. It was what we wanted to do though.

'It may not have been good career-wise but we were having fun. Bill must have been tearing his hair out because Cliff just wasn't around that much.'

During this time it appeared to close friends that Cliff was still mulling over his options. He spoke to married friends about the decisions he was facing and clearly saw marriage as a possibility. It had been while he holidayed in Bermuda though that he had more or less decided that he wanted to put the brakes on.

'I spoke to Sue on the phone from Bermuda because it's when you're away from people that you really start to think things through,' he says. 'I was feeling that I should curb it a bit. I don't really know why I felt that way. I still found her attractive and still enjoyed being with her.'

In 1988, he told *Woman's Own* magazine it had crossed his mind that 'marriage might be the outcome' but that one of the things that had decided him against it was an incident where Sue had become irritated when he had not told her where he was going one day.

'I suddenly realized that in the marriage relationship you no longer live for yourself,' he said. 'And, in the end, the love that I have for Sue was overshadowed by the fact that I love my lifestyle that much more.'

When Sue read this she was upset, not least because, as with Jackie Irving, during their time together he hadn't hinted that marriage was ever under consideration.

'We had a very close relationship for a few months but I needed to know someone for a couple of years before I thought of marrying them. I don't know whether he thought about marriage or whether he thought, "I've got quite close to this person – do I want it to continue? If it continues it's obviously going to involve making a decision."'

During a gospel tour of South Africa in 1981, which Cliff had played with Garth Hewitt and Nutshell (two British acts he had produced singles for), Bill Latham had struck up a relationship with an English woman who was a friend of the tour organizer. Her name was Jill Clarke, and she had emigrated to Johannesburg with her parents as a teenager. The following year Latham was in Sun City with Cliff and Jill drove up to be with him, by which time it was obvious to friends that something serious was starting.

In the summer of 1983, with Cliff apparently contemplating the possibility of marriage to Sue, Jill flew back to England to be closer to Latham. For several months she stayed with Sue at her flat in Wimbledon and she and Latham would go out on double dates with Cliff and Sue.

Close friends of Cliff and Bill felt that a double wedding in 1984 was definitely on the cards, during the same period if not on the same day. How things changed so drastically has never been adequately explained.

For Sue the most disappointing aspect was that it had seemed to change gear without warning. There were no explanations as to why the kissing had stopped and why the phone calls dried up.

'I had felt the need to put the brakes on but I certainly hadn't wanted it to fizzle out like this,' she says. 'I think Cliff felt it was all going too far although he wouldn't talk about it.

'It was almost as if he didn't want to confront it. Without us ever having sat down and talked about it, our relationship had gone into a different stage. It slowed down to a halt where there was no romance at all.'

They kept seeing each other, mostly for meals, but Cliff no longer displayed open affection as he had done prior to Bermuda. As far as the public was concerned, Sue and Cliff were still an 'item' and as late as July 1984 Sue was speaking publicly as though it was thriving as a romance.

'I love him, he's great and I'm sure we love each other,' she told one interviewer. 'But as for being in love, I'm not so sure, it's such a funny phrase. I don't think I'm in love with him and I don't think he is with me… We're still getting to know each other. Sometimes we don't meet for weeks on end.'

The truth was that although Sue was hopeful that there might be a future she could see that Cliff was unwilling to share a lot of himself. It might have drifted on indefinitely had Sue not started dating a fellow tennis star.

'I don't remember a particular conversation with Cliff to say we've changed but we did have a conversation to say this is it,' she says. 'I remember we were in a restaurant in Sydney in October 1984. I had met someone over here who I wanted to see more of and who didn't like the attachment I had with Cliff even though by this time we were only friends.

'We went out for dinner and I told him I had met someone else. He was really pleased. He said, "I suppose that means I won't be able to see you quite so much." And that was that.'

The relationship had lasted almost two years, second only to his time with Jackie Irving, although most of it was spent apart and only a fraction of it was truly passionate. It followed the same pattern of an early intensity followed up by a sudden cooling and a reluctance to progress towards commitment.

Those who only saw the public displays of affection tend to be dismissive of the relationship. They argue that it was just a convenient time for Cliff to be seen with a girl on his arm and that it boosted his image. But among his closest friends there was a genuine belief that something could have happened.

'I don't agree that Cliff has never found the right girl,' says Peter Graves. 'Sue Barker was the right girl. She was a Christian, she understood his show business commitments, she was madly in love with him and they looked fabulous together.' But again Cliff had weighed up his options and decided to stick with the decision that he'd first made in 1958, to put the career before the girl. Says Graves, 'Now he is married to his lifestyle and that has become more important to him than any woman could ever be.'

Above 1973: Cliff visiting Bangladesh with the relief agency Tear Fund

Above 1978: At home in Weybridge – (clockwise) Cliff, Cliff's mother Dorothy, Bill Latham, Bill's mother Mamie, Derek Bodkin (Dorothy's husband)

Left 1981: Baltimore, US – Cliff at a soundcheck

Right May 1981, Hammersmith Odeon: Cliff with Phil Everly at the Rock 'n' Roll special which was filmed for BBC TV

Below same concert. The first time the Drifters had met since Terry Smart left at the end of the fifties: (left to right) Ian Samwell, Norman Mitham, Terry Smart, Cliff

Right 23 July, 1980: Cliff with his mother Dorothy after receiving his OBE

Below Cliff with Alan Tarney, songwriter and producer of albums such as *Stonger* and *Always Guaranteed*

Above 5 July, 1982: Cliff with Sue Barker at Wimbledon during the height of their romance

Left Cliff at his villa in Portugal

Above The holiday gang in Portugal in the seventies – (left to right) David Rivett, Graham Disbrey, Glyn MacAuley, Bill Latham, Cliff

Left February 1989: Cliff and Sue Barker at a celebrity tennis match in London

Below August 1985: On holiday in Portugal – (left to right) Cliff, Bill Latham, Glyn MacAuley, Graham Disbrey, David Rivett

Above July 1989: Cliff's uniforms and gowns party – (left to right) Jill Clarke, Graham Disbrey, John and Carol Davey, Cliff

Above Elton John's Rocket Records gave Cliff his first US top ten hit when it released 'Devil Woman' in 1976

Right
October 1995: Cliff, after he received his knighthood at Buckingham Palace, with his three sisters: (left to right) Donna Gordon, Joan Pilgrim and Jacqui Harrison

Above July 1996: Cliff's impromptu performance at Wimbledon. Virginia Wade, former Wimbledon champion, sings along

Right October 1996: *Heathcliff* opens, starring Cliff, and Helen Hobson

Left New Year 2001, Dom Carlos Restaurant, Albufeira, Portugal: (clockwise from top) Cliff, Cherie Blair, Bill Latham, Glyn McAulay, Lizzie McCrossan, Pia Barchet, Tony Blair, Graham Disbrey, Roger Bruce, Alan Osman

Right Summer 2000, Portugal: Graham Disbrey (second from left) gives Cliff and Pia Barchet a still life art class

Below Cliff's holiday home in Barbados

305

twenty three
'CLIFF LIKES ANYTHING THAT KNOCKS AN AUDIENCE SIDEWAYS'

During the first half of the eighties Cliff was on the road for anything up to four months of the year in Australia, the Far East, Europe, Scandinavia, South Africa and America, as well as carrying out his annual gospel tours of Britain.

In this schedule he found time to make two further field trips on behalf of Tear Fund – the first, in 1982, a week-long stay in Kenya and the second, in 1984, a fortnight in Haiti. The purpose was to stay in touch with the charity but also to act as narrator and interviewer in two films: *Cliff In Kenya* and *It's A Small World*.

The conditions, particularly in Haiti, were far removed from the five-star luxury Cliff was used to on his tours where hotel managers fell over themselves to give him the best possible treatment and local record companies showered him with gifts.

There was starvation, poverty, disease, political violence and the threat of voodoo. In Port au Prince, the capital of Haiti, they stayed in a small hotel. On the small island of La Gonave, which could only be reached by a boat, they slept in a missionary bungalow.

'He is a tremendously adaptable person,' said George Hoffman, who had already travelled with him to Bangladesh, India, Kenya and Nepal. 'He never stands on ceremony. I've never heard him complain once, whatever the food we've been given and whatever places we've had to sleep in.'

In Kenya he reduced a group of Masai tribesmen to giggles by playing rock 'n' roll to them on his acoustic guitar.

'Their previous experience of white people was of development workers and missionaries who were all rather serious,' says documentary film director John Muggleton. 'To have this guy playing wildly on a guitar and rolling on the ground was quite amusing for them.'

Having revamped his approach to recording in the seventies, Cliff was starting in the eighties to think about his stage show. The new band were not expected to dress in black or hide behind their musical scores. He began to develop a more theatrical approach to performing: working out dance routines, acting out songs like 'Devil Woman' and incorporating ideas from science fiction films (especially *Close Encounters Of The Third Kind*) and West End musicals (especially *Starlight Express*).

Until the mid-seventies he had relied exclusively on light and sound equipment available at each venue which meant that he lagged noticeably behind the major touring acts of the day who were each trying to out-dazzle the other with the spectacular nature of their shows. Now he was investigating state-of-the-art systems: overhead trusses, motorized lights and lasers.

'Cliff liked anything that knocked the audience sideways,' says lighting engineer Bob Hellyer. 'He started to want to choreograph numbers, to have effects linked to particular lines in the songs, and so the show became part rock 'n' roll and part theatre.'

The tours abroad were almost always to countries where Cliff was established, with the exception of North America, where there were a couple of flings, and the Far East, which was sometimes fitted in for convenience en route to Australia. Japan, once a good market, had inexplicably gone off him since his comeback with 'Devil Woman'.

In his career he had played in every significant commercial territory in the world. He'd even played in places where there was little chance of selling records, such as Jerusalem, Beirut, Bangkok, Moscow, Calcutta, New Delhi and Belgrade.

The places where he was most successful were Britain, Europe (especially France, Holland and Germany), Scandinavia (especially Denmark), South Africa, Australia and New Zealand.

'It's all down to how much attention you give each territory,' said Peter Gormley. 'In the early days he would go anywhere, he would look forward to it and he would have fun. But as you get older you lose your enthusiasm for jumping on planes and switching all over the place.'

On tour Cliff maintained a proprietorial distance from the band and road crew, appearing for after-show meals but rarely hanging out with them and always travelling first class with his tour manager David Bryce.

Bryce had become an important part of the management team. Originally he worked on the road with Cliff on behalf of agent Leslie Grade and then, in the mid-sixties, worked directly for Cliff.

He had been around show business since the end of the war when he began work as a 'call boy' in West End theatres, knocking on dressing room doors before the curtain went up.

His brother was Dickie Valentine, the most popular male vocalist in Britain before the rock 'n' roll era, who was killed in a car accident. Through him he got into the Grade agency, going out on the road with such stars as Bill Haley and Buddy Holly. Well-muscled and prematurely bald, he had the effect of intimidating people without having to resort to violence. On the road he became the liaison between Cliff and the members of the band; if there was ever any trouble it was ultimately Bryce who had to sort it out.

Although no code of conduct was imposed there was an unspoken understanding that no one would risk tainting Cliff's good name by indulging in Led Zeppelinesque on-the-road antics. If the tabloid press could get the words 'Cliff' and 'Orgy' into the same headline it wouldn't matter how tenuous the connection.

People switched on their best behaviour when they were around Cliff anyway. 'A lot of the normal banter would stop when he came in the room,' admits guitarist Mark Griffiths. 'It was just out of respect for his views. I think the sort of humour that musicians enjoy would have been a bit too strong for Cliff. You just didn't want to involve him in it.'

If anyone blasphemed by saying 'Jesus Christ' or 'God', Cliff would brush it aside by saying, 'Right name. Wrong context', but obscenities made him feel uncomfortable. During recording sessions musicians would often retire to the bathroom for a quick five-minute swear before being able to carry on.

None of this was done through fear. His naïvety, particularly over sex, made them feel protective towards him. 'To swear in front of Cliff would be like swearing in front of your mother,' as one band member put it.

On tour in Hamburg, some of the band gathered in the foyer of the hotel in preparation for a visit to the Reeperbahn, the city's notorious commercial sex district. Cliff sauntered in, saw them about to leave, and asked if he could join them.

'We were all saying, "Well Cliff, I don't think you'll want to go where we're going",' said Graham Todd. 'There was a general feeling that we had to look after him which is a bit silly when you think he's a fully-grown man. He's not at all worldly in that respect.'

In Japan in 1974 he was told by someone in the band that he would be fine to have as much *sake* as he wanted with his meal, as long as he didn't switch to another alcoholic drink As a result he got drunk for the first time since his Italian experience in 1959.

'Naïve little me drank more than I should,' Cliff admits. 'The next day everyone said to me, "You were great! You were really one of the lads!" They were thrilled that I had got drunk. I felt dreadful. I hated it.'

Cliff was also kept in the dark about much of the practical joking that went on all around him on tour. It was assumed that he'd either disapprove or fail to see the humour.

He does have a good sense of humour – almost everyone comments on his readiness to laugh – but it was thought that some of their activities might be too much for his taste.

The bulk of the pranks centred on hotel rooms, and the priority of any touring band member was to keep his key with him at all times. Failure to do so could result either in a straightforward festooning with tea bags or the complete removal of all furniture.

Having your key didn't guarantee immunity. You could find yourself locked out by the simple trick of switching the plastic door numbers so that you tried the wrong door, or you could find yourself stuck in if a gang decided to apply adhesive 'gaffer tape' to the edges of your door.

When the management of an Edinburgh hotel released Alan Park from his gaffer-taped room it pulled away so much of the paintwork that they billed the Cliff Richard Organization for the damage and had the group banned from staying there again.

There was also no protection for those who were asleep. Keyboard player Dave Cooke woke one morning to find his room completely full of toilet paper and when Mart Jenner retired to his room after a heavy night of drinking the rest of the band took advantage of his comatose state to climb in through his window from a fire escape, strip him naked and cover him from the waist downwards with shaving foam.

'He didn't wake up until the middle of the night,' remembers Mark Griffiths. 'The window was open, he was frozen stiff and he had absolutely no idea what had happened to him.'

The undisputed master of the wind-up was tour manager Ron King, who'd first driven Cliff on the Kalins' tour in 1958. His practical jokes were legendary in the business because of their elaborateness. Once, while driving the coach for a British tour by American star Del Shannon, he arranged for two friends to dress up in uniforms as border guards and arrest Shannon by the roadside for attempting to enter Scotland without a visa.

His favourite joke with the Cliff band came when he discovered that Mart Jenner was involved in a dispute with his next-door neighbours and had one morning run over their son's bike with his car. Not wishing to be arrested for criminal damage, Jenner had cut the frame up and buried it in a field. His only mistake was to tell a member of the band.

While Cliff was on stage in London, King went outside the theatre and found an obliging policeman whom he brought to the side of the stage. When Jenner idly looked into the wings King pointed at him and mouthed the words 'That's him!' to the policeman who then left, his duty having been done.

At the end of the concert Jenner unplugged his guitar, leaped off the stage and ran terrified out of the theatre. He was so quick that no one could catch him. 'I couldn't get him on the phone at all,' says King, 'and then when I did get hold of him and told him what had happened he said, "Thanks a lot, Ron. You've just given me the worst weekend of my life!"'

Water bombing was the least elaborate prank the band members favoured. Plastic laundry bags were hoarded during a tour, then filled with water and released from hotel rooms. The resulting explosions were often loud enough to suggest a terrorist attack

In fact, water bombing became something of an art form for the musicians. They started dangling a microphone from the window so that the noises could be recorded and compared. Later they compiled stereo recordings by placing another microphone at the point of impact. Cassettes of the top plops would be circulated among interested parties.

In New Zealand Dave Cooke decided that Cliff might be a repressed water bomber. 'All the others were trying to keep me quiet,' says Cooke, 'because they never wanted Cliff to know anything, but I just asked him if he fancied doing a few water bombs that night and he said he'd love to. He thought it would be great fun.

'I'd collected about sixty bags and we started throwing them out of the window and Cliff just loved it. It was all very childish, but great fun.'

Nothing more was thought about this until an incident on a gospel tour with the singer Sheila Walsh, his latest gospel protégé, when a loud explosion was heard outside the hotel one night as the band congregated in Mark Griffiths' room.

Wanting to join in whatever fun was going on they began hurling bombs from the window with Sheila Walsh rapidly filling bags from the bathroom tap. One of the bombs, however, hit the roof of a van, creating an almighty noise which alerted the hotel management. Mark Griffiths, whose window had been noted as the source of the bombardment, was later questioned by local police.

The next day, in Manchester, David Bryce gave everyone a severe dressing down, threatening Sheila with the sack. 'Cliff's career could have gone right out of the window,' he admonished them, as they tried to stifle their giggles over his inappropriate metaphor.

'Cliff was standing there being unusually quiet,' remembers Dave Cooke. 'Two or three months later we discovered why. He had been the one to throw the first bomb.'

Sheila Walsh had been brought to Bill Latham for management by her husband Norman Miller, an executive for the Christian record company Word (UK).

A television show – called *Rock Gospel* and screened by the BBC – was built around her. She became the support act on the Tear Fund tours and Cliff began to produce her with Craig Pruess. But success in the secular world proved elusive.

A hit record seemed assured in 1983 when Cliff agreed to record a duet with her for the DJM record label but the result, 'Drifting', became one of his least successful records ever, reaching a highest chart position of 64.

'It was humiliating,' Sheila recalls. 'I was interviewed on Capital Radio just as the single was released and I was asked if I thought it would be a hit. I said of course it would be – Cliff could do a duet with Miss Piggy and it would be a hit. When it died a death I felt really stupid.'

Through knowing Sheila, Cliff came into closer contact with the Cobham Christian Fellowship, a non-denominational church led by Gerald Coates which practised a more informal style of worship and believed in such 'spiritual gifts' as speaking in tongues. Its meeting place was either a scout building or a school hall. The first event of theirs which Cliff attended (in 1979) was in a marquee.

The Cobham Christian Fellowship was an example of a recent phenomenon in evangelical Christianity known as the 'house church' movement. It was the fastest growing sector of the church and had started with people literally meeting in front rooms but had been forced to expand into larger premises.

One 'house church' in South London, for example, has 2,100 members. Cobham Christian Fellowship, which had started in 1971 with five people, expanded to a local congregation of 600, with a further 6,000 in associated groups.

Sheila and her husband Norman, who had sold their house for the sake of her career, had moved in with Gerald Coates and his wife Anona in their eighteenth-century home in Esher (formerly a residence of Clive of India), and it was here that Cliff developed a friendship with Gerald, whom he had first met at a social event in London.

Since leaving Guildford Baptist Church, following David Pawson's resignation in 1979, Cliff and Bill Latham had become irregular churchgoers. Initially they tried to fit in at Walton-on-Thames Baptist Church, but then tended to drift between churches.

Cliff's attraction to the Cobham set highlighted a major difference between him and Latham. Whereas Cliff fitted in naturally with uninhibited expressions of praise, believing that if it's alright to get visibly excited by rock 'n' roll then it's alright to get visibly excited by God, Latham is by nature a traditionalist who prefers the prayer-book worship of the Church of England. It was noticeable that Cliff quite often made his visits to Cobham alone.

'There was a two- or three-year period when Cliff clearly identified with us,' says Gerald Coates. 'He would come to our services, sometimes with Bill, sometimes without, and I know that he enjoyed our worship and teaching.

'Over that time Cliff and I would pray together. I think he was going through one or two things with those who were close to him and we were able to talk and I was able to advise. Bill encouraged these meetings.'

One of the hardest bits of news Cliff had to deal with during that period was the sudden death of Graham Jarvis, his drummer since 1978.

Unknown to Cliff, Jarvis had become a chronic alcoholic, sometimes polishing off a bottle of vodka before a show and another one back in his room late at night. On the last tour, which finished on 14 December 1985, the rest of the band were alarmed to notice that his skin and the whites of his eyes were turning yellow.

On 29 December he checked himself into a hospital detoxification programme in Croydon. Dave Cooke was the last group member to speak to him.

'I called him on the day before New Year's Eve and said I'd come along and play some backgammon with him,' he remembers. 'He sounded quite good. I told him I could either come that night or wait until the morning.

'I got a little Bible together for him as a present and at half past eight the next morning I called up to double check that it was OK to visit. The nurse answered and said, "Who's calling?" She then put me on to his wife Lorraine who was in tears. She said that he'd died half an hour ago.'

The shock to everyone came because they hadn't realized how seriously ill he had been. He hadn't lost his normal good humour throughout the tour and was never known to miss a beat. But, at 35 years of age, he was a victim of cirrhosis of the liver.

The funeral was in North London and all the band except Mart Jenner were there,' remembers Graham Todd. 'Dave Cooke had a song called "Where You Are" which Graham had always liked and Cliff was going to perform it. But when it came to the time he said a few words but he was just too choked up to sing. I think he felt that if he'd known about it he could have done something to get Graham off the booze but I don't think anything would have done that.'

It marked the end of an era. Cliff was already planning to change the line-up. He intended to be involved in a West End musical which was being put together by Dave Clark (formerly of the Dave Clark Five) and Jarvis' death provided a convenient opportunity to break the news. John Perry, Mart Jenner and Dave Cooke were phoned by David Bryce and told that their services would no longer be needed.

Taking part in a West End musical had been a long-term ambition of Cliff's. Since 1980 he had been specifically talking about a production which explored the possibilities of holographic technology.

'Having had a little experience in the acting world I would like to bring that together with the kind of singing I do to create the first real pop-rock musical,' Cliff said. 'In other words, get a really great story and pepper it with songs written by people like Terry Britten, John Farrar and Alan Tarney.

'Why shouldn't something like this happen? Why shouldn't the public go to a show and hear the top twenty live on stage, performed within the framework of a play? Why not? Why do we always have to have the traditional kind of musical? I'd like to do a show where every song gave me goose pimples, songs like "Miss You Nights", "Devil Woman" and "Dreamin'". I'd personally like to face that challenge.'

He had seen a lot of promise in a script sent to him by Chris

Hutchins, a Fleet Street gossip columnist who had once been publicist for Tom Jones and Engelbert Humperdinck.

It was a brilliant idea of a pop star who begins to tire of his career while at his peak and who one day meets a petrol pump attendant who is his spitting image. The star realizes that he can escape the pressure he's under by getting his lookalike to stand in for him by signing autographs at the stage door.

The story progresses with the lookalike taking over more and more areas of the star's life until he can perform his concerts. He then makes a move on the star's girlfriend. What excited Cliff about the idea was the possibility of having one of the characters played by himself in the form of a hologram. Unfortunately, a suitable ending was never found for the script and it was abandoned.

The project that Dave Clark approached Cliff with in 1983 was a science fiction musical, *Time*, which Clark had not only had a hand in writing but which he was keen to produce, using his own money. He had already been recruiting stars to contribute tracks to an album which would precede the theatre opening, people such as Julian Lennon, Freddie Mercury, Dionne Warwick and Stevie Wonder. Freddie Mercury had a posthumous hit in 1992 with 'In My Defence', from the musical.

It was a simplistic moral tale of the earth's judgment by the Time Lord Melchizidek – for the usual crimes of war and pollution – the fight for a reprieve organized by earthling pop star Chris and the wise sayings of the inscrutable Akash who, although apparently not meant to represent God, looked as though he'd have a hard time bowing down to anyone.

Its origins were in a musical called *The Time Lord*, with book and lyrics by David Soames and music by Jeff Daniels, which was put on at the Overground Theatre in Kingston-upon-Thames in 1978. Dave Clark didn't see it but he read the script and heard a tape of the songs, and thought he could do something with it.

Clark met with the two writers in 1980 and they began to forge something new. The story was altered, the songs were rewritten with Clark as an additional songwriter and a collection of new songs by outside writers was added into the mix.

The gist of the musical's message was that we'd all get on a lot better if we started being kind to the earth and kind to one other.

The more profound philosophical and theological issues raised by this homespun wisdom were ignored.

'It was a musical about caring,' says Dave Clark. 'Most of the bad things in life are caused through envy, bitterness and greed and unless you get yourself in order you are in no position to put the world in order.

'I believe all gods are one and that's what I tried to convey through the musical. I believe that everyone should have the right to believe in the way that they feel is right for them. As the song says, "It's in every one of us to be wise."'

In this respect Cliff's personal beliefs were at odds with the intention of the writers. But he was able to justify his role by claiming that while the musical fell short of presenting the whole truth, as he understood it, what it did say was true as far as it went.

When Akash, represented by a hologram of Sir Laurence Olivier's head, declared that love was everlasting and death was defeated Cliff felt he could add, under his breath, that this was so with Jesus. There was a sense in which it was 'in everyone of us to be wise', as the final song said, but only if we were 'born again of the Spirit'.

Some church people felt that the omissions constituted heresy rather than partial truth. The teaching that wisdom is to be found within, they pointed out, was uncomfortably close to the New Age doctrine that we need no outside saviour to reconcile us with God because God, or the energy source, is within us all.

There was a line in the original version which referred to a 'Time Lord' who went to Nazareth two thousand years ago. Cliff had this changed to 'a guiding light'.

'I respect Cliff for his religious beliefs and there was always a fine line to be walked,' admits Dave Clark. 'We had a lot of discussions about it and we ended up with no references to God at all. The challenge for Cliff was to play a part. I didn't want people to think that it was Cliff.'

Time, despite the involvement of top musical director Larry Fuller and top choreographer Arlene Philips, opened on 9 April 1986 to scathing reviews. *The Sunday Times* called it 'a spectacular load of bilge' and claimed that Cliff couldn't act his way into a deserted railway station.

Theatre critic Sheridan Morley considered it one of the

century's worst musicals and Milton Shulman thought it could only really be enjoyed by children. The only aspect of the production to be universally applauded were the sets created by John Napier.

Yet no amount of condemnation heaped on the musical – for its one-dimensional characters, its lack of drama and its unmemorable score – could prevent it from being a hit. Cliff fans were faithful to the extreme, treating it as if it was a twelve-month concert run, streaming to the front of the stage during the finale and waving their Cliff scarves in the air. When Cliff's term finished there had been over 700,000 tickets sold.

Time was a big commitment for a pop star in Cliff's position to make. It not only restricted him to one city for a year and a half but it meant being tied to a daily routine. He was on stage eight times a week, a total of over a thousand hours in a twelve-month run.

He would drive up to London each day in his Volkswagen Golf and got into the habit of eating his main meal after the show, often in the company of other members of the cast. He became particularly close to Roger Bruce, the production manager, and the dancers Wayne Aspinal, Jodie Wilson and Rosemarie Ford.

'We all found it terribly difficult to wind down after a show and we liked to do something different,' says Wilson. 'Sometimes we'd even play tennis. We'd go down to the David Lloyd Tennis Centre near Heathrow and would start a game at around midnight.'

Because Sunday was his only day off, Cliff would spend the time at home rather than attend church. It marked the beginning of a withdrawal from regular church-going, a move which worried his friends who could envisage the prospect of him drifting along without the affiliations which he himself had always recommended in his books as being essential to Christian growth.

His final night in *Time* came on 11 April 1987. Cliff was congratulated on stage by Dave Clark and then said a few words himself, some of them to the critics who had panned the show. 'You should write now that this is the greatest thing that has ever hit theatre,' he said.

Without Cliff, *Time* lost the focus of its commercial appeal. He was replaced by David Cassidy but six months later the show was taken off only to return for one night in 1988 to raise money for Aids charities. It was never to open in any other country.

twenty four
'ALWAYS LOOKING AHEAD'

Cliff had been without a smash hit album of original material since Alan Tarney worked the magic on *Wired For Sound* five years before. *Now You See Me... Now You Don't* (1982), a gospel album in disguise, had reached number four in the album charts but of the singles released from the album, 'The Only Way Out' just edged into the top ten and 'Where Do We Go From Here?' only reached number sixty.

Dressed For The Occasion (1983), which was recorded at the Royal Albert Hall with the London Philharmonic Orchestra, consisted mostly of back catalogue songs. *Silver* and *Rock 'n' Roll Silver* (1983), designed to mark Cliff's 25 years in show business, were a mixture of new material and old rock 'n' roll classics.

The Rock Connection (1984) was another of Cliff's 'co-productions', this time with his former engineer Keith Bessey. It only reached number 43 in the charts, his worst position since the *I'm Nearly Famous* comeback. The singles picked from it did no better. 'Heart User' made number 46 while 'Shooting From The Heart' didn't even enter the top 50.

It was David Bryce's suggestion to bring Tarney back as producer to arrest the slide.

Ever since hearing Michael Jackson's *Thriller*, which yielded five hit singles on both sides of the Atlantic, Cliff had nursed the idea of recording an album chock-full of hits – the ultimate Cliff Richard collection.

'I had dinner with David Bryce and I said to him that I felt I had never done the definitive Cliff Richard album,' says Tarney.

'"We Don't Talk Any More" should really have been on *I'm No Hero* and *Wired For Sound* was a hodge-podge of all sorts of writers. I felt I had never produced the album I could have done.'

Tarney's opportunity to do this came with *Always Guaranteed*. Recorded in September 1986 at R.G. Jones Studios while Cliff was still appearing in *Time*, it was one of his best albums ever, providing all his hit singles for the next year and the first of 1988. It was also one of his most commercial albums with sales of over 1.3 million copies.

It had been written in the studio. Tarney, who again played almost all the instruments, would arrive early in the morning to write and then Cliff would spend four hours each afternoon adding his vocals to the new backing track before disappearing to the Dominion Theatre.

'Alan liked to work on his own,' remembers engineer Gerry Kitchingham. 'He would start the day wandering around strumming the guitar and then he'd come up with a tune and he'd call me in and we'd get something on tape. That's the way he wrote "Some People". He came in with nothing and by the next day he'd got a hit song.'

Always Guaranteed illustrated Cliff's ability to come back with commercial cutting-edge pop after another period in the wilderness. Almost thirty years after his first hit he was still coming up with material that was effective competition for the chart acts of the day.

Although he was justly proud of his past achievements and would gladly recite chart positions and record sales, his main motivation was to do things of contemporary significance.

His most animated conversation was always about the music he was currently making, not about glory days gone by. He never basked in nostalgia, read books about himself and only reluctantly took part in reunions with the Shadows.

'He doesn't keep cuttings,' says Bill Latham. 'He has no interest in old photographs. He's just not interested in talking about the past. You would expect him to have all sorts of mementoes but he only has a few things hanging up on the walls because they happened to be there. If he lost them all overnight he wouldn't care two hoots.'

This was part of the key to remaining current. Too much attention to his own past and he would have found himself as a golden oldie, affectionately remembered but unranked. Part of his achievement had been never to recycle one part of his career and sell it back to the public.

He has never been one of those longing for a return of the excitement that surrounded the innovations of Elvis and Bill Haley. It genuinely bemused him when old Teddy boys came up to him and bemoaned the death of rock 'n' roll.

'There is a new excitement today,' he said. 'If I'm asked whether I prefer singing "Move It" or my latest hit I say my latest hit because it will have a different kind of excitement. I would prefer to be excited by today's noise than yesterday's.'

He needed to feel that he was a force to be reckoned with and he still regarded the singles charts as a battleground where reputations were won and lost and where newcomers needed to be seen off.

The stories are legion of Cliff's obsession with chart placings. When 'Devil Woman' entered the *Billboard* charts Bruce Welch walked across the stage during a concert in Hong Kong and whispered the news in his ear. In the summer of 1989, when the holiday gang were sailing off the coast of Croatia (then Yugoslavia), Cliff had his chart placings faxed to him on the boat despite the fact that all normal business was ignored during this period.

In 1990 he was delighted to have surpassed Elvis Presley's record of 55 British top ten hits, making him the supreme top-ten artist of all time in his own country.

The singles' market had become less significant than when he launched his career. Having a hit single no longer meant making a fortune. Yet the top thirty remained an effective shop window. It ensured radio and newspaper coverage, established the artist in the public consciousness and promoted forthcoming albums.

'He really wants to remain a contemporary artist,' says Alan Tarney. 'I think he sees any newcomer as a threat to him and it's really good for him to see things in this way. He responds immediately.

'Most people stop fighting but Cliff wants to get up there and be better. Whoever is the latest heart-throb, Cliff would like nothing better than to get up there and show them how it should be done. That's what keeps him going.'

Throughout the eighties he found himself in demand by major

artists wanting him to duet with them. Andrew Lloyd-Webber asked him to record a single of 'All I Ask Of You' with his then wife Sarah Brightman, which would draw attention to his new musical, *Phantom of the Opera*.

A & M Records approached him to duet with Janet Jackson, Dave Clark had his vocals added to a track from *Time* recorded by Stevie Wonder in California and Elton John invited Cliff to join him in singing 'Slow Rivers'.

It marked the rehabilitation of an artist who, although hugely popular with the public, had never been taken to the bosom of the rock aristocracy and had received a torrent of critical abuse over the years.

His beliefs were no more popular than they had been in 1966 but he had proved that he was a man of his word, unafraid to take the 'road less travelled', and integrity had its own reward. His music hadn't become more hard-edged or rebellious but there was no shame in being an unadulterated hit maker, especially if you had never made claims to be anything else.

'I think it takes a lot of strength of character to have Cliff's choices,' says Tony King, who is able to compare Cliff with his knowledge of working closely with such stars as Elton John, Freddie Mercury, John Lennon and Mick Jagger.

'In a way his choices are more daring because they are out of step with what everyone thinks you have to be in order to be a rock 'n' roll artist. They are braver choices in that respect. Mick Jagger's choices are certainly a lot easier for young people to identify with.'

The anarchic cult comedy show of the mid-eighties, 'The Young Ones', cast one of its main characters, played by Rik Mayall, as an ardent Cliff fan (hence the tribute in the title). When the cast came to record a single for the charity Comic Relief they chose to do a send-up of 'Living Doll' and asked Cliff to join in the joke. The record sold one million copies, almost as many as the original, and reached number one.

It was useful in keeping Cliff's name linked with contemporary pop cultural figures and also of showing him to be someone who could laugh at himself.

The only time he has been enraged by the mockery directed at him was in 1984 when the *NME* (13 October), carried a 'review' of his gospel concert at Hammersmith Odeon. It was little more than a piece of hate mail written in the style of a conversation between the reviewer and Satan.

It made no mention of the music but attacked Cliff, his fans and Christianity. It referred to Cliff as a 'Nazi', ridiculed his sexual morals and described his fans as 'two-dimensional masochists'. The final paragraph was an obscene insult.

Cliff responded by suing the paper for libel. He won and was awarded £5,000 damages which he immediately gave to the Arts Centre Group.

The most unlikely recording combination was that of Cliff and Van Morrison: the beaming pop star and the moody blues-soul legend. Where Cliff was smooth, Van was rough. Where Cliff was adored, Van was admired. Physically, temperamentally and artistically they were polar opposites, each revered for different reasons by different audiences.

Yet what they shared was apparently stronger than these differences. They had both started out in the skiffle era, were interested in spiritual issues and had doggedly followed their chosen paths regardless of fashion. It was on this level that they had first met at an Arts Centre Group supper party and a strong mutual respect had been forged.

When Morrison came to record his album *Avalon Sunset* he thought it would be interesting to contrast his tough soulful vocals with Cliff's sweet mellifluous voice. The song, 'Whenever God Shines His Light', was not one of Morrison's best, but it was one of his more clearly Christian songs in that it linked God to Christ, rather than to an anonymous natural force. It became his first top ten hit in Britain since, as a member of Them, he reached number two in 1965 with 'Here Comes The Night'.

Some purists thought that an artist of Morrison's stature should never have deigned to record with a mere show business creature such as Cliff. For them it was a like a member of the aristocracy slumming it with a Woolworth's checkout girl.

'Why did you choose to record a duet with Cliff Richard?' asked an incredulous *NME* reporter. 'Are you an admirer of his work?'

'Cliff Richard?' asked Morrison, making sure he'd heard the question correctly. 'You're joking, aren't you? You're kidding? I grew up with Cliff. He'd be on "Saturday Club". I was a teenager, you know...'

The same year that Cliff increased his credibility with the rock audience by helping Morrison back into the charts he had his first dance-floor hit with 'I Just Don't Have The Heart', a record produced and written by the Mike Stock, Matt Aitken and Peter Waterman team, which did wonders for Cliff-awareness among *Smash Hits* readers.

Stock, Aitken and Waterman had been dominating the charts with danceable pop tunes with programmed drum beats and vocals by singers such as Kylie Minogue, Jason Donovan and Rick Astley. For a while he team seemed invincible. The music critics hated their formulaic music and dippy lyrics but they sold by the truck load. By 1991 they had produced or written one hundred and six titles and seen fifty-two of them enter the top ten, making them the most successful team of producer-songwriters in British chart history.

As chart-orientated people, the SAW team and Cliff understood each other. Whereas Cliff couldn't see himself replicated in Mick Hucknall (from Simply Red) or Michael Hutchence (from INXS), he could see himself in Jason Donovan who presented a cheerful image, had an interest in musical theatre and made hit singles.

Stock, Aitken and Waterman met Cliff for the first time at the Ivor Novello Awards in April 1989 where they had won an award for writing Rick Astley's 'Never Gonna Give You Up'. Cliff was at the next table and he leaned over and said, 'If you ever come up with another song like that, give me a call.' They told him they'd love to work with him and took it from there.

'Usually we know the singers we work with very well but we didn't know Cliff and there wasn't time to find out what made him tick' says Peter Waterman. 'We had to imagine we were Cliff and dream up an appropriate story.

'I came up with the title. I said, "Just imagine Cliff had fallen in love with this girl and then met someone else. What would he do?" We thought, he's such a spiffing chap he wouldn't have the heart to tell her, and that's where it came from. That's what the song was all about.'

'I Just Don't Have The Heart' proved, if anything, that Cliff was the consummate British pop singer, able to surf any trend. The technology had changed but pop music, at heart, remained the same: it was melodic, rhythmic music, usually about love and usually with good harmonies. One sign of the new technology was that for 'I Just Don't Have The Heart' Cliff was taped doing his warm-up vocal exercises, then a sample of it was used effectively at the beginning of the single. 'When Cliff heard it,' says Waterman, 'he had no idea whose voice it was.'

Cliff has always produced his best work when surrounded by talented producers and writers looking for a vehicle. If he had been a singer-songwriter he would undoubtedly have run out of ideas by the early sixties but being an interpreter of other people's material meant that he was constantly able to recharge his career with the fire of other people's youth. The best songs throughout his career have been written by young men (and one woman) under forty.

The songwriters most successful with Cliff – such as Hank Marvin, Bruce Welch, Alan Tarney, Terry Britten and Chris Eaton – were those who'd worked with him as musicians and had passed songs on to him directly. They were also the first to learn what music he was currently fascinated with.

Terry Britten used to arouse Cliff's interest by rehearsing his latest riffs during band soundchecks. 'Cliff would then come over and say, "That's nice, Terry," and Terry would shrug and say, "Oh, it's just something I'm working on",' remembered Graham Todd. 'Then Cliff would say, "That would make a nice song." Terry was very smart in that respect.'

Cliff still prided himself on being able to spot potential hits, and argued that it was this instinct, even more than his voice, which had enabled him to stay on top for so long.

Chris Eaton wrote 'Saviour's Day' in October 1989. He brought a demo of the song to the office Christmas party despite having been told by Gill Snow, Cliff's secretary, that the whole of 1990 was already mapped out, with 'From a Distance' planned as the next year's Christmas single.

'I told Cliff that I wanted him to hear this song,' says Eaton, 'so we left the party and went to sit in his Rolls where we played the tape. He loved it straight away. He said, "This is a number one song." You've got to hand it to him – he does have a feeling for what's going to make it.'

His next collaborator was Paul Moessl who was spotted playing in the house band at Blazer's club in Windsor when David Bryce went along to see Jimmy Tarbuck. He thought he sounded innovative and arranged for him to deputize during *Time*.

When Cliff formed a new band in 1987 for his 'Beyond Time' tour he retained Alan Park as his musical director, Mark Griffiths on bass and John Clark on guitar but recruited the rest of the musicians from the ranks of the *Time* musicians, including Paul Moessl on keyboards.

A year later Moessl was suddenly summoned to David Bryce's office in Esher, for a 'little talk', and assumed that he was about to be sacked. He just couldn't think what he'd done wrong.

'Then they said, "Have a listen to this song,"' he remembers. 'It was "Mistletoe and Wine". I said, "Yeh, it's very Christmassy isn't it?" They said, "We want to record it and Cliff wants to give you the chance of doing it." I was completely taken aback.

'I don't know why they chose me. I put it down to youth. Cliff will always take a chance. I think he susses out young people and if he trusts that they've got an idea about what's going on he'll try and tap into that.'

'Mistletoe and Wine' went to number one and became the best-selling British single of 1988, and Paul Moessl had become the new blue-eyed boy who could carry on bringing new life to Cliff's recording career.

For *Stronger*, Cliff's follow-up to *Always Guaranteed*, Moessl was introduced as 'guest arranger' on two tracks – 'Joanna' and 'The Best of Me' – with Cliff credited as producer. 'The Best of Me', the first release from the album, went to number two and sold over 750,000 copies.

Because of the success, Moessl became arranger and co-producer for Cliff's 1991 Christmas album, *Together With Cliff Richard*, a UK-only release capitalizing on his unprecedented run of Christmas number ones, which included his part in the re-recorded 'Do They Know It's Christmas?' for Band Aid.

Instead of a great follow-up to *Always Guaranteed* and *Stronger*, his last two studio albums, he produced an uninspired collection of 'Christmas favourites' including 'Scarlet Ribbons', 'Silent Night' and, 'White Christmas'. It was as if the seventies and eighties had never happened.

In 1992 Moessl was given the chance to co-produce and arrange an album of original material – *Cliff Richard: The Album*. He even wrote two of the songs with Cliff. Released in April it topped the British album charts for one week and spawned the hit single 'Peace In Our Time'.

'The original title was *Access All Areas* (taken from the badges worn backstage by those granted unlimited access to stage, arena and dressing rooms), and reflected the idea that we tried to get different song styles onto the album,' says Moessl.

'Cliff was always looking ahead. He was into fresh ideas, fresh turnover and he's always trying to do something someone else hasn't done. He had a bad throat when we were recording and he started singing in a completely different way.

'It sounded so good that we recorded the album while it was in this lapsed state. When he got better he couldn't sing in exactly the same way again. It's a bizarre way of doing things but it worked and it shows his openness towards doing things in different ways.'

At the beginning of the nineties those working with Cliff were concerned that he was only now feeling the full effect of Peter Gormley's retirement a decade earlier even though Gormley continued to offer advice. Although he was already well-established by the time Gormley took over his career, there's no doubting the effect of this quietly spoken but rock-solid Australian in guiding him steadily through the ups and downs.

Gormley was a modest, unassuming man who valued instinct more than careful planning. He said he never did market research ('it's all bull'), never went out to create an image for Cliff ('image creation is a term that annoys me considerably') and had no philosophy of management that he could ever pass on to anyone else.

'You did what you had to do', he said simply. 'You worked according to your own judgment. It was purely a matter of instinct and judgment. There were no methods whatsoever. We never had any arguments about it. I presume we all thought alike.'

As a manager he was more than a negotiator, promoter and protector. He was a friend and father-figure to Cliff, and his instinct for what was right extended to the choice of singles.

'He has an incredible intuition about what is right and wrong for Cliff,' says Cliff's former producer Dave Mackay.

'Sometimes you'd be slaving away over something for Cliff, trying to get exactly the right feel, and he'd just walk in and stand at the back and say, "Hate those drums, son." You'd listen to it back again and he would always be right although he wasn't musical. He just knew Cliff and his audience.'

With Peter Gormley gone the management was divided between David Bryce (professional), Malcolm Smith (business) and Bill Latham (charity, Christian and media). None of them had Gormley's overall control. The fear expressed by those within the inner circle was that Cliff would now increasingly make decisions that went unchallenged and that this wouldn't be good for his career.

'Peter was the rock on which it was all built,' said one member of the inner circle who had worked with all three. 'Cliff and Peter Gormley were the greatest double act of all time. People always underestimate Peter but Cliff knew. He provided him with the ultimate platform. There is something wonderful about Cliff and Peter preserved that for thirty years. He kept it pure.

'Now he's lost that guiding figure. The next phase will be interesting to watch.'

twenty five
HEATHCLIFF

Typical of Cliff's desire to top his previous achievements and defy his critics was his decision, made in 1992, to commission, finance and perform in a musical based on Emily Brontë's 1847 novel *Wuthering Heights*. Unlike *Time*, this musical would tour, playing in Birmingham, Sheffield, Manchester and Edinburgh before coming to London.

Cliff had loved *Wuthering Heights* ever since being taught it by Jay Norris at Cheshunt County Secondary School in 1957. He was particularly attached to the character of Heathcliff, the foundling boy who in his pursuit of Cathy Earnshaw reveals dark and mysterious passions. It has even been suggested that it was his fascination with Heathcliff that favourably disposed him towards the name Cliff when it was first suggested in 1958.

Heathcliff was an unusual choice of fictional hero because he embodied many of the elements of Romanticism which ran counter to Cliff's personal beliefs. Heathcliff is the natural man, untamed by civilization, who strikes people as being an 'evil beast', possibly a 'devil', who has a 'half-civilized ferocity' lurking behind his brows – whereas Cliff, even prior to his Christian conversion, was never prone to wildness.

Cliff was obviously unconcerned about the philosophical undercurrents of the book. Although he admitted that it had 'depth and complexity' he was ultimately attracted to it as 'a tragic story, a pathetic failure of manhood; the story of a man obsessed with one woman to the exclusion of all else'.

When he first announced his ambition to play Brontë's tragic hero the press were quick to point out the dissimilarities between Cliff and Heathcliff. How could this clean-living Christian whose life had been famously free of passionate entanglements play the part of the 'fierce, pitiless, wolfish man'? Surely he couldn't hope to follow in the footsteps of Laurence Olivier?

Writing in *The Independent*, columnist David Aaronovitch said, 'Cliff as Heathcliff seems as incongruous as, say, Hugh Grant playing Falstaff or Jodie Foster's Lady Bracknell... Surely the man ought to realize that you cannot be one thing for most of your life, and then expect to be allowed to become another.' Comparable miscasting suggested by other journalists included Max Bygraves as Titus Andronicus, Bonnie Langford as Medea, John Inman as Ben Hur, Michael Jackson as Othello and Perry Como as the Antichrist.

Cliff's defence was that actors didn't have to have experienced the emotions they portrayed in order to be convincing. Wasn't that what acting meant? All they needed was insight into their own potential to behave in other ways. He asked whether it was necessary to kill someone in order to play the role of a murderer.

Yet the point being made by his critics was valid. There is such a thing as miscasting. The question was not merely whether Cliff could plumb the passions and cruelties he would have to act out, but whether his public image was so well defined that no audience would suspend its disbelief, even for an evening.

As always, the widespread conviction that he couldn't achieve something only spurred him on. He had wanted to play the part of Heathcliff for so long that no obstacle was going to stand in his way. He was even willing to sink his own money into the project so that no one but himself would lose if the venture failed.

'What goaded me on was the vehemence of the press,' Cliff admits. 'They kept saying that I couldn't possibly do this. "Mr Goody Two-Shoes? There's no way he can do it." I had thought that because we were doing something different and dangerous that they would support me. I had thought that they would at least say, "We don't think you can do it but we wish you the best of luck." But they didn't.'

He began by recruiting long-time friends as collaborators. John Farrar, who'd worked with Cliff as both musician and songwriter, was asked to do the music, and Tim Rice, who had been Norrie Paramor's assistant at EMI from 1966 until 1968, was invited to do the lyrics. Frank Dunlop, founder of the Young Vic in London and a former director of the Edinburgh International Festival, was asked to direct.

The book, which didn't aim to be a straight retelling of *Wuthering Heights*, was thrashed out in meetings between director and star. Dunlop's starting point was that he wanted the story to be told entirely in song but Cliff was adamant that he wanted dialogue. 'If I'm going to be in a show, I want to act,' he said. 'I want to speak-act, as well as sing-act.'

'Frank wrote out a basic scenario,' says Cliff. 'He's brilliant at that. Then every time I came across something in the book which I thought we had to have in I would tell him and he would slot it in. The only stuff that we had in the musical that's not actually in, *Wuthering Heights* is the journey abroad which attempts to fill in the missing three years of his life.

'That idea came from both of us. We wondered where we could take him. I thought that we had to have him in Africa because I wanted to include some African rhythms. He said that he would check out that possibility and he came back and said that the period we were covering was the time of Clive of India and that the Brits at that time were going to Africa, India and China. They would pick up gold and go on to China and buy opium. So we decided to take him through that.'

As the scenario was developed, Rice would be faxed with information on the pages in the novel which needed to be translated into song. 'We would tell Tim that we needed a song here, here and there,' says Cliff. 'We would let him know the actual page numbers. He would work by taking actual words and lines from the book. For example, "Dream Tomorrow" starts with the words "I shall think it a dream tomorrow" and that is a straight lift from the text.'

Rice (who lives in London) and Farrar (who lives in Los Angeles) met infrequently during the actual writing, both preferring to do their writing alone. Farrar was the first to get to work. He happened to have just read *Wuthering Heights* when Cliff called him and quickly wrote the music to three tracks which were then passed on to Rice.

'Whenever I've met Tim Rice over the years he has always chided me for never having recorded one of his songs,' says Cliff. 'So this time I rang him and said, "I know I've never done one of your songs – how would you like to do an album?" I told him about the project and he said that he would be delighted to be a part of it.'

It was in the spring of 1994 that the initial public announcements were made. Recordings of the first songs were started in Los Angeles and at Abbey Road. Cliff was pictured visiting Brontë country in Yorkshire in the company of Jay Norris. Press launches took place in London, Birmingham, Sheffield, Aberdeen and Glasgow. *Heathcliff* was booked to open in November of that year and tickets went on sale.

However, three months after the press launch, it was announced that *Heathcliff* was being postponed due to 'rehearsals being behind schedule'. In order to avoid the huge financial loss he would have made if he didn't use the pre-booked venues (a total of 27 days) Cliff swiftly arranged for a new tour to fulfil the dates and honour the tickets sold. It would be called 'Hit List' and would feature every top five single of his career.

A delay in rehearsals was the least of the problems facing *Heathcliff* at that point. The truth was that it had not yet been written and Cliff could see that there was no way that it was going to be ready by the anticipated opening night of 8 November. It was a great personal disappointment, but unavoidable in the circumstances.

'I knew that if I hadn't done something I would have been faced with a deficit of £5 million,' says Cliff. 'Tim and John are both people who don't take to being rushed. Quite right too. If you want quality you have to let it simmer a bit. Tim later said to me that five years is quite normal for a brand new musical.

'The interesting thing is, the bookings for *Heathcliff* had already stopped but after the 'Hit List' tour they tripled. People weren't going to come in their hordes to see the musical at that point because they hadn't yet heard anything from it. On the tour I then sang three of the songs and the bookings skyrocketed.'

The following year the singles 'Had To Be' (with Olivia Newton-John) and 'Misunderstood Man', and the album *Songs From Heathcliff* were released. The singles, which reached 22 and 19 respectively in the charts, didn't do as well as Cliff had hoped. He felt that this was in part due to a snub from BBC Radio 2, previously the natural home for Cliff 's music.

Although the success of the musical wasn't dependent on BBC

Radio, this action irritated him. The pop charts had been his natural home for so long and while not calling for special treatment he felt that his singles deserved to be heard by the public.

'"Misunderstood Man" didn't get any airplay,' he says. '"Had To Be" should have been number one, but it didn't get heard by anybody. Radio 2 wouldn't play it because they said it was "too dynamic". In other words, the song goes up and down. I can't understand this. I called a London radio station's phone-in programme and told them I couldn't understand this attitude. Of course, they then kept playing it and asking their listeners whether they thought it was too dynamic or whether the guitar solo was too loud.'

On 3 March 1996, at the Kensington Roof Gardens in London, Cliff finally announced the cast and the rescheduled dates. His co-star, playing Cathy, was to be Helen Hobson, and the show was to open in Birmingham on 16 October, going on to Sheffield, Manchester and Edinburgh, before coming to the Apollo in Hammersmith, London. Tickets were to go on sale the next day.

Almost immediately it was certain that *Heathcliff* was going to be a box office success. Fans were camping out overnight to make sure of getting tickets. By July, 300,000 tickets had been sold and the advance takings were estimated to be £8.5 million, a British theatre record. Cliff was invited to Tower Records in London's Piccadilly Circus to cut a celebratory cake.

When *Heathcliff* finally opened in October it received exactly the kind of critical mauling that Cliff had expected. While acknowledging that Cliff was an extremely capable singer and that the show was thoroughly enjoyed by his dedicated fans, the components of the show were mercilessly attacked. Frank Dunlop's production was 'awful', John Farrar's music was 'vapid pop pap' and Tim Rice 'didn't appear to have tried with his lyrics'.

'I wasn't surprised by the reviews,' says Tim Rice, who himself felt the production fell between two stools in that the music was rock but the staging was traditional. 'However, I think that a lot of the critics were unnecessarily vicious. If you're a part of something which is considered to be a hit – *Beauty and the Beast*, for example – then almost everything in it gets reviewed well.

'But there were songs of mine in *Beauty and the Beast* which frankly weren't any better than the songs I did for *Heathcliff*, but because *Heathcliff* was perceived to be an artistic mess by the critics, they slagged off the songs as well.'

The main point made by critics was that Cliff was miscast; too old for the particular role, too inexperienced in musicals and plainly out of his depth. His acting was wooden, his accent, in the opinion of one reviewer, wandered 'between Weybridge, Macclesfield and New York' and it was risible to see Britain's best-behaved pop star smoking opium, acting as a passionate lover and beating a pregnant woman.

However, none of this flak affected Cliff because he didn't read a single review. He remained unshaken in his convictions. The proof, as far as he was concerned, was in the box-office pudding. He did what he thought was right, the public came in their hundreds of thousands and everyone appeared to enjoy the evening. The critics, in Cliff's opinion, didn't understand public taste, whereas his career had been built on knowing what people liked.

'The critics were wrong about *Phantom of the Opera*,' he argues. 'They were wrong about *Cats*, *Les Miserables* and *Starlight Express*. They were four of the longest-running shows in the West End. It's obvious to me that the critics have no concept of what the public actually want and because they don't know, they don't understand what people like me are trying to do.

'I'm not interested in doing something that is only liked by myself and one critic. I've never run my career like that. That's why they've written me off so often but it's also probably why I'm still here. I get written off because I don't do what people think is the thing to do. The danger with reading reviews is that you read them and you become depressed. Then you try too hard.'

Cliff's fans, as ever, were likewise not perturbed by the opinions of the experts. *The Times* interviewed one fan who had travelled from Perth, Western Australia, to see it and another who had bought tickets for 22 performances. When it closed it had been seen by almost half a million people. Additionally, the two albums *Songs From Heathcliff* and *Heathcliff Live* went on to sell 300,000 copies while the video reached the top spot in the music video charts.

By the time it was all over *Heathcliff* had taken up five years of Cliff's life – an eighth of his career so far. It was a huge investment of his time, talent and money. 'At the drop of a hat I would do it again,' he says. 'But I don't feel that now the stage run is over that I have somehow let go of it. *Heathcliff* is mine.'

The years devoted to *Heathcliff* affected his achievements as a recording artist. Between 1994 and 1997 he released only five singles, one of which was a re-release ('Miss You Nights') and the rest were taken from *Heathcliff*. None of them made the top ten. Likewise, the only albums released were either compilations – *The Hit List*, *Cliff at the Movies* and *The Rock 'n' Roll Years* – or *Heathcliff*-related. His 1998 album *Real As I Wanna Be* was his first album of original non-*Heathcliff* material for five and a half years.

The lack of chart action didn't unsettle him. His normal pattern was to issue three singles a year to support an album. If there were no albums, it followed that there would be no singles. The compilation albums were planned by EMI. Cliff has no particular affection for compilations ('I can't understand who buys them') and didn't even listen to the entire box-set version of *The Rock 'n' Roll Years*, which consisted of four CDs and a handsome booklet.

His absence from the charts didn't mean a loss of visibility. If anything, his celebrity status rose. In 1995 he was chosen to sing for the VE celebrations in front of Buckingham Palace and to perform at the Royal Variety Performance and then, on 25 October, he became the first British pop star to be knighted by the Queen.

Even though Cliff had met the Queen many times before, he was still overwhelmed by the award. He went to the palace with his three sisters (his mother had seen him receive his OBE) and was given a brief rehearsal before walking in and kneeling on his right knee before the Queen and being dubbed on both shoulders with the traditional sword.

'It's only after you stand up again that she puts the award around your neck and then she speaks for the first time,' says Cliff. 'I can't think what she said to me. I was so emotional I could hardly talk. I got really choked. I think she said something like "It's been a long time coming," and I just mumbled because I couldn't talk.'

The knighthood, coupled with the OBE, gave him unprecedented access. Although he had always been a reputable figure unlikely to bring disgrace on any organization which chose to associate with him, he had now been elevated to the highest echelons of British society where he could mix freely with politicians, landowners, aristocrats, captains of industry and royalty. Watching the finals at Wimbledon in July 1997 he turned to his sisters and said, 'Do you think we could ever have imagined this? Here we are sitting in the Members' Enclosure drinking tea and eating scones and you're sitting with a knight!'

His journey from among the upturned packing cases of Bury Green Estate never ceases to amaze him. He knows that few of the people he now mingles with came from such humble origins.

'When you have achieved longevity you naturally become a little bit more establishment,' he says. 'It's nowhere near as bad as people make out. I don't know why people want to knock the establishment because it's a lot better than where I was.'

He was one of only a handful of pop stars (Sting, Elton John, George Michael and Chris de Burgh were the others) to be invited to attend Princess Diana's funeral. He felt honoured to have been considered. He was in New York to watch the US Open when she died and didn't expect to be invited.

'Because it was such a terrible shock to everyone the detectives had to go through her Christmas card list to find the names of people that should be there,' he says. 'Now, I wasn't on her list but I was someone who she apparently talked about quite a lot and they knew that she had enjoyed the times we had met up and had dinner together. So they put my name down as being someone that she liked.

'I knew her quite well socially but I couldn't say that we were close. We skied from the same hotel. I sang for her boys. In fact I did my first Royal Command Performance for William out in Austria! She was a fantastic girl. She wasn't perfect because none of us are but as people go, she was really special.

'She did care about people. I've met drivers who've told me that they'd driven her just once and she'd written to thank them. She was incredible and her death is a terrible loss. Even now I find it hard to take in. To talk of Diana in the past tense seems really ridiculous. I don't think I've ever met anyone who had such a wonderful effect on people.

'We were planning to work together during the celebrations for my 40 years in show business in London during 1998. She had called me to Kensington Palace to meet some people from the Leprosy Mission and some rich Asian men. I didn't know what was expected from me. I knew I couldn't sign cheques for millions. Then one of these guys asked me if I'd be willing to do a concert and Diana immediately said, "I'd come." So they said, "Do you mean that you'd patronize the evening?" She said, "Of course I would."'

It was never to happen. The next event to bring the two names together was the Diana tribute album, where Cliff's version of Paul Field's song 'All That Matters', produced by Alan Tarney, was put alongside contributions from such international megastars; as Paul McCartney, Bruce Springsteen, Michael Jackson, Barbra Streisand, Celine Dion, Whitney Houston and Luciano Pavarotti.

Besides being the year that he returned to active touring after being bound up with *Heathcliff*, 1998 was the fortieth anniversary of Cliff's entry into show business. It wasn't just 40 years since he cut his first single but 40 years since he turned professional, signed to EMI, made his big screen debut, first appeared in the charts, toured Britain and appeared on television.

However, Cliff was still not in the mood for nostalgia. He'd begun work on a new album that was being produced by Peter Wolf, an Austrian musician transplanted to America. A keyboard expert, Wolf had appeared on over 400 albums, played with the Mothers of Invention for four years and had produced American number one singles such as 'We Built This City' by Jefferson Starship, 'Who's Johnny?' by El Debarge and Wang Chung's 'Everybody Have Fun Tonight'.

Clive Black, former Managing Director of EMI Records, who had set up a production company, Blacknight, with Cliff, David Bryce and Malcolm Smith, had recommended Wolf after hearing his work on an album by Kristine Blond. Although Cliff's new record would be distributed by EMI, it would be a Blacknight production. 'The idea was to make an album that was honest,' says Wolf. 'It had to be what Cliff was. There was no grand plan other than to produce good music and present it in the most straight-ahead way possible.'

Unbelievably in light of his unparalleled track record as a chart artist, Cliff was now finding it difficult to make the playlists of the major stations. Without that sort of exposure, it would be hard to sell singles. Demographically, a 58-year-old singer wasn't considered suitable for Radio 1; even Radio 2, traditionally the home of adult-oriented rock, was revamping its image.

'There are four fantastic singles on this album,' Cliff said of *Real As I Wanna Be* while it was still in production. 'If I can get any airplay, they are certain hits. If I don't get any airplay, I would rather do another musical. I would rather do something where you plan, spend your money, do it and have the instant gratification of a large audience. Why should I waste my time recording if no one is going to hear what I do?'

When the album was released, he played a little game with the radio stations to prove his point that their refusal to play his music was because of his age, image and beliefs, not the quality of the music. He had some advance promotion white labels pressed of a remix of his next single, 'Can't Keep This Feeling In', attributing the recording to the as yet unknown artist Blacknight 001. The plan was to get the single accepted by saying it was the work of a young mixed-race boy from South London.

As Cliff had anticipated, this version of the single was given widespread airplay, especially on young urban stations that would never normally touch his material. E-Ze at Juice 105 FM declared it 'wicked rap'. Kurt Gee at Rebel FM thought it was 'cool'. 'It ended up number one on Climax Radio, Choice FM and all these cool urban stations,' says Clive Black. 'Eventually Cliff did a phoner with a DJ on Choice FM and the guy asked him to reveal who he was and he said, "I'm called Cliff Richard." It was very funny. I don't think they played it again but Cliff thought he'd made a point.'

Real As I Wanna Be was an accomplished album and Cliff's vocals were impeccable. The songs were rhythmically different, allowing him be more adventurous with his phrasing. Surprisingly, some of the better songs such as 'Even If It Breaks My Heart' and 'United For Evermore' with their Bee Gees-style harmonies were never released as singles. Instead the more mundane 'Can't Keep This Feeling In' (not the remix) and the gospel-flavoured 'The Miracle' were chosen. The album and the first single both peaked at number ten on the album's release in October 1998. 'The Miracle' failed to chart.

'Unfortunately it was the last album to go through EMI and so they didn't spend much time promoting it,' says Wolf. 'It didn't sell that well. As a good friend of mine once said, you can produce the best album in the world but it's only 30 per cent of the picture. The audience's perception of the artist is 30 per cent and the remaining 40 per cent is pure politics. You never have it under total control. In this case it was the politics that let the record down.'

For the first time, Cliff began talking about taking time off, something no one could ever have imagined him contemplating before this. The thought was always: but what would he do if he wasn't recording or performing? Although he always denied it publicly the critical reaction to *Heathcliff* had badly wounded him. This project had been so close to his heart.

So, in 1998, he would say: '*Heathcliff* was a career move. But I'd also like to do smaller things that were not career moves. I'd like to do a small part in a West End play or a short tour abroad. Things like that won't make me big money but I would enjoy doing them. I could still continue to relate to the fans and they would obviously still be able to follow me around.

'I'd like to slow down a little but I don't know how I would do it. I'd love to wipe out the diary and just work whenever I wanted to so that if I fancied taking a whole year off, I could.'

'MILLENNIUM PRAYER'

twenty six

Cliff's musings about the possibility of taking a year out seemed out of character. Ten years earlier, in his book *Single-Minded*, he had said that the only reasons he could imagine for 'ducking out' of show business would be the loss of his voice, a string of record failures or boredom. Even then, he believed his motive would not be to relax and indulge himself but to devote more of his time to 'specifically Christian activity'.

Although there were no signs of these impairments to his career, there were disturbances in his personal life that were causing him to rethink his priorities. The most significant of these was his relationship with Bill Latham. The two men had not only shared a home since 1965 but Latham had become his spiritual mentor, ghost writer, diary keeper, charity coordinator, personal organizer, publicist and close companion. Latham had protected him and guided him to such an extent that it seemed impossible to imagine Cliff without him.

Yet in 1998 cracks began to appear in their close friendship. In January, Latham suddenly terminated his seventeen-year relationship with Jill Clarke after becoming besotted with a secretary working at the Cliff Richard Organisation. Jill, who had been living at the house in Weybridge since the early 1990s, returned home one afternoon to discover a letter of dismissal on her bed. Having believed that they would eventually marry, she was absolutely shattered by the news. The new object of Latham's affections rebuffed his advances anyway.

It was left to Cliff to persuade Jill that it would be best if she left the house. To make the transition easy for her, the Cliff Richard Organisation bought a house nearby which she was given tenure of. Then, in July 1998, at the age of 60, Latham directed his attentions towards another woman, a 31-year-old Cliff fan from Germany named Pia Hoffman whom he had met in Mannheim two years previously when Cliff was promoting *Heathcliff* and she was working as a radio journalist.

Unknown to Cliff and certainly to Jill Clarke, Latham had been attracted to Pia during this time and had maintained contact. When he found himself single once again, he invited her to come to Britain. The relationship heated up and in January 1999, Pia moved into the house in Weybridge to be with Bill.

Those in Cliff's immediate circle were concerned at this new development. Some of them already knew Pia as a keen fan who as an eighteen-year-old had spent a year in London and had been a frequent visitor to the Dominion Theatre where Cliff was appearing in *Time*. She was a familiar figure, standing outside the dressing room doors at the end of each show and, after returning to Germany, had also shown up at European concerts.

The obvious worry was that she had locked onto Latham merely as a means of getting involved in Cliff's life. The fact that she had a background in radio journalism didn't help matters. Was it wise to allow a representative of the media to live in Cliff's home? Could she have a long-term ambition to write a 'warts and all' book about his life?

Others felt that Latham was being foolish. He was, after all, closer in age to Pia's mother and had only just emerged from a long-term relationship where he had found it impossible to make a commitment.

Christian friends were concerned that he would be accused of hypocrisy. Along with Cliff, he had always taught the uncompromising message that followers of Jesus were called to celibacy before marriage and to fidelity afterwards. He was the writer of Cliff's religious books and had helped define his views of sex and sexuality. 'There's a tendency today to be light on sin, to make excuses for it, and even sometimes to justify it,' he wrote in 1983. 'The story of Achan (told in Joshua chapter 7) gives me God's perspective and, uncomfortable though it is, I find that disobedience and sin – mine included – is unacceptable to him. Like a cancer which will destroy the whole body, it has to be located and removed.'

With the change in lifestyle came a retreat from the overt expressions of Christianity for which he had been known. The last Cliff book, *Single-Minded*, was written in 1988. The theological debates with Cliff that he had regularly conducted in churches throughout the country came to an end. He stopped attending church and privately admitted that he no longer had the spiritual certainties of his Crusader days.

Cliff wasn't happy with the new living arrangement, despite Latham's insistence that it was a temporary measure. By the summer of 1999, the couple had left the house and set up home together nearby. For the first time in his life, Cliff was living alone.

In October 1999, Jill Clarke did an interview with the *Sunday Mirror* in which she spilled the beans about her relationship with Latham and how poorly she felt she had been treated.

She told how she and Latham slept in separate bedrooms because Cliff disapproved of them sharing, that they couldn't be physically affectionate in front of him and that she had believed that Latham would marry her. 'In my heart I was committed to him,' she said. 'I felt I was married without having a piece of paper to prove it.'

Cliff and his management team were furious that Jill had spoken to the press, especially after having been given the house to live in. In situations where former partners of high-profile people are provided with accommodation, their discretion is usually assumed. 'It was the first time anyone from the inner circle had broken rank,' said one of them. 'I think she was actually caught on the hop. A journalist turned up on her doorstep, it was raining and Jill invited her in.'

Another disturbing event for Cliff was the death of TV presenter, Jill Dando. He had become close to her since being asked to surprise her during the filming of a *Holiday* programme in Vienna. Jill had been a keen fan since her teenage years in Weston-Super-Mare and yet had never met him so the production team set up an on-camera treat when she was presenting from the Royal Opera Ball. Expecting to be interviewing an Austrian prince, she instead turned around to see Cliff walking towards her and then sweeping her off in a waltz.

The two had a lot in common. Jill was well known from her fresh-faced look, her sunny disposition and her Christian faith. After years as a presenter on both the *Holiday* programme and *Crimewatch UK*, she remained unspoiled and humble.

She was returning to her home in Gowan Avenue in Fulham, West London, on the morning of 26 April 1999 when she was shot dead on her doorstep with a single bullet. The crime shocked the British public. That something so brutal and seemingly random could happen to someone apparently so good was inexplicable. Theories were developed about resentful former boyfriends, criminals who'd been trapped by *Crimewatch* and even international terrorists but they never led to anything. In July 2001 a local man, Barry George, who had an obsession with guns, celebrities and the BBC, was found guilty of the murder and jailed for life.

Cliff attended Dando's funeral at Clarence Park Baptist Church in Weston-Super-Mare on 21 May and later performed in a television tribute and at a service of thanksgiving. In interviews he professed bewilderment at the crime and for the first time admitted that his faith had been shaken. Why did God allow this to happen. Why wasn't she protected? 'Though the loss of Jill was tragic,' he said, 'for me it was another step of growth in life. If something like that happens to me I would like to think that my friends would philosophize and say, "Through this we can grow."'

A third blow to his life was the deterioration of his mother, now 79. Although she was in good physical health, she had succumbed to a form of Alzheimer's disease and was fast losing her memory. She'd had to be moved to a residential home in St Albans and, when Cliff visited her, she barely recognized him. This came as a great shock.

It may also have had the effect of releasing him from her expectations. As he had frequently explained, it was his mother's approval that often guided his choices in life. The simple question to himself 'Would mum like that?' had been his touchstone. Others have suggested that she affected his choice of partners. He would never have lived his life in a way that upset her.

He made the rather surprising confession in 1998 that he could imagine abandoning the single life. 'Now, for the first time, and I never thought I would feel this or say it, I can see that if the perfect partner stepped into my life, then I would change absolutely everything and re-order my life. I never considered it before. Yet, quite unexpectedly, I can sense that I could change my priorities.'

In 1999 he announced that he would be taking the year 2000 off. There would be no tours, no recording sessions, no television appearances and no album or single releases. Just as he had dreamed of doing, he would wipe the diary clean and would follow his own inclinations for twelve months.

Before the lull though, there would be a storm. In 1997 Paul Field had written a Christian musical, *Hopes and Dreams*, that was designed primarily for church audiences. The concept had been to explore the thoughts contained in the Lord's Prayer. The writer of the book, Stephen Deal, had thought that one of the songs should be a new setting for the Lord's Prayer itself but Field was initially resistant to the idea, arguing that it had been done too often. Deal pushed, saying that as the musical had the millennium in view, it would be good to match the prayer with a tune that people already associated with celebrations and new beginnings. 'As an example he suggested "Auld Lang Syne", says Field. 'It was pulled out of the air. It was almost said as a joke.'

Nothing was done about it for a while and then the notion began to intrigue him. 'I couldn't get the idea out of my head,' he says. 'I started to tinker around with it. I thought it was either the most cheesy, awful idea in the world or it was something that could actually fly. The truth is, it was probably both.'

In 1998 an album was made of the musical. Field invited Cliff to do the vocal on his song that combined the words of the Lord's Prayer with the tune of 'Auld Lang Syne'. 'At the time I suggested to him that it would make a great Christmas single but I got no response. I didn't hear anything else until a month before it was released when he played it to me after Jill Dando's memorial service at All Souls Church in London. By then it was all done and dusted.'

EMI, Cliff's recording company for 41 years, hadn't seen it as a single so David Bryce and Malcolm Smith had gone to Papillon Records, a label formed by Mike Andrews and Roy Eldridge from within the Chrysalis Group. 'They played the track to us and we assumed that this was Cliff's latest single and they were then going to try and interest us in another artist,' says Andrews. 'But they asked us if we wanted it. We couldn't believe that EMI weren't happy to go with it. Of course we jumped at it.'

Released in November 1999, it immediately sold 85,000 copies and became the subject of intense controversy. Leading radio stations such as Magic 105.4 FM, Virgin, Capitol, Capitol Gold and Radio 1 wouldn't include it on their playlists. Even Radio 2 declared that the track didn't have 'broad enough appeal' for its listeners. Some churches encouraged their parishioners to buy it because they felt that the Christian significance of the millennium had so far been underplayed. This enraged some non-Christian observers who saw it as a manipulation of the charts.

The lack of airplay was interpreted as a 'ban' by sections of the press and created a lively story about the clean-living singer who had recorded the best-known prayer in Christendom and was being censored by a secularized radio. Celebrities piled in with their denunciations of what they believed to be a piece of bad art. Melanie Chisholm, Sporty Spice, called it a 'pile of shit'. George Michael said it was a 'heinous piece of music' and he thought that the single and the way that church members had been urged to buy it was 'vile'.

Cliff seemed vindicated when 'Millennium Prayer' sold over a million copies, reaching number one where it stayed for three weeks. He was eventually toppled by the Irish boy band Westlife, whose version of Abba's 'I Have A Dream' reached the top for Christmas, but it gave him the unique achievement of having had number one hits in five consecutive decades and, along with the proceeds of a New Year concert in Cardiff, it raised £1 million for the charity Children's Promise.

Nevertheless the attacks on his choice of music still riled him. Interviewed by the *Daily Mirror* backstage at Birmingham's National Indoor Arena where he was starting a ten-day run of shows, his last before taking his break, he said, 'It hit me like a body blow. It left me feeling very, very low... What hurts me so much with these people slamming me is that it's so painful to know that it's all coming from my own industry, from people who I would regard as colleagues and fellow artists.

'I have been true to pop-rock throughout my career. But this has made me realize that maybe singers and musicians aren't one big unit. I'm a big boy. I'll get over it. But I won't pretend that I am not very hurt by some of the things people have said about me.'

Paul Field quite enjoyed the controversy surrounding his work. On the one hand, it earned him the distinction of being voted the creator of the worst single ever and the abuse of several pop stars; on the other, he obtained an Ivor Novello Award and sales of 1.3 million. 'It sold two or three times what a single normally sold to get to number one. Some of those sales might have been to Cliff fans but there aren't that many of them.

'I don't hold it up as a work of art. In fact, if someone else had done it I would probably have said, "What a terrible idea". But at the end of the day, it got the words of Jesus in front of millions of people and I don't think that can be a bad thing. The competition was a cover version of an Abba song by Westlife and something about a hamster. This was the best we could offer in terms of significant moments at the turn of the millennium!'

Fortunately for Cliff, he was about to embark on a twelve-month exile from the music scene. For the first time since he took off with Tony Meehan and Ronnie Ernstone to Italy in 1959, he was going to be able to travel without the baggage of fame and the worry about chart positions. His first destination was America, a country where, despite having had a handful of hits over the years, he could still live anonymously. He could pass through airports without needing special security, attend sporting events without being stared at and go shopping without having to sign autographs. He stayed in New York where he found he was able to walk along Broadway like any other British tourist. He visited friends in San Francisco. In Los Angeles he was a guest of John and Pat Farrar and also spent time with Olivia Newton-John.

One of the new friends he spent time getting to know was Father John McElynn, a 46-year-old Roman Catholic priest who was to have a considerable influence on his life. He'd first met McElynn the year before after Roger Bruce recommended that they link up because he thought they would have a lot in common. Not only was McElynn a bachelor who loved tennis but he was committed to a religious order, the Congregation of the Mission, that stressed solidarity with the poor. He'd spent time as a missionary in Panama.

In other ways it seemed unlikely that the two men would click.

He was a Catholic priest and Cliff a Protestant layman; he had taken a vow of poverty while Cliff was one of the richest men in Britain; he was politically to the left while Cliff was to the right. But somehow they got on, so much so that by the middle of 2000 it would be true to say that McElynn was Cliff's best friend and had taken up the mentor position in his life previously occupied by Bill Latham.

So who was John McElynn? He was born in Queens, New York, in 1953 to a fairly well off family and attended St John's Preparatory School in Brooklyn. He was ordained in May 1981, at the age of 27, and joined the Congregation of the Mission, an order that follows the way of St. Vincent de Paul (1581–1660). His vows committed him to a lifetime of stability, chastity, poverty and obedience. When Cliff met him in 1999, he was living in a Vincentian house in Southampton, Long Island, and working among Hispanic immigrants.

They probably got on so well with each other because of their differences. McElynn was not overawed by Cliff's fame because he knew nothing about it and this allowed him to be franker with him than most people feel they can be. Intellectually gifted, he was able to challenge some of Cliff's wilder speculations and Cliff, for his part, deferred to his wisdom. He also had a family – mother, sisters, brothers-in-law, nephews and nieces – who warmly welcomed Cliff into their circle.

When Cliff returned to England in the summer to fulfil a longstanding commitment to appear at a Christian festival at Glastonbury, McElynn was at his side. He'd been granted leave of absence by the Congregation of the Mission and had come almost immediately to England. In July he joined Glyn McAulay, Graham Disbrey, Roger Bruce and his partner Alan Osman, Pia Hoffman and Bill Latham at Cliff's home in Portugal.

Friends began to notice that Cliff had loosened up more since McElynn had been around. He appeared to be more comfortable with himself. For almost 35 years, his social life had focused on a small circle of Christians, none of whom were connected with show business. He now began to develop friendships outside that circle.

In October, Cliff turned 60 and celebrated in style by inviting 87 friends and family on an eight-day Mediterranean cruise that began in Nice and ended in Malaga. Half the bill was covered by *OK!* magazine, in return for exclusive coverage of the event, and the rest by Cliff.

The guest list wasn't perhaps as star-studded as *OK!* had hoped it would be (Olivia Newton-John was the only international star) but it accurately reflected the range of Cliff's interests. There were family, friends, neighbours, fellow musicians and entertainers, tennis contacts, employees of the Cliff Richard Organisation, British Airways stewards and members of his close Christian circle – all of them whittled down from an original list of 500. Notable absentees were his sister Jacqui (her son was ill), his mother (too ill to travel), Hank Marvin (as a Jehovah's Witness he didn't believe in celebrating birthdays) and Cilla Black (who was supposed to turn up at Monte Carlo but missed the boat).

During the first part of the voyage, there were high winds and choppy seas as the 4,250 tonnes *Seabourn Goddess I* sailed from Nice to Barcelona. Many of the guests were sick and had to be given injections. On the second night there was a 'somewhat risqué' (according to Gloria Hunniford) version of *This Is Your Life* that involved Roger Bruce dressing in drag as a hitherto unknown former girlfriend of Cliff's and Pia Hoffman wearing a mini skirt, stockings and suspenders as his hitherto unknown love child.

The following night, 14 October, was Cliff's official party, complete with a 60-candle cake and Shirley Bassey, who'd popped in for the night, singing 'Happy Birthday'. Cliff, wearing a black frock coat designed by Alexander McQueen, gave a short speech that hinted at the changes taking place in his life.

'I like myself at the moment,' he said, 'and it's because of you. I want to thank you for taking part in this celebration. Sixty is no different to any other number and inside I'm still a bubbling 18-year old. Society seems to think that if you're over 40 you can't have fun. Well, they wouldn't say that if they were here tonight.' Before the meal, he had asked Bill Latham to say grace. Now he asked John McElynn to close in prayer.

The weather brightened up when the ship reached Barcelona, allowing on-shore tennis and sightseeing. Somewhere between Majorca and Malaga, Cliff's keyboard player, Alan Park, 'married' his girlfriend Fiona in a ceremony on deck that was officiated by Garth Hewitt, a friend of Cliff's who, besides being a singer and songwriter, was an ordained Church of England minister. Cliff gave away the bride and the rest of the band was best man.

Cliff's other concern in 2000 was a new house he was having built in Barbados. His old friend, David Lloyd, the former captain of the British Davis Cup tennis team, was developing 47 acres of prime land at Sugar Hill in St. James that he wanted to turn into a luxury resort area. There would be colonial style mansions and town houses along with a club house, gymnasium, restaurant, swimming pools and tennis village. Sugar Hill was an old, run-down sugar plantation that, according to Lloyd, had 'a fantastic view of the sea, a cool gentle breeze and an amazing view of the sunset.'

Cliff was able to choose whichever plot he wanted and plumped for the one that he said 'had the best view'. On this site, that overlooked the Caribbean, he had ordered the construction of a sprawling house with five guest bedrooms and a large *en suite* master bedroom. The downstairs floors would be marble, there would be hanging chandeliers and outside there would be a swimming pool and landscaped gardens.

Everyone involved in Cliff's life agrees that the year 2000 was pivotal. Gloria Hunniford has said that it was the time during which he learned to 'spread his wings'. His mother was no longer there for him. Peter Gormley was dead. Bill Latham had left the house. David Bryce had retired. 'I think he learned to relax and in doing that he found something out about himself that he felt very much at peace with,' says another friend. 'I felt that he was his own person much more than he had been before. Maybe some people wouldn't like whatever it was he had found but for him that was quite an important moment.'

BACK TO BUSINESS

The year off had reinvigorated him. He'd not only had time away from the pressures of his normal life but he'd been able to get a fresh perspective on his career. Rather than following the constant treadmill of recording, touring and promotion, he decided to scale his work down to allow more time for developing friendships and leisure activities. The winters would be spent largely in Barbados, the summers in Portugal and each year he would pencil in the Australian Open, the US Open and Wimbledon.

He reasoned that he had spent most of his life giving to others and constantly moving. It was now time to slow down, take stock and develop roots. Show business was important, but it wasn't everything. There had to be the time to sit and wonder, to spend days ungoverned by the clock and to participate in such ordinary things such as gardening, shopping and watching TV.

At the same time he still wanted to record and perform. The ambition to compete with whoever happened to be in the charts and to receive applause from audiences hadn't left him. He just wanted to do it more on his terms – albums when necessary and concert tours interspersed with breaks.

He returned to the studio in 2001 with Alan Tarney, the man responsible for writing his best-selling single 'We Don't Talk Any More' and for producing three of his best albums from the eighties, *I'm No Hero, Wired For Sound* and *Always Guaranteed*. The partnership was obviously renewed because almost three years had passed since his last album and Tarney had a track record for reviving Cliff's career at crucial junctures.

Unfortunately, *Wanted*, which was released in November 2001, didn't provide the necessary kick start. Although it entered the chart at eleven, it failed to rise any higher and was generally regarded as lacklustre. It sold only around 200,000 copies. At a time when Cliff really needed something strikingly fresh and innovative, he had chosen a collection of songs that had already been hits for other people. Rather like David Bowie's *Pinups* in 1973, the idea was to pay tribute to tracks he wished he'd been the first to record.

There lay the danger. Because he hadn't been first to record them, every track existed in the shadow of its original. It was impossible to hear his recording of 'Moon River' and not to compare it to Danny Williams' version, or to listen to 'What's Love Got To Do With It?' and not hear Tina Turner at the same time.

What is more, the arrangements and instrumentation doused the fire of most of the songs. Without the distinctive jangling twelve-string guitar of the Searchers, 'When You Walk In The Room' sounds quite ordinary. Without the rolling piano and persistent heavy clicking, 'All Shook Up' sounds, well... unshaken. It left the impression that one of the downsides of his year out was that it had put him out of touch with current tastes.

The idea had come from Papillon, the record company behind 'Millennium Prayer'. 'We wanted a record that we could immediately TV-advertise and the golden rule of TV advertising is that you have to have a minimum of three hits so that there is a sense of familiarity,' says Mike Andrews. 'Because of the timescale, there was no way that we were going to get three hits before releasing an album. So we thought the other way of doing it was to ask Cliff to pick some classics that he had loved and always wanted to record. He embraced the idea.'

Tarney went along with the concept although he would have been happier creating new material. He knew that a collection of oldies wasn't likely to re-ignite Cliff's career and realized that his production would almost certainly be criticized. 'The problem with these things is that you're damned if you do and damned if you don't,' he says. 'If you change the songs – "Why did you change them?" If you don't change them – well, "You've just done them the same way." You're in a no-win situation.'

The problem with the material became evident when he commenced a world tour in October 2002. The first half of the show started well with 'We Don't Talk Any More' and 'Move It' but then featured six tracks from *Wanted*, none of which could be described as crowd pleasers.

'As his first set progressed, he seemed to lose the crowd,' wrote one Australian reviewer. 'In place of the expected lively numbers that would have had fans up and moving, Sir Cliff belted out ballad after ballad – none of them his own. They were songs from his new *Wanted* album. "Yeah, I've had my fair share of hits, but I want everyone else's as well," he told fans. The break between sets was a telling point. Many people packed up their gear and trudged for the entrance, with complaints ringing out.'

Many of the band members had seen better touring days with Cliff and felt that he could be in danger of losing his way. The spirit of camaraderie that had existed in the eighties and nineties had disappeared. Cliff frequently travelled separately from the band and stayed in more upmarket hotels with John McElynn and Roger Bruce. Often days or weeks passed without him socializing with the band.

This affected the social cohesion of the tour. There was no time spent with Cliff to discuss the previous night's mistakes or even to suggest reorganizing the set list. The musicians had to wear ill-fitting suits while Cliff took centre stage in the latest Italian designs. Only once in the six months of concerts did he ask them all out for a meal.

The tour was extensive, beginning with Britain, Scandinavia and Europe, breaking for Christmas and New Year, then continuing in Australia, New Zealand, Malaysia, Hong Kong, South Korea, Japan and Thailand. A month of rehearsals in England had preceded the European leg and a week was spent in Perth before touring Australia.

However, there were no longer the three- or four-night runs in major cities and some of the concerts were only 75 per cent full. His low public profile had had an effect as had the fact that it was four years since his last album containing original material.

The end of the tour coincided with the news that Pia Hoffman had broken up with Bill Latham and returned to her German boyfriend, Henry Barchet, with whom she'd been living before Latham romanced her. A friend of the couple told the *Daily Mail*: 'She was fed up. She was bored. I think you can say, given her attitude, it was inevitable. We were all so shocked when Bill fell for this girl. We thought he was crazy.'

She had wanted Latham to propose to her but he remained as keen to avoid marriage as he had been with Jill Clarke. When Pia got ready to leave, he changed his mind but by then it was too late. 'I don't think there was anything for her in Britain,' says one of her friends. 'She'd had a career and a nice boyfriend and she had given it all up to follow this dream and I think the dream ultimately proved less than satisfying. Bill was at work during the day and she was in the house alone. I think she just wondered where on earth she could go from there.'

Latham was devastated by the loss. Friends likened it to a second bereavement. First, he had lost his close friendship to Cliff and now he had lost his lover. Astonishingly, given the disruption caused by the affair and its break up, Latham remained close to Pia. When she married Barchet in October 2003, he was there to deliver the reading as was Cliff to give her away.

In August 2002, before the world tour started, Cliff had flown alone to Nashville for a meeting with music publisher, Val Jannsen. She published Chris Eaton, many of whose songs Cliff had recorded, and had just started a business partnership with Stuart Ongley who'd once run Cliff's publishing company, Patch Music. Ongley, Jannsen and Eaton had been talking together for some time about getting Cliff to America to record an album of new songs by American writers.

'I think we all felt that after *Wanted* he needed something fresh,' says Eaton. 'He'd always had an interest in America and I thought that if he came over he could be immersed in the lives and enthusiasms of some great writers and players. When I put the idea to him he said he'd do it if we could come up with a direction like "Shania Twain meets ZZ Top". I thought that was fantastic.'

When Cliff met with Val Jannsen she promised to get together a group of the best writers in Nashville to come up with songs specifically for Cliff and he committed to returning to Nashville for the first week in January when the writers would meet for the first time.

The 25 writers gathered at the Starstruck Building in Nashville on 4 January 2003 where Stuart Ongley gave a briefing. Most of them hadn't heard of Cliff and so he filled them in on his career and played them highlights from his greatest hits. Then each writer was given an envelope containing details of the writing room that they were assigned to that day. Only when they arrived at their rooms – which were at four different locations in Nashville – did they know who they'd been selected to write with.

'That was the most difficult thing,' says Jannsen. 'Stuart and I were up until the early hours of each morning deciding who we wanted to write together. We didn't want any competition between them or any weirdness. They worked mostly in groups of three and each day they would be with different partners. Some teams wrote two songs in a day. Some only managed one. No one ever failed to come up with anything.'

Cliff, on a break in his world tour, came in on the Tuesday and met the writers for the first time. He addressed them at a meeting. 'He basically shared his heart,' says Jannsen. 'He was so down to earth. People asked questions. How are you? What are you doing these days? What's up in your life? I think it was quite surprising for Cliff in some ways because these people have seen it all. They're not intimidated by fame. They were of course respectful but they think that their gift is to give the artist something that the artist wants.'

The idea was to write songs that reflected aspects of the way Cliff looked at life. He had talked about the fact that, despite his wealth and fame, the things in life that meant the most to him were moments of intimacy with friends shared over a cup of coffee. That resulted in the writing of 'Simplicity'. He spoke of his love of cars and inspired a number of road songs, one of which, 'What Car', he would record.

He also spoke candidly about his faith. 'He wanted what he thought of as his own song,' says Jannsen. 'That ended up being "Faithful One", a song written by Chris Eaton. It was very important to him to have that on the album.'

By the end of the week, around a dozen songs had been demoed and played to Cliff. On the last night Jannsen hired a local restaurant, The Boundary, and turned it into a songwriter's café. After a meal, the writers performed songs they'd written and then Cliff sang 'Move It'. 'It was the first time most of them had seen him sing,' she said. 'We all sat there in awe. We'd been around a lot of amazing artists but he was absolutely brilliant.'

Further songs were sent to Cliff when he returned home and, from a collection of twenty-eight to thirty to 30, he chose seventeen to record. 'First of all, I worked out which were the good songs,' he said. 'Then I put them aside and recorded only the best songs.' Over the next eighteen months, he would return three or four times to cut the tracks with Stuart Ongley and Val Jannsen as his executive producers.

As had been the case in New York, Los Angeles and San Francisco, he could wander around Nashville without being recognized. Chris Eaton took him down the Second Avenue 'strip' with its record stores, bars and souvenir stores. He went to the famed Bluebird Café, hangout of country musicians, and spent an evening at the Grand Ole Opry. He even went to church regularly.

There had been rumours that his spiritual passion had waned and even that he had been rethinking his theology. Concerns were raised when photos of the interior of his Barbados home featured in *Hello* magazine showed a giant statue of Buddha in the dining room. His later decision to sing backing vocals to Cilla Black's recording of 'Imagine', one of the most fervently atheistic songs in the rock canon, was viewed with dismay by some of his Christian fans.

Web sites were abuzz with speculation. Some contributors thought it indicated a drift towards universalism, others thought it was just a result of not thinking things through. 'I'm not trying to be judgmental here,' wrote one fan, 'but I'm genuinely concerned that he may be wavering a little from The Way.'

Chris Eaton has heard the rumours but believes that they are unfounded. 'I didn't see any chink in the armour,' he says. 'If anything, I think that going to Nashville renewed Cliff's spirit because there are a lot of Christian people there. Culturally it's much more acceptable to be a Christian and I think that when he's in a strong spiritual environment like that it allows him the chance to express himself.'

Working with writers and musicians he had never worked with before in studios he had never recorded in before helped to keep the creative experience fresh for him. He had worried that if he had recorded in England, he might have been lulled by the familiarity.

The result was a 13-track album, *Somethin' Is Goin' On*, that brought back some of the spark to his recording career. In Britain it went straight into the charts at number seven the week after its release, although it subsequently fell back out rather quickly. As always, Cliff thought it was his best album ever and his hope was that even at this late stage in his career, it might open up the door for him in America.

twenty-eight
'MY KINDA LIFE'

Forty-six years after his first (£200) tour, Cliff Richard is a wealthy man, although perhaps not as wealthy as some may imagine. In its 'Rich List' for 2004, *The Sunday Times* estimated that he was worth £40 million, a fortune that placed him at 950 out of 1000. In its list of music millionaires, he was joint bottom with Daniel Miller (owner of Mute Records) and Jay Kay.

Those who make the most in the music business are either entrepreneurs (Cameron Mackintosh, Simon Fuller, Chris Wright), songwriters (Paul McCartney, Sting, Tim Rice) or musicians in bands led by songwriters (Ringo Starr, Charlie Watts, Nick Mason). The only non-writing singers ahead of Cliff were Tom Jones (11 with £165 million) and Engelbert Humperdinck (26 with £75 million).

It has to be remembered that since the end of 1999 Cliff had cut down on touring, his primary source of income, and had put out only three singles. As a consequence, the turnover of his principal company, Balladeer Ltd, dropped from £5.6 million for the financial year ended April 2000 to just over £1 million in April 2001. In 1991, when he was touring heavily and enjoying high record sales, he was ranked number 182 by *The Sunday Times*, whose list then only included the top 200. He was already reckoned to be worth £50 million, although Cliff said at the time, 'When that story came out, I got a note from Malcolm Smith, my business manager, which said, "Don't spend it because I haven't found it!"'

His income comes primarily from ticket sales, mechanical royalties on albums and singles (he has made very little from songwriting), merchandizing and DVDs. In the early part of his career, he also earned from films and television. More recently, he has invested in a hotel, developed his own wine and given his name to a perfume.

Over the years, his singles sales have been phenomenal. 33 of them have sold over one million copies each and, in February 2004 when Channel 4 researched singles sales in Britain since 1954 for a programme titled *The Ultimate Pop Star*, it was found that Cliff had sold more records – 20,969,006 – than any other person or group. The Beatles were second and Elvis Presley third, although it has to be said that their careers as recording artists were considerably shorter. Cliff's albums also consistently made the top twenty from 1958 to 1966 and from 1976 onwards.

During the eighties and nineties, it was his live shows that showed the most rapid growth. He went from filling modest-sized Empires and Odeons in the sixties and seventies to large-capacity exhibition halls, with extended runs at places like Wembley Arena and the Royal Albert Hall.

Mel Bush, who promoted several of Cliff's tours in the eighties including 'The Event', which drew 72,000 fans to Wembley Stadium, believes that at the time he could have outsold any other act in the world. He was then one of only seven acts who had filled Wembley Stadium on the strength of their name alone. (The others were Michael Jackson, Madonna, Bruce Springsteen, the Rolling Stones, Genesis and U2.)

'If Cliff had the time and had wanted to do it, I think we could have had absolutely no problem in playing to a million people in Britain on one tour,' Bush said. 'When we played to over 400,000 in 1990, we played in only four centres.'

In 1992, his 'Access All Areas' tour had a total audience of 480,792, producing an estimated gross revenue of £9 million. Production costs were around £2 million but much of that was probably recouped by the practice of putting tickets on sale almost a year in advance so that a sizeable interest accrued.

Tours also generate income from merchandizing and the rejuvenation of Cliff's back catalogue. For the 'Summer Nights 2004' tour, for example, there were sixteen items of official merchandise on sale at each venue, ranging from a fleece jacket (£35) and a 'Please Don't Tease' T-shirt (£14) to a 'Summer Nights' picture mug (£7) and a signature badge (£5). There was a lavish concert brochure (£10), then two months later there was the DVD (£18.99).

Cliff's business is run by a 53-year-old chartered accountant,

Malcolm Smith, who joined the Cliff Richard Organisation as managing director in 1987. Before that he had worked for the City firm Touche Ross where he had handled Cliff's accounts for two years. He is a director of twelve companies, including Balladeer Ltd, the company into which Cliff's earnings pour. His fellow directors are Michael Simkins (Cliff's lawyer since 1960) and his colleague David Franks. Peter Gormley was a director until his death in May 1998 and accountant Philip Parker resigned in January 2001. All financial decisions are made jointly.

The Cliff Richard Organisation, based in Claygate, Surrey, has a permanent staff of five and two part-timers. Cliff himself only employs two people in England: his full-time gardener, Mick, and his housekeeper, Marion, who comes in three mornings a week.

His main assets are his home in Weybridge, bought for £1.4 million in August 1987, his Portuguese estate bought in 1992, the £3 million holiday home in Barbados, a cottage in North Wales with 125 acres of land and the Claygate building. He has three cars – a 2002 Mercedes convertible, a 1994 Bentley Brooklands and a Rolls Royce. One of his 'old' Mercedes cars was shipped to Barbados and his Range Rover is a courtesy car.

After being relatively frugal for most of his life, he has started to spend much more liberally. The Barbados home has absorbed a large amount of money over the past five years with the planting of an exotic garden and furniture being shipped in from around the world. His nineteenth-century farmhouse in Portugal, Quinto de Moinho, now has a working vineyard producing his own brand of wine. In 2004, 40,000 bottles of Vida Nova were produced.

Since March 1966, he has followed the Christian practice of 'tithing', giving away at least a tenth of his income to charity. This is usually done through the Cliff Richard (Charitable Trust) Ltd that has almost no administrative costs. Between 2000 and 2004, Balladeer Ltd donated over £1 million to charity. For many years he also donated a tenth of his time to charity and Christian events: making personal appearances, writing books and recording Bible tapes.

After leaving Tear Fund in 1978, Bill Latham became the manager of Cliff's Christian and charity affairs and then became his press officer. Together they would often appear at churches and religious gatherings where Latham would interview Cliff about his faith and his concern for the developing world and then Cliff would perform a few songs alone with his acoustic guitar.

Cliff is now so readily associated with charity work that it's easy to assume that it's an effortless enterprise. Bill Latham however believes that left to himself he wouldn't have chosen to involve himself in the pain and turmoil of faraway countries and that if he hadn't undergone a Christian conversion, he would probably have remained uninformed and unconcerned.

'I think that Cliff's concern for others has come about largely as a result of Christian self-discipline,' he says. 'I think that the nature of the Christian faith demands that one looks outside of oneself. I think he's forced himself to be aware of others. I don't think it's necessarily easy for him to do it because I think by nature he is more self-absorbed.'

In the days when he did gospel tours, the profits were automatically put into the Trust, as was income from his religious books. Half was given to Tear Fund and the rest to other charities. He continues to support the Arts Centre Group of which he is a patron. In 1971 he bought a huge country house in Great Dunmow, Essex, which he allowed the ACG exclusive use of as a retreat and conference centre. Sold a few years later, it was run by the Revd Jack Filby and his folk-singing wife Pauline.

'We get a lot of letters from people asking for money,' says Gill Snow of the Cliff Richard Organisation. 'The answer we give is that we don't help individuals because all of Cliff's giving goes through his trust and that is authorized only to give to registered charities.

'A lot of the stories are heartbreaking but if you give to one person then you're stymied. If we go through a recession, 90 per cent of the requests we get are mortgage-related. People lose their businesses and homes. I write back to them all individually and try to be as sympathetic as possible.'

Cliff can be generous to family and friends but is never impulsive in the way that Elvis bought Cadillacs for strangers he met in the street or that Elton John hands out jewellery. He set Donna's first husband up in business and bought homes for his sisters and mother. His favourite indulgences have always been holidays, homes and gardens. When he was living in Rookswood, he discovered that

Latham and Graham Disbrey were keen on tennis so he had a tennis court built, even though they were only able to use it twice before the house was sold.

In Totteridge and at Feather Green in Weybridge, he spent money on building extensions, then moved out when there was nowhere left to expand. At his current home in Weybridge, he has had the garages extended, a room added upstairs, a conservatory built at one end of the house with a lemon tree growing in it and an annexe created next to the kitchen.

In Portugal, one of his reasons for buying the vineyards around his property was to ensure that his home couldn't be peered at from public land. In Barbados, rather than fill in a coral stone quarry that stood in the way of constructing a driveway to his house, he had a gardener set it off with a variety of plants and then had a bridge built over it. He had sculptures flown in from Italy and paintings from Thailand.

It often irks his musicians that he has little idea of what it costs an ordinary person to live in Britain today. This is mainly because his bills are handled by his employees and his ready cash, supplied once a week in a brown envelope, is kept only for tips. Once at a band meal he said that he didn't see why people had such a hard time living on social security handouts because he seemed to manage on only a few pounds a week. One of the singers was forced to remind him that he didn't have to pay his mortgage out of the cash in hand that he gets once a week from the office. Neither did he have to pay any of his bills or buy food.

Up until his year off, it was safe to say that Cliff didn't live a very 'showbiz' life once he left the stage. His closest friends weren't fellow entertainers but accountants, teachers, engineers, tennis players, nurses, charity workers and vicars. He wasn't often photographed at first nights, although he did visit plays and musicals when he was preparing for *Heathcliff*. Neither did he entertain at home very much except with his trusted friends from his Crusader days.

Recently this has changed quite dramatically. He sees much less of the friends he first met when he became a Christian and much more of show business associates such as Gloria Hunniford, Cilla Black, Michael Ball, Graham Dene and Mike Read.

For over thirty years his holidays have followed the same pattern, that of two or three weeks in the sunshine with the 'holiday gang' where he swims, plays tennis and sunbathes. Most often these holidays have been taken in Portugal but there have been trips to California (1968), Israel (1972), Madeira (1973), South Africa, Bermuda (1983) and Florida. In 1987 and 1989, a London art dealer, David Mason, gave Cliff and friends the free use of his ocean-going yachts, *Lindsay Jane* and *Lindsay Jane II*. On the first trip they toured the Greek islands and on the second the coast of Croatia (then Yugoslavia).

The holiday gang shrunk after the marriages of Peter Graves and David Rivett but the style remained unchanged. When Bill Latham was with Jill Clarke, she was allowed to come to Portugal with the gang over the New Year period but never during the summer. This was an inviolable bachelor-boy break. However, in the summer of 1999, Pia Hoffman accompanied Latham, breaking the pattern. The following year Cliff brought John McElynn. In subsequent years, Cliff no longer stayed in Portugal for the full holiday period. In 2004 he visited earlier in the summer with his newly-acquired friends and left before Latham and Disbrey arrived. Glyn McAulay didn't go.

Tennis remains Cliff's favourite sport. Ever since playing badminton as a boy, he has enjoyed racquet games. After meeting Sue Barker, he changed from being a 'pat-a-cake' player to a deadly serious competitor with all the grit and determination he once displayed on the rugby field. He started playing regularly at the David Lloyd Tennis centre where he was also coached. Soon after, he became a common sight on the British tennis social circuit: a fixture at Wimbledon, an organizer of pro-celebrity tennis tournaments and, through his charity the Cliff Richard Star Search (tennis) Limited, a financier of future tennis stars.

Now when he travels, he ensures that he is booked into hotels with tennis courts and on some tours he travels with a tennis pro. He plays doubles with the likes of Chris Evert Lloyd, Steffi Graf and Ilie Nastase. Virginia Wade is a neighbour of his in Barbados and frequently uses his court.

'He became infatuated with the game,' said Sue Barker. 'He couldn't accept not doing it well. I kept telling him that children mimic and can pick things up quite quickly but that he had no hope of doing this at his age. I think he then approached it in the spirit of trying to prove that I was wrong.

'He still doesn't look like a natural player, like someone who has been playing all his life. There is always a distinction between someone who started as a child and someone who has taken it up much later in life. You can see it in the flowing motion of the shots. The result is still the same, but you can feel that it's manufactured rather than natural.'

In 1992 he and Bill Latham went to Lech in Austria with Charles Haswell, an old tennis partner, and there he tried skiing for the first time in twenty years. He was on the beginners' slopes for just two days, graduated to the blue runs and by the end of the fortnight's holiday was confident enough to come down red runs and do parallel turns.

His involvement with skiing again illustrates the depths of his determination. He is never content to dabble. He has to attain complete mastery, confounding those who doubt his capability. He thrives on a diet of fresh challenges, however apparently insignificant they may be.

One former producer, when asked why Cliff had never married, reputedly said, 'How can someone so in love with himself ever fall in love with someone else?' The remark sounds quite cruel but contains a kernel of truth. How could someone so in love with their current lifestyle ever make room for the demands of another individual?

He has admitted as much himself, repeatedly saying over the years than whenever he has contemplated marriage, he has been deterred by the thought of what he would stand to lose by committing himself to someone else. He cherishes the absolute freedom to do whatever he wants whenever he wants and acknowledges that this would not be possible if he entered into a binding relationship.

Bill Latham put it like this in 1993: 'There is no way Cliff could have lived the life he has lived, contributed what he has contributed and achieved what he has achieved if he had been married. There is no question of that. Although he loves his home, he doesn't feel tied to it and that freedom has meant that he has been able to do much, much more than if he had a family.

'It's also partly to do with the enthusiastic approach he has towards everything he touches. He always goes the extra mile. If he was to have a relationship, he would give it everything. There would be no half measures.

'So because his commitments have been his career, his faith, and, more latterly, tennis, he has given himself wholeheartedly to those three activities. There has been no room for anything else.'

He hasn't had a girlfriend since 1984, although there has never been a shortage of women willing to be Mrs Cliff Richard. Some of them have been able to get very close to him. They have visited him at home, cooked him meals, accompanied him to the cinema and eaten out with him. But there has always been a final barrier. As soon as he senses that they want more from him than he is able to give, he cuts them off.

It's back to that scene in *Summer Holiday* where Cliff says, 'Girls are all very well, but date them once and then run. Date them twice and they get serious... Next thing you know, you're hooked and wondering what's hit you. No. No girl is ever going to own me.'

He enjoys female company, though, and the women that have been close to him are always rapturous over his kindness, his consideration, his charm, his cheerfulness and his gentlemanly behaviour. They also like the fact that he's more interested than most men in such 'girly' subjects as designer clothes, hair products, perfumes, furnishing, weight maintenance and botox treatments.

For most of his career, he has explained his singleness by saying that he was just waiting for the right girl to come along. But as he entered his fifties he began to admit that the truth was that he wasn't the marrying sort.

'Maybe I have lived through all the things I needed to live through to find myself and what I want out of life,' he said. 'I don't think marriage is one of those things. I don't feel I'll ever get married now. I don't think I'm unique. I still have enough female company and it's fine.'

Then in 1998, as he headed towards his sixtieth birthday, he made the surprising comment that if 'the perfect partner' stepped into his life, he could imagine making all the changes necessary to accommodate them. 'If it happened, it would be very exciting,' he said. 'If it doesn't, that's fine too. I have to meet the right person first.'

The fact that he has spent most of his adult life without a girlfriend and has always shared his homes with unmarried men has led people to assume that he is homosexual, despite vigorous denials over the years. While the denials are still there, his attitude towards homosexuality appears to have changed.

In the seventies he was clear that sex outside marriage was wrong 'because God says it's wrong and I have to assume that he knows better than I do' and that homosexual practice was 'a deviation from God's original intention'. Perhaps to avoid rumours, there were no known homosexuals in his inner circle; as a result he was even the subject of attacks by campaigning groups like the Gay Liberation Front who accused him of homophobia. In 1991, while he was rehearsing for a gospel tour at Bray Studios near Windsor, a group of extras working on Derek Jarman's film *Edward II* invaded the band's soundstage. They waved placards carrying gay rights slogans and urged Cliff to 'come out of the closet'.

However, during the nineties he became less wary, including at least seven or eight openly gay men among his closest friends. He even went on holiday cruises with some of them and all were included on the guest list for his sixtieth birthday party on board the *Seabourn Goddess 1*.

Although he has never made a public statement admitting to a change of view, in December 2003 he was asked by a TV documentary team about comments he had made about homosexuality during the time he identified with the Festival of Light. At that time, he had denounced homosexual practices as 'an abomination'. He said, 'Certainly in my heart now I embrace almost everything. I don't have the right to say, "This is wrong." People nowadays will often bring up something from 25 years ago and say, "You said this." I'll say, "Wait a minute. Aren't we allowed to change?" If you come out of some kind of stimulating discussion, there will be something changed in you. You may not even notice it until a long time has passed and you'll suddenly think, "Oh well. I used to be downright against this but now I'm not so sure."'

But accepting homosexuals into his circle of friends is not necessarily an acknowledgement that he has shifted his theological position and certainly not an admission that he is himself gay. It may be, as some suggest, that he is now more confident and can mix with a variety of people without fearing that his Christian convictions will be diluted. At his age a high proportion of the single men that he's likely to find a lot in common with will necessarily be gay.

The question of Cliff's sexuality is a reasonable one for people to raise because his whole career has been based on the premise that he is a clean living, heterosexual guy who would love to find the right girl. He recognized this early on which is why he ditched his girlfriends in favour of his career. He knew that the essential components of his image were his (mainly female) fans' perception of him as a handsome, caring but lonely guy and his potential availability to each one of them. His songs, and even his film roles, have all fostered this image which remains essentially unchanged. At 64 he is still ostensibly the youthful man who'd give it all up for the 'right partner' and the majority of his songs are still about love.

The public is therefore intensely interested in whether the reality matches the image. Is he really as youthful as he seems? Is he really still longing for love? Is he really a courageous romantic who can only share himself sexually with that one perfect woman or is there some other reason for apparent lack of desire?

One of the first questions anyone who has known Cliff gets asked is 'Is Cliff gay?' Cliff is rarely asked the question directly. The normal approach of an interviewer is to ask how he feels about people insinuating that he's gay. In the early days he offered flat denials. 'I'm asked if being single suggests that I am gay,' he once said. 'Well, I am not. God made us male and female and there are obvious ways in which male and female interact.' He would also denounce those people who suggested otherwise, calling their comments 'snide' and saying that their publications were from the 'gutter'.

More recently he's changed tack, preferring just to say that he doesn't care what others say about him because he knows the truth. In the 2003 TV documentary he said of the 'gay thing': 'Now I find it really rather fun. You know, I'm an "enigma". Once I looked that up I thought "I like this." They didn't understand me and long may it reign! I don't intend to talk about everything in my life and you're naïve if you think that when I'm asked questions I'm going to give all the answers that you want to hear. There will be things that I'll take to the grave with me.'

When I interviewed Cliff for this book in 1992, I was as forthright as I could possibly be with my questions and he was equally as forthright with his answers. My tentative conclusion, based on having spoken to all the key people in his life at that point, was that he was asexual. It was obvious that he had no powerful urges towards women and, equally, there was absolutely no evidence that he had ever had a relationship with a man or had even shown the slightest interest in having one.

I started by asking him to argue his case in the face of the accusations that he was gay. 'I can't see what there is to argue about,' he said. 'I'm always saying to people that I've denied it since the idea was mooted when I was eighteen. In the early days, they were either trying to prove that I was a sex maniac or that I was gay.

'It didn't seem to matter which one was true. So really early on I saw that there was not much I could do. Even now there are people who are married and people will tell me that they are gay and I'll say, "They can't be gay. They're married and they've got children." They'll say, "Oh, that's a cover."'

It seemed naïve for someone of his age and experience to deny knowing that there are married men who have gay sex lives. I mentioned the then recent case of the married actor, Denholm Elliot, who, after his death, had been revealed as having had gay relationships. 'I don't know about that,' said Cliff. 'So, even if I got married tomorrow there would be a group of people who would believe what they wanted to believe. There is no point in justifying everything you do. All that counts is what your family and friends know and they all trust and respect me. What the people outside think, I have no control over.'

I became more specific. I asked him whether the thought of being gay had ever crossed his mind. 'Have you ever looked inside yourself and thought, "Am I gay?" To this he simply answered 'No.' Had he ever contemplated the possibility that he might be gay? 'No,' he repeated. 'I mean, you wouldn't, would you? I mean, have you ever thought that? Surely you wouldn't have done! I read a lot of things about myself and I laugh. One of the best things about me is that I really don't care any more and haven't done for fifteen or twenty years. In the end it doesn't matter what the outside world thinks.

'This year I will play to 400,000 people and I don't know what they think about me. I just know that they love me at the time and in the end that's all I'm there to do. When I'm away from them it doesn't really matter any more.'

I then explained what I thought might lead people to think he was possibly gay. I said that he had a background that some psychologists think is typical of someone who develops homosexual attachments – a strong, attractive mother to whom the son is unusually close and a remote, slightly ineffectual father whom the son finds it impossible to regard as a role model.

'But I could find people with attractive mothers and distant fathers who aren't gay,' he countered. 'When I see people, I don't think about whether they are homosexual or heterosexual. I don't assume anything.'

For years, many people supposed that his close friendship with Bill Latham was evidence that he was gay. The two men shared a home, after all, and Latham, like Cliff, was a bachelor. But those close to the couple knew that Latham was anything but gay. He'd had women in his life for years and it's unlikely that he would have remained single if he hadn't met Cliff and decided that his role in Cliff's life as companion and mentor was a calling that required certain sacrifices.

'I had never set my mind on being single,' Latham told me. 'I've had relationships in the past and have been under constant pressure to marry but I don't feel that I would want the upheaval. In one sense I would like to have had a family but, because my life has been so fulfilled in so many other ways, it's not something I lose sleep over or become depressed about.'

When they were sharing the house in Weybridge, the relationship between the two men was close but not suffocatingly so. A lot of the time they spent together was because of work. When Cliff was recording or touring, Latham carved out his own life. Their interests were quite different. Latham had never been a big fan of rock 'n' roll; he preferred cricket to tennis and couldn't stand the electronic games that Cliff played. When Cliff first went to Austria, Latham sat out the skiing sessions in local coffee bars. When the next trip was arranged, he elected to stay at home.

Among close friends, they often allowed these tensions to

surface. 'I've been at meals where there were almost fights between him and Bill,' said one friend. 'Bill talks a lot of common sense but Cliff will come out with comments about the unemployed and homeless, and I think it drives Bill to despair. I don't think Cliff understands.'

For years Cliff's politics were always unashamedly right wing but in the nineties he declared that he was 'smack in the middle'. Although he enjoys a close relationship with Prime Minister Tony Blair, friends say that when they're together they never debate politics and no one is sure that his approval of Blair as a person has resulted in him becoming a Labour supporter.

Their relationship deepened in January 2000 when the Blairs were in Lisbon with the British ambassador to Portugal and came to the Algarve for an overnight stay with Cliff. The holiday gang was there with Pia, Roger Bruce, Alan Osman and Lizzie McCrossen. The Blairs, who had security staff in attendance, seemed relaxed. After a morning walk, Tony Blair played tennis with Cliff. For lunch, the whole group walked half a mile to the Atlanticos restaurant in Guia where a table for twelve had been booked.

As a result of this meeting Cliff, Glyn McAulay, Bill Latham, Graham Disbrey and Pia Hoffman were invited to 10 Downing Street for tea with the prime minister and were given an official tour of the property. Cherie returned to Cliff's home in Portugal for a short break with her mother and her newly-born son, Leo, in July 2000 and then in 2003 and 2004 the entire Blair family spent their summer holiday at the Sugar Hill mansion in Barbados.

It would be an interesting debate if the conversation between prime minister and pop star ever strayed into politics. In his time, Cliff has advocated birching, called for stricter censorship and suggested that the unemployed could help out in hospitals. He was a big supporter of Margaret Thatcher and then John Major. He also dismayed many of his music business colleagues by continuing to play South Africa during the apartheid era, a move that earned him a UN blacklisting and a bomb threat while touring Scandinavia.

His attitudes are the inheritance of the child of the Raj and the poor boy made good from a council estate in the Britain of the 1950s. Thatcherism appealed to him because, through determination and talent, he has gone from having nothing to having millions. His tacit assumption is that anyone with similar single-mindedness could lift himself or herself out of poverty.

He can be quite vocal about people he regards as 'slackers' who don't seem to 'pull their weight'. Apparently oblivious to his own privileges, he can even complain about those who simply work to make money. His background in India forged a strong, often uncritical, allegiance to those in power. At times when other pop stars have questioned police behaviour, been critical of royalty or protested against British foreign policy, Cliff has remained unstintingly loyal to the establishment.

Colleagues have often been shocked by his ignorance of the harsher aspects of ordinary British life. This is not entirely his own fault. Since 1958, he has led a life that has cut him off from what used to be called 'the masses'. His encounters with the public and with officialdom are superficial because the situations are controlled and he is always treated with a respect not offered to ordinary citizens. It's difficult to come up with informed views about a world that you only ever see through a tinted screen.

Having been the focus of attention all his adult life, he finds it natural to assume that people he meets want to hear him talk about himself. He rarely asks questions of others about their work and family but can spend hours reeling off facts about his chart positions and record sales.

'One of the causes of our disagreements is the blind spot I feel he has over the pressures in society today for people just to exist,' Bill Latham admitted. 'He doesn't really understand the pressure of a mortgage, interest rates, unemployment and so on. I often feel he doesn't have enough empathy with people. I would like him to go to some inner-city areas in Britain to see just what people there face.'

Since Latham left the Weybridge home in 1999, the relationship between the two men has shifted gear. Although Latham still organizes Cliff's charity and media work, it is as an employee rather than a mentor. 'It's much more distant and professional now,' says a friend. It's now John McElynn who shares Cliff's home, organizes the diary, picks up the mail, opens the emails and acts as the new gatekeeper even though (as of December 2004) he is still officially a member of the Congregation of the Mission on an extended leave of absence. He will soon have to decide whether to remain with the order or to depart.

Like Latham had been, McElynn is the organizer in the relationship. Although not employed by Cliff (as an American he is only allowed to stay in Britain on a visitor's visa), he took control of the house in Barbados from the start. When it was being built, he dealt with the architects and then the builders. Once it was completed, he played an important role in choosing the interior design. In 2004 he joined Malcolm Smith and the property developer Subash Arora as a director of Arora Manchester Ltd, the company running the 141-bedroom Arora International Hotel in Manchester that Cliff has invested in.

Cliff's life today is an enviable mix of work, sport, holidays, travel, gardening and socializing. He has health, wealth, fame, acclaim and access to the most powerful people in the country. His looks are amazingly intact and he is the recipient of undiluted adoration from his fans. He realizes that he has been incredibly blessed. As he surveys his beautiful holiday homes, his achievements in the record industry and his standing in British society, he can only shake his head in amazement that it all happened to him. As he once told me, at times like this all he can say to himself is, 'I can't believe all this is happening. I'm only a boy from Cheshunt.'

twenty nine
'REAL AS I WANNA BE'

If Cliff had been asked in 1958 what he would liked to be doing in his sixties, he would probably have said 'singing'. But he could never have dreamt that his wish would come true.

That year his father was 53, a gaunt, balding man with an austere Victorian demeanour. It would have been impossible to have imagined someone of his age shaking a leg, swivelling a hip and performing a song like 'Move It' to an audience of excitable ladies.

Realistically, Cliff envisaged a career that might last throughout his teens before his audience deserted him and he was forced to get a 'proper job'. By the time he was twenty, he was admitting that he was saving up for the inevitable day when 'the bubble burst'.

The bubble never did burst. He has been through trying times. He has put out ill-advised records. He has been out of the charts and off the radio. But never in 47 years has he been less than a major star in Britain. He has had such an uncanny habit of climbing back to the top just as he's been written off as irrelevant that few are brave enough to compose his career obituary.

What makes his career even more remarkable is that he has never contented himself with playing his greatest hits. He has continued to want to be known for his latest material.

His first decade in the business was spent establishing himself as a singles artist and then as a film star. During his second decade ending in 1978, he emerged as a television host and, for the first time, as a creator of substantial albums.

But even by then he hadn't done everything. In his third

decade, while producing his biggest-ever single, 'We Don't Talk Any More', he developed his stage show to new and spectacular dimensions. In his fourth decade he made the huge leap to conceive, finance and star in the multimillion pound production of *Heathcliff*, the book of which he also co-authored.

His fifth decade has been characterized by a renewed attention on his personal growth where he has decided to make the music fit in with his personal life rather than the other way round. It has been a time of re-evaluation, of cutting old ties and nurturing new interests.

How has he survived so many changes in musical fashion? It would be flippant to say that it was all down to talent. If that were so, the Rolling Stones and Paul McCartney would have had equally consistent careers.

Part of the answer is that most performers who established themselves in the sixties were songwriters as well as singers. Their fates have therefore been tied to their ability to come up with fresh and exciting material. Broadly speaking, they produced their best work when they were in their twenties and thirties. Cliff, who has only ever been an interpreter of songs written by others, has not been affected in this way.

Another part of the answer is that because of his singleness, Cliff has been able to devote his life to his work. He has been able to maintain his youthful enthusiasm because he hasn't had to shoulder the normal responsibilities of adulthood. He is one of the most fiercely determined singers in the business, although because of his easy-going manner this quality is often overlooked by observers. The fighting skills he honed in the playground have never really deserted him.

The help of top-rate colleagues has supplemented this devotion to his work. In a business noted for sharp practice, he has been extremely fortunate with those who have influenced his career. Very early on he found himself working with good, honest men such as Norrie Paramor, who gave him strong fatherly direction as well as enough space to be himself. In the Shadows, he had the backing of one of the best guitar groups of the period and men like David Bryce and Bill Latham effectively gave their lives for the sake of his career.

Undoubtedly, however, his greatest asset has been his pure and well-rounded singing voice. It is distinctive (you can tell a Cliff record within a few notes), he has maintained it well (he took voice lessons in 1991 and now always tunes up before a concert) and is in harmony with what the public know of his character – warm, smooth, compassionate, reassuring.

Cliff has always known what he wanted. Although he has been supported by good musicians, songwriters and producers, he deserves the credit for seeing the potential in these people. He has an eye for talent just as he has an ear for hit songs. But more than even the music itself, his continued success is due to his warm personality and to the unique relationship he has built up with his fans.

Many performers are content to churn out singles on a 'take it or leave it' basis and refuse to do anything more than the minimum of publicity. Cliff has always unashamedly given his public what it wants and has allowed himself to 'belong' to his fans.

Because he recognizes that he is an entertainer, he has never adopted the attitude that if he likes a song it is the job of the audience to learn to like it. As far as he is concerned, entertainers are not employed to confound expectations and alter perceptions. They are there to provide pleasant distractions from the harsher realities of life.

From the start Cliff talked of 'doing what the fans want me to'. In 1960 he actually brought a group of fans to Abbey Road studios to choose his next single from a collection of 21 newly recorded songs (they chose 'Please Don't Tease').

Asked in 1977 what he would do if faced with a choice between personal artistic satisfaction and pleasing the public, he said he would compromise. 'I would compromise with quality songs though,' he said. 'I don't want to cut the parents and grandparents out.'

Although he values his privacy, he makes himself available to his fans, both in person at signing events and sometimes outside his concert venues and through newspaper interviews and chat shows. Many performers come to view their dealings with the media as a chore, but Cliff genuinely believes he owes his public these opportunities to 'meet' him and he still approaches it all with the same zest with which he records his singles. The result is that those who follow him hold him in great affection. This is obvious to anyone who has attended his concerts where the rapport is that of one between friends rather than that between salesman and customer.

Given Cliff's huge following in the UK and many other regions, his failure to really crack America seems surprising. This must be due, in part, to the fact that the American public knows nothing of Cliff's personality. Each time he has a minor hit, there is no legend attached. The songs are heard in isolation from each other and are bought when they're strong and ignored when they're weak. In Britain there are fans who'll buy ten or twenty copies of each single simply to get Cliff in the charts. They see record-buying as a duty to Cliff because by doing this they are giving him the one thing they know he wants.

He may be too mild for American tastes. The performers who succeed in America tend to be larger than life. They are known for their extravagant costumes or for lives of excess. It's a country where you have to shout louder to get noticed. It's not enough simply to make 'good' records.

Cliff's image in Britain is well defined and well known, although he has never employed an image-maker. Publicity, in Cliff's case, has always been a matter of sending out press releases and answering queries from journalists. Although outside publicists have been hired for different projects, there has never been a strategy to shape the public's perception of him. The closest thing to image-creation was when Jack Good encouraged him to 'smoulder'.

The strongest elements of the image that people have of him are his decency and his youthfulness. Most of what is revered or reviled about Cliff can be traced back to them. His decency was established from the beginning. Here was someone who was kind, polite, honest and caring. He didn't swear, didn't drink, wasn't found groping girls, dressed smartly and had a ready smile. He was frequently cited as an example that not all teenagers were bad.

This wasn't exceptional at the time because even the wildest pop singers emphasized their love of milk and mother. It would have been career-suicide in 1959 to swear during an interview or to brag about having been drunk. The difference with Cliff was that the image happened to be true. This boy really did love his mother, look after his sisters, like milkshakes, respect policemen and go to bed early. There was no need to fabricate anything.

What is amazing is that the image has persisted. All who meet him are impressed by his 'niceness'. He makes people feel comfortable in his presence, never bitches and always appears cheerful and optimistic. 'You feel you are a much better person after having met him,' says actor Anthony Andrews. 'His outlook on life is so positive that it always has an effect on you.'

When he is criticized, it is not for being phoney but for being 'too good to be true'. His decency is sometimes perceived as a character weakness, as though he doesn't have the guts to be nasty or to disgrace himself publicly.

The truth is that, although he has a naturally even temperament, a lot of his 'niceness' is the result of grit rather than spinelessness. He says that he believes it is important to love others even when he doesn't feel like loving. He struggles to be gracious, even when it would be more convenient to be rude.

'In the Bible, Paul says that there is an "evil me" that is constantly trying to override the "good me",' Cliff explains. 'If I can let the "good me" win in front of the public as often as possible, I consider that a success rather than a fault.

'The fault is that I can't always control my thoughts, and I can't stop thinking that I'd rather be doing other things. I'd rather smash some people in the face because they really annoy me, but it's a success that I don't smash them in the face!'

It's often said that such restraint has protected him from the traditional show business excesses that could have prematurely aged him. It's probably true to say that his facial features reflect his ease with himself. He doesn't appear to carry the baggage of guilt or resentment and he believes that he is part of a bigger plan.

His involvement in the Christian world during the time of the great social upheavals of the sixties and seventies preserved his innocence. Whereas many of his contemporaries bear the marks of having lived through this era, Cliff still manages to give the impression that he has sprung fresh from the pages of an Enid Blyton novel where policemen cycle down country lanes and people still say 'crikey' and 'gosh' while sipping fizzy drinks.

His single status is also essential to this impression of eternal teenage. It's important that he should appear available, that his typical fan can still entertain the hope that they might be that 'special person' he says he would alter his life for. If he had a wife, children and grandchildren, he would no longer be seen as able to give himself totally. In his most popular songs, he shows himself as lonely and vulnerable, a man still searching for love.

Yet the fantasy is quietly romantic rather than ferociously sexual. He is not Tom Jones or Mick Jagger coming to offer a wild night but a sensitive boy who wants nothing more than to hold his girl tightly and whisper that he'll love her for ever. A night with Cliff, every girl knows, will end with a kiss on the doorstep.

As a consequence his followers don't respond to his hip thrusts by throwing hotel keys on stage as they did for Elvis. The letters that come to the office show that very few imagine doing naughty things with him. They see him instead as someone who would understand them, unlike their present partners.

None of this would have happened if he'd grown old and grizzly. The fact that he still looks and acts young is vital to his image. 'I wish somehow I could be Peter Pan, the boy who never grew up,' he said wistfully during an interview in 1960. 'I'm going to stay young for as long as I can.'

Yet despite his unparalleled achievements in terms of record sales, ticket sales and career longevity, it still irks him that he hasn't received the critical acceptance he thinks he deserves. That a sizeable proportion of the British record-buying public likes what he does is beyond doubt, but he knows that he has never won the respect of those who decide his place in rock 'n' roll history. He remains surprisingly sensitive to the way in which his contribution is frequently dismissed.

For American rock historians he only exists as a footnote to the career of the Beatles. The *Rolling Stone History of Rock 'n' Roll*, for example, gave him only three passing mentions, none of which were in reference to his music.

Rock critic Dave Marsh in the *Rolling Stone Record Guide* gives a typical career summary from an American perspective:

'Before the Beatles, Cliff Richard was England's answer to American rock,' he wrote. 'He began as a sort of mini-Elvis, with a back-up group called the Shadows, who included a guitarist, Hank Marvin, an important influence on many British guitarists of the sixties. But Richard converted to England's variety of fundamentalist Christianity, and whatever spark of spunk had been in his music was

376

snuffed, though he continued to make the British charts through the sixties.'

British critics are frequently as harsh. A review of his CD back catalogue in *Q* magazine concluded, '... these are 24 albums of limp-wristed tosh... Maybe he should have quit after "Move It".'

Overlooked in these summaries is the importance of his role in British rock between 1958 and 1962 during which he and the Shadows helped to create the climate out of which the 'beat group' phenomenon developed. With their self-written songs and reliance on British craftsmanship, they sent messages to Liverpool, London and Newcastle that it was possible to create a home-grown version of rock 'n' roll.

Cliff did imitate Elvis, but then so did almost everyone else at the time. For most aspiring rockers, Elvis *was* rock 'n' roll and therefore to copy his style, intonation and movements was to follow the maker's instructions.

Cliff was also the first British singer to create scenes of mass hysteria – teenage expressions of delight that were to climax in Beatlemania.

Also overlooked is his mastery of the pop ballad. His inclusion of slower, softer material is often pointed to as a betrayal of the promise indicated by 'Move It', whereas when the Beatles recorded 'Yesterday', 'Here, There and Everywhere' and 'Hey Jude', they were praised for the range of their material.

Undoubtedly the decade following Cliff's Christian conversion harmed his reputation because his music lost its passion and he didn't respond to the creative explosion of the sixties. For a while it looked as though he would remain the televisual equivalent of an end-of-pier entertainer, dishing up something for everyone. That only altered in 1976 with his artistic renaissance.

Today he is more of an inspiration than an influence. There are no mini-Cliff's trailing behind him, but he remains a tremendous inspiration because of his absolute professionalism, his longevity as a hit-maker and the weight of his history. Young performers on *Top of the Pops* are still overwhelmed to shake his hand and inevitably call back home to tell their mums who they've just met. Gareth Gates, runner up to Will Young in the first British *Pop Idol*, went to him for advice early on in his career.

He has also been one of the most visible Christians in the country and the best public example of someone trying to integrate his faith with his work. In 1999 a survey discovered that in Britain he was the best-known living Christian, beating the Archbishop of Canterbury, Billy Graham and the Pope.

Although his career has slowed down since 2000, there's no sign of him giving up. He would never want to give up. There is still that record to make that will establish him in America and the album that will secure his place in rock and pop history. There's also his first number one hit of the 21st century. Whatever it is, there will always be one more unrealized ambition that will fire Cliff Richard's enthusiasm and take him back again into the studio.

POSTSCRIPT

(Added to first paperback, 1994)

Cliff read the manuscript for this book some months before it was first published in hardback. Although he had no creative control over the project, I wanted to be sure that I had the facts right.

He's not a voracious reader and not much interested in accounts of his own life, but he read a chapter of this biography each night before going to sleep. The first report I heard was that he was enjoying it. The particularly heartening news was that he considered it 'a good read'.

Biographers of living persons have ambiguous feelings about the response of their subjects to what they have written. If there is too much delight it could be because flaws have been overlooked. On the other hand, if there's too much rancour it could be because the biographer has over-emphasized weakness.

Cliff didn't disappoint me with his reactions when he finally 'phoned me up. He was enthusiastic, but had the natural reservations of a private person seeing his life unfolded before the public. He appreciated the depth of research – much of it uncovering things he either didn't know about or had long forgotten – but prickled at some comments made by former colleagues.

He felt his father had been portrayed a little too severely, that some of those who had worked with him were claiming too much glory for their roles in his success, and that he, at times, appeared weaker than he knew himself to be.

To his credit, he never even suggested that I should alter my findings to please him. I thought that this in itself proved his enormous strength of character. All he suggested I might like to change were a few factual errors relating to dates, chart positions and musicians involved in sessions.

The parts I thought he might protest about – the digging up of old romances – he didn't mention, although he later told the Irish Times *that his one criticism of the book was that 'too much attention is paid to things that happened to me years ago, in one case 32 years ago'.*

The quote he graciously gave me for use in the book's publicity campaign was revealing in what it implied about these events. 'This book has been a learning experience!' he wrote. 'I found out more about my family tree, for instance, than ever I knew before and it revived memories I had long since buried.

'Even though I found it a good read, it's never easy to accept criticism about oneself or one's family. But then maybe that's what decent biographies are about.'

Six months after publication I asked him what he now thought. We both knew that he'd always resisted a detailed independent biography, and that I'd only finally succeeded in writing one because I'd made the point that if I didn't do it now then someone else would.

'Anything that deals with personal things makes me feel uncomfortable,' he admitted. 'I wouldn't like to have another book done – not immediately anyway! The most difficult thing is reading other people's opinions about you. Most people don't actually confront you with them.'

I wanted to know how he had reacted to the comments of those who had concluded that the mystery of his sexuality was explained by a low sex drive. Did it bother him to read people saying this? 'No,' he said, 'because it's all speculation.' This was a perfect Cliff answer, which displayed unflappability while neither confirming nor denying the observation.

Adding to the confusion over this issue was the fact that Carol Costa, his only sexual partner, had contacted me after publication of the book to say that Cliff had not been the poor innocent seduced by a married woman, as some had suggested. He was a more than willing partner. Was she right to claim that she hadn't been his seductress? 'I don't think she was [a seductress],' he agreed.

The most recent speculation had been over his romance with Una Stubbs. I had described it as a 'flirtation' in the book. The newspapers, almost thirty years after the event, had turned it into an 'affair', implying that 'nice boy Cliff' had been guilty of more than he's previously admitted.

'It was a flirtation,' he confirmed. 'My memory of it was that it was a sweet little time. She was having an unhappy marriage and we did a lot of holding hands. And that was it really. I did a lot of comforting. But it wasn't an "affair". We didn't go to bed together.'

Cliff is always referred to as 'born-again Christian Cliff', even when what is described happened long before his conversion.

'The thing is, I wasn't even known as a Christian in those days,' he *pointed out in connection with the Una Stubbs story. 'I've been telling the press for years that I know I've changed because I know what I was like in those days.'*

He finds it hard to comprehend the press's apparently insatiable appetite for personal details of this kind. I suggested it was because he remains a mystery. No one seems able to believe that what they see is what they get. People are searching for clues which they hope will resolve the mystery.

'But everyone is a mystery to everyone else,' he argued. 'I don't know anything about you, but it doesn't change anything. It's not as though I need to know. Everyone I know is a mystery to me really. You only know what they want you to know about them, and they'll never have the kind of speculation that I have as a public figure.'

Could it be that Cliff is genuinely unaware of the power of the enigmatic? This air of mystery, of which speculation is a vital component, has worked well for him. It's kept him front-page news in Britain for forty years, despite a lifestyle not given to colourful excess or nail-biting unpredictability.

'Most people don't spend their lives trying to figure me out,' he said. 'The biography brings it up or an article brings it up, but in between times nobody is bothered by me as an enigma or whether I'm a mystery or not. I either make good records and do good concerts, or I don't.'

My point is that pop stars do not live by good records alone. They need star quality. There has to be something unresolved into which the public invests its imagination.

Cliff didn't think so, and cited the example of the black American singer Morana King, whom he rated highly in the sixties, but who snubbed him when he met her in America.

'She was horrible to me. She turned her back on me and told someone else to answer my questions about her. But it didn't change my opinion.

'So I think we are what we are as people, but what we are as artists is almost something else. No one needs to know anything about me other than whether they like my music, and whether I make them feel good at a concert or whether I can act or dance or sing.'

Yet people will always want to know more. If they like what they see on stage and hear on record, they assume they will like what goes on backstage and behind the curtains at home. The performance has whetted rather than sated the appetite.

The biographer's task is to supply answers to the question, 'What's he or she really like?' The performer's task is to decide just how much of themselves they can afford to let go. If you distribute too much of yourself to too many people, you can be left with a void at the centre of your life.

'Everyone needs privacy,' Cliff said. 'If you had to live under public scrutiny the whole of the time it would be horrific. Psychologically we need things that are ours alone. We need our own space.'

Cliff has managed better than most to give to his public and also to hold back an inviolable private life.

I respect him for that as I know he respects those of us who take it upon ourselves to find out where that dividing line is.

APPENDIX CONTENTS

QUESTIONS TO CLIFF (1994)

It's difficult to ask Cliff anything he hasn't been asked before. Steve Turner fired a volley of one-liners at him in the hope of uncovering something new.

Which famous person have you been most excited at meeting?
I think it was Billy Graham. I was more nervous about meeting him than anyone else.

At what moment in your life were you most in love?
They've all felt the same to me. Each time it's happened I've thought, 'This is it.'

When were you most depressed about your career?
I've never been depressed about my career. There were times just before we kicked off again in the mid-seventies when I wondered what was happening, but I wasn't depressed. Things weren't going badly. It was just that I didn't quite know where to go. I was torn between straight acting and getting back to music. I wasn't sure if I was being any good at either of them.

What has been your most frightening moment?
I suppose it was in a plane when we flew over Nashville and the pilot circled the airport twice and we realized something was wrong. He then said that the light hadn't come on to tell him that his wheels were in position. We had to land with fire engines racing down the runway beside us. Fortunately the wheels had come down, all right. It was the bulb that had broken! I prayed a lot.

What has hurt you most?
All the sexual speculation is very painful for me. It's hurtful that of all the things I do in life, so much is aimed at the sexual side of things. That area hurts a lot.

What is your favourite city?
I have a great soft spot for Lisbon in Portugal. I had a fantastic holiday there with a whole load of students one year. I enjoyed the place so much.

What do you carry in your wallet?
Some money, although not a great deal. I carry credit cards, a driver's licence and a credit card sized calculator.

What book have you enjoyed most recently?
Recently? Probably a Stephen King book.

What's the worst thing about getting older?
I suppose physically at the moment I don't notice much. I'm still fairly active. But obviously on the tennis court if I'm playing someone much younger, I'm aware that I am slower than I ever was.

What is the best thing about getting older?
Having the head you've got. I love knowing all that I know. I spoke at some churches the other day in Essex, and I was talking about age and I said that the one thing youth has is energy, but what it doesn't have, and can never have, is wisdom. You have to get older to have wisdom. I feel that as you get older you gather wisdom – so although I'm not as wise as many people I've nevertheless collected a certain amount of stuff that could be called wisdom. Certainly I'm wise enough for me and my life.

Can you remember when you first looked in the mirror and thought that you were no longer young?
That hasn't happened to me yet!

Do you have any repeated dreams?
Only one where I fly. I first remember having it as a child. There used to be a conker tree at the bottom of our close and we'd run along and jump and throw sticks into it to get conkers down. In the dream I did that and I found I flew. The more I flapped my arms the higher I flew. That has happened on and off quite a lot. I like it – it's a nice dream.

Do you ever dream of old girlfriends?
No, never.

When did you last travel on an underground train?
I think I've only ever done it once. It was in 1958 from Oxford Circus to St John's Wood.

How much is a loaf of sliced bread?
I've no idea.

A pint of milk?
Don't know.

The *Daily Mail*?
I don't know.

A first-class stamp?
Twenty-one pence?

What photos do you have in your bedroom?
I've got a photo of me holding a Bangaladeshi child whose finger Bill Latham had trodden on while we were both out there. It screamed and I picked it up. Then I've got a picture of my mum and a painting.

Are you getting better at tennis?
I am improving, but it's a slow process at my age.

When did you last check your bank account?
I don't check my bank account. My accountant tells me when I've overspent.

Who was the last pop star to shock you?
I don't think I've ever been shocked by any of them. They don't shock me at all. I find the things they call shocking are not really shocking. Is Madonna shocking? She doesn't shock me.

Which current actress is your ideal type?
Michelle Pfeiffer is pretty cool. And Kim Basinger.

Do you have one childhood memento that you cherish?
No, I don't actually.

If your house burned down while you were away on tour, which possession would you most miss?
I'd probably miss my Nintendo machine. Assuming that the dogs got out that is.

When is the last time you chatted up a girl, and what is your most successful line?
Do you know, I don't think I've ever chatted up a girl. Chatting up suggests going out of your way to pick a friendship up. It's always happened very naturally for me, so I haven't got a best line.

Where will you retire?
I don't think I'd like to retire away from Britain, but I wouldn't mind having a second home which is probably what I will have with my latest house in Portugal.

How did the rumour that you wear a colostomy bag begin?
I don't know. We think that some medical person somewhere who has had to deal with someone who was worried about having to wear one of these things has said, 'Well, famous people do have them – Cliff Richard's got one.' I suppose it's brought comfort to somebody. Funny thing is, I play tennis in all this clobber and they all see me wearing swimming trunks and it still doesn't kill the story!

FAMILY TREES

Baron Joseph Jensen—m....?

Charles Woodfall—m....?

James Smart—m.—Amelia Brill

Thomas Webb—m.—Mary Taynton
(b.1805)   (b.1807)

Gertrude Jensen—m.—James Woodfall
(b.1854)   (b.1836)

Amelia Sophia Smart—m.—Thomas B. Webb
(b.Stratford 1842)   (b.Limehouse 1841)

Donella Eugenie Woodfall
(b.Negapatam 1875)

m.

Frederick William Webb
(b.Woolwich 1872)

Rodger Oscar Webb
(b. Rangoon 1904)

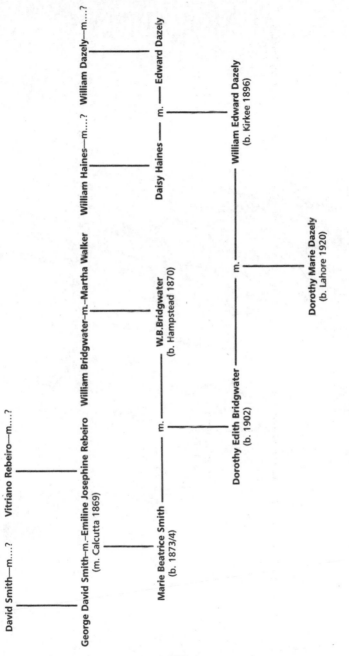

David Smith—m....?   Vitriano Rebeiro—m....?

George David Smith—m.—Emiline Josephine Rebeiro
(m. Calcutta 1869)

William Bridgwater—m.—Martha Walker

William Haines—m....?   William Dazely—m....?

Daisy Haines —— m. —— Edward Dazely

Marie Beatrice Smith —————— m. —————— W.B.Bridgwater
(b. 1873/4)   (b. Hampstead 1870)

William Edward Dazely
(b. Kirkee 1896)

Dorothy Edith Bridgwater —————— m. ——————
(b. 1902)

Dorothy Marie Dazely
(b. Lahore 1920)

389

90

20/9/57

We, the undersigned (members of Dick Teagues Skiffle group) hereby agree not to leave the group to take an individual engagement with any other musical concern without previously discussing the matter with the full group and its controlling manager.

Signed:—

Cliff's first contract

CLIFF RICHARD AND THE DRIFTERS

Telephone: HERtford 3817

51, London Rd.,
Hertford Heath,
Hertford,
Herts.

17th June, 1958

Dear Mr. de Villiers,
                        Many thanks for giving CLIFF RICHARD AND
THE DRIFTERS the opportunity to play at the "Freight Train" last
Sunday evening.

        Despite the late arrival of your staff they thoroughly
enjoyed the evening and were pleased by the most appreciative
audience.   Unfortunately playing for almost three hours proved
rather too strenuous this was, however, compensated by the addition of eight new members to our "Fan" club.

        Should you require our services in the future we shall be
pleased to hear from you.

        Assuring you of our best intentions at all times.

                        Yours faithfully,

                        (J. FOSTER)
                        Manager

Letter to the manager of the
Freight Train coffee bar in Soho

May 1959: debut issue
of the fan club magazine,
edited by Jan Vane

THE OFFICIAL CLIFF RICHARD FAN CLUB

30 Southend Road,
Rainham,
ESSEX

Dear Cliff Richard Fans,

I hope you will enjoy this, our first
magazine.   I have tried to make it as interesting
as possible, and Stan Edwards, a personal friend of
Cliff's, has contributed two fabulous articles for
us.

I would like to hear whether you
liked the magazine and if you have any ideas for
future editions.

Your friend,

JAN

P.S. Sorry for delay but I was waiting for the
theatre leaflets to come through.

FORTHCOMING EVENTS

Regal Ballroom, Ripley

4/-

7.30 until 11 p.m.

Saturday— BLUE JOHNS SKIFFLE GROUP
Plus Dancing to Keith Freer's Dixielanders 2/6

(Club Members Only)

Sunday— Club Four Skiffle Group and Top Records 2/-
Club Four Rock Group and Top Records

Monday— MODERN BALLROOM DANCING 2/6

Tuesday— KEITH FREER'S YOUNG MEN OF MUSIC 2/-
ROCK 'N' ROLL TO RECORDS 3/6

Wednesday— 7.30 (until 11 p.m.

Thursday— OLD TIME DANCE 2/-
M.C.: E. Stanton and The Gaiety Players

Friday— ROCK 'N' ROLL TO RECORDS

Saturday, 3rd May—
Direct from the famous Soho 2 i's Coffee Bar
CLIFF RICHARD and the ORIFTERS
Plus Keith Freer and his Dixielanders

1958: Cliff's first
billing as Cliff Richard

The *Sunday Pictorial*
advertisement that
inspired Lionel Bart's
writing of 'Living Doll'

ON THE RECORD . . . . . by Patrick Doncaster

NEW RECRUIT FOR THE DISC WAR

● Cliff Richard . . . a Presley fan.

NEW records are few, because of the holidays. All seems quiet on the Discland front.

But it's just a front . . . Behind the scenes the battle for the autumn—when the big guns open up again—is being planned.

Making a battle-eve sortie into the Columbia camp this week. I spied a new name due to spark off on August 29. . . .

Cliff Richard, a seventeen-year-old dark-haired, dark-eyed singer and guitar twanger from Cheshunt, Herts.

He is a Presley-ish type with so much promise that he has been given a big long-term contract by orchestra leader Norrie Paramor.

Norrie is Columbia's guiding light (he looks after — among others— Michael Holliday, The Mudlarks and Eddie Calvert).

"Cliff is a rock 'n' roller." said Norrie.

But isn't the rock on the rocks ?

"Not quite," said Norrie. who knows what he is talking about. "I just can't see the kids giving up these personalities with a beat "

HER Verdict

Norrie has great faith in his new find. He took home a test side of the boy to let his daughter Carolyn, nearly fourteen, hear it.

A test side lasts about thirty plays. Carolyn liked it so much—that it is now worn out.

The titles: "Schoolboy Crush" and "Move It."

I think Cliff Richard, born in Lucknow, India, has a personality that shines through the grooves. He could succeed in Discland.

His favourite artist is Presley, his favourite actor is Presley. And his ambitions are (1) to win a gold disc for a million sales and (2) to meet Presley.

Daily Mirror, 31 July 1958
– Cliff's first mention in
the national press

October 1961: Cliff's letter
to Delia Wicks ending their
relationship

MELBOURNE
AUSTRALIA.
21ˢᵗ OCTOBER

Dear Dellia,

I know I haven't written
for a long time, but I've been so
confused in my mind about you
& about myself.

I've had to make, probably, one
the biggest descisions, I'm ever going
to make & I'm praying that I won't
hurt you too much.

Dellia, I want you to try and
understand the position I'm in.
Being a singer I'm going to have

to give up many things in life.

But being a Pop singer I have to give up one very priceless thing — The right to have any lasting relationship with any special girl.

Delia, you must find someone who is free to love you, as you deserve to be loved, and is able to marry you.

I couldn't give up my career, & besides the fact that my mother & sisters, since my fathers death, rely on me completely, I have showbiz in my blood now & I would be lost without it.

"D" all I can say now is, goodbye & don't think too badly of me.

Love —

Cliff

1959: Cliff's letter to Dave
Lilley organizing the purchase
of Hank Marvin's first Fender
Stratocaster

Hippodrome Birmingham

Dear Dave,
We've decided to
have the with "Red" Fender Guitar
A. Three pickups
B. With Tremolo lever.
C. Gold plated hardware

The guitar is a "Stratocaster"
Have marked in catalogue.
When you send for it please
order spare set balanced strings and
also a "Fender Case"
Well Dave thanks a million
All the Best
Cliff.

1960: Cliff's
billing on his first
tour of America

POP STARS CLASH ON RELIGION

A CONTROVERSIAL clash between two of our leading pop stars has been recorded in a television programme which will be shown this evening.

In it Paul Jones, the 24-year-old former lead singer with the Manfred Mann group, claims that Cliff Richard is letting himself be exploited by the Church.

The programme, ABC's *Looking For An Answer*, pulls no punches from its opening shots.

It begins with a scene from the film *Privilege*, which stars Paul Jones as a pop star cynically exploited by religion and cuts to a real-life shot of Cliff Richard singing at a Billy Graham rally.

"Is the Church," asks interviewer Robert Kee, "exploiting Cliff Richard, too?"

This is the first of many hard questions for Richard in the programme.

Eight years ago he burst in on the pop scene—sideburned feather-cut, his thin husky voice and hip-wriggling raising hysteria among his girl fans.

His values

Two years ago, despite fame, a £30,000 country mansion and a £1,800 a week salary, he discovered a need for spiritual values. Now he appears with bishops at meetings, sings Gospel songs for Billy Graham and wants to teach divinity if he can finish his O levels.

He is single, a non-smoker and never touches spirits.

Jones went to university, and lived till recently in a converted garage in Cricklewood. He is married with two children.

Kee asks Richard if he questioned his own motives when he saw what happened to the pop star in *Privilege*?

"Did it embarrass you the slightest bit seeing that film? No one questions your sincerity as a Christian doing this. But you *are* using the mass you're able to command through your pop singing and bringing them along to a church."

RICHARD: "I put myself in God's hands and say, look, if this is the thing I ought to do I shall do it. The Church is just, I think, a front. You know, it's a name. We are always fooled by words and names and things."

JONES: "Well, one of the bishops in *Privilege* says when he is accused of using the pop singer to further the ends of the Church: 'Once they used a Spanish Inquisition and this is less painful.' You know, it's exactly what you have just said, really."

RICHARD: "Before I came

WESTON TAYLOR'S SHOWPAGE

● Cliff Richard and Paul Jones argue about the Billy Graham campaign

on the scene, you know, Graham packed out places like Earl's Court. He doesn't need me."

JONES: "But people don't know what they're coming for. Billy Graham knows why people go to his meetings is the same reasons why people in America spent 125,000,000 dollars in one year going to fortune tellers. They are insecure; they're unsure. They don't know what they're going for.

Just a show

"Right, so you say: 'We are giving them Christ.' Well, I say you're not. You're giving them a show.

"Billy Graham said in the film I've just seen of the Earl's Court thing: 'Let the bombs drop—we have joy inside.'

"You know, this is pie in the sky. This is absolutely ludicrous. If the bombs drop, you've got joy nowhere."

RICHARD: "If you become a Christian you must start

immediately thinking peaceable things. Before you can ban the bomb you should know about the rest of mankind. We know that mankind, Biblically, is not going to save the world—we just know it.

"We rely on Christ's strength: so what we do first is to make the world Christian. I mean, this is what counts."

JONES: "Is this what it's all about. Until everybody's on your side. . . ?"

RICHARD: "No, no, no—again you're using words. If I'm at all convinced, Paul, I've gotta say, 'Look, something's happened to me. I've become a Christian. I've

accepted a thing called salvation which means if I die I can look forward to an eternal life of peace and joy and no pain; and things like this.'

"If you ask a psychedelic what-not, or the drug-takers what they get out of it, you can treble it and multiply it by a thousand—and that's how I feel all the time."

JONES: "You know, if you ask somebody from any religion—even if his religion is acid—he'll tell you, I mean, the basic answer any religion will give you is it's the final unification of the many with the one. I mean, that's religion, that's Christian religion, and that's LSD."

KEE: "And what's your answer?"

JONES: "I say, let's get on with making the world a nicer place."

DISCOGRAPHY (UK)

singles

1	Move It/Schoolboy Crush	Aug 1958
2	High Class Baby/My Feet Hit The Ground	Nov 1958
3	Livin' Lovin' Doll/Steady With You	Jan 1959
4	Mean Streak/Never Mind	Apr 1959
5	Living Doll/Apron Strings	Jul 1959
6	Travellin' Light/Dynamite	Oct 1959
7	A Voice in the Wilderness/Don't Be Mad At Me	Jan 1960
8	Fall In Love With You/Willie And The Hand Jive	Mar 1960
9	Please Don't Tease/Where Is My Heart?	Jun 1960
10	Nine Times Out Of Ten/Thinking Of Our Love	Sep 1960
11	I Love You/'D' In Love	Nov 1960
12	Theme For A Dream/Mumblin' Mosie	Feb 1961
13	Gee Whizz It's You/I Cannot Find A True Love	Mar 1961
14	A Girl Like You/Now's The Time To Fall In Love	Jun 1961
15	When The Girl In Your Arms Is The Girl In Your Heart/Got A Funny Feeling	Oct 1961
16	The Young Ones/We Say Yeah	Jan 1962

17	I'm Looking Out The Window/ Do You Want To Dance?	May 1962
18	It'll Be Me/Since I Lost You	Aug 1962
19	The Next Time/Bachelor Boy	Nov 1962
20	Summer Holiday/Dancing Shoes	Feb 1963
21	Lucky Lips/I Wonder	May 1963
22	It's All In The Game/Your Eyes Tell On You	Aug 1963
23	Don't Talk To Him/Say You're Mine	Nov 1963
24	I'm The Lonely One/ Watch What You Do With My Baby	Jan 1964
25	Constantly/True True Lovin'	Apr 1964
26	On The Beach/A Matter of Moments	Jun 1964
27	The Twelfth Of Never/I'm Afraid To Go Home	Oct 1964
28	I Could Easily Fall (In Love With You)/ I'm In Love With You	Dec 1964
29	The Minute You're Gone/Just Another Guy	Mar 1965
30	Angel/Razzle Dazzle	May 1965
31	On My Word/Just A Little Bit Too Late	Jun 1965
32	The Time In Between/Look Before You Love	Aug 1965
33	Wind Me Up (Let Me Go)/The Night	Oct 1965
34	Blue Turns To Grey/Somebody Loses	Mar 1966

88	Please Don't Fall In Love/Too Close To Heaven	Nov 1983
89	Baby You're Dynamite/Ocean Deep	Mar 1984
90	Shooting From The Heart/Small World	Oct 1984
91	Heart User/I Will Follow You	Jan 1985
92	She's So Beautiful/She's So Beautiful (instr.)	Sep 1985
93	It's In Every One Of Us/Alone (instr.)	Nov 1985
94	Born To Rock 'n' Roll/Law of the Universe (instr.)	May 1986
95	My Pretty One/Love Ya	Jun 1987
96	Sonic People/One Time Lover Man	Aug 1987
97	Remember Me/Another Christmas Day	Oct 1987
98	Two Hearts/Yesterday, Today, Forever	Feb 1988
99	Mistletoe and Wine/Marmaduke	Nov 1988
100	The Best of Me/Move It	May 1989
101	I Just Don't Have The Heart/Wide Open Space	Aug 1989
102	Lean On You/Hey Mister	Oct 1989
103	Stronger Than That/Joanna	Feb 1990
104	Silhouettes/The Winner	Aug 1990
105	From A Distance/Lindsay Jane II	Oct 1990
106	Saviour's Day/Oh Boy! Medley	Nov 1990
107	More To Life/Mo's Theme	Sep 1991

Albums

1	Cliff	Apr 1959
2	Cliff Sings	Nov 1959
3	Me And My Shadows	Oct 1960
4	Listen To Cliff	May 1961
5	21 Today	Oct 1961
6	The Young Ones	Dec 1961
7	32 Minutes And 17 Seconds With Cliff Richard	Oct 1962
8	Summer Holiday	Jan 1963
9	Cliff's Hit Album	Jul 1963
10	When In Spain	Sep 1963
11	Wonderful Life	Jul 1964
12	Aladdin And His Wonderful Lamp	Dec 1964
13	Cliff Richard	Apr 1965
14	More Hits By Cliff	Jul 1965
15	When In Rome	Aug 1965
16	Love Is Forever	Nov 1965
17	Kinda Latin	May 1966
18	Finders Keepers	Dec 1966

SOURCES

Most of this book was researched from original sources. I conducted over 240 interviews with 205 people, the majority of whom had never been interviewed about Cliff before.

The research from interviews was supplemented by archive material from the following organizations:

BBC Written Archives, *Billboard*, British Film Institute, British Library, Broxbourne Borough Council, Butlin's Holiday Camps, Cheshunt Public library, Chiswick Public Library, Companies House, Diocese of Calcutta, EMI Archives, Equity, Eurovangelism, Ferguson Ltd, Granada Television, Indian Tourist Board, India Office library, Musicians Union, National Newspaper Library, National Maritime Museum, National Sound Archives, Office of Population and Censuses, Peninsular and Oriental Steam Navigation Company, Performing Rights Society, Press Association, Public Record Office Screen, Actors Guild, SOCAN, Spotlight, Sutton Public Library, Tear Fund.

There have been over thirty books written about Cliff so far although only a handful have been biographies. During research I made use of the following:

Driftin' With Cliff, Jet Harris, (Charles Buchan, 1959)

Cliff Richard (Fan Star Library, 1959)

It's Great To Be Young, Cliff Richard (Souvenir Press, 1960)

Cliff Richard: Baron Of Beat, Jack Sutter (Valex Products, 1960)

Me And My Shadows, Cliff Richard (Daily Mirror Publications, 1961)

Cliff Around The Clock, Bob Ferrier (Daily Mirror Publications, 1962)

The Wonderful World Of Cliff, Bob Ferrier (Peter Davies, 1964)

New Singer, New Song, David Winter (Hodder & Stoughton, 1966)

The Way I See It, Cliff Richard (Hodder & Stoughton, 1968)

The Cliff Richard Story, George Tremlett (Futura, 1975)

Which One's Cliff?, Cliff Richard (Hodder & Stoughton, 1977 and 1990)

Cliff, Tony Jasper and Patrick Doncaster (Sidgwick & Jackson 1981 and 1992)

Cliff Richard and the Shadows, Dezo Hoffman (Virgin, 1985)

Cliff Richard In His Own Words, Kevin St John (Omnibus Press, 1991)

You, Me and Jesus, Cliff Richard (Hodder & Stoughton, 1983)

Jesus, Me and You, Cliff Richard (Hodder & Stoughton, 1985)

The Cliff Richard File, Mike Read (Roger Houghton, 1986)

Single-Minded, Cliff Richard (Hodder & Stoughton 1988)

Cliff Richard; The Complete Recording Sessions, Peter Lewry and Nigel Goodall (Blandford, 1991).

Other books which mentioned Cliff were useful in their observations. Among these were:

Big Beat Scene, Royston Ellis (Four Square, 1961)

The Shadows By Themselves, ed. Royston Ellis (Consul, 1961)

Love Me Do: The Beatles' Progress, Michael Braun (Penguin, 1964)

Crusade '66, John Pollock (Hodder & Stoughton, 1966)

Awopbopaloobop Alopbambboom, Nik Cohn (Weidenfeld & Nicholson, 1969)

Revolt Into Style, George Melly (Allen Lane, 1970)

Land Aflame, Flo Dobbie (Hodder & Stoughton, 1972)

Spre-e '73, David Coomes (Coverdale House, 1973)

Rock 'n' Roll, Chris May (Socion, 1974)

The Guitar Greats, John Tobler and Stuart Grundy (BBC Publications, 1983)

The Story Of The Shadows, Mike Read (Elm Tree Books, 1983)

Days In The Life, Jonathan Green (Heinemann, 1988)

Rock 'n' Roll – I Gave You the Best Years of My Life, Bruce Welch (Viking, 1989)

Music Collector magazine no. 21, (January 1991)

Funny Old World: John Henry Rostill, Rob Bradford (Rob Bradford, 1992).

Articles about and interviews with Cliff are legion. Other than all the British national newspapers I consulted the following periodicals during my research:

Billboard, Boyfriend, Cheshunt Weekly Telegraph, Disc, Lucknow Pioneer, Marty, Melody Maker, New Musical Express, Newsweek, Radio Times, Record Mail, Ripley and Heanor News, Rolling Stone, Shepherd's Bush Gazette, Sutton Herald, The Stage, Tear Times, Valentine, Wallington and Carshalton Times, West Lancashire Evening Gazette.

INTERVIEWEES

Following is a list of my main interview sources for each chapter. Some sources have been left unattributed at the request of the interviewees.

CHAPTER 1
Roger Bruce, Shane Guy

CHAPTER 2
Vincent Bridgwater, Pete Bush, Joyce Clarkson, Rodger Cooke, Elsie Dazely, Joyce Dobra, Olive Gregory, Edna van Haeften, Gertrude Woodfall

CHAPTER 3
Dorothy Bodkin, Vincent Bridgwater, Olive Gregory

CHAPTER 4
Dorothy Bodkin, Pete Bush, Ivy Clare, Brian Cooke, Patricia Cookson, Ted Davy, Vincent Dickson, John Harris, Jacqui Harrison, Bob Henrit, Richard Holmes, Linda Lazarri, Norman Mitham, Jay Norris, Gladys Pearcy, Christine Poynter, Frances Slade, Mrs Slade, Mrs Tonks, Dorothy Willis

CHAPTER 5
Ruth Dickson, Jacqui Harrison, Betty Longhurst, Christine March, Marie Mitchell, Norman Mitham, The Rev. M.J. Bannister, Jay Norris, Terry Smart, John Vince

CHAPTER 6
Sheila Bateman, Jimmy Grant, Terry Harness, Chas McDevitt, Brian Parker, June Pearce, Frances Slade, Terry Smart, Dick Teague, Kathleen Teague, Mick Teague, Walter Teague, Wally Whyton

CHAPTER 7
Janice Berry, Dorothy Bodkin, Brian Cooke, Terry Dene,

John Foster, Jacqui Harrison, Paul Lincoln, Norman Mitham, Steve Nichols, Ian Samwell, Terry Smart, Jan Vane

CHAPTER 8
Malcolm Addey, Janice Berry, Peter Bown, Franklyn Boyd, Frank Clarke, Stan Edwards, Mark Forster, John Foster, George Ganjou, Georgine Ganjou, Jack Good, Margit Good, Derek Johnson, Chas McDevitt, Norman Mitham, Caroline Paramor, Joan Paramor, Carl Perkins, Ian Samwell, Ernie Shear, Terry Smart, Tulah Tuke

CHAPTER 9
John Foster, Rita Gillespie, Jack Good, Jet Harris, Wee Willie Harris, Hal Kalin, Ron King, Hank Marvin, Paul McCartney, Mickie Most, Ian Samwell, Terry Smart, Maggie Streader, Bruce Welch, Wally Whyton, Marty Wilde

CHAPTER 10
Franklyn Boyd, Jess Conrad, Stan Edwards, John Foster, David Lilley, Ray Mackender, Tony Meehan, Sammy Samwell, Tulah Tuke, Marty Wilde

CHAPTER 11
Lionel Bart, Janice Berry, Dorothy Bodkin, Franklyn Boyd, Tito Burns, Jess Conrad, Carol Costa, Ronnie Ernstone, John Foster, Jet Harris, Wee Willie Harris, Andrew Ray, Maggie Streader, Jimmy Tarbuck, Cherry Wainer, Marry Wilde, Terence Young

CHAPTER 12
Lionel Bart, Roy Bennett, Tito Burns, Freddie Cannon, Jess Conrad, Yolande Donlan, Royston Ellis, Val Guest, Father John Oates, David Lilley, Ray Mackender, Wolf Mankowitz, Josie Pollock, Ian Samwell, Father Shergold, Maggie Streader, Sid Tepper, Diana Ward, Bruce Welch, Mark Wynter

CHAPTER 13
Sheila Bateman, Tito Burns, Mike Conlin, Carol Costa, Royston Ellis, Ronnie Ernstone, Jacqui Harrison, David Kossoff, Jerry Lordan, Vicky Marshall, Tony Meehan, Steve Race, Cherry Wainer, Diana Ward

CHAPTER 14
Roy Bennett, Stanley Black, Tito Burns, Ron Cass, Brian
Crompton, Peter Gormley, Kenneth Harper, Jet Harris, Melvyn
Hayes, Derek Johnson, Hank Marvin, Barry Ronger, Herb Ross,
Cyril Simons, Sid Tepper, Bruce Welch, Delia Wicks

CHAPTER 15
Dorothy Bodkin, Vincent Bridgwater, Ron Cass, Mike Conlin,
Royston Ellis, Adam Faith, Peter Gormley, Kenneth Harper, Jet
Harris, Melvyn Hayes, Brian Locking, Ray Mackender, Hank
Marvin, Tony Meehan, Lauri Peters, Victor Peterson, Una Stubbs,
Bruce Welch

CHAPTER 16
Brian Bennett, Dorothy Bodkin, Ron Cass, Mike Conlin, Graham
Disbrey, Royston Ellis, Kenneth Harper, Bill Latham, Hank
Marvin, Jay Norris, Bruce Welch, David Winter

CHAPTER 17
Pete Bush, Mike Conlin, John Davey, Graham Disbrey, Nigel
Goodwin, Peter Gormley, Peter Graves, Olive Gregory, Paul Jones,
Bill Latham, Tony Meehan, Jay Norris, David Winter

CHAPTER 18
John Davey, Graham Disbrey, Dave Foster, Peter Graves, Cindy
Kent, Bill Latham, Bill Martin, Tony Meehan, Olivia Newton-John,
Larry Norman, Bruce Welch, David Winter

CHAPTER 19
Anthony Andrews, Terry Britten, Barrie Guard, Eric Hall, Kenneth
Harper, George Hoffman, Bill Latham, Dave Mackay, Olivia
Newton-John, David Pawson, Trevor Spencer, Alan Tarney, Liz
Hutchison

CHAPTER 20
Terry Britten, Tony Clarke, Eric Hall, Christine Holmes, Tony
King, Dave Mackay, Larry Norman, Trevor Spencer, Dave
Townsend, Bruce Welch

CHAPTER 21
David Bryce, Tony Clarke, Chris Eaton, Phil Everly, George Hoffman, B.A. Robertson, Trevor Spencer, Graham Todd, Alan Tarney, Bruce Welch

CHAPTER 22
Sue Barker, Terry Britten, David Bryce, Stu Calver, Jill Clarke, Dave Cooke, Carol Costa, Chris Eaton, Paul Field, Alan Godson, Nigel Goodwin, Don Grierson, Mark Griffiths, Jet Harris, Garth Hewitt, Carol Illingworth, Bill Latham, Phil Lloyd, Hank Marvin, Norman Miller, John Perry, Craig Pruess, Mike Read, B.A. Robertson, Dan Slater, Gill Snow, Alan Tarney, Bruce Welch, Muriel Young

CHAPTER 23
Dave Clark, Gerald Coates, Dave Cooke, Mark Griffiths, Bob Hellyer, George Hoffman, Ron King, Norman Miller, John Muggleton, David Soames, Graham Todd, Sheila Walsh, Jodie Wilson

CHAPTER 24
David Bryce, Peter Gormley, Tony King, Gerry Kitchingham, Bill Latham, Paul Moessl, Alan Tarney, Graham Todd, Peter Waterman

CHAPTER 25
Tim Rice, Clive Black, Peter Wolf

CHAPTER 26
Mike Andrews, David Bryce, Paul Field

CHAPTER 27
Alan Tarney, Clive Black, David Bryce, Chris Eaton, Val Jannsen

CHAPTER 28
Sue Barker, Gerald Coates, Graham Disbrey, Charles Haswell, Bill Latham, Gill Snow, Gerald Williams

CHAPTER 29
Dorothy Bodkin, Peter Gormley, Bill Latham

INDEX

Crombie, Tony 100, 102, 119, 135

Crosby, Bing 33, 159

Crouch, Allan 67–68

Crusaders 215–218, 229–233, 235, 237, 246, 294, 360

d

Dallas Boys 112

Dando, Jill 341–342

Daniels, Jeff 315

Davey, John 15, 232, 235–237, 246–247

Dazely, Olive Queenie (aunt) 14, 27–33, 35–37, 49, 182, 231–232

Dazely, William Edward (grandfather) 26–28, 389

Delamar, Mickey 132, 182, 184

Dene, Terry 86, 88–89, 119, 138, 204, 236

Denne, Michael 267

'Devil Woman' 266–269, 271, 273–274, 279, 307, 314, 320, 405

Diana, Princess 245, 325, 335–336

    funeral 335

    tribute album 336

Dickson, Dorothy see Bridgwater, Dorothy Edith (grandmother)

Dickson, Richard 28–29, 43

Dickson, Vincent 43, 61

Disbrey, Graham 15, 216–218, 232, 235, 294, 346, 360–361, 368

Dobra, Joyce 14, 24–25, 34, 45, 52

Donegan, Lonnie 64, 68–70, 73, 76, 202

Donlan, Yolande 156

Dore, Charlie 280

Douglas, Craig 158

Douglas, Josephine 111

'Dream Tomorrow' 330

'Dreamin' 19, 314, 406

Dressed for the Occasion 318, 411

Drifters 86, 88–89, 93–97, 100–102, 107–109, 113, 116–122, 124–127, 132, 134–137, 154–155, 284

    Butlin's Holiday Camps 107

    Foster, John 88–94, 96, 100, 108–109, 115, 121–122, 126, 131, 135, 157, 284

    Ganjou, George 96, 100–101

    new name 161

    play at 2 I's 90–91

Driftin' With Cliff (Ellis and Harris) 153–154, 413

Duncan, Johnny 135

Dunlop, Frank 329–330, 332

Eager, Vince 122, 126, 128, 135, 204

Earl, Andy 17

Eaton, Chris 19–20, 285, 324, 352–354

Edwards, Stan 108, 125

Ellis, Royston 15, 153–155, 159, 170, 179, 194, 200, 209, 414

Epstein, Brian 169, 205

Ernstone, Ronnie 141–143, 155, 170, 345

Eurovangelism 247–249

Eurovision 244–245, 255, 265, 275

'Event, The' 8, 284, 357, 411

Everly Brothers 64, 86, 117, 161, 164

    Phil and Cliff 284, 408

Every Face Tells A Story 275, 277, 410

Expresso Bongo 123, 155–156, 159, 163, 165, 175

f

Faith, Adam 128, 204, 235

'Faithful One' 20, 353

Farrar John 245, 251, 314, 329, 330, 332

Farrar, Pat 251, 345

Ferrier, Bob 36

PICTURE
ACKNOWLEDGMENTS

Every effort has been made to trace the copyright holders of the photographs in this book, but one or two were unreachable. We would be grateful if the photographers concerned would contact us.

SECTION 1

page 77: Vincent Bridgwater

page 78: (top & middle) Joyce Dobra; (bottom) Vincent Bridgwater

page 79: Joyce Dobra

page 80: (top) Dorothy Willis; (middle) Joyce Dobra; (bottom) *Waltham and Cheshunt Weekly Telegraph*

page 81: (top) John Vince; (middle & bottom) Jay Norris

page 82: Jan Goring

page 83: Jan Goring

page 84: (top) Terry Smart

SECTION 2

page 145: (top) Franklyn Boyd; (bottom) Ian Samwell

page 146: (middle) Popperfoto; (bottom) Royston Ellis

page 147: (top) Ray Mackender; (bottom) Holton Deutsch Collection

page 148: (top) Rex Features; (bottom three) Ron Ernstone

page 149: (top three) Ron Ernstone; (middle), Topham Picture Library; (bottom) Ray Mackender

page 150: David H. Hawley

page 151: (top left & right) Ian Samwell; (middle) Rex Features; (bottom) EMI Records

page 152: (top) Delia Wicks; (bottom) Topham Picture Library

SECTION 3

page 221: (top) Popperfoto; (middle) Topham Picture Library; (bottom) Rex Features

page 222: (top) *Daily Express*; (middle) Kenneth Harper; (bottom) Camera Press

page 223: Graham Disbrey

page 224: (top) *Daily Express*; (bottom) Joan Paramor

page 225: (top) Graham Disbrey; (middle) Rex Features; (bottom) Dave Foster

page 226: (top) London Features International; (bottom) Popperfoto page 227: (top) Hulton Deutsch Collection; (bottom) Rex Features

page 228: (top left) Joan Batten; (top right) *Daily Express*; (bottom) Rex Features

SECTION 4

page 298: (top) Tear Fund; (middle) Ray Mackender; (bottom) Steve Turner

page 299: Steve Turner

page 300: (top) Hulton Deutsch Collection; (bottom) Rema Pictures

page 301: (top) Syndication International; (middle & bottom) Graham Disbrey

page 302: (top) Topham Picture Library; (bottom) Graham Disbrey

page 303: (top) Graham Disbrey; (bottom) Topham Picture Library

page 304: (top) Topham Picture Library; (middle) Rex Features, London; (bottom) Mark Bukowski

page 305: Graham Disbrey